Global Power Structure, Technology and World Economy
in the Late Twentieth Century

Global Power Structure, Technology and World Economy in the Late Twentieth Century

by Mihály Simai

Pinter Publishers, London

Joint edition with Akadémiai Kiadó, Budapest
First published in Great Britain in 1990 by
Pinter Publishers Limited
25 Floral Street, London WC2E 9DS

This is the English version of *Hatalom, Technika, Világgazdaság*
published by Közgazdasági és Jogi Könyvkiadó, Budapest
Translation by Pál Félix

British Library Cataloguing in Publication Data
A CIP catalogue record for this book is
available from the British Library

ISBN 0—86187—998—8

© Mihály Simai
© English Translation by Pál Félix

Printed in Hungary
Akadémiai Kiadó és Nyomda Vállalat

Contents

6

Part Three

Part Four

Part Five

Introduction

The main issues in this book are the politics and economics of global changes. The world economy is in a process of major transformation. A new technological revolution is spreading rapidly, resulting in what may be fundamental shifts in the global distribution of production capacities in output and consumption patterns. Changes are taking place in comparative advantages, thus influencing and even transforming the international division of labour. National economic policies face qualitatively new challenges and requirements. The hierarchical position of different countries is changing too. The old and new actors on the world economic stage, with their special interests and problems in this evolving environment, are forcing countries to re-interpret their roles and possibilities in the process of adjustment, looking for new opportunities and trying to avoid new perils.

The changes in the world economy are important sources of structural transformation within national boundaries too. Traditional links between various activities have been broken up and new linkages have been established. Politics and society are also in the process of being reconstructed. Inefficient and autocratic regimes in certain countries are being replaced by new ones; in others, more conservative groups have come to power. The social stratification that has characterized most of the century is also being replaced by new structures. New social groups are appearing and new skills emerging.

The sources, consequences and mechanisms of the above changes are analysed in this book which is the result of research work undertaken by the author in the first half of the 1980s.

The work synthesizes three important projects:
(1) the changes and new era in the world economy in the late twentieth century;
(2) the new characteristic features and trends in the world technology market;
(3) structural changes and disturbances in the world economy and its global consequences.

The first part, which deals with the new regulating forces of the world economy and their influence on changes which have taken place since the early 1970s in the developed Western countries, in the Third World and in the socialist countries, reveals the underlying trends behind the two recessions and provides an analysis of the debate on the crisis in a way which is confronting the various old and new ideas with reality.

While trying to avoid any prefabricated elements in the diagnosis and in the projections, the author arrives at the conclusion that the nature of the changes and the weakness of the institutions and policies could be blamed basically for the troubles which emerged.

The second part of the book is entitled: "The Changing Global Power Structure in the World Economy in the Late Twentieth Century". In this part, the author analyses the global role of the changes in the power structure, the mechanism of transition from one regime to another and the consequences of this in the present world of military bipolarity and economic and political multipolarity.

The conclusion is that the role of economic power is on the increase and that competition in this sphere has a much greater global role now than it had in previous decades of the century. This characteristic of economic power implies, however, important global political shifts and problems.

The third part of the book deals with the new technological revolution in the global economic system. Technology has, of course, always been an important source of global changes and problems. At this stage, the nature of the revolution, the pervasive character of the new technology, the special role of a handful of countries in the hierarchical system, and strategic factors have upgraded the role of technological change. Monopolies and efforts to preserve them, competition, cooperation and different degrees of dependence will remain longer-term characteristics of the technology market. It is extremely important for the whole of mankind, that in this situation the necessary minimum of global cooperation and control should be established.

The fourth part of the book is in a way a comprehensive overview of the present system and of the main trends in international economic relations, world trade, capital movements, etc., from a structural point of view: and how the structural changes of output and consumption influence international economic relations. The new forms of cooperation are also analysed from this point of view. Special attention is paid to the role of the service sector and to some important areas, like agricultural raw materials, microelectronics, transport equipment, etc.

One of the important conclusions is that the structural disturbances and other imbalances will remain with us and, therefore, in order to avoid the collapse of the international system, new forms of global cooperation are needed, which assist not only national adjustment policies, but also facilitate coordination of policies leading to the changes.

The fifth part of the book, which deals with the present and the future of global cooperation raises some fundamental questions about the existence or absence of interests in global cooperation. It confronts two possible approaches: one, which assumes international cooperation based only on national interests and the other which assumes cooperation from a global point of view. The international monetary system serves as a case study to show the conflict between the two approaches. The conclusion of this part is that those policies which are aimed at maximizing national advantages and disregard the interests of other countries and of mankind, if implemented, are much more dangerous and disruptive today, in an independent world, than they were in the past. Countries that are strong and can directly influence the international system through their policies and actions, therefore bear a much greater responsibility than ever before.

The author expresses his thanks to all those who helped him with advice or criticism: especially Professors József Bognár, János Berecz and Tibor Erdős from Hungary, and William Diebold and Professor Robert Manley from the Unites States.

Part One

The New Regulating Forces of the World Economy and the Nature of the Changes

International events interlaced with conflicts and crises and the actions of states in the 1980s already contribute in many respects to the shaping of the twenty-first century. The necessity to transform international relations is professed and declared by many statesman, scientists and experts. The need to develop new conditions is voiced almost like a platitude, at the meeting and discussion of international organizations. Yet, the unfolding of the necessary changes seems to be rather slow. If a nuclear world war does not break out, if mankind succeeds in avoiding the disaster threatening its very existence, and if the world economy does not disintegrate as a result of crises and disturbances—then at the end of this century and in the world of the period beginning in the next century new approaches for the solution or mitigation of our cumulating worries, troubles and disturbances will emerge. The formation of these new approaches has to spring from our present world, which, as regards its basic structure, will presumably not change to a great extent. The exploration of ways and means has begun and has already provided us with many important implications.

1. Economic Problems of a Period of Global Changes: Old and New Theories, Longer Term Consequences of the Recession and the Recovery of the 1980s

The 1970s and the 1980s were characterized by serious world economic problems, much beyond the recessions of the 1970s and the early 1980s. It was not just a traditional economic crisis which hit or influenced all the countries adversely. It can be interpreted as a global structural crisis. The nature of crisis can be defined as a grave and significant disturbance of a given system which aggravates its conflicts and, or incidentally, prevents its normal functioning (i.e. its functioning according to the prevailing conditions and scale of values), its reproduction and development, and increases its conflicts and contradictions making them unmanagable so that its contradictions become insoluble, and could result in its eventual collapse.

A crisis can develop under the influence of internal factors of the system, as a consequence of external factors, or as a result of the combination of internal and external conditions, i.e. as the resultant of objective and subjective causes. A crisis is not identical with the disintegration of the system but—as pointed out—can result in its collapse. Such a situation can occur if the factors of the crisis are not recognized in time, if the powers controlling the system are unable to solve the contradictions or at least to mitigate their effects or to create conditions which make it possible for the essential elements of the system to function even in a crisis situation.

All over the world heated discussions have been going on regarding the causes, the characteristics and the consequences of the world economic crisis and about its relation to the recessions of 1974–75 and of 1982–83. Experts tend to agree that neither the recession of the mid-1970s nor that which started in the early 1980s could be characterized as a traditional cyclical one. However, views differ considerably as to the character of the crisis.

The heated and many-sided debate can be explained first of all by the fact that the crisis broke out in a number of sectors of production and in the system of international relations, i.e. not just a single country or group of countries was affected but the world economy as a whole was hit. A number of long-lasting economic and social problems formed the background to the outbreak of the crisis. The economic policies of the governments played an important part among its direct causes. The recession of the early 1980s reflected especially clearly the long-term problems. This was the most serious global economic crisis since World War II.

World production was affected in many ways by the factors which led to the outbreak of the recession in the early 1980s, which started in the developed capitalist countries and resulted in the most serious economic difficulties since World War II. Although world output as a whole did not decline in any single year of the recession (as a result of the increasing production of the socialist countries), a drop in production was experienced in the developed capitalist countries which was accompanied by a major showdown in the Third World states (Table 1), with a decline of GNP in two regions.

Gross national product fell in the USA and Great Britain in 1980, in the FRG, Italy, Britain, Belgium, Denmark, Norway and Switzerland in 1981. The gross domestic product diminished in ten developed capitalist countries in 1982; in the USA it dropped by 1.9 per cent, in Canada by 4.4 per cent, in Switzerland by 1.7 per cent and in the FRG by 1.1 per cent. In 1983, however, the gross domestic product decreased in only two developed capitalist countries: Italy and Switzerland.[1] From among the developing countries, GNP declined in the Middle East (in 1980 and 1981) and in Latin America (in 1982 and 1983).

The decline and the drop in industrial production assumed even greater proportions. Industrial production of the developed Western countries decreased by about 4 per cent between 1980 and 1982. While the gross domestic product fell by 1.8 per cent in the USA in 1982, industrial production decreased by 8.2 per cent. The decrease went to 4.9 per cent in the FRG, 3.8 per cent in France and 2.9 per cent in Italy. Of all the developed capitalist countries, it was only in Japan and Denmark that industrial production increased, though the rate of increase slowed down.[2] For the first time since the end of World War II the growth in industrial production of the developing countries fell. The decline was recorded mostly in the mining sector but in Latin America occurred also in manufacturing. The under-utilization of industrial capacity reached 80 per cent in some of the developing countries. In 1982 26–33 per cent of the industrial capacity of the developed Western countries remained unused and moreover

Table 1.
Growth of World Output*

	1971—75	1976—80	1981—85	1986—87**
Western industrial countries	3.1	3.5	2.3	3.1
Eastern Europe and the USSR	6.3	4.1	3.0	3.4
China	5.5	6.0	9.8	8.3
Developing countries	6.1	4.9	1.4	2.8
World	4.2	3.9	2.7	3.1

* For the Western economies, Gross Domestic Product, for Eastern Europe, USSR and China Net Material Product.
** Preliminary estimates.
Source: U.N. World Economic Survey 1986. International Monetary Fund: World Economic Outlook. Revised Projections. October 1986, 87.

the industrial production capacity of the USA was utilized only to 68 per cent even as late as February 1983.[3]

The number of firms which went bankrupt increased considerably—it was the highest since the 1929–33 crisis. (Their number increased in the USA by 43 per cent in 1981, by 49 per cent in 1982, and the losses written off amounted to nearly $6 billion.) Following 1981, the percentage of loans on which borrowers proved unable to pay interest or instalments came to 4 per cent in the USA (prior to 1981 this had amounted to only 3.1–3.2 per cent) and the ratio of "not-yielding" loans was still 3.4 per cent in 1984.

The number of bankruptcies in the Federal Republic of Germany increased by 2.7 per cent both in 1981 and 1982, it increased in France by 20.3 per cent and in Britain by 26.4 per cent. Several famous great firms went bankrupt or were rescued only by substantial public subsidies. There emerged also a particularly serious problem: the number of unemployed in the developed Western countries doubled between 1979 and 1983, the number of those without jobs growing from 5 per cent (15 million people) to 10 per cent (more than 35 million). The number of unemployed has been underestimated by official statistics because they do not take into account those (for instance many women and young people) who have removed themselves from labour force statistics having sought for work in vain; these people have become homemakers or students at the expense of the income of the breadwinners.[4]

Probably the whole of the 1980s will be characterized by slow growth which in some countries may be interrupted by short intervals of rapid economic boom. Global economic imbalances will be a source of major difficulties and uncertainties.

The international debate on the crisis reflects not only the recent experience and complex nature of the problems but also the capability of the different "schools of thought", in economics to evaluate scientifically the causes and consequences and to define the course of action needed. Experts who looked for explanations for the severity of the recession during the early 1980s set out primarily from the theories of the traditional Western schools of economics, only sought for short-term interpretations based on direct causes. They generally did not investigate the effects of deeper and more lasting factors point out the long-term consequences and implications of the crisis.

Thus, the 1983 World Economic Survey of the United Nations stressed that the unexpectedly serious drop in demand in the wake of the anti-inflationary policy initiated by the major industrial countries in 1979 and 1980 resulted in a considerable slowing down of world production and trade in 1981, and the deflationary effects became even more serious in 1982.

 This situation served as an emphatic reminder for the industrial countries that their economies were strongly interrelated with those of other nations. An uncoordinated upswing is continuing currently in an atmosphere of uncertainty. If this cannot be stepped up into a healthy and lasting prosperity then interdependence—now serving as a bond between developed and developing countries—could increasingly become an obstacle to progress an the cause of searching for new industrial development.[5]

The causes directly responsible for the recession as well as the significance of interdependent relations were correctly recognized by the UN experts. However, these specialists did not bestow enough care, for instance, on the fact that the background, i.e. the growth conditions of the individual countries, had also considerably changed by the early 1980s; moreover, this was just one of the reasons for the "uncoordinated" and "uncertain" nature of the upswing which began and unfolded in 1983. The upswing is uncertain and contradictory in almost all important industrial countries.

The 26 leading economists of fourteen industrial and developing countries who published a joint declaration in 1982 under the title "Promoting World Recovery" did not reckon with the changes either.

The authors of this declaration—just like the statements of the UN—emphasized the grave and serious character of the crisis which had developed in the early 1980s but regarded it as basically a short-term recession which, therefore, could be overcome within a short time if appropriate measures were taken for checking it. They considered the crisis to be the result mainly of the monetary restrictions which were imposed by the governments anxious about inflation following the second oil shock. What serious consequences restrictions made simultaneously—and often on a greater scale than necessary—would have had on the network of international relations was not understood.[6]

A complex analysis was also given in the second report of the so-called Brandt Commission on the crisis and its effects. "The protracted recession of the developed industrial countries" was regarded as the basic cause of the crisis, the root of which was once again seen in the anti-inflationary policy of the Western industrial countries. According to the report the exaggerated monetary restrictions were combined with an incorrect budget policy.

Treating mainly the conditions of a global upswing, the report drew attention to a number of other grave problems of the world economy, e.g. the disturbances in international monetary relations and world trade and the deficiencies of the institutions; but all this was done first and foremost from the aspect of the North-South relationship.[7]

The Polish economist Pajestka voiced an individual view regarding the crisis in the debate among the economists of the socialist countries. According to him the events of the 1970s and 1980s were the result of a deliberate policy of adaptation by the developed Western countries. The real value of the immense sums gained by the OPEC countries in the wake of the increase in oil prices was reduced with the help of inflation and the previous increase in the real incomes of the working classes was also counterbalanced.

He regarded the rise of the real rate of interest in the 1980s as "the counterrevolution of capital". To his mind the owners and operators of capital wanted to counterbalance the previous negative real rate of interest in that way and, at the same time, to stimulate capital supply. Relying on this thesis he was more optimistic than the majority of Western economists in evaluating and predicting long-term trends because he thought that the above-mentioned efforts had been basically successful and had turned development in the desired direction, at least according to the logic of the scale of values of the capitalist states: all the world was compelled to adapt itself accordingly. But Pajestka also stressed that these phenomena had proved to be harmful to the world economy and could in the long run cause more serious problems to the Western capitalist countries than those which they were striving to avoid.

Outside the circle of Marxist economists there are quite a few economic experts who view the economic recession of the early 1980s as part of a long-term, "more general" crisis or crises which are rooted in the capitalist system, in the crisis of capitalist accumulation. In this theory, special attention is paid to the fact that the process of global capitalist accumulation has become more difficult, and also to the problems of the incipient disintegration of the colonial division of labour.

The majority of the so-called radical American economists hold the view that it is the traditional capitalist structure which has undergone a crisis. The term "structural crisis" indicates that it is not the cyclical phenomena which are of vital importance. Of the causes of these phenomena, the insufficiencies of the institutions of the world economy are emphasized by some who regard the present conditions as a global management crisis.

Another recurrent conception of the analyses is the crisis of socio-political conditions as an independent factor. The renowned Mexican economist Wioncek in his contribution at the VIIth Congress of the International Association of Economists argued that we were facing not a single crisis but a whole crisis system, afflicting both the various parts of the world economy and its forms of relations. He considered the crisis to be of multifold and multiform character being rooted in the last resort in the structure of the world market.[8]

The late Raul Prebisch, former Secretary General of UNCTAD, also regarded the present-day world economic conditions as a structural crisis. In his view this crisis of capitalism was of a structural nature, and it was deeper and more complex than the great slump he had experienced as a young economist in the 1930s. That one had been a cyclical crisis, a serious crisis but one which had been overcome. The present crisis, however, originated from the inherent logic of the system, from the very structure within the bounds of which the system functioned. It was pointed out by Prebisch that the most disturbing characteristic of the crisis was the structural disequilibrium between increased consumption and the increase in the accumulation of productive capital. He emphatically stressed the term "productive capital" meaning such capital as increased employment and productivity because accumulation had other damaging forms as well.[9]

Prebisch set out in detail that, by using the term "disequilibrium" he wanted to emphasize that because of its structural position the ruling class was able to monopolize the profits of increased productivity based on technological progress. This renders it possible to accumulate capital and to maintain the privileged system of the consumers' society. Within that given system the rate of productive capital accumulation is surpassed by that of exaggerated consumption and accumulation serving non-productive objectives (e.g. in the defence industry).

Prebisch, however, did not restrict his definition to the recession which had begun in the early 1980s. Structural disequilibrium was regarded as a long-term cause and was interpreted in a broader sense. Though the factor he mentioned is undoubtedly an important one, it seems too generalized to give a justified explanation for the causes of the world economic relations which came into being at the beginning of this decade.

Highlighting the more comprehensive, long-term interrelations of the world economy in the early 1980s, Soviet economist Bogomolov set out from the hypothesis that mankind is probably undergoing the most complex and difficult period of its history. Until now it has never had to face such a dreadful challenge: it is threatened by nuclear devastation and the arms race has assumed unprecedented proportions. The world economy is critically ill, the consequences of which are difficult to predict. The stability of international politics and economy has been undermined by unceasing conflicts and clashes. Unsolved global problems—nutrition, energy, raw materials, environment, etc.—have resulted in serious trouble. Scientists and politicians even doubt whether there is any possibility for the survival of mankind. According to Bogomolov, it is important for just this reason that the world community should be able to overcome the present dangerous and critical situation of which the world economy is an integral part.[10]

A Hungarian economist, Tamás Szentes, stresses the importance of the holistic and global approach. He points out that the sources of the present crisis of international economy should by no means be considered as some "special" or temporary factors, and neither is it merely a "normal" cyclical crisis in the developed market economies. In his view it is a structural and institutional crisis of the world economy as a whole, i.e. a crisis rooted deeply in certain fundamental contradictions and inequalities of the modern world order. The crisis was triggered off by the unbalanced nature of the international division of labour, by a spontaneous industrial redeployment of labour, by the increasing confusion of state control of the national economies, by the growth and demonstration effects of the wasteful consumers' society, and finally by the internationalized armaments race and militarism.[11]

The causes and consequences are analysed from many aspects and angles in the paper by Szentes. He, too, is one of those authors who interpret the crisis in a more comprehensive way and as a long-term process. The justification of the holistic and global approach seems indisputable.

However, there are many experts who blur or confuse important details under the pretext of a global approach, and substitute generalizations, platitudes of economics for analysis. Both their diagnosis and their suggestions for overcoming the crisis tend to be too general and therefore are unfit for influencing concrete action. Another and often recurring problem is the fact that owing to the global and multifold character of the problems, even such phenomena as actually are only minor disturbances of the world economy or of one of its segments are declared to denote a crisis. Thus not only has the heart of the matter been blurred but also the difference between the crisis and other problems, disturbances also, which renders it more difficult to seek for a way out.

It seems obvious that many of the vital problems—among them global problems—of the world originating from its divided nature and inequalities could be solved or mitigated only in the long run. Of the economic difficulties, however, some could be eased in the foreseeable future. Thus a relevant and coordinated international economic policy could achieve significant changes in the market within two or three years. A common action to strengthen international economic cooperation and eliminate protectionism could also lead to rapid improvement in economic development.

In the course of the debate on the crisis a very specific view is voiced by the adherents of long cycles. The attention of some economic experts was drawn once again to the notion of long economic cycles by the development of the crisis and in general the events of the 1970s and 1980s: the sudden rupture following the heyday of the 1950s and 1960s, by stagflation, i.e. the slowing down of development going hand in hand with an extremely fast rate of inflation, as well as by growing unemployment and other phenomena characterized as factors of the crisis. These experts tried to find answers to the problems of causes and phenomena mainly in the investigation of long economic cycles.

As is well known, the theory of long cycles surfaced in various forms in the 1920s and 1930s. The conception itself is associated mainly with Kondratiev who examined the tendencies of long-term development primarily as a function of price and interest rate movements, and also tried to find other indices (e.g. raw material consumption, wages, etc.) to back up his views on the development of production. Incidentally, no statistics on world production were available in the 1920s.[12]

According to Kondratiev the development of the capitalist economy is not of a linear but of a cyclical character. However, the 7–11 year cycle is not the only one in the economy. There are also shorter waves lasting from one- and a-half to three years, and there are long cycles lasting for about fifty years which make economic development more complicated than ever. As a result of his studies he drew the conclusion that in the rising phases of long cycles the periods of growth are more frequent whereas in the descending stages depression is dominant as a rule. It is particularly agriculture which suffers in the descending phase. Quite a few new inventions are developed during that phase and introduced in production and transport and communications; however, their adoption *en masse* begins only at the beginning of the next upswing. In the rising stage of a long cycle gold production increases, markets expand and new countries are drawn into the circulatory system of the world economy. The rising phases of long cycles are also periods of growing tensions among economic forces. Mainly due to the struggle for markets, it is in this phase that devastating wars and revolutions break out which themselves have a complex influence on economic development.

For the sake of historical truth it should be mentioned that it was not Kondratiev who dealt first with the long cycles of capitalist development but the English economist Hyde Clark, and later on the Russian Marxist Alexander Helphand (Parvus)[13] in the 1870s and 1890s. Clark analysed railway construction, while Helphand's field of research was protracted agricultural depression. As a matter of fact Helphand defined the role of technological development in long cycles in a more comprehensive and scientific way than Kondratiev. But others also had reached the notion of long cycles prior to Kondratiev (e.g. the Dutch economist S. Van Gelden).

More recently, in connection with long cycles some economists—among them such famous scientists as Schumpeter—have concentrated their attention on the significance and role of innovations.[14]

In Schumpeter's opinion the upswing in the first Kondratiev-cycle was due mainly to the spread of steam as a driving force (1790–1813). Railway construction had the leading part in the second upswing (1844–1874), whilst the third was the result of the spread of electric power and the motorcar (1885–1916).

The examination of the so-called innovation cycles was begun by Mensch in the Federal Republic of Germany in the last decade; he attributed the emergence of adverse world economic conditions in the 1970s mainly to the stagnation of technological development. Mensch plotted technological development over 200 years and at four dates he found innovations of vital importance from the point of view of the economy in 1770, 1825, 1885 and 1935. After that date he found no significant innovation.[15]

Mensch regarded as fundamental those innovations which yielded entirely new social benefits: they made it possible to introduce new types of services and industrial products in the public or private sectors of the economy, for which there existed real demand and the production and distribution of which required the opening up of new markets; and at the same time, they contributed to creating a great number of new jobs and profitable investment opportunities.

The American economist and economic historian W. W. Rostow considered the development phase beginning with the early 1970s as the descending part of a "long cycle" of the world economy. His comments are noteworthy since many experts—particularly in the Western countries—hold similar views. Rostow, however, tends to be more scientific than the uncritical adherents of the theories on long-term cycles. According to him, since the mid-1960s and particularly from 1972 onwards, the world economy has entered the relatively long fifth period of rising raw material prices following a period of 20 years of absolute and relative price fall beginning in 1951. This phase was the end of the fourth so-called Kondratiev-cycle. On the strength of this analysis Rostow himself does not agree with the views regarding the applicability of the Kondratiev-cycle. Nevertheless, he regards the cyclical correlation between the price movement of raw materials and finished goods as significant. His opinion on cyclical price movements cannot be plotted as a simple sine curve, though certain similarities could be detected in the deviations.

He did not regard the 1983 drop in raw material prices as significant from the point of view of long-term tendencies and proclaimed that the stage of increasing raw material prices had not yet come to an end. Both in production and in development activities further investments will be needed leading to substantial decrease in the use of raw materials and energy per unit of output. This would further reduce raw material prices.

Thus, according to him, the primary cause of the crisis situation is the rise in raw material prices which coincides with the unfolding of the fourth industrial revolution and the industrial transformation accompanying it.[16]

It is not the intention of the author to review the various ideas and debates regarding long cycles or to criticize the theory itself. However, from the aspect of the situation evolving in the 1980s it seems important to draw attention once again to the criticisms which had been voiced with good reason as early as in the 1920s and 1930s.

These criticisms had chiefly stressed the following inadequacies of the theory:

a) The development of the capitalist world undoubtedly has periods of deceleration and others of acceleration the fundamental causes of which are, however, so different that exactly recurring causal relations could not be pointed out particularly, the social conditions of economic development which are very different.

b) Effects and causes are mixed up in the arguments of Kondratiev and other adherents of the long-cycle theory. They often allude to factors (e.g. to price movements) which are just the consequences of the development of the given state of the system. These undoubtedly could become active factors themselves, later on. Nevertheless, development is characterized much more by the fact that specific (and not cyclical) historical situations and conditions have emerged (or previous ones have changed) in the wake of which the conditions of economic development, too, have altered.

c) As regards opinions on the role of innovations, it seems an undeniable fact that certain innovations have played a significant economic part. It is impossible to point out their direct effects on the single stages of world economic relations. They always function in a specific social and economic environment, and their dispersion, too, has had extremely complex effects. In addition, innovations tend to be a continuous process. Scientific discoveries and inventions can appear both suddenly and by leaps, but their application and mass dispersion can take place only gradually. The more industrialized the world, the more complex the structure of production, the more intricate will be the growth effect of one or another major invention.

The character of the changes is particularly clearly indicated by the new scientific and technological revolution unfolding in the 1980s and based on microelectronics as well as on the deliberate industrial and agricultural application of biological processes. The effect on economic development unfolds not as a result of the scientific inventions and industrial activities built directly upon these but by means of comprehensive application in the ranges of production and services. There are boundless possibilities in this respect. The inequalities of economic conditions and the training of experts, venture capital, differences in public subsidization, priorities in making use of funds (e.g. military or civil objectives) are all sources of major divergencies.

d) As regards the views of W. W. Rostow on the development of raw material prices, it is undeniable that in the early 1970s the oil price shock had a part in triggering off a crisis the causes and consequences of which, however, cannot be considered independently of the actual economic and political conditions and the subjective relationships.

The second oil price explosion which was caused, not by shortage, but by the policy of the oil producing countries has proved precisely the significance of the subjective conditions. Analysing the development of the raw material situation a number of factors have to be taken into account—among others the problems and role of the developing countries, which have been largely disregarded by Rostow. Actually, these countries are not only producers but, to an increasing degree, consumers as well.

This, however, has nothing to do with the long cycles since new world economic conditions have evolved which were not fully revealed previously. There had been no analogous situation in the modern history of mankind. (Since the disintegration of the colonial system more than 120 new states have started on the road of deliberate economic development.)

In my opinion the new conditions which have arisen in the world economy by the beginning of the 1970s are not the result of long cycles. Since the end of the 1960s and the beginning of the 1970s a peculiar change in the world economy has taken place.

As a direct economic consequence of World War II and the transformation of the established world economic system, a new phase of development has begun.[17] Different views were formulated both regarding the question of change or stages of the world economy and the interpretation of the term, respectively. In the course of various professional debates of recent years some historians deemed it doubtful whether we could speak at all about a new era or change. They declared that the "change of eras" was brought about by the French Revolution and the October Revolution. Other historians and economists, however, interpreted the eras in terms of long periods. They held the view that the period which is coming to an end in our times began in the seventeenth century (i.e. with the era of colonialism), whereas the disintegration of world economic relations based on colonial exploitation has started essentially with the fall of the colonial empires. The development of prices, too, has reflected this process, and therefore they spoke about a price revolution which indicated the end of the era of cheap raw materials and energy carriers.

The author of this book interprets the development stages of the world economy differently. He holds the view that changes of phases in the world economy take place within long historical and economic-historical eras. Following the end of World War II there began a new stage in the world economy and it lasted till the end of the 1960s and the early 1970s. In this sense the unfolding of the new phase of world economic development has taken place within a long historical era. But it seems probable that the changes of some elements of the present longer eras coincide with the shorter developmental changes of periods. (For instance, the beginning of the disintegration of the colonial-type division of labour following the political collapse of the colonial system.)

According to my studies the shorter phases are determined by some major factors, so-called "regulating forces" in which the causes and consequences are naturally mutually interlinked in many ways and also linked with the socio-political conditions of our age, including the circumstances of the simultaneous existence and interrelation of the two social system.

a) *The international political and economic power structure of the given period.* The most important factors from the point of view of the enfolding of the new development stage are the following: the coexistence of 170 states (among them of 120 new countries) on our globe, the emergence of the Soviet–American military equilibrium and its influence on international affairs, the contradictions between the bipolar world (from the aspect of military force) and the multipolar economic power relations, the strengthening of regional power centres in international affairs (this problem will be treated in greater detail in Part Two of this book).

b) *The characteristics of scientific and technological development.* In this respect there have emerged new directions of development, new conditions have been brought about in the relationship between man and nature. Since the end of the 1960s micro-electronics has rapidly gained ground and mankind has arrived at the threshold of the "biological revolution". A new stage has begun in the fields of utilization of materials and the production and use of energy. New materials and combinations of materials were recognized. The new conditions are also indicated in the recognition of the weapons of mass destruction, the deterioration of the natural environment and the focus on global problems. (The problems of scientific and technological development and their international connections will be analysed in Part Three of this book.)

c) *The conditions of economic growth.* The conditions of economic growth have changed by and large simultaneously in the three main country groups of the world (developed capitalist, developing, and socialist countries.) The role of the different sectors (industry, agriculture, services) has changed and so have the factors behind the increase of demand.

Supply conditions, too, have changed. There were two major energy price increases and a fast decline of prices within 10–12 years. At the same time new technology has become more expensive. The relationship of economic policy and economic growth has changed. The international coordination of economic policies has became indispensable as the effectiveness of economic policies based on the philosophy of Keynes in a national framework has diminished in the developed capitalist countries, and new schools of thought emerged. In the socialist countries of Europe the tasks of intensive development came to the fore where the reserves of extensive development were exhausted. In the developing countries the intricate tasks of economic adjustment to the new global conditions represented major challenges.

d) *The character and conditions of international cooperation.* Changes commenced in the system of international economic cooperation. The strengthening of interrelationship and interdependence among the states as well as efforts aiming at the elimination of a colonial type of division of labour have brought about new conflicts in international cooperation. The emergence of new economic problems and new conditions has made organizational frameworks established in the previous stage partially obsolete. The necessity of fashioning new forms of cooperation has been put on the agenda. (These problems will be treated in connection with the structural changes in Part Five of the book.)

The development of the regulating forces of the new stage is uneven. The situation of the different groups of countries—and within them that of the different countries—varies to a considerable extent. The survival of the old frameworks and the conflicts under the new conditions bring about serious tensions and crisis situations.

The oil price explosions (in 1973 and 1979) and following decline are themselves partly the consequences of the changes in the world economy (and have naturally taken the form of an independent factor from the point of view of economic development).

The joint action of the oil producing and oil exporting countries (OPEC) has undoubtedly been a highly important milestone in the development of the world economy in the 1970s. Quite apart from the future of OPEC, and oil prices, for the first time in the modern history of mankind a group of developing countries has proved capable of organizing its forces effectively and enforcing concessions resulting in a significant redistribution of world national income by means of the mechanism of oil prices. This was made possible, of course, by the specific international conditions, particularly by the disintegration of the colonial system and by the military balance of power between the Soviet Union and the USA. The UN resolution about the declaration and programme of action for the "New World Economic Order" also reflected the effects of OPEC. In this respect we may witness further similar efforts in the next decade. It should be mentioned as a characteristic of the world economic situation at the beginning of the 1980s that the share received by developing countries from the world market sales prices of raw materials produced by them was 25 per cent. The nationalization of their extractive industries somewhat increased their share. However, the position of each individual raw material in the world economy is rather different and so are the positions of the developing countries. Up till now it was only a handful of developing countries which was able to make gains simply by nationalization. Taking a stand against the transnational corporations (which had traditionally dominated the extractive industries), the developing countries demand not only political determination but also adequate organizational (marketing) measures; currently there are few developing countries which are able to meet these requirements.

Actually the direct cause of the economic recession which began in the early 1980s was the second oil price explosion and/or the reactions of the states all over the world. The effects on the world economy of the changes in prices in the wake of the price explosions of 1973 and 1979 were quite considerable.

Table 2 illustrates the changes in the price index of the major commodity groups of world economy between 1960 and 1985.

As in the previous price explosion, considerable material means flowed from the oil importers to the oil exporters and also the total demand in the developed capitalist countries had to face a sudden deflationary pressure. The annual surplus income of the oil countries (the deficit of the OECD countries) reached the sum of $110–120 million, i.e. 2 to 3 per cent of the gross national product of the OECD states. From the point of view of the main protagonists of the world economy this was not such a shock for the developed capitalist countries as the first price explosion since they were aware of what they had to reckon with and decided to regard action against inflation as the most important task.

The world economy, however, was in a much weaker position than at the time of the first oil price explosion, which had been preceded by a considerable boom and which brought about a great demand for labour, raw materials and finished goods (in certain cases there was even a shortage of such goods). At the time of the boom following the recession accompanying the first oil price explosion, economic development slowed down and became more contradictory as unemployment had been fairly high in a number of industrial countries even before 1979. Following the second oil price explosion the reaction of the majority of the leading capitalist countries to the sudden external deficit and the internal inflationary pressure was a series of measures aimed at curbing economic growth.

In the early 1980s the first singificant recession of the world economy occurred, which was characterized—among other things—by the adverse effects of the relatively intensive conditions of interdependence. In the earlier (favourable) development stage

Table 2.
Price Index of Commodity Groups in International Trade 1960—1985

(1970 = 100)

Year	Raw materials (oil excluded)				Crude oil	Industrial finished products
	Total	Food stuffs	Metals	Agricultural raw materials		
1960	89.0	84.3	69.7	128.3	115.7	83.5
1961	85.6	81.6	69.5	119.5	111.7	85.2
1962	83.8	83.2	67.9	114.6	109.1	85.2
1963	89.1	98.4	66.8	117.2	108.3	85.2
1964	95.1	95.7	83.0	117.3	102.5	87.0
1965	93.2	88.9	91.4	113.9	102.5	88.4
1966	96.2	88.9	98.2	116.8	102.5	90.6
1967	90.1	90.7	83.9	106.1	102.5	90.8
1968	89.4	87.8	86.2	103.4	100.0	90.8
1969	96.5	95.0	94.9	109.8	98.4	94.9
1970	100.0	100.0	100.0	100.0	100.0	100.0
1971	94.3	102.0	84.6	99.5	127.2	105.6
1972	107.5	116.8	86.6	130.1	146.3	114.8
1973	165.6	179.8	127.1	233.2	208.3	135.2
1974	211.5	288.0	158.8	224.9	752.1	164.8
1975	173.4	226.8	128.0	180.5	826.5	185.2
1976	195.3	185.0	135.7	224.2	887.6	185.2
1977	237.7	178.2	145.7	231.4	956.2	201.6
1978	226.6	203.2	153.8	248.9	979.3	231.5
1979	263.8	231.8	199.6	383.6	1308.3	264.8
1980	289.4	310.7	220.9	316.1	2209.9	287.0
1981	247.0	268.0	191.0	285.2	2505.8	272.5
1982	207.2	187.6	166.2	248.1	2398.1	267.1
1983	219.2	199.4	166.2	265.5	2155.8	255.0
1984	223.0	208.0	160.8	270.8	2125.0	258.0
1985	211.0	179.9	154,2	235.8	2061.0	260.8

Sources: UNCTAD Trade and Development Report 1982, p 134., 1983, pp 3,4.
U.N. World Economic Survey, 1984. E. 1984/62, p 40. Commodity Trade and Price Trends.
World Bank, 1986, Edition ISSN: 0251–401 X

of the world economy the intensification of international cooperation was both furthered by the consequence of rapid economic development. A quarter of the total industrial and agricultural world production was marketed internationally. World economic development was furthered by the close interrelationship of the world's money markets. At the time of the recession which developed by the early 1980s the great international concentration of accumulated global effects of the major financial centres had strengthened, particularly owing to the fact that accrued total international (bank, public and enterprise) debt had reached 10 per cent of the world gross national product.

✳2. The Economies of the Developed Industrial Countries of the Western World

The recession of the early 1980s clearly demonstrated that the internal situation of countries and country groups which play an outstanding part in world production and exports is reflected faster and more intensively than before in effects on other parts of the world. Their national economic policies, their achievements and errors, too, had a much more intensive international influence than ever before.

The causes of the changes in the conditions of growth, how deep and how long-lasting the economic troubles would be, have been frequently and hotly disputed. The favourable supply and demand conditions and the institutional structure, which had benefited economic development in the 35 years following World War II undeniably grew weaker or even ceased to exist by the beginning of the 1970s.

The circumstances which had served as the basis of the West German, Japanese and Italian "economic miracles" are spoken of as the "golden age of economy" by Western economic literature. Indeed, specific conditions had developed at the time.

The accumulated purchasing power at the time of World War II, the many years of missing of "postponed" civil consumption and investments, developed an immense potential market, an effective demand in the United States and in some other capitalist countries as well. To realize this demand incentives from various (internal and international) sources were needed, too, in certain countries, for instance in the FRG and Japan. Economic growth received its significant initial "impetus" from this state which existed in the twenty-five years following World War II.

Meanwhile—particularly in the 1960s—the almost continuously expanding market stimulated also by the rapid technological developments in the range of capital goods and consumer goods has resulted in the rapid growth of productivity and incomes. On the basis of these it became possible to increase simultaneously consumption and investments.

In both industry and services of some Western European countries the influx of peasants, housewives, former owners of small businesses, refugees and later many millions of guest workers has guaranteed a cheap labour force for a long time and also kept wage rises within "manageable" limits. In Western Europe the increase in wages and their ratio in the national income—despite the mass influx of guest workers—has accelerated only since the beginning of the 1960s. By that time full employment had become fairly general and the number of job opportunities has exceeded that of job seekers. True, not all Western European countries were able to create such favourable conditions. Thus Great Britain, because of her domestic organizational problems and her considerable dependence on foreign trade as well as her deteriorating competitiveness, had to grapple with almost permanent difficulties: between 1950 and 1970 the growth of Britain's gross national product was a mere 2.8 per cent per annum as opposed to the average of 4.9 per cent of the 16 most industrialized capitalist countries.

Favourable external (world economic) circumstances, too, backed up the "golden age" conditions. The system of fixed exchange rates brought about a certain degree of discipline in the field of world market price fluctuations. In the 16 industrialized capitalist countries consumer prices increased only at an annual average rate of 3.8 per cent between 1950 and 1970. Considerable credits were available at favourable terms facilitating the survival of countries grappling with transitional payment difficulties. Until 1966 the utilization of resources in the economy of the most important capitalist country, the USA—the currency of which, i.e. the dollar, had a fundamental part in the system of international finance—was not particularly high, resulting in a relatively low rate of inflation. The greater liberalization of trade policy among the developed capitalist countries contributed to the growth of international trade in manufactured goods and particularly in capital goods. New and rapidly expanding markets were opened up by the commencement of industrialization in the developing countries. Exports from the developed capitalist countries increased by four and a half times (calculated using current prices) between 1950 and 1970. Exports increased most rapidly in countries where the growth of the price of export goods was slowest. Export prices in the 16 developed capitalist countries increased by an annual 1.5 per cent between 1950 and 1970, i.e. the rise was much slower than that of their domestic prices.

The international flow of capital assumed immense proportions. Immediately after the war part of the shortage in consumer goods was surmounted by means of state funds from the USA through the Marshall Plan and its Japanese counterpart. Thus, the consumer market was brought up to standard and internal stabilization was bolstered up. Both the Marshall Plan and, later on, public aid to developing countries were a considerable contribution to the increase of exports of the donor countries. In the course of the 1960s the capital investments of transnational corporations amounted to many times the capital which had flowed to Europe by means of the Marshall Plan, and at the same time a significant volume of new technology, too, was brought to a great number of countries in that way. Raw material prices remained stable between 1950 and 1970 (with the exception of the years of the Korean war), moreover the price of gold did not change either. Economic recessions were neither significant nor of a lasting character.

Change in the conditions of economic growth is a process comprising both disadvantageous and potentially advantageous factors. The latter are particularly related to the development of new trends in technological progress but are still not strong or broad enough to serve as the basis of a lasting world economic growth process. Under the given circumstances the realization of reserves through economic integration has become more difficult, too.

Particularly serious are the troubles in certain Western European industrial countries, because their internal political and economic conditions do not allow such flexibility as is the case in the USA and Japan, and thus major shifts in their economic policies are more difficult to achieve, in many respects explained by the role played by strong political and economic groups, often with conflicting interests. Following World War II, specific political conditions emerged in the majority of the industrial countries of Western Europe which facilitated the strengthening of social security and the raising of living standards of relatively broad strata of the population. At the same time, the position of the ruling elites has not become weaker either. A radical transformation of economic relations did not constitute the economic core of the political struggles but rather the reason for this conflict was the maintenance and strengthening of hard-won positions. This was achieved partly by means of the system of objectives and incentives of public economic policy. As a result of the freer movement of goods, capital and labour, the openness of the countries and their international "vulnerability" was enhanced by integration.

As regards the consequences, similar changes have taken place in the American economy. The intensity of these changes, however, was less than in Western Europe. The direct causes, and the mechanisms too, were for the most part different.

Changes were of outstanding significance in the following areas:

a) the process of defining wage costs and the functioning of the labour market;

b) the definition of nominal prices;

c) the relations between the internal and external changes;

d) the relationship between the state budget and the economic processes.[18]

As a result of the above factors regulating processes on the macro scale has become more difficult.

Wage costs (wages + social security contributions) were increasingly determined by autonomous processes. Wages have not been influenced "in the traditional way", by the labour market. The importance of indexation increased, which limited the impact of current changes on the development of wages. The increase of social allocations was brought about by the growing number of people insured growing unemployment and the attitudes of households. Under the influence of these factors the ratio of wages in costs has increased everywhere by 1982/1983, and the share of transfer payments for social objectives has increased in the national income. Enterprises were stimulated by increased wage costs to adopt labour economizing technologies, and this led to the development of a specific situation in the labour market. While the security of the so-called central part of the labour force (organized and highly qualified manual workers, engineers and technicians), as well as of a certain percentage of the numerically increasing staff of economic management was enhanced, uncertainty at the periphery of the employed population grew, unemployment increased, living standards sagged. As a result the labour market became even more polarized. The inequalities in the labour market increased.

A similar situation emerged in the case of price movements. Actual and expected rises of costs could still be shifted to the consumers by oligopolies and enterprises operating in so-called protected sectors. As the central groups of workers succeeded— irrespective of the disadvantageous conditions on the labour market (e.g. oversupply)—in keeping wage rises on the same level as the rise in living costs, so the most important protagonists of economic life were able to adapt themselves faster to actual and expected changes than the others. As a consequence, the monetary regulation of economic life could influence macro processes only under the circumstances of slow growth or a stagnating economy with a high level of unemployment and at the expense of the poorer groups in the countries concerned. These costs of anti-inflation policies are high and the policies which have been adopted have not provided any real solution.

The third change is related to the strengthening interrelationship of the USA, the Western European and particularly the EEC—countries and their closer relations to other parts of the world. The openness of the countries in question has promoted international trade. As a result, the surplus or deficit of the trade balance represents a considerable percentage of the gross national product, and considerable fluctuations are possible in the trade and payments' balances.

The adjustment of economic policy by the traditional means is hindered by such fluctuations. The problems are related mostly to the peculiarities of changes in the structure of consumption and imports.

The price elasticity of non-competitive imports is low in the short run, and its income elasticity is negligible. Competitive imports, mainly industrial goods, are on the other hand characterized in these countries by high income and price elasticity. For this reason the effect of exchange rate fluctuations on imports and the trade balance has decreased. At the same time, the influence of capital movements on the balance of payments has increased and the effect of international capital flows on interest rates has accelerated as is reflected for instance by the influx of capital into the United States at the beginning of the 1980s. Changes in exchange rates result in shifts in the direction of foreign trade more quickly than in modifications to the level of imports or exports. Accordingly, the macro-economic possibilities of economic regulation have become more difficult.

The conditions of regulation on a micro scale have changed, also, as a result of increasing interdependence. Economic activity is once again restructured in the new phase of technological revolution at an uneven rate. Cost relations are altered, particularly with the introduction of the achievements of microelectronics. The whole way of life is transformed, new needs and demands emerge, new structures of the labour force and new skills come into being.

The transformation of the structure of final demand is affected by changes beginning with households and spreading to enterprises, and by changes in investment which affect the cosumers. The uneven character of the process has a varying influence on demand in different countries.

All those changes in the developed industrial Western countries, particularly of Western Europe altered the conditions of international competition. The impact of changing cost relations led to an increasing inflow of goods from the developing countries and Japan. These became important factors in increasing the dangers of protectionism as a traditional instrument of economic adjustment.

The considerable divergences and constraints of state budget policies also played a part in the greater difficulty in regulating macro-economic processes. Problems were intensified also by the differences in the factors behind the formulation of national economic policies of the various governments.

In determining the actual objectives and means of public policies the social struggles of the given countries, the balance of class forces, also had a major part. The disagreements of the so-called "left-wing" and "right-wing" Keynesians for instance could chiefly be explained by this fact. Of the major manifestations of left-wing Keynesianism the most important one was the development of the "welfare state" structure based on social political programmes. The chief policy of the right-wing Keynesians was the increase of military expenditure and the specific economic system of stimulation based on an increase in military contracts. In the case of both trends specific mixtures emerged and there were no truly "pure" models on either side. Thus, the above classification indicates only basic trends. There were considerable differences also in the directions of state countercyclical policies (stimulating or retarding tendencies) and in their results. Serious mistakes were made in many countries as regards the scale and timing of measures. In some countries the unambiguous and definite passing or implementation of regulations was made impossible by domestic struggles (e.g. in Great Britain). All these differences hindered and in some cases made it impossible to synchronize national economic policies internationally on the necessary scale.

The member states of the Common Market, too, preserved the decision-making autonomy and priorities of national economic policies on such fundamental questions, as their reaction to external effects. Considering the priority of realizing objectives and the means serving this aim, differences were aggravated by the conflicting trends in home policies.

State (central as well as local) budget expenditures increased considerably in all developed industrial countries. In the 1960s the average ratio of state budget expenditures in the developed Western industrial countries amounted to approximately one third of the gross domestic product, though the range tended to be fairly high (Japan 19 per cent, Sweden 40 per cent).

On average in 1980 the share of state budget expenditures was 46 per cent[19] (Japan 34 per cent, Sweden 62 per cent). Thus, the increase was extremely fast, and this means that the role of the state budget has grown (and that of revenue and of expenditures separately, too) as an influence on business life.

The high proportion of public expenditure in GNP also meant that the economic significance and political importance of outlays and revenues increased as well. The economic and political processes influencing the development of the structure of the budget, which are indicated by the character and rate of income taxes and by their breakdown by social class as well as by the magnitude of social, military or other expenditures, exert their influence generally not as short-term effects but rather by political electoral cycles. For this reason certain budget allocations have become rigid, on one hand, and a self-activating effect of varying intensity could be felt on the other hand (depending on the share of different lobbies or on the nature of the expenditure). This also had the consequence of narrowing the manoeuvring possibilities in the budgetary policies of governments as they tried to restrain the fluctuations of business life (countercyclical policy) or to solve long-term problems.

In 1883 German economist Adolph Wagner declared the tendency of state budgetary expenditures to grow as a specific economic law.[20] According to him, with social progress, economic development, growing urbanization and broadening public education, as well as other demands, state budget expenditures necessarily have to increase.

Objective economic and social conditions and needs, too, are a background of growing budget expenditure. In different periods many Western economists and decision-makers of economic policy have come to the conclusion that the increase in budget expenditure has been exaggerated.

The well-known economist Colin Clark predicted in the 1930s that the economy would collapse if taxes exceeded 25 per cent of the gross national product.[21] Since then it has been proved that the economy can stand even double that tax burden.

It is also true, however, that the possibilities for public redistribution are limited. Results depend mainly on the economic effectiveness of state budget expenditures and to what an extent a given country is able to organize—in the broad sense of the term—its public finances. The effectiveness of budget expenditures depends in the last resort on how much they stimulate the productive basis of the economy in question, the growth of its productivity and its international competitiveness and how much they improve the "social mood" by promoting employment and strengthening the feeling of social security. Naturally it is important from the point of view of effectiveness what influence the structure of state revenue has on the economy. It is an economic truism that beyond a certain level the raising of taxes functions as a brake on the performance of the taxpayers. Empirical examination has proved the fact that investments, exports, employment, productivity and innovations are influenced by the degree and kind of taxes. It is, however, also a fact that the growth of public debt caused by accumulating deficits in the wake of expenditures exceeding budget revenue has an unfavourable effect as well, since it puts considerable interest burdens on the economy while the high interest rates necessary for financing the deficit could "drive" some private investment away from production.

The economic effects of the state budget are considerably influenced by the budget deficit and by the substantially increasing public debt. The rate of budget deficit in the member states of the European Common Market grew from 1 per cent of the gross national product in 1970 to 5 per cent in 1981. (In the United States the relatively fast growth began in 1982 and reached 3–4 per cent of the gross national product in 1983 representing 30 per cent of the net accumulation of the country.)[22]

Not only savings, interest rates, private capital investments and the network of financial relations are influenced by budget deficits in the countries affected, but so are international economic cooperation and, in particular, the international flow of capital. Thus the enormous budget deficit of the United States has an effect on the interest rates of all other leading capitalist countries as well, keeping them on a high level.

Economic policy has developed differently in Japan. Japanese economic policy has tended to be systematic and comprehensive: at the level of the national economy, the monetary and budgetary-political means were linked with the targets of the individual sectors of industry. At the time of rapid economic growth, for instance, Japan had no independent monetary policy because the stock-market was rather underdeveloped and the Bank of Japan was the tool of the Ministry of Finance. Credits were used by the government for the stimulation of certain sectors of industry. Some other measures were used to support the growth of accumulation, the restriction of consumption and the stimulation of productive investments. Moreover, macro and selective micro-economic objectives were blended in a peculiar way in Japanese economic policy.

Stimulating and restrictive measures were adopted by the government on the basis of forecasts—founded on consensus—from the big enterprises and public institutions, and their cooperation was enlisted in the correction of mistakes. (Thus, in the 1960s and 1970s considerable surplus capacity was called into being on the basis of exaggeratedly optimistic estimates; labour on such superfluous capacity was put out of use and dismantled by joint effort.

Economic policy measures have changed, too. In certain periods general measures influencing all branches of industries were in force such as training of cadres, improvement of the information system, establishment of a stable macro-environment, while in other periods selective measures were preferred (e.g. at times when the encouragement of a switch-over became a priority).

Thus, state budget policy did not take the form of an independent, autonomous system of measures. The rate of inflation, too, was considerably lower and manifested itself in a different context in the Japanese economy, a phenomenon that can be explained by the fact that the wage level was low and exports were relatively greatly important.

Inflation—which was made the most of particularly by the neo-conservative forces—became one of the key issues of domestic political struggles related to economic policy in the USA and Western Europe, because of its connection with budget deficits and their effects, and also because of other structural characteristics of the economies of the developed capitalist countries. Social unrest and discontent related to inflation played a vital part in bringing these neo-conservative forces to power.

Inflation has multiple social and economic, domestic and international causes. Its political connections, are, however, fairly simple. The high rate of inflation is regarded as a peculiar "tax-collector" by the broad masses. At the same time, it is a means for the redistribution of incomes for those favoured by the economic policy. The direct causes and consequences of inflation were different in the United States and in Western Europe, and there were also differences among the European capitalist countries in this respect.

The background of the post-war American inflation was the so-called credit-economy, i.e. the established system of financing economic development. In this system the financing of expenditures (and the deficit) of the state budget was closely linked with the credit policy of the private banks and the state (cooperative) bank system. This was supplemented by enterprise financing, private consumption and mortgages. From 1946 to 1969, i.e. in the period of a lower-rate inflation, gross national product (at current prices) increased from $ 208.5 billion to $ 932 billion, the state debts from $ 269 billion to $ 380 billion, whereas private debts grew eightfold, exceeding $ 1200 billion. In those 23 years the dollar lost about half of its value. Between 1970 and 1984 the gross national product had increased by 2.6 times (current prices), state debts rose by 2.6 times, private debts doubled, the dollar once again lost half its value but at a much faster rate than in the previous period.[23]

The credit economy became the fundamental means of demand stimulation, it increased consumption and the financing of considerable budget deficits.

Inflation, which is essentially a macro-economic phenomenon, was closely linked to processes in the microeconomic sphere. As was proved by economic developments in the United States, economic, social and psychological causes were equally responsible for the appearance of inflation (such as the effects of inflationary expectations on the wage struggles of working people or on enterprise decisions). Under the influence of the pressure of certain political and economic circles of modern American society state budgetary expenditures steadily increased and regularly exceeded revenues. Pressure exerted on the system of the Federal Reserve Board in the interest of financing deficits resulted in an increased money supply. However, other specific causes, too, have contributed to increased inflation.

The movements of the inflation spiral as well as the credit economy were influenced decisively by military expenditures. The effects could be felt most directly through the relation of demand and supply. Military expenditures brought about purchasing power and effective demand but did not contribute (at least not directly) to the creation of productive capacities serving future consumption. Thus, a kind of additional demand was created which had the effect of increasing prices all over the economy. The growth of military expenditures not only contributed to the increase in the budget deficit (these expenditures were not fully covered by the revenue) but also had a part in the unfolding of a mechanism generating inflation via public monetary and credit policy. This mechanism could be particularly keenly felt at the time when the economy was "overheated". Thus, the inflationary wave in the United States at the end of the 1960s was related to a great extent to the above mentioned facts. From other aspects, too, military expenditure was an important stimulant of price increases generating the inflation spiral and related to rising costs.

Wages are higher and grow faster in the defence industry as a rule because here resistance to increasing wages and salaries is weaker. Increased expenditure is accepted by the military sector readily since these can be shifted quickly and easily to the "consumers". The military expenditure of the state budget is therefore always higher than the original allocation. In most capitalist countries the military sector operates on contracts which assume from the very outset that production costs and profits will be covered; cost increases are interpreted less strictly than in other sectors of industry.[24]

It was revealed by the US Government Accounting Office in 1979 that in the decade following 1969 real costs were on the average double the original price calculations forwarded to the Pentagon. Not a single case could be found of costs being underestimated or allocations having been calculated correctly.[25] These findings were corroborated by investigations in 1984.

Price increases in the defence industry rapidly spread to other sectors of the economy as well. The increase in military expenditures actually drains away resources from civil production, slows down its possibilities for expansion and thus makes the economy as a whole vulnerable to the impact of inflation.

The rapid growth of military expenditures in the early 1980s—combined with an unprecedented budget deficit—did not trigger off an inflation simply because there were enormous untapped production capacities in the economy, and unemployment was rather high.

Incidentally, there were three periods of major price increases in the United States in the past three decades. The first was related to the Korean war, the second occurred between 1956 and 1958, whereas the third lasted from the end of the 1960s to 1982; the subsequent two oil shocks played a great part in the last one. The third inflationary wave was the longest and also—in peacetime—the most intensive inflationary period in the history of twentieth-century American economy. Consumer prices increased by 5.5 per cent between 1940 and 1950, by 2.1 per cent in the following decade, by 2.7 per cent in the 1960s, and by 8.2 per cent in the 1970s. The inflationary wave of the 1970s was accompanied by a peculiar economic stagnation and slow growth.

The American economy was sapped by this inflation. The growth of investment slowed down since inflation increased the risks of investments and made it impossible to envisage and plan real profits adequately. It had a particularly damaging effect on investment demanding long-term commitment and on research and development allocations. Inflation added to the raising of taxes since it artificially inflated incomes, and under a progressive tax system more money was automatically taken from the taxpayers. Thus, savings were reduced, too. The recessions of the 1970s took the form of specific inflationary recessions.

It was partly inflation which was responsible for the slackening of the growth rate of productivity since it had an adverse influence on investment.

Though it was first of all the working masses who suffered under the impact of inflation contradictions sharpened within the business sector as well. Some industrial groups made great profits out of inflation whereas others fared less well, since—with the exception of the high-tech sectors of industry—the replacement of previously invested capital and modernization demanded more funds than the amounts which had accumulated out of amortization. As it was mentioned above, according to certain opinions, inflation was consciously and rather successfully made use of by international big capital after the first oil shock as a means of reducing the value of the currencies flowing from the developed capitalist countries and of the real incomes of the oil producing countries.

Despite the high interest rates which reached an all-time record since the American Civil War (the official interest rate had been about 2–3 per cent at the time of the Korean war, reached 7–8 per cent between 1966 and 1969 and surpassed the 20 per cent ceiling in 1981), a considerable section of bank capital, the proliferating consumers' and other credit institutions were affected unfavourably by the inflation. Incidentally, high nominal interest rates are equal to lower real interest rates when inflation exists.

A certain rise in prices is unavoidable in a dynamically developing market economy. The modern capitalist economy is able to stand an annual 4–5 per cent rise of prices without serious problems even for a longer time. However, it is unable to overcome inflation on a considerable scale without major economic shocks. Under certain conditions, of course, this, too, would have been possible by means of restoring the balance of the state budget, reducing of military expenditure, stimulating productive investment, introducing an income policy by which it would be possible to control and coordinate the activities of the main protagonists of business life through wages, prices, profits, taxes, etc. as well as by backing the elimination of the bottlenecks of economic development (e.g. energy). Certain governments have tried to adopt some of the above mentioned measures. Their complex implementation, however, was not undertaken because of the conflicting interests of different groups of countries. As a result, inflation had become public enemy No. 1 in the United States by the end of the 1970s. As it is well-known, at the elections in 1980 the Reagan administration came into office with the help of slogans proclaiming the termination of inflation, the curtailing of federal expenditures held to be largely responsible for inflation, and the elimination of budget deficits.

Similar slogans were professed by the British government and the governments of other developed Western countries. They curtailed social expenditure and tried to make a rise in unemployment acceptable.

What Has Happened to Inflation: Lasting or
Temporary Improvement?

A basic question for the future is the following: how long will the lower level of inflation last or how could disinflation be harmonized with a significant future boom? Fear of the direct and long-term consequences of inflation has played an outstanding part in the economic policy of the majority of the Western industrial countries ever since the end of the 1970s. Curbing inflation has become the priority of economic policy particularly in countries wielding considerable economic power.

Of the factors contributing to the slowing down of the rise in prices it was actually of great importance that despite the high rate of unemployment in most of the industrially developed capitalist countries the anti-inflationary economic programme was continued in the first half of the 1980s.

Most of the restrictions were upheld or only slightly relaxed. The increase of wages and salaries in the public sector was checked and sometimes even blocked. In addition to the high rate of unemployment this put a break on the wage demands of those working in private enterprise, too. Thus, real wages in the USA in 1982 did not reach the level of 1967.[26] It also became more difficult or even impossible for enterprises to shift the burden of wage rises to the consumers by raising prices. At the same time, the growth rate of productivity increased, and this had a beneficial influence on the increase of profits.

The declining price of imported goods, primarily of raw materials also had an important part in curbing inflation.

The threat of inflation or the danger of a new wave of inflation is especially great in countries where there is a considerable budget deficit. In the United States, for instance the inflationary effects of the $ 200 billion budget deficit was balanced by a substantial influx of foreign capital amounting to about $ 100 billion as well as by an import surplus of another $ 140 billion in 1985, leading to lower prices. (Table 3 illustrates the price movements, Table 4 increases in wages and consumer prices in some capitalist countries.)

From the point of view of future price increases an important question concerns the trend of raw material prices, wages and profits should faster economic growth occur. For instance, will oil prices increase again as they did during the 1970s and how long will the organized workers show "self-restraint" and when will major new wage struggles, break out and finally, how long would the present favourable conditions for profits last? The "future" of inflation will be influenced in the long run by the balance of state finances, the amount of budget deficits and the way such deficits are financed. There is of course a problem of a different nature. Disinflation may produce stagnation. When prices are not increasing there is no pressure to buy. Decision-makers in business deposit their money in banks or speculate in financial markets instead of speculating with inventories. In this situation, such issues as of synchronizing the economic and social performance of the countries with their capacity, will appear again but from a different direction. The most meaningful solution is to improve the efficiency of production and consumption by significant and coordinated structural changes, to strengthen the position of the countries in question in international competition by accelerating technological progress. Disinflation as a

Table 3.

Changes in Prices as Compared to the Previous Year

Country	1980			1981			1982			1983			1985		
	1	2	3	1	2	3	1	2	3	1	2	3	1	2	3
USA	13.4	13.5	13.5	7.7	9.2	10.4	1.3	4.6	6.1	1.2	1.6	3.2	2.9	2.1	4.3
FRG	14.0	7.0	5.5	11.6	6.0	5.9	3.4	4.8	5.3	-0.5	1.5	3.0	5.0	2.8	2.4
United Kingdom	8.5	14.0	18.0	9.2	9.5	11.9	7.3	7.8	8.6	7.0	5.4	4.6	9.6	6.1	5.0
France	8.8	16.3	13.6	11.0	12.8	13.4	11.1	11.5	11.8	11.0	8.8	9.5	13.3	7.6	7.4
Italy	22.8	17.5	21.2	18.1	17.0	16.5	12.9	14.8	14.7	7.9	12.2	17.0	8.1	10.1	10.8
Switzerland	5.8	4.4	4.0	6.2	5.6	6.5	2.3	3.7	5.6	-0.7	1.1	2.9	3.4	3.0	3.0

Note 1 — price of intermediate products; 2 — final output prices; 3 — consumer's prices
Source: U. N. Economic Commission for Europe. Economic Survey 1983, pp. 20, 23, 24, 1984-85. pp. 43-49.

Table 4.

Annual Changes in Hourly Earnings in Manufacturing (1) and consumer's prices (2)

Country	1980		1981		1982		1983		1984		1985	
	1	2	1	2	1	2	1	2	1	2	1	2
USA	8.5	13.5	9.9	10.4	6.4	6.1	4.0	3.2	4.0	4.3	3.7	3.5
FRG	6.2	5.5	5.3	5.9	4.9	5.3	3.2	3.0	2.3	2.4	4.1	2.2
United Kingdom	17.8	18.0	13.2	11.9	11.1	8.6	8.9	4.6	8.7	5.0	9.4	6.
France	15.1	13.6	14.5	13.4	16.0	11.8	11.5	9.5	8.1	7.4	6.4	5.8
Italy	22.5	21.6	23.7	16.5	17.2	14.7	15.0	17.0	11.4	10.8	11.4	10.8
Switzerland	5.2	4.0	5.1	6.5	5.6	5.6	6.8	2.9	1.8	3.0	3.3	3.4

Source: U. N. Economic Commission of Europe. Economic Survey 1982, 1983, pp. 20, 21. 1984-85 p. 43, 49; 1985-86 p. 37, p. 39.

disadvantage means the slowing down of consumption and the growth of budgetary revenues. Imports are also endangered. In this situation, the most conservative forces attack social expenditure first of all, and the socioeconomic structure established under the banner of the "welfare state".

Naturally the debates concerning the "welfare state" were more comprehensive and deeper in the economic policies of the developed Western states and were not related solely to the economic recessions of the 1970s, or to the disinflation. They were interrelated with structural changes, the take-over of a new generation and other factors influencing social development in the Western industrial countries.

One of the most important of the so-called "direct roots" of the welfare state was the fact that under the influence of the pressure of the broad masses of the Western countries—and also prompted by their own socio-political interests—the ruling circles started to expand the social services considerably as an answer to the mass discontent and demands accumulated in the course of the Great Depression of the 1930s and World War II. The motives of the various political groups were different in this respect, too. (Thus, the idea of the social democratic parties was to establish a comprehensive welfare state by a considerable extension of the existing elements of social benefits. More moderate objectives were formulated by other, middle-class political organizations. As a final outcome, however, the ratio of social outlays in the gross national product substantially increased and resulted in the large-scale redistribution of the GNP.)

The considerable rise of living standards in the developed industrial countries after World War II and the strengthening of social security has changed the priority of the social scale of values. In addition, this redistribution has radically curtailed the incomes principally of the middle strata.

A number of criticisms were voiced relating to the welfare state even prior to the neo-conservative attacks. It was primarily its "expensiveness", its "character affecting economic stimulation in an adverse way" and "mounting red tape" which were stressed.

As long, however, as the Western economy developed satisfactorily, alternatives opposed to the "welfare state" were not formulated in the conflict between those in favour of social policy and the protagonists of economic performance. This situation underwent a change during the recession of the 1970s. At the time it was strongly emphasized that industrial expenditure should be increased at the expense of social outlays, because that way weak competitiveness could be strengthened and employment improved.

The Commission of the European Economic Community, reflecting the above views, pointed out in its 1982 annual report on social development the following: the social insurance system of the member states showed a great number of common problems and the time was ripe to compare experiences and seek adequate solutions in the light of budgetary restrictions. Though the Commission emphasized the point that it did not want by any means to bring about a set-back in social progress, it wanted to initiate a broadly based debate on social expenditure and the effectiveness of the system.[27]

In a number of Western countries the reduction of social expenditure actually began. This, however, could not be a large-scale reduction since at a time of growing

unemployment the various relief and compensation payments were an important
means of maintaining social peace. Without this it would have been much more
difficult for the Western countries to beat an unemployment rate of 32 million afflicting
almost 10 per cent of their population of employment age. The purchasing power
created by social benefits was not a negligible economic factor any more in a period of
decreasing demand. Even more important were the political factors which almost
prevented the realization of the programmes originally proclaimed. Though social,
health and educational expenditures were reduced the scale of reduction was less than
planned.

It is undeniable that irrespective of social systems an adequate balance is needed
between economic performance, resources and social policy. Social welfare, however,
is not simply the result of the "voluntary" decision of the Western world but it is also
the achievement of a hundred years of social struggles. Tensions which have developed
and intensified between economic performance and budget expenditures were related
less to the increase in social welfare expenses than to the growth of military
expenditures. This has become especially characteristic in the 1980s in some important
Western countries, primarily in the USA where first of all the neo-conservative
"supply-side" oriented school launched sharp attacks on social benefits.

The other great issue in public expenditure is the size and dynamics of defence
allocations. Their economic consequences—as mentioned above—are closely linked
to the strengthening of the "inflationary inclinations" of the economy—to a much
greater extent than to social welfare outlays since they are essentially of an
unproductive character.

In estimating the economic effects of armaments costs the starting point is the size of
the defence budget and its share in the gross national product of the countries. As all
the experts know very well the international comparison of military expenditure is a
highly intricate task. Such a comparison is rendered difficult and almost impossible to
interpret (in the economic sense of the term) for technical reasons—the composition of
the budget, the different interpretation of the individual items, the dissimilar nature of
the cost factors, the possibility of concealing some items which are of a military
character in the long run, the distorting effect of the exchange rates taken into account
in the course of conversion, and many other factors.

Between 1980 and 1985 the share of the developed Western countries in total of
military expenditure (amounting annually to some $ 800 billion) was 48 per cent. This
represented nearly 3.8 per cent of the gross national product of the developed industrial
countries in 1983 or one sixth of their total budget expenditures.[28] The ratio of their
military expenditures in the gross national product had actually diminished between
1969 and 1978, but it has been on the upgrade ever since.

The economic effect of military expenditure varies in the developed western
countries.

i) The percentage of material resources used for military purposes is quite dissimilar
in the countries in question. Military budgets represent 3.8 per cent, i.e. more than the
average ratio, of the gross national product of the developed western countries
(OECD states). (The average was around 6 per cent in the NATO nations in the early
1980s.) It was higher in the United States (6.9 per cent), whereas it was lower in Great
Britain (3.4 per cent), the Federal Republic of Germany (3.4 per cent), France (4.2 per

cent) and only about 0.9 per cent in Japan. From the point of view of judging the effects, comparative figures regarding per capita gross national product and per capita military expenditures are highly interesting. Of the $ 10. 480 per capita gross national product of the NATO countries $ 529 were spent on military purposes in 1982.

ii) The ratio of the strength of the armed forces related to the population in employment age is different, too. The population of working age in the OECD countries was 500 million in 1982, the strength of their armies 5.9 million, i.e. nearly 1.2 per cent of the population in employment age. In the NATO countries this ratio was 1.5 per cent, in the United States 1.6 per cent, in Great Britain 1 per cent, in the FRG 1.1 per cent, in France 1.4 per cent and in Japan 0.3 per cent. Although adding the number of people employed in the defence industry would change the above ratios by orders of magnitude, the comparative position of the individual countries, would remain unchanged.

iii) The percentage of defence spending within the state budgets also reflects considerable variance. The ratio in the OECD countries—taking the annual average between 1967 and 1978—was 21.3 per cent. Within this period the rate was highest in 1969 (27.7 per cent) and by 1978 it had decreased to 16.3 per cent. The average of the NATO countries was 23.4 per cent, and this also showed a diminishing tendency until 1978. The decline reflected primarily the changes within the USA where defence spending within the Federal budget dropped from 44.1 per cent in 1969 to 24 per cent in 1978, but has increased again ever since.

The data in Table 5 compare per capita defence, health and educational expenditures of the NATO countries in 1982.

Comparisons of the impact of defence expenditure in the individual countries from the point of view of inflation or stagnation indicate great differences. Moreover, though the percentage of military expenditures in the gross national product in the 1970s was not too high (at least it was lower than the peak values of the Cold War period or at the time of the Korean and Vietnam Wars), nevertheless these countries spent close to $ 2 000 billion on armaments (reckoned at 1977 constant prices), i.e.

Table 5.
Comparison of Budgetary Expenditures (US dollars) per capita in 1982

	Gross national product	Military expenditures	Public health expenditures	Educational expenditures
World	2.789	147	115	140
NATO, total	10.480	529	548	562
USA	13.160	845	589	686*
United Kingdom	9.580	488	508	525
FRG	12.280	414	798	625
France	11.520	482	738	462
The average of 114 developing countries	827	43	14	32

* Total of federal and local governmental organizations.
Source: World Priorities: World Military and Social Expenditures. Washington, 1985.

about one third of the world total that had been spent on military purposes in the years of World War II (also reckoned on the same price basis). Defence expenditures of the NATO countries totalled $ 1500 billion in the 1950s compared with $ 1886 billion in the 1960s.

The absolute amount (reckoned at constant prices) of military expenditure between 1950 and 1980 increased from decade to decade though the increase tended to be rather uneven in the individual countries and years. The increase was stepped up particularly in the USA from 1980 on and by 1985 it had reached globally (reckoned at current prices) $ 1 000 billion.[29]

The volume and development of military expenditure proves the fact that considerable economic and political interests have crystallized around the armaments industry in the developed Western countries (first and foremost in the NATO countries), and the defence contracts of the industry, which come to about half the armaments expenses, are significant factors in the economies of the countries in question. From the point of view of the world economy the armaments' race is a highly significant factor.

The effects of the armament industry on the United States were defined very instructively by General Eisenhower in 1961 when his term as President expired. His statements have come true many a time since then. He pointed out that the United States was compelled to establish a gigantic permanent war industry. These military establishments directly employed three and a half million men and women, and spent annually more on military objectives than the net annual profits of the American corporations. (The sum of military expenditure in 1980 was higher by one third than the net profits of all corporations. — M. S.) In this connection there emerged a new phenomenon in American business life: the relationship between the powerful military group and the defence industry. According to General Eisenhower, the influence of this complex was of an economic, social and even spiritual nature and could be felt in all cities, all local authorities and in all the authorities of the Federal government. The necessity for change was well understood but its serious consequences could not be left out of consideration. He stressed the point that this phenomenon had become the vital problem for American jobs, resources and livelihood, i.e. it became a matter of the structure of American society.[30]

Defence expenditure, however, cannot be regarded as purely or even decisively a matter of economic motivation. The increase or decrease in international tension is connected first of all to politics. Expenditure on armaments cannot be justified without the stimulating effect of foreign policy. However, the developed Western countries have not switched over to peaceful production to an adequate extent in the past 25 years, though they have had the possibility of such a change (e.g. after the Vietnam war, in the period of détente). After a considerable rise in expenditure on armaments has somewhat dropped from time to time or has remained stable but—as pointed out above—has not receded to the previous low level.

As was illustrated by the situation in the United States in the early 1980s, the economic stimulation effects of defence expenditure can be substantial if, simultaneously with considerable unused (material and human) capacities, military spending is growing faster than the gross national product (or effective demand in the civil sectors) or if obsolete weapons or weapon systems are rapidly replaced by new ones.

Thus at the time of economic recession in the early 1980s leading circles of West European countries with relatively highly developed war industries were prompted by decisions on the modernization of traditional strategical weapon systems to increase (within the framework of NATO) the share of their countries in military contracts. Postwar developments, however, repeatedly proved that when the volume of defence expenditures have risen to a relative considerable extent and their increase has become more difficult or the economy has become overheated anyway, military expenditure becomes highly detrimental and its adverse economic effects become increasingly conspicuous. One of the reasons for the disadvantageous consequences is the fact that in the long run military expenditures compete with other, peaceful items within the state budget. They compete not only with social allocations but also with industrial investment and the development of an infrastructure, which means that public funds for the improvement of economic efficiency become more and more scarce as a result of the military expenditure. There are, however, other problems, too. Some of these were pointed out in a study by the American Council of Economic Priorities, a liberal middle-class group concerned with the most important economic and social problems of the United States. Analysing the adverse economic consequences of military expenditure, the economic experts of the Council pointed out in the December 11, 1981 issue of *The New York Times* that long-term effects were of much greater importance than short-term problems bringing about various industrial and monetary tensions. Such effects are the decrease of investment and the distortion of technological progress. A country participating in the armaments' race sacrifices its possibilities of developing its civil industries.

The Council's study compared the economic performance of 13 developed Western industrial countries in the twenty years between 1960 and 1980. It was emphasized that countries which have spent a smaller proportion of their production on defence objectives developed faster, invested more and increased productivity to a greater extent. Of the developed capitalist countries those which spent the greatest sums on armaments, i.e. the United States and Great Britain, developed slower and their competitiveness diminished. Better economic performance was achieved by Japan, Austria and Canada, which spent least on military objectives. Therefore, it is not social expenditure or high wages which are responsible for unsatisfactory economic performance. The United States, for instance ranked first from the bottom in the ratio of social expenditure to GNP but was in the middle of the ranking as regards increases in wages over the same period.

The considerable growth of defence spending in the USA in the 1990s (and also in the other Western countries if they follow America's lead) could become a source of new economic difficulties, including a new wave of inflation. Incidentally, neither in the United States nor in any other economies of the developed Western world did radical changes take place as would exclude the possibility of a recurrence of inflation, and neither did they solve the dilemma between the alternatives of rapid upswing, full employment, and inflation, stagnation, unemployment and disinflation.

Despite the problems mentioned, the developed Western countries were able generally to expand their production, to shift most of the burdens of recession— among them the costs of the necessary adjustment—to the other regions of the world and to start the process of structural tranformation based on the latest technological and scientific achievements. But their development paths became rather different. The second longest upswing after World War II following the most serious economic recession in the postwar period bore the marks of the inequalities related to the structural characteristics mentioned above.

Some Economic Policy Issues of the Recovery

In the second half of the 1980s the most important (and difficult) issues of a strong global recovery are connected with the readiness of the major industrial countries to give priority to growth instead of continuing restrictive measures in their economic policies. The first major Western industrial country which went through a rapid economic recovery, the United States, has been able to stimulate economic growth in a comprehensive way. The budgetary deficit served as a major fiscal instrument to pump purchasing power into the economy. Other measures were also important. Monetary policy took a radical turn in the summer of 1982 and became more expansive. Under the influence of this change the nominal rate of interest was temporarily reduced, and therefore the consumers who had not undertaken any major purchases, being afraid of unemployment and loss of income, found considerable financial means at their disposal, and suddenly stepped up their purchases. The net financial means of the households increased by $ 1 000 billion between the middle of 1982 and the end of 1983. The possibility of deducting interest payment from taxes proved an important stimulant, particularly in the higher income brackets of the population, and as is well-known, the economic significance of this social layer is considerable in the USA. The income of this layer was further increased by the Republican Administration's reduction of taxes, under the slogan of "supply-side measures". Employment experienced a fast rise, too. One of the peculiarities of the recovery was that the un-precedentedly rapid increase of real interest rates, which was most spectacular in 1983, did not crowd out investment in industry. Owing to the growing demand for money, the interest rate increased generally in that period of recovery. In the USA, however, the increase in real interest rates was stimulated mainly by the all-time high budget deficit. The economic development in the other capitalist countries was adversely influenced by the high interest rate in the USA; this had particularly grave consequences in the highly indebted countries. An enormous volume of foreign capital was attracted to the United States by the high interest rates. The other important feature of American economic recovery has been the considerable revaluation of the dollar, partly as a consequence of the great volume of capital influx. As a result of the overvalued dollar the current account deficit of the USA reached about $ 140 billion by 1985, which also contributed to the curbing of inflation.

Thus the slow pace of economic recovery in the Western European countries finds a partial explanation in the economic recovery of the United States. Part of the capital was syphoned off to the USA as a result of the high interest rates in America. The overvalued dollar supported the increase of exports to the USA from Western Europe, too, though to a lesser extent than from Japan or other countries of the Pacific region, and added to the costs of oil imports and sometimes to those of other raw materials as well. The main export markets of the developing countries, the European region and the West European countries faced serious difficulties. The driving force in the USA therefore, meant only a moderate stimulation for them.

Economic recovery, however, was also impeded by considerable domestic economic problems. In its early stage arose a moderate stimulation from the increased consumption of the population since the volume and intensity of the surplus consumption of the population was rather low. Unemployment remained permanently high, and this, too, had an adverse effect on the incomes of the population. The governments, grappling with great budget deficits and fearing inflation, did not change their economic policies in time (incidentally, for a number of reasons such a change is a rather difficult matter, anyway). Recovery was rendered generally weaker and more uncertain in Western Europe by the slow expansion of external and internal markets, the moderate dynamism of investments and the resulting slower increase of profits.

The decline in oil prices stimulated domestic consumption and savings in the developed industrial countries of Europe and in Japan. Its impact, however, had to be supplemented by proper government policies.

The phenomenon to be avoided is termed "the pitfall of slow growth" by the well-known Canadian economist Sylvia Ostry, who pointed out that this is a pitfall which has many unforeseeable difficulties: because of the obsolescence of vocational training, and lack of job experience, cyclical unemployment becomes permanent and assumes a structural character. Deficits, too, assume a structural nature. Effectiveness, productivity and flexibility are diminished by the rescue of bankrupt enterprises, subsidies and neo-protectionist measures. The decrease in investment adds to the bottlenecks in business life. The attitudes of the entrepreneurs is determined by orientation to slow growth. To avoid such pitfalls, business investment ought to become the driving force of growth in Europe.[31]

Ostry's views are shared by others, too—though for different reasons. A renowned West German banker, Otmar Emminger wrote, for instance, that it was widely believed that not just temporary stimulation was needed which could be supplied by public investment programmes, but also the creation of permanent jobs by means of the expansion of the productive capital of the economy. In the Federal Republic of Germany half the number of those currently unemployed could not be given jobs even with full-capacity utilization of capital and the real growth potential is about 2 per cent; therefore, he emphasized, the expansion of the productive capital stock is a very urgent task.[32]

The extent of accumulation under conditions of the 1980s has been too low in most of the developed Western countries to make a considerable recovery of investment permanently possible.

It was understood that to reduce unemployment to the 1980 level, 20.000 job opportunities ought to be created daily in Western Europe between 1984 and 1990. At the beginning of 1984 the creation of a new job cost DM 20.000 in the FRG.[33]

How and from what sources and with what kind of stimulants could the Western European countries increase the productive investment in their economies?

Though the possibilities for the individual countries are obviously different, the basic precondition is everywhere the same: to increase the share of investment in the gross national product. (Correlations are illustrated by data on some developed capitalist countries in Table 6.)

Thus, the ratio of savings and investments to GNP should be increased. This, however, has significant structural effects and in a case of slow economic growth it

Table 6.
Investment Ratios, Growth and Productivity

	Share of gross investments the Gross Domestic Product				Growth of the Gross Domestic Product (annual average)				Growth of productivity in the economy*			
	EEC	FRG	USA	Japan	EEC	FRG	USA	Japan	EEC	FRG	USA	Japan
1967–73	22.5	24.5	18.3	34.3	5.0	5.3	3.6	9.6	4.3	4.5	2.5	8.0
1973–80	21.1	21.6	18.3	32.0	2.3	2.3	2.3	3.7	2.0	2.4	1.3	2.7
1980–86	20.0	20.3	17.4	30.1	1.7	1.5	3.1	3.6	1.5	1.6	2.2	2.9

* Average annual growth of the per capita Gross Domestic Product.
Sources: OECD and national statistics. *Die Presse*, 18. Oct. 1985, World Bank, 1989.

seems particularly difficult to increase savings at the expense of consumption. Tax reduction or tax allowances granted to those in high income brackets result in an increased deficit of the budget if expenditures cannot be reduced or revenue cannot be increased from other sources.

From the point of view of internal productive investments the movement of interest rates is of great importance, too. For instance if the American interest rate is high, part of the European accumulation continues to be enticed to the USA. Within the country itself, however, the high and tax-free interest on gilt-edged securities drains capital away from production.

The stemming of inflation, too, stimulates the increase of productive investments only if low interest rates obtain. Stimulation of investment, however, needs adequate and secure market demand, including expanding export possibilities and a greater supply of capital, which is increasingly willing to take risks. In the background of all these, important stimulative measures are needed from the governments, influencing demand conditions in such a way as would promote expansion and still maintain the required long-term stability.

Conditions in Japan were more favourable. In the first half of the 1980s the ratio of wages and salaries to the value of production was about 60 per cent, despite the fact that wages have risen considerably since the 1960s. In the member countries of the European Common Market the ratio of wages approaches 70 per cent, mainly for the reason that additional (social, etc.) wages were substantially higher and also rose faster.

Though the Japanese economy was affected less by the recession than those of the other Western industrial countries and the economic growth of this country has remained relatively fast compared with other nations, the Japanese economy, too, has reached a peculiar situation by 1986. As a result of the increasing value of her currency, the Japanese exports appeared more expensive. Following the years of rapid economic development based chiefly on exports, Japan has increasingly been compelled to exploit her internal market. This could result in new demands, first of all on her monetary and fiscal policies.

Internal changes in economic policies are, however, important but not sufficient conditions for creating a lasting and balanced global economic growth. More efficient coordination of national economic policies would be needed, which take into account the interests of other countries as well. Due to sharpening competition and the domestic problems of the individual countries, this seems more difficult today than in the past. The pressure of the problems may still force these countries to take more meaningful steps in the coming year to overcome the constraints on global growth.

They must understand the global consequences of their actions.

Ever since World War II the considerable difficulties of the industrial capitalist countries, having an outstanding part in the system of world economic relations, world trade, international capital flow, financial and technological-scientific relations, have had great influence—because of the intensity of the economic relations—on the other countries of the world as well. It was they who exported inflation, later on economic recession, the effects of high interest rates, and it was their protectionist measures which, impeded imports, so significantly precipitating the indebtedness of a great number of developing and socialist countries.

44

3. The Crisis, the Recession and the Developing Countries: the Interplay of Internal and External Factors

In the early 1980s the world economic recession had an extremely impropitious effect on the developing countries, revealing new social and economic problems and thereby further worsening the difficult situation of these nations.

The troubles of the Third World countries have dramatically increased in number. Their difficulties are of a highly complex nature and differ from country to country but they are rooted in the very same problems. The position of the least developed countries, which had been pressing from the very outset, continued to worsen.

As regards the effects of the recession on the developing countries, an UNCTAD report of the early 1980s pointed out that the developing world is now experiencing its gravest crisis since the great slump of the 1930s. The recession—just as in the past—is the result of the defective economic functioning of the industrial countries with developed market economies, and is still more aggravated and intensified by the disturbances of the trade and financial systems. The development crisis is fuelled by the network of poor growth indices and therefore it may drag on for years. It was emphasized by the report that the international environment, too, changes in a way which narrows down the possible development alternatives of the Third World countries and reduces the effectiveness of the given economic policies.[34]

The second report of the Brandt Commission, too, shifts the responsibility for the dramatical worsening of the developing world to conditions in the developed capitalist countries.

By the beginning of the 1980s the situation in the developing world differed in many respects from that pertaining in the 1960s and 1970s, though some fundamental features have remained unchanged in and characteristic of the countries in these regions: such were backwardness, the gap dividing them from the developed industrial countries, the distorted economic structure and the "enclave" economy (modern industrial islands in the sea of backward economic conditions). At certain places, however, even these phenomena and characteristics differ from the earlier situation. Nevertheless, the new features are also interwoven with the consequences of traditional relations. Certain—sometimes highly important—changes have taken place in the world economic position of the developing countries, and the international conditions influencing these positions have undergone changes to a certain extent as well.

Developing countries, taken as a whole, have been characterized by relatively fast economic growth ever since the 1960s. Per capita incomes had grown at an annual average of about 3.1 per cent between 1970 and 1980 (growth had amounted only to 2 per cent in the 1950s) and within that the rate of growth was 3.4 per cent in the 1960s. These data are particularly noteworthy if they are compared to the historical tendencies experienced in the developing countries. Structural changes were stepped up in the economies of the developing countries. The production of the manufacturing industries grew by about 7 per cent at an annual average between 1960 and 1980, and in spite of the fact that agricultural production increased only by 2.8 per cent in the period under survey, the modernization of agriculture is going on at a fast pace in many countries. Having overcome the initial difficulties of industrial development, some of these countries are able to tackle even highly complex technological tasks. In the processing industries substantial industrial productive capacities and export potentials have been established which are up to international standards. As a consequence of the growth of the economies of the developing countries and the changes accomplished, the institutions of these countries were transformed, too. Both in the public and private sectors huge industrial corporations have been established. National bank systems have been built up having gained experience both as regards domestic and international finance. Experience of economic planning has been gained. The potential for scientific research has strengthened in a number of developing countries.

Despite their structural weakness, the developing countries today—though to a different extent—have greater possibilities of making use of state power, and better economic organization and infrastructure than before to defend themselves against adverse external influences. The economy became more self-sustaining in a number of countries. In some cases the dependence on monocultures was diminished. At the same time, it is obvious that owing to their world economic positions and the character of their economic, financial and technological relations with the developed industrial countries, the majority of the developing nations are not only highly sensitive to external economic developments but have become vulnerable in new areas and they are still structurally dependent on the developed Western countries.

Notwithstanding the changes, the part of the developing countries in the international trade in raw materials has remained highly significant. In the early 1980s more than two thirds of the raw material and the fuel exports of the world came from the developing countries. Their share in oil, rubber, bauxite, tin, manganese, cotton and a number of foodstuff exports was 50 per cent, and nearly 50 per cent in the exports of copper and iron ores. Fifty-six per cent of raw materials imported by the developed capitalist countries originated from developing countries. Accordingly, the deterioration of the situation on the raw material markets affected these countries rather keenly.

Demand for raw materials has decreased. In addition to the decline in consumption of raw materials per units of output the developed capitalist countries need less raw materials because of the slowed down development. The production of the manufacturing industry of the world increased by an annual average of 7 per cent, the exports of raw materials and energy carriers by 7 per cent between 1963 and 1973. Between 1973 and 1979 the production of the manufacturing industries increased by 4 per cent, the exports of raw materials and energy carriers by 0.5 per cent. At the time of recession both production and demand dropped conspicuously.[35]

Nowadays it is much more difficult to sell industrial finished goods on the markets of the developed Western countries partly because of the slower increase of demand, and partly as a result of protectionist measures. Today 45–50 per cent of the exports of developing countries exporting finished goods are afflicted by the new wave of protectionism. Some developing countries, however, (as will be discussed in Part Three) were able to develop their technology rapidly and became participants of a new division of labour in microelectronics. These countries are, of course, in a dependent position: not only in the field of technology from the new innovations but also financially because of the higher costs of adjustment.

The chaotic situation of international finance has affected the economies of the developed Western countries and has sapped the purchasing power of the currency reserves of the developing countries; the real earnings of the new oil raw material exporters have been reduced by about 45 per cent between 1980–85 whereas their imports have become more expensive.

How strong then were the autonomous forces which strove to uphold economic growth in the developing countries? Some of the major developing countries actually have such dynamic driving forces. Enhanced economic cooperation among the developing countries does also promote autonomous development to a certain extent. Though its volume and significance has increased in the past decade, world economic recession has seriously harmed the overwhelming majority of the Third World countries and, therefore, they could not avoid the effects of economic difficulties.

According to the calculations of UN economists every 1 per cent decrease of the gross national product of the industrial Western countries brings about a 1.5 per cent decrease in the developing countries. As regards some of the raw material producing and exporting countries the economies of which are dependent on monocultures the induced decline is even greater, the ratio being about $1:10$.[36]

Incidentally, the recession did not have the same effects on the different regions of the Third World and within those on the individual countries. Discrepancies were due not only to different export possibilities or to the different extent of the narrowing import potential. The discrepancies in the effects were related also to the character of the economic policies established previously and the degree of efficiency of the capacity to control the economy.

The economic life of some oil producing and exporting countries may serve as typical examples. Inflation, huge budget deficits, the development of low efficiency industries needing public subsidies, wage rises which are in no way connected with the rise of production and/or productivity, neglect of other industries capable of exporting—all these can be defined as general problems.

Only in some of these countries were the governments able to organize the process of economic growth efficiently on the basis of the oil revenue. In eight of the thirteen OPEC countries the share of the oil sector in the gross national product kept on rising even after 1973 (this ratio increased to 90 per cent in some countries).

External vulnerability and the distorting effects of oil dependence can be clearly demonstrated by Nigeria, a specific African example. As an outstanding oil exporter this largest country of tropical Africa had made considerable profits from the rises in oil prices in the 1970s. But the poorest classes of the population got nothing at all from the huge oil incomes. The proportion of destitute people increased even in the years of the greatest oil price increases. Oil export earnings were spent on low-efficiency investment and, in addition, agricultural production dropped and food imports increased. Shrinking agricultural production brought rural incomes down and enhanced the migration to towns and cities. The number of the inhabitants of urban slums rose by leaps and bounds. Earnings from oil exports diminished as a result of the world economic recession: it was still $ 91 billion in 1980 but dropped to $ 70.8 billion in 1981, while per capita gross national product diminished from $ 1010 to $ 870. Despite the huge international credits, imports decreased by 11 per cent in 1982, and the development allocations of the state budgets, also shrank markedly.

The position of the Arab oil countries, too, deteriorated because their production decreased. Therefore they cancelled or rescheduled their orders to a later date and generally slowed down their development activities. They ceased to be spot cash payers. The deteriorating situation of these states affects the position of the other developing countries and even that of the highly industrialized countries. Since there were not enough experts and labour force available they had to import practically everything. In 1982 the leading oil exporting Arab countries and Iran paid $ 122 million for imported goods, and a further $ 70 billion for technological and other services. In the years to come the development of this region will be more limited even if there should be an upswing in the world economy. In marked contrast the so-called oil producing countries with less import-absorbing capacity have continued to play an important role on international money markets. They are the owners of 90 per cent of the $ 395 billion worth of capital of the OPEC countries invested abroad: Saudi Arabia owns $ 170 billion, Kuwait $ 80 billion and the Arab emirates $ 40 billion.

Data in Table 7 reflect the deteriorating positions of the developing countries.

Lagging for behind all other Third World regions the developing countries of the African continent have got into the most difficult position, irrespective of what kind of statistical indices are analysed. In the 1960s the growth of per capita gross national product in tropical Africa (i.e. in areas south of the Sahara) was only one third of the average for all developing countries (1.3 per cent as against 3.5 per cent). The growth rate continued to decrease in the 1970s (to 0.8 per cent as against the average 2.7 per cent). Per capita production has diminished by 6 per cent in tropical Africa since 1979. Numerous factors had a part in the deterioration in the situation: the deterioration of external conditions was worsened by natural calamities, internal and external armed conflicts, weak and poorly organized public administration, corruption, *coup d'états* and tribal strifes. The terms of trade of the countries of this region deteriorated by 30–40 per cent between 1978 and 1983. A typical example is Zambia. After it had gained independence this country was one of the richest in the region whereas after 1964 it suffered many a serious setbacks. The drop in copper prices (they decreased to the lowest level in 50 years) went hand in hand with the increase in the prices of oil and other imported goods, and all this resulted in a deterioration of the terms of trade by 75 per cent between 1970 and 1982. In addition, there were a number of political and geographical factors: the liberation struggles in South Africa and the transport difficulties of the country. Between 1976 and 1981 the losses of the country came to three times the national income. Per capita gross national product between 1974 and 1981 dropped by 52 per cent (in terms of real value). The import possibilities of the country have been restricted by these changes and have led to chronic payment difficulties. Chronic scarcity of basic materials and consumer goods made it practically impossible to control the economy of the country, more specifically its public finances. The government was obliges to reduce expenditure of the state budget by 75 per cent.

A further example of African countries is a serious situtation in Tanzania. The crisis of the country began in 1973 when it was stricken by a grave drought and at the same time, oil prices and import prices increased. The deficit on the balance of payments trebled by 1974, the deficit on the budget doubled. The financial position of the country was further aggravated by the military intervention of Tanzania in neighbouring Uganda. Because of the lack of foreign currencies scarcity of energy and raw materials,

Table 7.

Contraction of Economic Growth in the Developing Countries

	Number of developing countries reporting decrease of the gross domestic product (GDP)						Number of developing countries reporting decrease of per capita GDP						
	1979	1980	1981	1982	1983	1984	1985	1987	1979	1980	1981	1982	1983	1984	1985	1987
Number of countries	10	17	26	41	34	26	18	19	25	32	38	55	51	45	49	34

Source: U. N. Department of International Economic and Social Affairs, 1986, 1988

a drop of the level of industrial capacity utilization to 20–30 per cent was experiencel. Shortage of consumer goods increased, too. Public expenditure diminished by 74 per cent between 1977 and 1982. Nevertheless, the country strived to defend its social achievements and structure and has therefore considerably reduced its development programme.

A peculiarly contradictory situation has emerged on the Asian continent. Some countries have profited directly or indirectly from the increase in oil prices. Many others, suffered serious losses because of the price rise. Though international loans supported development, growth rates were low. Since the Japanese economy continued to develop dynamically (rapid increase in its international trade in industrial goods, fast and efficient internal switchover and the relatively considerable expansion of agricultural production brought about spectacular economic progress in the 1970s), the smaller developing Asian countries with close connections to Japan have felt the effects of the recession to a lesser degree. The development of the economic position of three countries—India, Sri Lanka and South Korea—also indicates cases of an opposite nature.

India, too, is one of those countries which, owing to its huge population, high-degree of self-sufficiency and relatively minor dependence on imports and exports, has weathered the world economic recession without a serious drop in growth rate or a considerable deterioration in the terms of trade. Yet, the recession contributed to the increase in the deficit of her trade balance and slowed down development to a certain extent. The deficit of the trade balance increased from $ 1 billion in 1977 to $ 6 billion in 1981. Deficits in the balance of payments and state budget increased as well. However, the internal economic conditions of India proved to be sufficient to guarantee adequate autonomy to maintain growth even under the circumstances of deteriorating world economic conditions.

The economic problems of Sri Lanka were aggravated in the 1970s mainly by the deteriorating terms of trade. The drop in tea prices was combined with the rise of prices of imported goods necessary for the economic functioning of the country. The price development of the other two export articles—rubber and coconuts—was also characterized by incertainty and fluctuation. Under the influence of economic difficulties the rate of unemployment rose while that of production declined. Food shortages assumed serious proportions. The situation was further worsened by the rise of oil prices in 1973. After a turn in the political life of the country significant measures of economic policy were taken to alleviate the difficulties by strengthening capitalist market relations. The national currency was devaluated, imports liberalized, price controls and food price subsidies were terminated, capital flow liberated. As a result, the influx of direct investments took unparalleled proportions. Foreign capital was enticed to the country by various benefits and guarantees as well as by the advantages offered by the relatively high level of education of the population combined with extremely low wages. Under the influence of the influx of foreign capital and domestic investment, economic growth was stepped up (from 3 to 6 per cent). As a result of all these changes Sri Lanka was able to curb her imports and increase the extent of autarky. At the same time, however, the distribution of incomes has changed to the advantage of the rich and foreign capital. Internal inequalities increased, real incomes of the poorer classes dwindled.

The economy of South Korea represents a typical example of an export oriented development policy adapted to world markets. The annual growth rate reached an average of nearly 10 per cent between 1963 and 1978, which is quite considerable even on a world scale. Economic growth was stimulated by the production of manufacturing industry and by the expansion of exports. Exports of the country increased by an annual average of 35 per cent in the 1960s and 20 per cent in the 1970s and early 1980s. In 1985 exports were equal to 36 per cent of GNP. Unemployment was reduced from an annual 8 per cent in 1962 to 3.6 per cent in 1976. The South Korean economy suffered the first heavy blow after the second oil shock in 1980. Gross national product decreased then by 3.6 per cent, per capita real income by 10 per cent. While South Korea had been able to react to the first oil shock by stepping up her exports, considerably, in 1980—owing to the general deterioration of her world economic position—she could not avoid the effects of the recession in the same way. Under the new conditions the stimulation of growth based on domestic demand was attempted and the government started to introduce a serious adjustment (including measures to attract more foreign capital) programme in order to increase competitiveness. The increase of the rate of domestic savings, the restructuring of debts, and restriction on wage increases were important components of this policy. This policy proved successful, and as a result exports and economic growth have accelerated, the economy of the country became at the same time more sensitive to the global economic changes and especially vulnerable as far as protectionism is concerned.

Following a highly successful economic development after World War II, the majority of the Latin American countries, too, got into considerable economic difficulties in the 1980s. According to the Review of the UN Economic Commission of Latin America the region suffered (and continues to suffer) from the severest and most prolonged recession since the 1930s after successful progress lasting four decades. Between 1960 and 1980 per capita gross national product in the countries of this region increased from $ 780 in 1960 to $ 1400 in 1980. Since then, however, it has tended to diminish, and in 1984 it was 8 per cent below that of 1980.

The economic recession of 1974–1975 had slowed down economic growth in Latin America, too, but, with the exception of four countries, it has not put an end to it. The four disadvantaged countries at that time were: Argentina, Bolivia, Peru and Venezuela. But the economic recession which started in 1980 hit the region as a whole. In Brazil, the biggest economy of the region, the rapid industrialization policy was continued in the 1970s despite the rise of energy prices; export orientation and elements of import substitution were relatively smoothly blended by this policy. Following 1979, however, the economy was afflicted by an unparalleled crisis of debt service.

In spite of the significant differences in the situations of the individual countries there has been a common characteristic of all Latin American countries ever since 1976—increasing external indebtedness. Cheap money stimulated the drawing of external credits even in countries (e.g. Venezuela) which had considerable oil revenues at their disposal. Meanwhile under the effect of world economic recession and high interest rates, the burdens of debt service increased to an unprecedented extent.

According to the data of the Inter-American Development Bank the burdens of debt service came to 47 per cent of the export earnings between 1976 and 1980. (In Brazil they exceeded 82 per cent in 1982.)

As a result of their increased international payment obligations and their losses from the terms of trade, the non-oil-exporting countries payed an annual 6 to 7 per cent of their gross national product to foreign countries in the early 1980s (calculated on current prices this sum reached $ 120–140 billion.) This huge amount of money flew from the developing world to the highly industrialized capitalist countries and OPEC states.[37]

This loss was moderated to a decreasing extent by the new influx of capital and international aid. While the actual capital influx (i.e. net transfer minus the amortization of the loans) in 1980 had been still $ 3 billion, the net outflow reached the $9 billion level in 1983, not to mention the losses on the terms of trade.

As a consequence of the recession, social conditions, too, have worsened in many developing countries. Less children went to school than before. Diseases checked long ago have spread once again, and streets were crowded with beggars. Thus the pressure of acute social problems increased. As reflected by the growing number of bankruptcies, high interest rates brought ruin to an increasing degree to the middle classes which had begun to emerge and gain strength. The statement of the UN Economic Commission for Latin America made in 1983 is virtually characteristic of all the regions of the developing world. It was pointed out that the most direct consequence of the recession and diminishing economic growth—afflicting the overwhelming majority of the countries—was the deterioration of the social conditions of the population. This fact is reflected by increased unemployment and underemployment, diminishing real wages, the perpetuation and even increase of inequalities and extreme poverty afflicting broad classes of the population. It is emphasized by the report that in the periods of economic upswing or at the time of dynamic economic progress incomes, the fruits of economic growth, are distributed in an unequal way, and employment does not grow adequately either. At the time of economic recession on the other hand, the low income sectors are affected to the greatest extent by the adverse factors.[38]

The effects of the recession have actually hit the masses of the Latin American countries very hard in the early 1980s since earlier economic development had gone hand in hand with unprecedented inequalities in this region. In other regions of the world growth had resulted in a certain improvement of the situation of the poorer classes in preceding years. In Latin America, however, this was not true: the low-income 40 per cent of the population had received a mere 8.7 per cent of the total income in 1960. By 1975 this percentage has decreased to 7.7 per cent while the wealthiest 10 per cent of the population enjoyed 50 per cent of the income. Of the population of 378 million of the region 150 million were reduced to absolute destitution.

Factors influencing the development of an economic recovery in the developing world were particularly contradictory in the second half of the 1980s. Demand for raw materials and some price increases in certain raw materials were favourable changes. These were, however, not strong enough to counterbalance losses originating from the burdens of debts which were further aggravated by high real interest rates. The export of finished goods was hindered both by the protectionism of the developed industrial capitalist countries and by the slow increase in demand. Net capital influx, too, has diminished considerably, and private capital tends to escape from a number of countries. Because of this the stepping up of the rate of economic growth (and occasionally even the new start of growth) is impeded by the unavoidable restriction of imports. The public sector, which plays an important part from the point of view of economic development in some countries, has been plunged into a particularly difficult situation. The reduction of public expenditure—and first of all of public investment—has afflicted private enterprise, too. There are, however, significant differences in the situation of the individual countries. Thus, particularly great efforts are made to promote a new structural switch-over to improve the conditions of economic development in some newly industrialized countries of the Pacific region which have joined the new international division of labour. China, India, and some other major developing countries too, try to step up the pace of transformation of the structure of their economic production, primarily in the range of industry. Most of these programmes are, however, highly cautious and set only moderate targets.

The countries of the tropical zone of Africa, which are in a very difficult situation as a result of the recession and for other reasons as well, proved unable to master their troubles in the second half of the eighties, and dragging out these difficulties could become the source of new internal tensions.

The economic difficulties of the Third World countries naturally react upon the developed capitalist countries and even upon the European socialist countries. Under normal world economic conditions an increasing volume of goods and services is bought by the developing countries from other countries of the world. The import needs of the expansion of their production will remain considerable for a relatively long period irrespective of the (import-substituting or export-oriented) development strategy adopted. The developing countries had played an outstanding part as buyers' markets even at the beginning (1970) of the slowing down of the development of the world economy and exports. In the course of the 1970s their share in the industrial goods exports of the developed industrial countries continued to grow, when the problems started influencing their import capacities, the industrial world also suffered. In the second half of the 1970s 31 per cent of the machine and equipment exports, 30 per cent of the chemicals exports, 29 per cent of the iron and steel exports and 31 per cent of the total industrial goods exports of the developed capitalist countries were directed to Third World countries. Eighteen per cent of industrial goods exports of the European socialist countries was purchased by developing countries.[39] This shows that the other part of the world cannot do without these relations and the prospect of their further development. It is for this reason, among others, that the development of the situation of the economies of the Third World countries tends to be a significant problem for the other parts of the world, too.

4. The Autonomous Growth Potential of the Socialist Countries and the Global Recessions

The situation of the European socialist countries was affected by the changes in the conditions of the world economy and by the global recessions in a peculiar way. As could be seen in the case of the developing countries the problem of to what extent they could dispense with autonomous development dynamism—taking into consideration the character of their links with other parts of world economy and the extent of their dependence—came into the limelight.

Similar questions took shape in recent years in connection with the socialist countries as well. It is of outstanding importance whether the conditions of their economic development have changed, and to what extent, under the influence of other parts of the world economy.

Since the mid-1960s the European CMEA countries have had to face three major changes which have affected them to a different extent. In the first stage (the 1960s) the possibility of continuing the process of economic growth as it had been previously hindered by the increasing perception of or effects on the countries' economy of the system of centralized, direct, mandatory plan targets and the extensive development model which served as a basis of this system. Though the need for reforms came into the fore everywhere through the problems which cropped up, a complex reform was introduced only in Hungary, but here, too, the progress of reform slackened in the early 1970s.

The price changes and later on the oil shock in the second stage (in the early 1970s) affected the CMEA countries in various ways. World economic changes—first and foremost because of internal supplies of raw materials and energy and/or export capacity—had various influences on the CMEA countries. Having at its disposal 60 per cent of the coal, mineral oil and natural gas supplies of the world, 41 per cent of iron ore and 83 per cent of manganese supplies, the Soviet Union achieved a better position than before in the wake of the rise of raw material prices since these resources added considerably to its hard currency earnings and improved its terms of trade. The conditions for the development of Poland and Romania (the other two raw material and fuel exporters) too, improved for a short time. The positions of the German Democratic Republic, Czechoslovakia and Hungary, however, have considerably worsened, particularly since 1975; by that time the effects of world market prices had caused serious difficulties.

The third stage is related to the foreign trade and international monetary effects of the world economic recession following the second oil shock. These effects had a very adverse influence on the economies of some CMEA countries which had become extremely indebted by that time; some smaller CMEA countries highly dependent on foreign trade were also hit hard. Per capita foreign trade turnover in the East European CMEA countries is almost three times that of the Soviet Union, and a considerable percentage of the vital sector of their production depends on foreign trade.

Owing to its vast size and complex economy it is only the Soviet Union (of all CMEA countries) which in principle would be able to achieve lasting economic growth if isolated from the other parts of world economy, relying entirely on its own resources and the internal driving forces of its market. Yet, even in the course of the development of the Soviet economy, the significance of international economic relations has increased. Relations other than those with the East European socialist countries (i.e. relations with developed capitalist and developing countries) also played a part in the increased importance of foreign trade. The effects of external conditions on the Soviet economy too, increased, especially after the fall of oil prices in the mid 1980s. The Soviet Union is still in a better position to influence directly the scope and intensity of her international trade. The other CMEA countries have no such chance. The high degree of external structural dependence had been borne out also by the failure of the efforts to maximize autarky in the 1950s.

At the time of the recession in 1929 the rapid and spectacular development of the Soviet economy had markedly stood out against the situation of the rest of the world economy at that time, with mass unemployment, the mass-scale under-utilization of material and human values and possibilities, while on the other hand, through economic connections (which were sought after by all countries in those years) the economic development of the Soviet Union had a beneficial influence on Western markets. This beneficial effect could be felt at the time of the 1974 recession and later on, too. However, at the beginning of the 1980s (and partly since the late 1960s) difficulties multiplied in the economies of the European socialist countries. Among the causes of the problems of the socialist economies, the increased influence of the economic development of the Western nations—and in general of the non-socialist regions—on the CMEA countries gained in significance. After 1948 the socialist countries became isolated from the other parts of the world economy to a great extent, which was the result partly of their own policy and partly of the Western embargo policy. As a consequence, the structural transformation of the economies of the CMEA countries took place on the basis of autonomous decisions whereas impulses from the world market had but little influence on this process. These changes led to new international relations and to a novel type—mainly superimposed—of dependence on external economy. From the 1960s the situation changed gradually: by the middle (or rather the end) of the 1970s the European CMEA countries have established stronger links than ever with the other parts of the world economy. These relations are still relatively small-scale but are nevertheless more significant than before. At the beginning of the 1980s 30 per cent of the exports of the European CMEA countries were directed to Western industrial countries and about 10 per cent to developing nations. Of their imports 37–38 per cent originated from capitalist countries and about 5 per cent from Third World countries. As a result of East-West cooperation it was particularly the modern branches of industry of the socialist countries which became more than ever dependent on Western technology, materials and components. The strengthening of the trend towards world economic integration has been most explicit on the international money markets.

CMEA countries which have integrated to a greater degree into the other parts of the world economy naturally have to feel the unfavourable effects (e.g. diminishing demand, protectionism) faster and more intensively because their economies are structurally still introverted, relatively less developed, and their competitiveness is generally poor. Moreover, the conditions of relationships—mainly with the developed

Western countries—are highly unfavourable and thus restrict structural cooperation (integration).

A more intensive linking up with the world economy has developed actually under specific conditions: on the basis of the different nature of the systems of relations, the asymmetry of interests and the occasional considerable differences of direct objectives, and under the circumstances of a low-efficiency, rigid cooperation among the CMEA member states. A further unfavourable effect is the fact that owing to the difficulties in East-West relations, these countries have more difficulties in meeting their obligations within the CMEA as well. The harmful effects, therefore, manifest themselves in a cummulative way. Not only are their "hard" commodities directed to the Western markets but they experience difficulties in the supply of their raw materials and spare parts, too.

The external difficulties of the CMEA countries aggrevated the crisis of their development model.

There are a number of individual problems among the difficulties of these countries related to the specific situation of a particular country. There are, however, some more general difficulties characteristic of all countries. Thus, for instance, the effectiveness of economic growth has diminished in almost all CMEA countries. The measure of deteriorating effectiveness is illustrated in Table 8 in respect of labour productivity, marginal capital productivity and the coefficient of capital and production.

In the socialist countries the growth rate of production and productivity has decelerated, the introduction of new technology has slowed down, and the technological gap has grown in some industries. As a result of increasing internal imbalances the quantity of consumer articles has diminished in the shops as compared to increased money incomes, and often the quality of these goods has deteriorated, too. In some of the CMEA countries tensions developed in the supply of goods to the population and in basic consumer articles. Two socialist countries were compelled to introduce rationing for certain food produced which—under normal conditions—was an unprecedented measure in the case of similarly developed countries. At the same time, in many of these countries the stock of unsold goods has increased. Internal disproportions and equilibrium disturbances had a part in the growing external indebtedness of some CMEA countries.

The internal reasons for the evolution of difficulties, disturbances, and tensions are rather wide-spread. The arms-race imposed increasing constraints on the economies of the countries. The driving forces of the extensive development phase and the system of planning and management are unable to provide adequate dynamism for the development of these countries. In addition, a number of individual errors of economic policies or mistakes of planning have cropped up. Some of the mistakes, however, are themselves the results of exaggerated extensive growth and have only aggravated disturbances which would have occurred anyway. History has put the furthering of the emergence of a new development phase on the agenda in the socialist countries.

Society accumulated new demands and unsatisfied requirements. New needs appeared in economic development as well as in the mechanism of the economy and society (including the political system).

a) Modernization based on the latest achievements of technology, cutting back of older industries and/or their considerable reshaping became necessary simultaneously

Table 8.

a) Changes in Labour Productivity in the European CMEA Countries
(average annual growth)

	1966–1970	1971–1975	1976–1980	1981–1985
Bulgaria	6.6	6.2	4.6	2.9
Czechoslovakia	5.4	5.9	4.2	2.2
GDR	6.0	6.2	4.3	3.7
Hungary	3.4	6.1	5.0	3.7
Poland	4.9	7.3	4.5	1.5
Romania	7.4	6.2	5.8	2.8
Soviet Union	5.5	5.8	2.8	3.0

b) Changes in Marginal Capital Productivity
(average annual growth)

	1971–1975	1976–1980	1981–1985
Bulgaria	−1.0	−1.8	−3.1
Czechoslovakia	−0.1	−1.3	−2.6
GDR	−0.5	−1.5	−1.2
Hungary	−0.5	−3.2	−2.6
Poland	−1.1	−3.5	−5.9
Romania	−0.5	−0.6	−5.1
Soviet Union	−2.8	−2.8	−2.9

c) Changes in the Incremental Capital
Output ratio (average annual growth)

	1971–1975	1976–1980
Bulgaria	3.6	4.3
Czechoslovakia	3.5	5.8
Poland	3.0	8.3
Hungary	4.8	8.4
GDR	4.6	5.8
Romania	2.7	4.0
Soviet Union	3.6	4.6

Sources: National statistics and estimates of the ECE. UN Economic Commission of Europe. *Economic Survey of Europe,* 1982, 1986.

in all socialist countries. These are significant preconditions for the solution of their internal tasks but the further development of their international relations are not possible either without the considerable stepping up of their technological advance. A decisive requirement for structural changes is the development and acceleration of the changes in product structure within the industry. Another highly important target is the further development of productive and non-productive infrastructure, primarily that of the network of transport and communications (internal communication). In the Soviet Union, for instance, 600.000 square kilometres of new roads ought to be built and the majority of the roads bituminized. However, taking into account the given standards of economic efficiency, investment demands related to meeting the new requirements surpass both in the productive and non-productive spheres the internal resources of the socialist countries in the present situation.

b) The new phase of development has brought about significant changes in the demands on economic policy, economic control and planning, too. An improvement in the effectiveness of the mechanism of the national economy has become an absolute necessity in all CMEA countries. The direction and intensity of the reforms is not the same in all these countries since their actual tasks are different, too. A considerable part of the problems and tasks, however, are common or similar; let us mention here but a few of them:

— a more responsible, more efficient management and utilization of the national capital stock (partly by greater democratization of ownership forms);

— a better satisfaction of economic and social needs on the basis of the economic possibilities;

— the achievement of a more balanced growth in the national economy, by the improvement of macroeconomic management and the better harmonization of micro and macro policies;

— a better, more efficient supply of basic consumer articles and services to meet the changing requirements of the population;

— better coordination of the interests of enterprise and the national economy; an improved, more efficient stimulation both of individuals and enterprises; the establishment of new systems of incentives based on quality requirements;

— strengthening of democracy in economic life in order to draw the broadest masses into economic building work on the basis of the new conditions, and to mobilize all their creative qualities to realize the targets of the present complex phase.

c) Significant new tasks emerged in this new phase as regards the further development of the institutions and political mechanisms of socialist society. This is partly related to the fact that socialist society has become more differentiated and the interests of social classes, strata and groups are more difficult to coordinate. A number of questions are formulated more sharply regarding the relationship of individuals and society, thus, for instance, the possibilities of the individual to influence and control social changes, decisions and institutions under the new conditions. As compared to previous major social transformations, social mobility has decreased, and its mechanisms, too, have undergone modifications.

The above-mentioned internal problems and changes emerged in the CMEA countries simultaneously with the deterioration of international conditions.

The increase in oil prices in the 1970s taxed the economies of the socialist countries highly dependent on imports. These countries reacted in different ways to the changed internal and international conditions, and, as a rule, their reaction was not rapid and efficient enough. Since in the 1970s there were no radical changes either in the economic policy or in the system of planning and management (an essential change had taken place only in Hungary), the previous trends continued. All East European socialist countries (among them Hungary, too) realized only belatedly that the capacity of their economies was not strong enough simultaneously to solve the problems of importing the necessary volume of energy, raw materials and technology, to realize the investments demanded by further growth and to set the raising of living standards as a target. In accordance with the targets set previously, these countries continued in the 1970s both their development policy requiring an increasing volume of investments and their programmes aimed at the raising of living standards. The policy directed to maintain the stability of the internal price level was continued for rather a long time, practically until 1981 by some countries, though in the meantime prices have risen on the world market by 9–10 per cent annually. Even between 1976 and 1981 consumer prices rose only by an annual average of 0.2 per cent in the GDR, 1 per cent in the Soviet Union, 3 per cent in Czechoslovakia, 1.8 per cent in Romania. This laid immense burdens upon the budgets of these countries, which, in order to bring about a switch-over in their economic structures did not avail themselves of the fact that higher prices for its oil exports were enforced only gradually by the Soviet Union. The terms of trade deteriorated rapidly, i.e. for imports of the same volume as in previous years they had to pay with more exports because of the price movements in the opposite direction; in a number of CMEA countries this absorbed almost the whole increase of their national incomes. The raw material exporting countries—as for instance the Soviet Union—on the other hand, owing to their internal conditions and difficulties, were unable to utilize their surplus incomes resulting from the rise of export prices in a way which would have helped them considerably to comprehensively solve their domestic problems. Thus, poor harvests forced the Soviet Union to import great volumes of grain.

The considerable increase in the international indebtedness of the CMEA countries took place overwhelmingly in the period after 1974 because of their maintaining an economic growth of the previous structure and intensity. A slackening of the pace of economic growth could be observed from 1977 on in the East European socialist countries and from 1978 on in the Soviet Union.

As is illustrated by data on the net material product in Table 9, this slackening of the rate of growth became large-scale in the Soviet Union following the second oil shock in 1979.

The European CMEA countries reacted to their domestic and international economic problems in that period first and foremost by slowing down economic growth, moderating domestic consumption and increasing imports as well as by stepping up their exports. Investments dropped by 14 per cent in 1982 and thus fell below the level of 1978. In 1983 growth increased in the majority of the countries of the region but the main obstacle to a stepped-up rate, just as before, were organizational difficulties which had emerged in the previous period. At the same time, investments were increased in all CMEA countries in industries important for technological progress and/or for exports, whereas a relatively great percentage of investments were assigned to update productive equipment of operating enterprises. Programmes aimed at a certain degree—to varying extent—of revision of their planning and management systems were elaborated in all CMEA countries. The chief directions of these programmes were as follows: improvement of planning methods, putting quality indices in the fore instead of quantitative ones, improvement of individual and enterprise incentives, increasing the independence of enterprises, transformation of enterprise organization within the framework of the traditional centralized guidance

Table 9.
Average Annual Growth of the Net Material Product

	Soviet Union	East European CMEA countries	East European CMEA countries (Poland excluded)*
1976–1980	4.3	3.9	5.0
1979	2.2	2.5	4.5
1980	3.9	0.7	3.2
1981	3.3	−1.1	2.7
1982	2.6	−1.1	2.3
1981–1985	3.6	2.2	—
1986	4.1	4.6	—
1987	2.3	3.2	—

* Since 1982 separate calculation for the five countries has been discontinued.
Sources: Calculations based on national statistics; UN. Economic Commission of Europe, *Economic Survey of Europe, 1982, 1985, 1986, 1987–88.*

system. Only the Bulgarian reform measures and the Soviet attempts at the enterprise level represented something similar to the Hungarian reform introduced in 1968.

Simultaneously with the announcement of programmes stressing decentralization, a certain centralization was introduced in some CMEA countries, justified by their economic difficulties. In some cases these were declared to be but of transitional nature, nevertheless their effects proved to be of a lasting character. At the same time, it is also an undeniable fact that following 1983, mainly as a result of restricting investments, not only was indebtedness brought to a halt in the European CMEA countries, but their external debts were even decreased. Thus the growth rate of production was enhanced and internal development, too, became more balanced.

The short and medium-term measure in the early 1980s, however, were but seldom in harmony with the objective of switching over from an extensive type of economic growth to an intensive one. In the second half of the 1980s the situation may change, however, if the reform program in the U.S.S.R., the continuation of the changes in Bulgaria, Poland and Hungary, the elaboration of new changes in Czechoslovakia, etc. and the reform of the mechanism in CMEA cooperation could bring substantial improvements in the mechanism of the economies.

The conditions which characterize the European CMEA countries in the mid-eighties indicate the fact however that constructive programmes evolve but slowly. The force of inertia at the stage of extensive development is extremely strong in both political and economic public opinion and in the institutions, though the tasks are often more complex than they had been at the initial stages of socialist construction. Moreover, social and economic tasks are closely interrelated. The economic situations of the CMEA countries are different, the degree of agreement about which tasks ought to be solved differs, too, and the will and capacity for the necessary social activity vary as well. As has been pointed out, the world economic situation is not favourable either to bring about changes to a full extent, and without strengthening international cooperation the solving of the tasks is absolutely impossible. Perfecting the efficiency of CMEA cooperation has become a basic high priority issue.

The future of the region will be determined, however, by the interaction of political and economic changes in the U.S.S.R. and other socialist countries. The political and economic crises which evolved during the 1980s have created new conditions demanding radical reforms.

It is indicated by the general tendencies of the development of the world economy, the considerable tensions, and unbalanced conditions in production, finances, employment and international trade as well as the specific difficulties of single countries and country groups that mankind has entered a considerably more contradictory and difficult period in the late twentieth century. It would seem impossible to improve the situation by the individual action of one or another country. Joint actions are needed to roll back protectionism, to give more support to multilateral financial institutions and to harmonize macro-economic policies in a growth-oriented way. All these, of course, must still be supported by proper national adjustment policies. The improvement of the world economic situation is particularly impeded by greater world political disturbances and tensions since these put obstacles in the way of international cooperation. Incidentally, mutual dependence and interaction have become stronger not only between the countries but between international problems and processes as well, and it is particularly the interactions of world economy and international political relations which have strengthened. Bringing about conditions needed for a faster and more harmonious development of the world economy—and the significance of such conditions has become more and more obvious in the wake of increasing difficulties—has become one of the fundamental tasks of the coming years. The feasibility of this task depends first and foremost on the actions of the protagonists of the present-day world order, i.e. on the leading powers.

Part Two

The Changing Global Power Structure in the World Economy of the Late Twentieth Century

Changes in the international system constantly reproduce or extend inequalities but seldom along the previous lines. The changes in the relative economic position of the countries as regulating forces in the global economy are of course subordinated to different factors. No country can change her place in the international economic power structure by declaration or through resolutions in intergovernmental organizations. The economic and political events of the last decades also proved that in the international system or world order of the late twentieth century, in spite of increasing interdependence, the hierarchical structure and the concentration of economic power determine the framework in which the weaker countries have to "adjust". For many of them this is basically a difficult, often a hostile environment. Without understanding the nature and the trends in the power structure it is not possible to perceive the present (or any) international system and its future.

1. The Concepts of "World Order" or "Global Systems"

The concept of "world order" is not fully defined. Categories, the interpretation of which are heatedly discussed, are often used in social sciences. What exactly the world order is and how it should be interpreted in terms of economics or political science is also disputed.

The causes which had resulted in the internationalization of economic development—under the conditions of capitalism at that time—were comprehended and elucidated by Marxist political economy more than a century ago. In their Communist Manifesto published in February 1848[40] Marx and Engels pointed out the fact that by exploiting the world market the bourgeoisie has internationalized the production and consumption of all countries. They stressed the part of modern industry in processing raw materials coming from faraway regions and manufacturing goods which are consumed all over the world; thus, a manifold mutual dependence of nations has taken the place of national isolation and autarky. They added, that this process takes place not only in material but in non-material production as well, and that the intellectual products of the individual nations have become common treasures.

Colonial conquests had a vital part in the development of the world order characterized by capitalist relations. The characteristic features and perspectives of the world order developed in the era of imperialism were summed up by Lenin. The Marxist analysis of imperialism explored and revealed not only the characteristics of the world of a given era but threw a light on the causes of the disintegration of the established world order. Since Lenin approached the character and fate of the world order from the aspect of social relations, he did not regard its hierarchical power elements as absolute. He did not simply identify imperialism with conquests. He interpreted dynamically the established order and its components by revealing the interrelationships of internal and international relations, economic and political processes. For this reason the method of Marxist analysis is suitable for the comprehension of the characteristics of the present world order, of the components determining its development and of the changes of these components as well and often borrowed by other schools of thought.

In their analyses and suggestions the Marxist and bourgeois social scientists of today dealing with international problems increasingly set out from the complex structure of the "world order". However, this is interpreted in different ways or only some of its elements are stressed. The still popular concepts of "centre and periphery" and their several variations are based for instance on the characteristics of the productive forces and international division of labour. However, owing to their static approach, they often distort actual conditions. The classification according to "North and South"—a fashionable definition used by UN organizations—does not render much help in achieving a realistic interpretation of present relations either. Though structuring the world into industrial and underdeveloped regions represents a more dynamic alternative of the concept of "centre and periphery", in many respects it blurs the differences—emerging in the wake of differentiation—between the industrial and developing countries as well as of those within the latter group.

At the same time, more and more Western scholars tend to agree that the approximately 170 countries co-existing today are not an amorphous, anarchic formation but are "structured" and try to change their positions according to the effects of certain regulating forces. The two social and economic systems, their conflicts, the differences in development, power relations and coalitions, the ever strengthening links of mutual dependence and the institutional reflection of these relations (e.g. in the UN or other international organizations)—all these are often mentioned in the works of different social scientists but are rarely linked to analysis of the world order based on a uniform approach.

The late French historian Raymond Aron accepting and to a certain degree developing the "traditional theory of Clausewitz", has characterized in one of his works the conditions of the world order in the 1950s and 1960s.[41]

a) Within the international system or "world order" the leading part is played by some independent states. The others, the dependent countries, are not protagonists but mere "pawns" in international relations. This does not mean that there are no interrelations and no connections among the states. These, however, are of a voluntary nature and can be altered, and interrelations (trade, etc.) do not influence either political relationships or the system of decision-making or the means necessary to activities in the fields of domestic or foreign affairs (military power, economic means, subversive activity, etc.).

b) The national interests of the protagonists of international affairs are determined not only by their domestic needs but also by the needs and objectives of their foreign policies, which in turn are conditioned mainly by their geopolitical situation, their competition with other countries and their diplomatic traditions. In the course of this, they attempt to extend and strengthen their positions.

c) The "game" within the international system is overshadowed by the possibility of an armed conflict. There exists a strategic competition the main structure of which consists in the military alliances, the coalitions of forces with the aim of deterring or defeating the adversary in the long run. The basic feature of the system is the existence of two categories: allies and adversaries, and these change places from time to time.

d) It follows from the above that the main means of the system is military force, power. Power is the sum total of the resources available and the capability of mobilizing them for war production and combat (manpower, materials, bases). Power as a means of control is the capacity to get hold of the positions of others and to defend one's own position.

e) The hierarchy of the system is of geostrategical nature. It is the great powers which at all times dispose of the most significant military and economic might (France and Russia in the eighteenth century, Austria and later Germany in the nineteenth century, the USA and the Soviet Union in the second half of the twentieth century), which have the power to conquer key positions or to defend them in any part of the world.

The theses of Raymond Aron were not entirely new or original even at the time of their formulation, yet his views have gained popularity and continuously crop up as variants in the statements of different authors and politicians.

The left-wing ideologists of the Western countries have been influenced considerably by another "theory of world order", the system of ideas of Immanuel Wallerstein which might be summarized as follows.[42]

a) The basic organizational unit of the world order is the capitalist world economy which is of a global character and the sub-systems of which are linked to the central "core".

b) The changes within the sub-systems originate from the contradictions of the system as a whole, i.e. the structural contradictions of the capitalist system are the main sources of the problems of the whole system.

c) Since the sub-systems are positioned as a concentric circle around the central core, peculiar interrelations come into being between the external forces and the active forces within the subsystems. Though the movements of the sub-systems within the system have some measure of autonomy, it is the external effects which dominate in the interrelationships.

d) Since the world order is in effect the world market and within that the exchange relations are the chief components of the sub-systems, the world order can be defined fundamentally by the capital flows permeating the whole system.

e) The main characteristic of the world order is its global nature. There is no feudal system in the world economy, and likewise there is no socialist system in world economy either. The world order is essentially capitalistic.

f) Within the framework of the capitalist system no sub-system can turn socialist. A sub-system can change only when the system as a whole changes as well.

Thus the concepts relating to the world order as elaborated by Aron and Wallerstein differ in many respects. They are, however, identical in so far as actually both of them deny the existence of the socialist world system. Aron regards the power relations as absolute whereas Wallerstein considers essentially the exchange relations of world economy determinative, and he also puts the part of the Soviet Union on a level with that of the United States. He virtually regards both of them as belonging to the "central core" with some qualifications as to the socialist countries. These latter he thinks to be partly central and partly peripheral elements within the framework of the capitalist world order. Wallerstein has little regard for both political (power) relations and institutions. Mutual relationships of dependence, too, are absent from his theory, and by regarding the hierarchical elements as virtually absolute, he distorts the actual situation.

The theory of world order elaborated by R. Aron is distorting, too, but from another aspect. He and his adherents are correct in pointing out that within the international system—which is a peculiar contradictory medium—power relations are one of the regulating forces. However, the world order is a much more complex phenomenon, the power system is only one of its aspects, and even this does not consist of rigid static relationships and unchanging centres. Simultaneously contradictory effects, too, assert themselves in the international sphere promoting the centralization and concentration, the decentralization and diffusion of power. The intensity of these effects tends to be different.

The terms "force" and "power" have appeared as traditional political-military categories in the system of international relations. However, to be able to analyse present-day relations (be it world economic or international political relations, or their correlations) it is necessary to interpret the system itself within which such relations have developed and have exerted their influence.

The reason for the ideological confusion regarding the notions "system" and "world order" lies undoubtedly with the fact that they can be interpreted in more than one dimension. Thus, the present-day world, our planet and even the universe can be seen as a "system" in the astronomical sense of the term. (And within that, for example our solar system could be regarded as a separate little system.) In the social sense of the term our globe—i.e. the sum total of the countries having come into being on it—can be treated as a system with a definite structure. Though the countries are divided by the conflict of the two groups of countries living under antithetical social and economic conditions there are still some interrelations between them and they are linked by a number of common problems. (Such are the natural conditions of the planet and the finite character of these, the threat of the capability of mutual destruction, etc.) In this sense the concept of a uniform "world order" seems justified in our given era, too, though it has of course some socio-economic, military-political and even sociocultural components as well. However, both existing societies also constitute systems in themselves and have a specific hierarchy of values and power structures. As regards international economic conditions, they live, develop and establish relationships within the framework of the same world market but the system-specific values effect the essential nature of their relations, too. The socialist countries, for instance, strive to create other norms of international cooperation than those characteristic of the traditional world market but they can achieve these goals only partially. From a socioeconomic point of view, however, the approach that considers the existent two social systems to be two sub-systems of the traditional global order cannot be substantiated since their common existence is the result of the disintegration of the previous world order.

Despite the fact that the two social systems appear in the social and ideological sphere as the negation of each other, they show a number of similar characteristics. Similar categories exist in their economy.

Their common feature is the fact that the productive forces, technology, science and economic life in general have become internationalized and this process has been accelerated by up-to-date industrial development, particularly by the scientific and technological revolution taking place in our times. The existence of the national states has been upheld in both of the social systems.

The contrast between the trend of internationalization and the upholding of the framework of the states is a characteristic feature of both social systems. The intensity and forms of these contradictions, their consequences and the means and possibilities of mitigating them are important issues in both systems. As a result of the similarities in the problems and in the available institutions similar international organizational forms could emerge as well.[43]

A fundamental issue in the development of the present world order is the relationship between the countries of the two systems.

The conditions of the development of the two systems amidst the present power relations, military and political realities of the nuclear age as well as on the basis of the universal interests of humankind provide for strong incentives to emerge in both systems in favour of peaceful coexistence and cooperation. Nevertheless, the threat of a global military conflict has not been eliminated. Under the conditions of the system of international relations in the late twentieth century this threat is kept alive by the rising spiral of the armament race under the pretext of "mutual deterrents". Since lasting coexistence and the development of mutual relations is the only acceptable prospect in the interest of the survival of humankind and the world, all present and future international organizations, political and economic institutions are bound to reckon with the system of competition and the compulsion of coexistence or even cooperation. However, neither the tendencies based on the conditions of cooperation nor those of conflict can be extrapolated separately.

Neither of the two social systems are homogeneous. Of outstanding importance among the reasons for their heterogeneous nature are the characteristic features resulting from the historical development of the states belonging to one or the other system, their internal economic and social relations, the differing level of their economic and social development. The highly complex and vastly differentiated group of developing countries which have chosen the capitalist road of development is held together rather by the common colonial or semi-colonial past of these countries and by the common tasks resulting from the elimination of this past than by some kind of common future. Their underdevelopment and backwardness is partly due to the international economic relations of the given system. However, the developing countries have a specific position within the socialist world system, too, since owing to their social and economic conditions they have to grant priorities to other tasks than those in the more developed countries. Their direct economic interests and aims are, therefore, not entirely identical with those of the more developed industrial countries belonging to the socialist system. (Thus, they are more interested in the international redistribution of resources.)

Hence "world order" is the sum total of the relationship among its components (elements) or the total effect of the regulating forces determining development, international movements and relations in a given period, and in the background of which the social and economic relations can ultimately be found.

Within the scope of world order "politics", "economic power" and "relations of interdependence" represent specific and overlapping dimensions, and relations among the states are influenced in different ways by them.

2. Politics, Economy and Interdependence in the Changing World System

The relationship between politics and economy, the correlation between political and economic power is a fundamental problem for the functioning of any world system. If contradictions develop between the political and the economic structures, the political power has—according to historical experiences—to adapt itself to economic realities and necessities, which in the last resort further economic development though the disintegration of the established order and the creation of new conditions. These changes are, however, not necessarily fast, automatic or even free from shocks especially in the case of world economic relations where the partners are states. In the system of international relations politics has a vital part in shaping the economic "framework", in establishing states, the inhabitants of which produce, consume and cooperate with other countries. It is also an important political problem how the leading powers enforce their international economic ends. In the course of history all dominating powers have struggled to organize their international economic environment according to their own interests and objectives.

The precondition of interdependence is that it is states which are related with each other, and that these states have national borders and adequate political institutions. Thus, it excludes international relations within empires, relations between politically oppressed people and their oppressors. The interpretation and the subject matter of "interdependence" is highly complex. It means first of all that the existence of the states is interwoven in a complex way by the consequences of the existence of other states. As a result, their objectives (and among their frameworks the objectives of the individual social classes and groups) can be realized only by taking into account the existence and effects of the other countries both in politics and in the economy.

In economic terms interdependence means that the international flow of goods, services, capital and the migration of labour as well as international financial relations influence not only the growth and distribution of the national income (and through this the level and structure of employment) but also effect the mutual relations of classes, thus influencing the political sphere as well, in different countries. The international interconnectedness of scientific and technological development has also a vital part in the economic processes. In an interdependent structure the inter-state economic relations are based on joint interests, and more often than not develop simultaneously with political-military alliance systems—or at least with common interests manifesting themselves in this field, too.

Inter-state relations have become somewhat more stable. Interests and ties and the forms of cooperation are naturally modified in the course of time. However, the consequences of breaking off relations among the states participating in the system are considerable, the costs of such steps are extremely high. Common interests naturally do not preclude the possibility of dissent, or differences of opinions as to how these states could or should jointly act.

The intensity of interdependence may vary greatly between the individual countries. Interdependence influences the degree of autonomy of the decisions by governments and mostly in an asymmetrical way. This is true only in respect of states which are unable to influence their international environment and simply absorb the effects of international events, but also (to a lesser extent) of those which, owing to their economic strength, are able to directly influence international trends. Therefore, it is necessary that in an interdependent framework the states should be prepared adequately for external effects and be ready to act appropriately (to make use of or to curb their consequences). It follows that the economic structures and institutions of the states in an interdependent world must have proper policy instruments and coordinate their actions.

The increase of interdependence has taken place in a peculiar way. Perhaps the most clear-cut example is the system of relations among the highly industrialized Western countries. The economies of these countries became more "international" in recent decades and, at the same time, the role of the governments has grown in influencing or regulating their domestic economic processes. While these efforts sometimes included certain protectionist measures as well, the developed Western countries increasingly made use of foreign technologies, capital and raw materials, and exported their industrial commodities to a growing extent.

Industrial division of labour demands long-term commitment for internationalization and a given degree of market freedom. Governments, therefore, have to give each other mutual guarantees that no restrictions will be put into force against the other party. This factor had had a part in the establishment of the European Common Market as well as in the outcome of customs negotiations within the framework of GATT.

Inter-governmental agreements have in the long run considerably furthered the possibilities of external penetration and, at the same time, have put restraint on the measure of economic control within their boundaries. This very fact has brought about quite a number of problems, too. The problems have been aggravated by the increased activities of the transnational corporations by further restricting the sphere of influence of national decisions as regards economic policies. These corporations are able to take an effective stand not only with respect to the national instruments of demand management; they are also in a position to evade or elude restrictions put on currency or capital exports, and render it more difficult to defend the exchange rates of national currencies. International raw material markets can be influenced in various ways by their speculative transactions. The conditions of technological development and world trade in technologies can also be affected in various ways by the business strategies of the transnational corporations. In many a critical sphere of the economy the question has arisen whether the highly industrialized Western countries are able to make autonomous decisions at all?

If the opening of the borders, and the scale of dependence had an equal effect on all states there would be better prospects for the elaboration of some kind of a common policy based on compromises. However, the individual countries are not affected to an equal degree by external influences. These problems are well known to the small though highly industrialized Western countries, such as the Netherlands or Sweden. It had been realized, however, long ago by these countries that in spite of all the difficulties the economic closing of their borders would be a more costly affair for them.

The gigantic proportions of the US economy and the "loop-holes" in economic legislation have rendered it possible to bridge many a problem. The problem is most pressing for the middle powers (Britain, Japan, France and the FRG) as regards the coordination of conflicting objectives.

The functional regulation of cooperation the bringing about of international cooperative systems and organizations, is rendered necessary by the growing intensity in the development of inter-state relations. However, the joint decisions of the states as a rule materialize mostly by means of the decisions of the governments of the participating member countries or of some other national participants in international affairs, i.e. through "national filters", and thus tend to become distorted as compared to the original notions. This by the way is a major problem of integrating groups, in spite of the fact, that the communities enjoy special supranational power.

Interdependence among the socialist countries had developed under specific conditions.

Prior to World War II, when there was no socialist world system, the Soviet Union represented a rather closed, isolated entity in the world economy. The system of its international economic relations developed in connection with and subordinated to the objectives of development as set by the state. The Soviet Union deliberately strove to minimize its dependence on the world economy, which was considered as basically hostile. As is well known, it succeeded outstandingly in achieving these ends. The model thus elaborated considerably contributed to the internal integration of the Soviet Union, to the intensification of the division of labour among the socialist Soviet republics and territories.

Following World War II, at the end of the 1940s the East European states which had entered on the road to socialism were not presented with the possibility of developing a novel type of socialist community, becoming integrated in the field of economy on the basis of similar social conditions as well as common economic and political interests.

They became interdependent politically. Certain plans were elaborated also to create a customs union and to coordinate the development of some branches of industry.

The deliberate establishment of an integrated socialist economic community, which would have realized the various developed forms of international economic relations in a planned way, could not be achieved because of the given historical circumstances.

Thus economic relations among the socialist countries have not developed according to a common plan, nor as a consequence of an internationally coordinated production process. The direct aim was to create the external conditions under which production could develop favourably even on the basis of isolated state plans. In this respect the forms adopted truly exerted an influence: they helped the growth of independent national economies and the surmounting of temporary difficulties. An exceptional part was taken by the Soviet Union in these developments. It was the Soviet Union which supplied most of the necessary raw materials, it was capable of supplying machines and equipment in many an industrial branch, and at the same time it guaranteed a market for the commodity surplus of the socialist countries.

The relationships among the socialist countries were characterized by a new type of connections based on equal rights. The fact that the partners were sovereign states, the owners of the produced commodities, has not at all, or only to a minor degree, restricted parallel industrial development, the unfavourable consequences of which had manifested themselves as acute problems even by the end of the 1950s. The instruments to organize well-structured and complementary division of labour were not developed. Unrealistic prices and exchange rates, the lack of convertible currency, and other shortcomings of the system of planning and management also restricted international cooperation. Following the exhaustion of the reserves of import substituting industrialization the established new branches of industries—often with low efficiency and small capacity—had made the economies of a number of countries competitive in many respects (from the aspect of exports). The system of international economic relations of the socialist countries is still influenced by the characteristics of this period although the importance of international economic relations has increased in the course of economic growth, and this fact has been reflected in state planning beginning with the early 1960s.

It can be seen from the above that the possibilities and means of strengthening the process of interdependence are in many respects different in the two world systems. The specific features of the socialist and the capitalist countries bring about different possibilities and in certain cases may justify the implementation of differing methods in the future, too, as regards the organization of inter-state relations. In the socialist countries with planned economies—irrespective of the actual economic mechanisms—the part of the central state authorities is going to remain significant in the development of international economic relations.

The contemporary Western economic and political literature characterizes the relations between developing and developed capitalist countries as "interdependence" and tends to project this term to the past as well. As for the past, however, relations enforced by political and economic domination cannot be interpreted as interdependence. The developing countries had been forced in the colonial era, mostly by political means, to become the food and raw material suppliers of the industrial, particularly of the colonial, powers. As a result, their economic structure has become distorted and they have become monocultural producers and mono-exporters. This one-sided dependence prevails in their international relations up to this date and—

though certain links of interdependence, too, have come into being—hinders their economic development in many ways.

In the relations between the socialist and the industrialized Western countries there are strong interactions but not of symmetrical nature. The socialist countries, for instance, exert a many-sided influence (with their mere existence, development, results or difficulties, and possibly with their errors) on the internal evolution of the Western countries. The Western countries, too, exert a certain political and military effect on the socialist states. Thus, the effects and interrelations are broader than would be assumed on the basis of East-West economic relations. Economic relations have become also more intensive, since the 1960s. Trade, inter-firm relations and financial cooperation have increased. On the basis of these developments and in connection with some global problems, certain elements of interdependence have developed between the socialist and the industrialized Western countries as well.

3. The Power Structure of the Contemporary World System and Future Trends

Similarly to the relations created by interdependence, so the role of both military and economic power can be examined as an independent set of issues, too. Their analysis is actually desirable in spite of the fact that their influence—just as in the case of interdependence—does not make itself felt in an abstract medium and cannot be isolated. Thus the antagonism between the social systems appears as a vital factor in the background to the conflicts between the two leading world powers. In the wake of socialism's gaining ground and the emergence of the two social systems, common interests and dependence has developed within the framework of the power elite in the Western world, which, in the long run, restricts and limits the sharpening of their conflicts and at the same time, promotes and encourages compromises. Their relations with the developing countries are influenced in many respects by the defence of the general interests of the social system (e.g. it makes them interested in preventing socialism from gaining ground in these regions of the world by means of joint actions). Within the socialist world, too, the joint interests and cooperation of the states is a major power factor.

The characteristics of the world order are naturally not of a static nature, particularly from the point of view of power relations. A significant characteristic of the present world order is, for instance, the great number and highly differentiated nature of the "participants". Today, more than 170 states exist which is a new and essential characteristic as compared to the era preceding the disintegration of the colonial system. According to their positions, roles and capacities, the states can influence the system to different extents. For the majority who have only minimal resources, the maintenance of a workable system of international relations is a matter of life and death. The overwhelming majority of currently existing states is characterized by vulnerability, though this fact does not eliminate conflicts and competition from the system, indeed it may develop new sources of these (e.g. in the relations between raw material producing and raw material exporting nations or in those between the states developing new industrial structures). Every state is interested in the dynamic development of the world economy and scientific and technological development is also of vital interest for all of them. They are also interested in avoiding rampant inflation, environmental pollution, the exhaustion of natural resources, devastating economic crises and, naturally, a nuclear world war. None of them has an interest in the disintegration of the world economic institutional system and in protectionism becoming a general phenomenon.

However, there are important differences among the states as regards their possible losses in the case of a world economic crisis or to what extent they would be capable of shifting the burden or their losses to their neighbours, partners of the other members of the international system.

There are also differences—and these are not permanent ones either—as to how the benefits resulting from the smooth functioning of the system and the development of the world economy are distributed. The fundamental conflict of the present-day world order is the conflict between the two systems determining international relations. However, the increasing interdependence among the states has brought about a new situation even for the major powers of the Western world. Direct political conquest, full or partial annexation of other countries, which had characterized the previous history of mankind, has become very difficult to achieve, whereas the significance of military power has survived not only because of the existence of the socialist system but also as a political means in their relations to the developing countries.

As a result of the strengthening of interdependent relations, the influence exerted by the states on each other has increased, too. Mutual interest has increased particularly in the basic stability of relations within the system and also in the general world economic stability. None of the countries can regard its own international economic system of relations as a zero sum game, when the losses of its adversary could be considered pure advantage or, vice versa, its own advantage a pure loss to its adversary. This, however, does not eliminate competition, or conflicts, but restricts the intensity of rivalry.

The growing number and differentiation of the states, i.e. the diffusion of power, naturally increases the heterogeneity and manifold character of the states, and results in the emergence of new power centres,

The main question from the point of view of international power relations is not only how these relations change but also how these changes affect existing relations, how the regulating forces connected with power relations within the international system are modified by the changes.

Naturally, the transition from one power structure to another cannot be independent of the working mechanism of the world order. It is quite obvious that, for instance, in the world order characterized by the colonial empires the transition from the specific role of the British world empire to the development of the hegemony of the United States took place rather differently from the changes in world order in the present day when two global powers dispose of dominant political and military power and there are 170 political entities in the world.

Two basic views on the interpretation of the development of power structure are contrasted by the Finnish economist and political scientist Raimo Väyrynen: one stresses chiefly its economic aspect, the other the political one. The latter one does not necessarily deny the importance of economic elements in the process of transition but imputes an independent significance to the military (strategic) dimension of power.[44]

According to historical experiences, political uncertainty increases as a consequence of changes in power relations; tension grows, conflicts and wars break out within the system, international relations are restructured and all these events contribute to the emergence of a new dominating power. As stressed by Väyrynen, economic and political changes manifest themselves as an interrelationship in the course of this process.

It was first of all Germany which attempted to overthrow the given system (according to the analysis cited above, this was the system based on British hegemony). Germany failed in this attempt in both of the two world wars. As a result of the total effect and interrelationship of domestic and international conditions, it was only after World War II that the United States got into a position where it was capable of striving for global hegemony or to cite the American political term: "to accept global leadership".

Global Powers in the Contemporary World System

The power structure of the present world order is different from the previous ones and is unprecedented in modern history because 170 conflict ridden countries coexist on our planet. One of the institutional guarantees of their existence and survival is the UN structure based on the sovereign equality of the states and its background of a system of power relations. This system has a decisive part in the calling into existence and the survival of this great number of states among which there are many small, mini- and micro-states. One of the most characteristic features of the present-day world order— from the point of view of international power relations, has been the fact that two opposing global powers have existed and coexisted concurrently for a relatively long historical period. The term "superpower", a borrowed word in Western political slang, which, taken as a pure term, has no derogatory meaning, does not seem adequate to characterize these two powers. It does not reflect the actual situation within the power relations. The attribute "super" merely refers to the concentration of power whereas the term "global" stresses the comprehensive significance of interests and actions and reflects the capacity of force (primarily military force) on a global scale.

A truly immense force is concentrated in the two global powers. Both of them have vast territories at their disposal abundant in raw materials and energy endowments. As regards territory and endowments, the Soviet Union by far surpasses the United States. But it is also beyond argument that these resources are more difficult to exploit owing to their geographical location. Until the second part of the twentieth century the United States was practically self-supporting in almost all mineral raw materials and moreover, it had a considerable export surplus of them. The importance of imports increased in the sixties and seventies, not only as a consequence of wasteful raw material and energy consumption, so that some of the resources of the United States have become exhausted, but also because it was cheaper to cover its needs from other—mainly developing—countries or because mining had to be stopped in certain regions to protect the environment. The United States still disposes of great reserves and depends less than any other developed industrial Western nation on the imports of energy carriers and raw materials, consuming about 36 per cent of materials produced all over the world. In an emergency the US would be able to meet its own consumption for a long time by means of increasing domestic production and further improving the efficiency of consumption.[45] In changes in the part taken in world affairs by both of these powers the number and the "quality" of the population is of considerable importance. Both the Soviet Union and the United States have large and highly qualified populations; following China and India, the Soviet Union and the United States are the two greatest countries as regards population. In the early eighties the population of the United States approached the 230 million mark, proliferating at a rate of 1.6 million annually.

The workforce in the United States has several favourable characteristics from the point of view of economic development.

First: the educational level of the labour force is high and increases relatively fast. This is accompanied by a broadening of production experience and culture. Of the population in employment age amounting to roughly 100 million, only 18 per cent have completed less than eight classes (as against 30 per cent twenty years ago), and about 15 per cent of them are college or university graduates, their percentage being almost double that of twenty years ago.

Second: the regional mobility of manpower is high, which eases structural shifts in output. One-third of the employed labour force do not work in their native states. Interregional mobility is particularly high among juveniles.

Third: manpower switches over from one trade to another with relative ease. This is rendered possible by high educational standards since manpower has become more versatile. Various retraining systems have become wide-spread. People have become accustomed to the fact that they have to change not only jobs but professions perhaps several times in their lifetime. Nearly a third of the American workforce has changed professions in the seventies.

Fourth: together with the highly qualified workers, unskilled workers willing to take difficult work requiring physical effort are also present, and a further supply is available through immigration. A relatively great number of people are willing to accept part-time jobs (2 or 3 hours a day) and to perform qualified work for rather low wages (e.g. some housewives take part-time jobs in services or offices).

The nearly 280 million population of the Soviet Union is distributed regionally more unevenly as a manpower source than in the United States, and the supply of labour force to Siberia continues to be a considerable problem. As regards professional composition, the quality of manpower has greatly improved between 1960 and 1980. The number of highly qualified experts and of those graduated from highschools has almost doubled, and the breakdown by educational level has become by and large similar in the various regions of the country and also within the two sexes (the percentage of the highly qualified workforce included).

As regards the number of people working on scientific and technological development jobs the Soviet Union outstripped the United States in the sixties, and as regards their percentage in the total labour force it outdistanced the USA in the seventies.

Despite the significant decrease in the number of workers coming from traditional sources of labour (agriculture, households), which have migrated to other sectors, and of those entering employment age, a more efficient utilization of the work-force could become a further great resource of economic development. The differences in industrial production potential, on which—among other things—national defence is based, has become a significant factor of global power status. While the volume of production of the Soviet Union is about 60 per cent that of the United States, the differences in labour productivity or in the technological conditions of some sectors are in favour of the USA. However, the differences are smaller today than they were in the fifties. Particularly in the fields of research, technological development and production connected with national defence the gap has narrowed, though it is still considerable and has even widened in civilian industries. Certain strategical advantages of the Soviet economy (easier mobilization, the speed of organizing the switch-over to defence purposes and its possible effect on the civilian economy) moderate to a certain extent the advantages of the United States in volume, quality and efficiency of production.

The comparison of military powers is a highly complex task. The gap between the U.S. and the Soviet Union in the volume of production, development level, technological level and in the level of personal consumption increased since the early 1970s. On this basis one must judge the importance of the fact that since the end of the sixties a certain degree of strategic equality developed between the Soviet Union and the United States in the military field (aerodynamics, fluid dynamics, nuclear and conventional warheads, laser technology, etc.), which are the most important areas of deterrence.

The situation of the two countries is similar also in the respect that as both of them are the leading powers of the contrasting social systems, their internal development and international actions have not only a general influence on world development but also affect the conditions of the two systems to a great extent, which makes them of direct international significance. Therefore their responsibility, too, is greater than that of the other powers because, among other things they control between them about 95 per cent of the nuclear destructive power accumulated in the world (meaning about 40 000 warheads) and both of these powers dispose of enough nuclear armaments to destroy the conditions for life on our planet. Thus, their mutual relationship is of great importance from the point of view of the "functioning" and prospects for the present-day world order, and even problems, which incidentally would be only of bilateral interest in their relations, are highly important.

The history of Soviet–American relations—practically ever since 1917—are characterized by lasting periodic tensions, sharp confrontations and relatively short-period cooperation. In the period prior to World War II, Soviet–American relations had begun with military intervention against the socialist forces which had come to power. American intervention had been triggered off by the fear of the spread of proletarian revolutions and its aim had been the elimination of the Soviet state since this had been regarded as their main antagonist by leading American circles. The Soviet Union was officially recognized by the United States in 1933. An improvement of relations was experienced in the thirties, economic co-operation increased, and the two powers fought within the same alliance system against the Axis powers in World War II.

After 1945 their relations gradually deteriorated leading to the Cold War which lasted till the end of the sixties. Four years after the end of World War II, the secret document NSC-68 (National Security Council Document, No. 68:1950) approved by the American president of that time, Truman, pointed out that American political leadership considered the United States the only country in the world which, owing to its economic strength, would be able to establish a world order organized according to its own interests. Emphasizing that the Soviet Union was regarded as the chief opponent of this world order, it was pointed out in the same document, that the strength of the United States should be further enhanced in order to enforce a fundamental change in the Soviet system, to stimulate the growth of the seeds of decay in that system, and to create and support unrest and uprisings in some of the satellite countries of strategic importance, and further such development by all means, overtly or covertly, by force or without violent means. The authors of this document added that the increase in military expenditure in the USA would not result in a decrease in living standards and, therefore, would not bring about social or political unrest.[46]

From the late 1960s and the early 1970s new conditions developed in Soviet–American relations. As a consequence of a balance in nuclear power, certain common interests emerged in Soviet–American relations, mainly as regards the avoidance of a nuclear world war or a world situation (brought about either by the spread of nuclear armament or by other—incidental—reasons) that might plunge the two world powers into war. Moreover, a growing number of global problems came to light where the two powers did not confront each other but their co-operation could clearly further the solution of these problems (e.g. improving the conditions in the developing countries, natural environmental protection, etc.).

In the period under review two trends of opinion within the leading circles of the United States collided: on the one hand that sharply opposing the Soviet Union, and on the other hand that preferring a compromise, and it was the latter which gained the upper hand in American foreign policy. In 1972, for the very first time, the leaders of the two powers formally codified and in joint declarations formulated the aims which they agreed upon and regarding which their interests coincided, and at the same time they acknowledged that the worldwide contest between them continued.

Recognizing the necessity of the principle and practice of peaceful coexistence, the following objectives were set by these declarations and agreements, respectively:

— limitation of strategic nuclear weapons, the setting into motion of the SALT process.
— prevention of the outbreak of possible wars due to accidents, miscalculations or broadening conflicts in the developing countries;
— reduction of tension in Europe;
— prevention of the spread of nuclear weapons;
— development of Soviet–American economic relations;
— promotion of functional cooperation in environmental protection and space exploration;

— strengthening of scientific cooperation;
— extension of cultural relations.

The Helsinki Final Act defining the main principles of peaceful coexistence and cooperation among the states was signed by the leaders of both powers. Thus the road was opened up for long-term and comprehensive cooperation in Soviet–American relations.

The period of cooperation, however, once again proved to be short-lived. The highly complex political changes in the developing countries, the Egyptian–Israeli war of 1973, the African situation brought about by the collapse and disintegration of the Portuguese colonial empire (the former Africa colonies of Portugal have chosen a socialist-type development) as well as other regional conflicts in the seventies, have resulted in new tensions between the two global powers. These tensions coincided with the gradual gaining of ground by neo-conservative and aggressively anti-Soviet forces in American domestic and foreign policy. All those events led directly to the objectives of the Reagan Administration; establishment of American superiority, a qualitative change in the American armament programs, the increasing subordination of the international economic policy of the USA to American military-strategical objectives.

These changes had a highly adverse effect on world politics as a whole, increased tensions again and even enhanced the effects of the existing crisis centres. The summit of November 1985 reflected the awareness of both powers to the grave dangers of their confrontation in the increasingly complex global environment. Political changes that have taken place in Soviet–American relations since then mark a new stage, and a beginning of a new era of cooperation.

Global "bilateralism", the bipolar character of military power and political influence, has assumed such an extent that no other power could be in a position to counterbalance it in the foreseeable future. Global political processes cannot be treated—beyond a certain level—independent of the development of Soviet–American relations. But it is also an undeniable fact that since the end of the sixties the increasingly independent interests and ambitions of the regional great powers as well as the established groupings of minor powers associated with them (these groupings e.g. non-aligned countries, Islamic states, etc. have been brought about on the basis of different regulating forces) have introduced increasing instability into the political structure of the bipolar strategic (power) system. Behind the emergence of new centres of conflict, of the restructuring of old ones, of their changing relations to the main power centres are not only elements in the dynamism of the conflicts between the two systems but often independent, new or newly defined power interests as well (e.g. the Iran–Iraq conflict).

Changing international power relations make themselves felt increasingly in the world economic sphere, too. On the basis of strategic-military bipolarism within the present world order it is highly important that the significance of the diversification of force and power has increased. As a result of the limited possibilities of using military power, the significance of economic strength and economic power has greatly increased as compared to the past. This upgrading is not only the consequence of the fact that the arms race as one of the major factors and instruments of contemporary international relations requires and absorbs immense economic energies in both the

Soviet Union and the United States. Since the overwhelming majority of the states is vitally interested in international economic cooperation then, economic dependence, economic leverages and economic warfare have become important factors in international relations.

The Role of Economic Power

In the system of contemporary international relations economic power is a highly complex category. In international political relations military power is concentrated in the states and the use of such power is primarily the function of the states. The other direct international participants in political relations (e.g. international organizations or movements) do not dispose of direct military power independent of states, and national liberation movements fight for the establishment of their independent statehood.

To a certain extent economic power, too, is tied to national flags. At the same time, it is a much debated question whether such participants in international economic relations as international private organizations, transnational corporations and international banks should or should not be regarded (and if so, to what an extent) as independent participants. Direct participants in the world order were defined by two well-known experts of international relations, the Americans Keohane and Nye, as follows: the problem should be decided on the basis of whether such participants are able to influence by their decisions resources and values and establish interactions with other participants of transnational relations.[47]

Another American economist, D. Holzman, gives a different definition of economic power. According to him two things should be understood by the term "economic power." First, there is the classical monopolistic market power by which the seller (or the buyer) has sufficient control over the supply (or demand) to be able to influence the conditions of the transaction. Second, economic power can also originate from the fact that a certain government is in the position to control the flow of an immense volume of resources.[48]

Accordingly, economic power can be made use of for two purposes: to acquire such economic advantages which could not be realized under other conditions or to enforce political advantages. It should be stressed, however, that Holzman's definition of economic power is not comprehensive enough either.

On the strength of both definitions the transnational corporations, too, can be categorized as independent participants in international affairs. However, the differences between the degree of autonomy of the governmental and non-governmental organizations within the international system are blurred by these definitions. Moreover, all these participants act within the bounds of a medium moulded by the actions of the states, and often they, too, are the means of the policy of the states (although sometimes state power is made use of as a means in their "parent" countries). The exertion of economic power—contrary to political power—is more complex because its basis is more comprehensive.

Political and military power are interrelated. The volume of natural resources and their composition, the level of technological and scientific development, the magnitude and breakdown of the research and development, the size of population and its composition according to age and professional qualification, the size, productive capacity and switch-over flexibility of the economy, the measure of the supply of the population and the way of satisfying their demands and needs—all these are highly relevant factors from the point of view of both military power and military strategical vulnerability. As mentioned above, the military power of the Soviet Union and the United States (strategical and tactical nuclear weapons, traditional weapon systems, transportation facilities and equipments furthering military mobility, etc.) are based on both sides on a powerful economic foundation within which the scientific basis and development capacity are of outstanding importance from the point of view of the armaments race.

The basis of economic power is, however, much more manifold than that of direct military power. Its main components are scientific and technological development, the innovative capacity of society and economy (introduction of new products and productive processes, renewal and restructuring of institutions), availability of natural resources and the capacity to exploit and transport them, the capacity to export products competitively, the possibility of investing and using working capital abroad, the role played on international money markets, and the position in world trade. The latter one is reflected by the capacity to mobilize production, services and capital accumulation internationally. Efforts to centralize military power internationally tend to exert an adverse influence on the above factors. Thus, it is a well-known fact that major powers which concentrate the greatest part of their research and development expenditure on military objectives often fall behind in many fields of world market competition. At the same time, the forging ahead of Japan can be explained partly by the fact that only a relatively small part of Japanese forces was invested in unproductive ventures.

Both the objectives and methods of implementing economic power are different from those of military power. Under the manifold and contradicting circumstances of the internationalization of economic life, science and technology, even the front lines between the opponents are not easily drawn.

Between normal (i.e. from the political aspect, friendly or neutral) partners economic power is asserted generally in the sphere of enterprises. Offensive or defensive management strategies are supported by the states by means of their international economic policies. (Such a means could be the founding of intergovernmental organizations or integration.) However, in developing and asserting national economic power, a state's economic policy is of vital importance. The state has a particularly important part in the political implementation of economic power, partly by extending the "economic net" as a means of political influence, and partly by economic sanctions with the help of which it attempts to induce certain states to do or to abstain from something.

Owing to the peculiarities of the contemporary world, under the conditions of the existence of the two systems and the two global powers, political rivalry and conflicts have resulted in smaller or greater wars almost exclusively in the developing world, whereas the danger of a global nuclear war between the Soviet Union and the United States has been mitigated by the military balance of power between the Soviet Union and the USA. The most important conflicts among the leading Western powers have been concentrated on the economy.

The Characteristics of the Hegemonic Economy

The most direct source of the realization of economic power is the emergence and functioning of hegemonic economies. According to the French economist François Perroux[49] hegemonic economies—from the point of view of the volume of production—exert great influence on all other economies because of their great scale, technological development and the extent of their international economic transactions (to a certain extent this influence is unrelated to their intentions). The changes in the internal balance of such economies—economic growth, employment, rate of interest, structure of consumption, etc.—extends to the others, too, through the system of international relations. The United States was regarded by Perroux as the typical example of a hegemonic economy.

It has already been made obvious in earlier decades of the twentieth century that the changes in the economy of the United States, the great world economic significance of this country and its enormous economic power have not remained simply the domestic problems of the American economy. These changes have in many ways affected the position of other countries as well, and not only that of those nations which had closest contact with the United States. The famous byword attributed to Lloyd George is dated also from this time: "If America sneezes, Europe catches the flu."

No doubt, the share of the United States in the gross world production has changed a number of times in the twentieth century before now. On two occasions—after the First and the Second World Wars—its share increased but lately this advantage has gradually declined. However, the United States has retained its superiority all through these years.

The future possibilities of the dominance of the American economy have been evaluated on the basis of historical experience by many experts. According to them, hegemonic economies have emerged in the world in the past, too. Great Britain occupied such a position in the world economy of the nineteenth century though she was able to perform this function in the circumstances of increasing competition among the powers even before World War I. Following the war, Great Britain proved unable to remain the "stage manager" of international economic relations. Since the disintegration of her colonial empire she has become a mere regional power. To what an extent could the British experience be applied to the position of the United States? The example of Britain has proved that it is not only overwhelming world economic predominance which characterizes the dominating power and not merely the comparative prosperity evidenced by its gross national product which is the only decisive factor, although lacking these, the bringing about of such a position would be inconceivable.

The emergence of American hegemony was the result partly of the uniquely advantageous conditions of the internal development of the United States, and partly of the weakening position of the other powers. This latter factor was true not only in the relative but in the absolute sense.

Rich natural endowments played an important part from the very beginning in the economic development of the United States of America. Right up to the end of the past century huge free territories were at the disposal of the settlers. This not only facilitated the settling of the empty regions of the United States but also furthered and contributed to the development of capitalistic agricultural relations on a broad basis and to the rise of a well-to-do farmer stratum as well. Incidentally, agriculture as a raw material source and a buyers' market created highly favourable conditions for industrial development, too. (Thus, the textile industry, for instance, was founded on cotton produced on the Southern plantations.) As a result of its considerable exportable "surpluses" the United States is the leading agricultural exporter even at the end of the twentieth century.

The country is extremely rich in mineral resources, too. Almost all raw materials necessary for modern industrial development are in abundance, and since settlers received the land so to speak gratuitously they had to provide only for the labour force and transport vehicles. Despite changed conditions, it is still the United States of all the developed capitalist countries which is least dependent on raw material imports.

Almost from its earliest days the United States represented a relatively great and rapidly expanding market. Foodstuff, clothing and other consumers' articles as well as housing had to be provided to an ever increasing extent for the immigrants. Even the early manufactures of New England were produced in greater quantities than similar enterprises in contemporary Europe produced. Many industries had been founded on mass production in the United States almost from the very beginning. The farmer stratum mentioned above by itself formed a vast domestic market. The significance and effect on efficiency resulting from the large scale of the enterprises was greater in the American industry than in any other region of the world from the very beginning and particularly after the 1860s. The huge American market was of great importance for the development of the world economy as a whole, and the extensive broadening of this market (its extension to ever new territories in this vast country) was further accelerated following the railway construction. By the turn of the century the United States had become the greatest producer and consumer of the world, and has upheld this position to this very date. In the middle of the 1980s its gross national product—reckoned in current prices—has approached $ 4000 billion. (Reckoned on constant prices this has increased by more than five times in the past 50 years and has doubled within the last 20 years.)[50] Simultaneously with the growth of the territory and production of the country, the American economy, once broken up into small isolated units, had developed over a long period into an immense integrated, complex system.

As a consequence of its huge and highly differentiated domestic market, the United States has a considerable economic edge on the present-day world economy consisting of 170 political entities (mostly small and medium countries), and this is true in respect of any of its competitors, the Common Market—consisting of smaller national units—included, though as regards the latter's total volume it is almost equal with the United States. Japan as a domestic market is about 35% of that of the US and the Federal Republic of Germany is about a quarter of the United States.

Another significant factor from the point of view of the world economic position and the future of the United States is her technological development and innovative capacity. The technological development potential of the Unites States—as is pointed out in detail in the chapter on technological development—surpasses that of the joint capacity of Japan, the Federal Republic of Germany and Great Britain. Incidentally, right from the beginning of modern economic development there have been advantageous conditions for relatively fast technological development in the United States.

Manpower shortages, higher wages than in the European countries and domestic and international competition were all factors which goaded American entrepreneurs to mechanize production rapidly and to modernize the whole process of production.

The vast domestic market and the multiple applicability of machines made it possible to introduce an extraordinarily high standard of specialization in American engineering. This raised the technological standards not only in the given industry but also furthered the implementation of experiences and acquired technical skills—for instance in the field of designing special machinery—in other sectors of the economy as well. Innovations in the pioneering industries became important sources of technological development of other branches, too. Technological development was facilitated and stimulated also by the fact that abundant and relatively cheap natural resources were available (as opposed to capital and manpower) and, therefore, technology could be concentrated on their application with maximum efficiency.

Technological imports, too, were of great significance in the technological development of the United States. Immigrants brought with them a great intellectual stock of knowledge and experiences. Often whole enterprises moved over to the United States from Europe with all their entrepreneurs, engineers, technicians and skilled workers, thus establishing new industries in the United States. This source tends to be of great importance up to the present day. Many an important invention or innovation (made in Europe or other parts of the world) is actually put into use first in the United States.

From the aspect of introducing innovations and diffusing them, the roles of the entrepreneur, organizer and capital are naturally of equal importance. The part of the capitalist entrepreneur willing and capable to shoulder considerable internal investment and risks is still greater in the United States than for instance in the European capitalist countries.

In the past the United States had a highly advantageous, strategically almost ideal, position in the system of international economic relations. Until the 1960s international economic relations had an insignificant part in the economic development of the USA, while its economy was, nevertheless, a determinant factor from the point of view of the majority of its partners since they were unable to influence the functioning of the American economy whereas the USA proved to be able to influence its partners by economic means as well.

Though by the end of the 1970s and the early 1980s to a certain extent new conditions emerged in this respect, international economic relations are still of lesser importance in the American economy than in the economies of the other Western industrial countries. At the same time, events of the seventies have proved once again that external economic sensitivity can result simultaneously in vulnerability and in the strengthening of economic power if the country in question represents considerable economic force and at the same time is capable of reacting flexibly to the changes in external conditions.

The power of the USA is still strong in global economic relations. Dollars cannot be converted in fixed rates to gold and the previous fixed exchange rate of the American currency has ceased. In spite of the collapse of some other pillars of the Bretton Woods system the dollar keeps on playing a key role in international monetary relations. No other Western country has been capable and willing since the end of World War II to enhance the international role of its national currency to such an extent as the United States.

From the point of view of the dollar, the economic and political strength of the United States (as well as the difficulties of the others) is still a favourable factor. Even abroad the American dollar is the currency available in greatest amounts in the world economy, with a continuously fresh supply. Neither the SDR (Special Drawing Rights) nor the currencies of other capitalist countries have been able to replace the dollar fully in the complex system of international monetary relations. Ninety per cent of inter-bank clearing transactions were effected in dollars in 1983. The overwhelming part of the currency reserves of all the other countries consists of dollars, and most of the loans granted on international monetary markets are dollar loans. The dollar is still the most frequently used currency in the world. Fifty-five per cent of world trade is effected in dollars, 14 per cent in German marks, 7.5 per cent in pounds sterling and 6 per cent in French francs.[51]

The conditions of the world economic dominance by the United States have changed—as compared to the situation following World War II—less because of the absolute weakening of its domestic economic foundation than as a result of the relative strengthening of its other capitalist partners and competitors.

Main Trends of Changes in the Economic Power Structure

The changes in the situation of the main regions and countries of the world since the end of World War II can be characterized by some important indices. Table 10 shows the share of the leading nations in the gross national product produced in the world.

From the point of view of global political and world economic relations the events which have taken place since the 1960s are of particular importance.

The share of the developed Western industrial countries in the gross production of the world (Gross Domestic Product) was 68 per cent in the early 1960s, whereas at the middle of the 1980s it dropped to 62 per cent. The share of the United States has decreased from 29.2 per cent to 26.9 per cent, that of the member countries of the European Common Market from 25 per cent to 21 per cent. Within the Common Market the share in world production of the Federal Republic of Germany, Italy and Great Britain has fallen back while that of France has slightly increased. The share in world production of non-Common Market developed Western countries— particularly Japan—has increased from 5.7 per cent to nearly 10 per cent. At the same time, the share of the developing countries in gross world production has risen from 11.1 per cent to 16.5 per cent. Of the Third World countries the share of oil exporting countries has increased from 3.2 per cent to 4.7 per cent, while that of the rapidly developing industrial goods exporting countries has risen from 2.3 per cent to 3.6 per cent. As regards the cumulated net material product of the socialist countries— converted into gross domestic product and added up within world production—the changes are as follows: their share between 1960 and 1962 was 20.9 per cent, between 1980 and 1985 21.5 per cent. Within this group of countries the share of the Soviet

Table 10.
Share in the World Gross National Product (GNP) (per cent)*

	1950	1960/1962	1980/1982	1985/1986
USA	39.3	29.2	27.0	26.9
Japan	1.5	5.7	9.2	9.9
FRG	3.0	7.6	7.0	6.7
United Kingdom	6.0	5.0	4.4	4.2
France	4.0	4.2	4.7	4.9
Italy	1.6	3.0	2.2	2.0
Soviet Union	10.0	13.0	14.0	14.4

* Calculations of the author based on U.N. and national statistics.

Union has risen from 13 per cent to more than 14 per cent, that of the other socialist countries (Yugoslavia included) has increased from 3.5 per cent to 4.0 per cent. The share of the Asian socialist countries has changed from 2.4 per cent to 3.5 per cent.[52]

Analysing the modifications of the geographical distribution of world production it seems noteworthy that the share of Japan has risen by 75 per cent within twenty years, that of the oil exporting countries by about 30 per cent and that of the rapidly developing countries by 56 per cent. A considerable part of world economic changes has been the result of modifications to the positions of these three country groups.

Since the above changes have taken place at a time when world production and demand has slowed down generally and the world economy experienced a serious economic recession, the effect on the system of international relations has sometimes assumed dramatic dimensions.

The military power position of the USA, the scale of its economy, its technological development and financial role, as well as several other factors, continue to guarantee her a key position in the system. However, even the United States is not strong enough to disregard the interests and objectives of its allies, partners and adversaries, or to be able to shape world economic relations unilaterally.

The changing geographical distribution of industrial production reflects especially strongly the emerging new international economic and power relations and the development of cooperation on both macro and micro level. (Table 11). According to global data, the share of the developed capitalist countries in the new value produced by the industry dropped from 73 per cent to 68 per cent between 1960 and 1985. At the same time, the share of the developing countries increased from 8 per cent to 11 per cent, that of the European socialist countries from 17 per cent to 20 per cent.[53]

It should be emphasized that the share of certain regions increased very rapidly in some industries. The share of the developing countries exceeds the average in most of the labour and material intensive industries. Their share in world food industrial production in 1980 was 16 per cent, in tobacco industrial production 33 per cent, in textile industrial production 19 per cent and in oil refining it was 35 per cent, i.e. their average share has grown considerably.

Characteristic changes have taken place in the geographical distribution of the steel industry. The share of the developed capitalist countries in the crude steel production of the world in 1950 was 17 per cent, that of the socialist countries was 19 per cent

Table 11.
Changes in the Regional Shares of Industrial Production.
1960–1980 (percentage of value added)*

	1960	1985
North America	31	22.5
Western Europe	34	31.3
of this: Common Market	30	26.2
Japan	4	11.3
Oceania and other	4	1.6
Latin America	4	5.4
Africa	0.5	0.4
Middle East	0.5	1.5
East and South-East Asia	3.0	3.3
Industrially developed socialist countries	17.0	21.3

* Calculation of the author based on U.N. and UNIDO statistics.

whereas that of the developing countries was a mere 1 per cent. By 1987 the share of the developed capitalist countries had dropped to 49 per cent while that of the socialist countries had grown to 39 per cent. Within that, the Soviet Union supplied 22 per cent of world production (previously 14 per cent) and the developing countries 12 per cent.

In 1950, 46 per cent of world crude steel production came from the United States, 1.2 per cent from Japan, 6.3 per cent from the Federal Republic of Germany and 0.4 per cent from Brazil. In 1987 11 per cent of world crude steel production was supplied by the United States, 13 per cent in Japan, 5.4 per cent by the Federal Republic of Germany and 3 per cent Brazil.[54]

The changes in the geographical distribution of industrial production has had significant world economic results.

First: New industrial countries have emerged in regions which previously had been almost absolutely dependent on imports to meet their demand for industrial goods demand. Nevertheless, the scale of world industrialization and the quantities of industrial goods produced in the individual regions has remained highly dispropor-tionate, though the newly emerged industrial districts are important bases of further industrial development and the socio-economic transformation accompanied by such an evolution.

Second: Industrial development and the emergence of new industrial regions have resulted in the appearance of new outlets creating new demand for capital goods, technology and materials, etc. Import substituting industrialization has not resulted in a general decrease in imports either, however, it has changed the structure and composition of imports affording possibilities for the broadening of a new intra-industrial division of labour. This tendency was strengthened by the significant part played by transnational corporations in industrial development. In the case of the industrial nations the development of the division of labour within the industry has taken place as a rule on the basis of reciprocity, while the measure of reciprocity in the less developed countries has been much lower.

Third: The increasingly global scale of industrialization has furthered the development of the infrastructure (the building of ports, railways, roads, the extending of transport and communication, international warehouses, stores and marketing systems as well as of telecommunication systems) in previously underdeveloped regions of the world economy. Thus, the further development of industry has become possible, and also a more intensive participation in the international division of labour has resulted in new and increasingly broadening markets for the industry of the world.

Fourth: World market competition has been further intensified by the disproportionate character of industrial development. This holds true particularly in the case of industries and/or products where the comparative advantages have shifted in favour of the newly industrialized countries or have further strengthened the positions of some developed countries. Almost in all industries new conditions have developed in international competition as a result of the above changes.

This problem will be dealt with in greater detail in Part Three on technological development. However, taking into consideration the experiences of the leading Western countries and the newly industrialized developing nations some important conclusions can already be drawn (these are based on the period 1960–1980 but are valid for the future as well).

a) In the case of all the countries (or enterprises) surging ahead spectacularly, the realization of efforts aiming at a radical cutting of costs and at the stabilization or improvement of quality has played a vital part.

b) An analysis of the role of raw materials and energy necessary for production indicates that it is generally not those countries with abundant resources or those able to exploit such resources relatively cheaply which are capable of bringing about advantageous situations for themselves but those which can secure favourable innovations, marketing and transport conditions: they can buy guarantee their supplies in great quantities by means of long-term agreements, and pay in exchange with valuable industrial products manufactured by themselves and eagerly sought after by exporters of raw materials. Thus the leading developed Western countries have been able to counterbalance increasing oil prices by additional exports to the OPEC countries as follows: USA 28 per cent, Japan 35 per cent, France 43 per cent, FRG 76 per cent, Italy 64 per cent, Great Britain 61 per cent (U.S. Commerce Department Trade Series Ft. 210; Ft. 610). Countries which were able to reduce their specific raw material and energy consumption significantly and rapidly also succeeded in gaining considerable advantages.

Thus, the steel producers of the United States have access to cheap foundry coke whereas Japan uses 20 per cent less coke than the USA to produce a ton of crude iron.

c) The role of research, development and innovation in strengthening competitiveness has proved to be rather complex. Great expenditure may result in negligible output. The products of successful research and development can be exploited to a greater extent by countries (and enterprises) which have highly developed sales (distributing) systems or broadly based such international networks. Such countries and corporations are able to keep a firm hand on different "generations" of products. Their rivals can only succeed in competition by means of better quality and lower prime costs (and rarely by means of lower selling prices).

The capacity to extend the sphere of adjustment has also proved to be an important factor in the case of standard products. This has manifested itself in two forms: the manufacturers were able to adapt a given product (technology) to the demand of different buyers, and they also made it possible to use basic equipment in a great variety of ways. The latter feature is particularly important in electronics.

d) Automation is of primary importance in international competition. Not only is unskilled manpower replaced by high technology but the productivity of highly skilled labour has been considerably enhanced.

e) Direct production costs are particularly important from the point of view of competitiveness. The extension of the scale of production, the stepping up of mass production, and quickly, the capacity to adopt efficient, new technologies play a considerable part both taken together and separately. (The latter factor, for instance, gave special advantages to small and medium enterprises in certain industries.) However, the complex nature of manufacturing industry resulted in highly differentiated enterprises in the course of competition, according to the advantages mentioned above.

f) The magnitude of capital, the maintaining or creating of a vertically or horizontally integrated company organization from a single country or a group of countries has been a highly important factor in the changes in international competitiveness. It partly facilitated the combination of the above mentioned factors on an international scale, and partly rendered it difficult for weaker companies to surge ahead. The significance of the marketing departments of global organizational networks has increased in direct proportion to the sharpening of competition. Specific marketing organizations and strategies compete with each other. Forms modelled on Japanese experience, i.e. forms combining production, financing and marketing, have gained ground increasingly. The significance of competitive strategies combined with protected markets is also growing. Founding productive enterprises operating in the national markets of the chief rivals has gained added importance as well as the thorough knowledge of a given market, the securing of available financial, technological and other possibilities in order to weaken the positions of the rival companies (or occasionally to reach an acceptable agreement with them).

g) The importance of making use of public means to strengthen international competitiveness has also increased. Supporting research and development activities, hand-outs for switching over and restructuring, direct and indirect subsidies, furthering marketing activity abroad—all these indicate the importance of government assistance in international competition. And in addition, we are witnessing protectionism—this peculiar brand of public support—which has greatly strengthened in the 1980s.

Thus, changes in industrial development had an outstanding part in the establishment and strengthening of specific new centres. Japan, for instance, has become an increasingly important world economic factor, first of all owing to her enhanced industrial strength. A number of significant structural changes have been effected in the past 35 years. In the 1950s it was still products demanding mainly unskilled labour which were predominant in Japanese production and exports, in the sixties capital intensive goods came gradually into the fore, and since the 1960s research intensive goods have become rapidly dominant in both production and exports.

Rapid technological development played an outstanding role in the forging ahead of Japan since it was combined with considerable capital investments and also transformed the composition of employment. Of all invested capital the share of Japan was only 7 per cent in the early 1960s, whereas that of the United States was 41 per cent and of the Federal Republic of Germany 9 per cent. By the end of the 1970s the share of Japan has risen to 15 per cent, that of the United States has been reduced to 32 per cent and that of the Federal Republic of Germany to 8 per cent. In the 1960s and 1970s invested capital per worker has risen by 10 per cent annually. (Invested capital per worker has risen faster only in South Korea.)[55]

As regards the ratio of skilled and qualified manpower, Japan occupies the second place behind the United States on the list of capitalist countries (in global statistics Japan takes the third place behind the Soviet Union): her share was 8.5 per cent at the end of the 1970s. Her position in capital invested in industry has considerably improved as compared to the United States, while it has hardly changed in respect of skilled and qualified manpower, though some advance has been witnessed here, too. In the 1960s the advantage of the United States as regards the share of capital was almost sixfold and as regards skilled and qualified manpower fivefold, whereas in the latter respect its lead has shrunk to a mere threefold in the race with Japan.

As regards the adoption of pioneering technologies the position of Japan has considerably improved according to a highly important index—that of the number of scientists and engineers per 10,000 workers. In 1965 this index had been 64.1 in the USA, 24.6 in Japan, 22.6 in the Federal Republic of Germany, 21.4 in Great Britain and 21 in France. By the end of the 1970s the ratios have changed as follows: USA 57 (i.e. the United States has retained its leading position), Japan, 50 (the lag has diminished considerably), the FRG 41 (it has also caught up somewhat with the USA.), France 30 and Great Britain 31.[56] It is noteworthy that the Soviet Union which in 1965 had ranked second behind the USA with a ratio of 42.6 took the first place at the end of 1970s with a ratio of 66.

Obviously not a single factor but the combination of different causes resulted in the fact that productivity increased rapidly in Japan and she was able to exploit her advantages. As can be seen from Table 12, the increase in productivity in Japan between 1965 and 1973 was more than threefold as compared to that of the United States. Under the difficult world economic conditions of the 1970s the differences between these two countries kept on increasing.

In the 1980s Japan has been undergoing a further phase of industrial development. Some experts compare the significance of this fact to the Meiji restoration or World War II. Partly as the result of the rapid development of heavy industry, and particularly of the chemical industry, fundamental structural changes have been brought about in the Japanese industry, and presumably these changes will continue until the end of the century or even beyond the year 2000.

a) In order to lessen the dependence on foreign technology, Japanese companies and institutes make huge investments to establish and develop an independent research basis.

Table 12.
Changes in Industrial Productivity (per capita Production of Employed Population)

	1950–1965	1965–1973	1973–1979	1979–1984
Austria	5.7	5.7	3.6	3.6
Belgium	6.1	6.1	6.5	5.0
Finland	4.1	4.1	3.7	4.6
France	5.7	5.7	5.2	4.2
United Kingdom	2.2	3.5	1.5	3.8
FRG	5.2	4.3	4.3	2.7
Italy	5.7	5.7	3.3	3.6
United States	2.4	2.9	1.5	2.6
Japan	7.2	9.9	3.7	5.6
Soviet Union	5.5*	5.5*	2.8**	2.4***

* 1966–1970
** 1976–1980
*** 1980–1984
Sources: U.N. Economic Commission of Europe.

b) They try to use various alternative energy sources in addition to oil, and this endeavour is combined with a less energy intensive production and consumption.

c) The introduction of new materials is enthusiastically continued thus making it possible to make use of solar energy, to develop micro-electronics and to strengthen the basis of space technology.

d) Biotechnology is increasingly employed in producing new drugs, in raw material processing, energy economizing production processes and also in the more efficient protection of the natural environment (genetical combinations, cell fusion, bioreactive development, etc.).

e) By utilizing large integrated circuits the output of machines and products is considerably enhanced. Automation as well as medical electronics are developed rapidly.

f) With the help of production cooperation with the military industry of other developed western countries, particularly with that of the United States, Japan has made great strides towards acquiring experience regarding the production of highly sophisticated military technology. This connection is of particular importance in the field of electronics and new materials.[57]

g) The new conception of production is the linking up of computer-aided design (CAD) and computer-aided manufacture (CAM) which is more productive and flexible than the existing production systems, economizes on energy, needs less space and releases considerable amounts of labour for other purposes. The Flexible Manufacturing System is particularly suitable for the automation of the production of medium-sized series and increases the competitiveness of small and medium enterprises by leaps and bounds.

As regards industrial restructuring, the structural links established between Japan and the nations of the Pacific region are highly important. These latter countries are simultaneously raw material suppliers, industrial cooperative partners, production bases and markets for Japan. Japan has switched over to the new phase of industrial development at a time when similar plans and ideas have been elaborated in other highly developed capitalist countries as well. Great efforts are made to realize such plans in countries which are major rivals of Japan, such as the Federal Republic of Germany, France and Great Britain, which would like to make use of the Common Market to strengthen their world economic positions. It is highly probable that as a consequence, competition on the world market will come to a head among the major Western countries calling into existence new forms of cooperation which will tend to strengthen mutual dependence as well.

The forging ahead of Japan, the considerable improvement in Japanese competitiveness—taking the lead in some branches of technological development—has caused serious changes in world trade as it can be seen from the data in Table 13.

Though the weight of Asian power is increasing, it plays a minor role in world politics and international affairs—particularly as regards military strategy—taking into account its economic strength and significance. A strange difference has developed between the part it has in world politics and in the world economy. The experience of history—especially Japanese history—indicates that such tensions do not tend to be long-lasting. The question of whether in the present world order such forces could or could not make themselves felt is important not only because of the position of Japan. In the 1980s the politicians who have come to power in Japan have committed themselves to an increase in the defence sector. This is partly connected with the economic expansion. It is mainly in some branches of microelectronics that Japanese industry has been integrated with the American military industry. As a result and in the process of this integration and organizational details as well as production information relating to military technology, which was previously almost inaccessible. In certain domains, e.g. in rocket technology, remote control and the nuclear industry, Japan itself is engaged in significant research work. However, Japanese ruling circles have to take into account a number of hard facts in their endeavour to increase the political, strategic side of their country under the present overall Asian balance of power. Such

Table 13.
The Largest Exporters and Importers
(Shares in World Trade)*

	1960–1965		1981–1986	
	Exports	Imports	Exports	Imports
USA	14.2	11.4	11.1	15.5
Japan	4.4	4.0	8.8	6.3
FRG	8.9	8.7	10.2	8.4
United Kingdom	7.1	7.9	5.2	5.4
France	5.1	5.1	5.4	5.9
Italy	3.7	3.6	4.2	4.5
Soviet Union	5.1	3.9	4.3	3.8

* Calculations of the author based on the statistics of UNCTAD, International Monetary Fund and the GATT elements are for instance the military power of the Soviet Union, the regional importance of the Chinese People's Republic, the increasing strength and growing significance of a number of important countries (first of all of India) which as member countries of the Asian region do not sympathize with the military strengthening of Japan.

All things considered, even the leading circles of the United States are interested in the stimulation of Japanese rearmament only in so far as this would probably curb the further increase of the economic power of the island country and would also exert a favourable influence on the American military potential. Japan serves also as an example for the double character of international interdependence. The country is extremely vulnerable. Of all the leading Western countries it is Japan which depends to the greatest extent on foreign markets, raw materials and energy. Though Japan can lessen this dependence by a structural flexibility, there is no way to change the situation fundamentally. It seems, however, highly probable that this Asian country will have an important part first of all as an economic superpower in the system of international relations in the years to come, while furthering also the sharpening of power conflicts as a result of its economic expansion.

The well-known American economist and economic historian, W. W. Rostow in one of his studies dealing with the future of Japan as a world power raised the question of whether the emergence of the world economic hegemony of Japan should be taken into consideration after the end of the era of British and American domination. In his opinion the most probable prospect would be the diffusion of leadership under future world economic conditions. He emphasized that in his views there would be no dominant state in the era of the fourth industrial revolution, and there would be a number of leading powers in the world economy, the characteristic feature of which would be a peculiar kind of cooperation and competition.[58] At the same time, the influence of Japan would increase in the world economy.

If interdependence were to increase among the states, the distribution of economic power relations were to become more equal and the "openness" of world economic relations were to remain at least at a level characteristic for the early 1980s, this prospect would seem a probable course of events. A considerable improvement of institutionalized international cooperation and the raising of the level of such cooperation would be a requirement for such a development. However, historical experience in the Western world does not indicate the development of this more "harmonic" world in the twentieth century. It is also a fact that the strengthening of new economic power centres continues within the framework of the system of international relations.

The Federal Republic of Germany, too, has developed into a peculiar "economic superpower" by the end of the 1970s. The changes in the position of the FRG can be seen from the data of Table 14, which reflect the tendencies of development not as global changes but treating the data of the five leading Western countries as an index of 100, thus relating the characteristic data of these countries to each other.

Though as a consequence of the rapid growth of Japan the position of the Federal Republic of Germany has deteriorated as regards the gross national product and the output of the processing industries of the five leading countries, it still ranks first in exports of finished goods, outdistancing even the United States. But even in this respect way Japan has caught with the leading powers seems a remarkable trend.

Table 14.
The Relative Position of Five Leading Western Countries (per cent)

	Year	USA	France	FRG	United Kingdom	Japan
Gross national product	1960	57.0	9.0	13.0	11.0	11.0
	1985	58.0	7.0	9.0	7.0	19.0
Industrial production (value added)	1960	57	7	16	10	10
	1985	51.4	7.7	12.7	5.6	22.6
Exports of manufactures	1950	37.0	13.0	10.0	35.0	5.0
	1960	29.0	12.0	26.0	24.0	9.0
	1980	24.0	14.0	27.0	15.0	20.0
	1986	18.5	18.2	21.6	18.2	23.5

Source: Dualité, Change et Contraintes Extérieures dans Cinq Economies Dominantes, La Documentation Française, 1983, p. 21.
UNCTAD: Handbook of International Trade and Development Statistics. 1987. pp. 414–415, 434–445. 136–157.

In international competition the Federal Republic of Germany had concentrated its efforts on industries which have traditionally been the solid basis of its progress in foreign trade in the postwar era. In the fields of research, development and investment in mechanical, electrical and electronical engineering West Germany has considerable advantages. Since the end of the 1970s the FRG has worked to reduce its time lag rapidly in the fields of microelectronics and some other branches of industry implementing highly sophisticated technologies because its position has deteriorated within the world export of engineering, whereas that of Japan has improved as compared with the 1960s.[59]

Though the increase in the economic power of the Federal Republic of Germany has come to a standstill in recent years, it has remained an important element in the rearrangement of power relations. The process of modification took place under peculiar circumstances, i.e. under the conditions of the establishment of two German states and of the Common Market membership of the FRG. The economic and military strategic position of the country has also become more "rigid" not only compared with the situation prior to World War II, but also compared with its major rivals within the system of international relations.

Less spectacular, though significant from the regional aspect are the changes—from the point of view of the global rearrangement of economic power relations—which have taken place in some of the developing or medium developed countries and which have made themselves felt particularly in certain sectors of world trade. Regional powers, e.g. the Chinese People's Republic or India, have an increased part in the system of international relations not only because as the two most populous nations in the world they represent as a matter of course considerable potential but also because they cover enormous territories.

Both of these countries have carried out economic development programmes of great importance and as a result, they have increased their share in world production as well: their joint ratio approached 4 per cent in 1985. Both countries have economies based on complex internal development within the framework of which there functions a relatively modern industrial sector, too.

There were some other types of economies which emerged or further developed and became significant on a regional scale in some Asian and Latin American countries. Brazil and Mexico particularly have considerable development potential. The share of Brazil in the gross national product of the world more than doubled between 1960 and 1980, reaching almost 2 per cent. The share of ten to twelve developing countries in the gross production of the Third World has risen to more than 85 per cent by 1980. These countries have evolved into specific and significant regional economic great powers, and the small nations of their regions are able to orient themselves to them economically. Thus, new economic-industrial regions could develop in the world economy, and these represent a potential challenge from the point of view of future economic power relations.

In a certain stage of their export-oriented development activity these countries were able to get capital relatively easily partly from banks and partly through transnational industrial companies. They could easily and readily obtain the most up-to-date technologies in the textile and clothing industry and steel production as well as in engineering and the chemical industry. In all these industries poorly paid but relatively highly skilled manpower was available which could be concentrated to an adequate extent and in addition, a great number of semiskilled or quickly and easily to be trained workers with very low wages were to be found.

In the earliest phase (in the 1960s) they began to export textiles, shoes and toys. However, in the 1970s they began to switch over to industrial activities which turned out greater new value; thereafter they became competitive in many branches of industry, ranging from steel and shipbuilding to the production of household electronics, radios and calculators.

Another change followed at the end of the 1970s and the early 1980s. The trend is now in the direction of more complex audiovisual electronics, electromechanics and highly sophisticated branches of engineering while there has begun a rapid "migration" of the shoe, the textile, and the lower grade electronics industries to the less developed countries such as Malaysia, Thailand, Sri Lanka, etc. where manpower is still cheap.

The economies of the newly industrialized countries were assisted by the fact that in many developed Western countries they were able to build up considerable retail chains rendering it possible for them to obtain rapidly a relatively large share of the market. International transport became faster and cheaper, which proved another helpful factor to them, particularly the fast spread of container transportation.

A great number of household electronics, goods marketed under the label of Philips, Sony or General Electric are produced or assembled in Hong Kong, Singapore or South Korea. Blueprints and component parts are supplied by some West European or Japanese corporations, production is financed by Japanese, American or West European banks, whereas distribution is done by integrated international retail enterprises in response to the orders of the electronics companies. This process takes place smoothly however, only until serious troubles arise as a result of competition among the producers and the protectionist policies of the developed industrial countries, as happened, for instance, in the early 1980s.

Another type of concentration of economic power took place following the growth of the economies of some OPEC countries which directed their efforts towards international finance. The total value of the foreign capital investment of three or four Arab countries approaches $ 400 billion i.e. these are only about $ 100 billion less than the direct foreign capital investment of the developed industrial capitalist countries. Theoretically these countries could have a significant role in the international financial system; however, owing to the weakness of their national production bases, they themselves are extremely vulnerable and, when all is said and done, they are dependent on international economic relations.

The changes in interstate economic power relations are reflected also in the world economy, the microsphere—i.e. in the world of relations among the enterprises—and the modifications in world market competitiveness, thus influencing in many ways international concentration and centralization of capital.

The Transnational Corporations as Power Centres

The various forms and characteristics of the international "transnational" economic organizations—rooted in the major economic centres of the contemporary Western world and interrelated in many a way—reflect fundamentally the increasing internationalization of capital and production. Production, finances and services are controlled to a growing extent by a couple of hundred international companies. The interlocking of capital assets, the "incorporation" of rivals, the buying up or founding of companies abroad and the organization of control is not a harmonized, smooth process in the current world situation either.

Competition is sharp and bitter and its main instrument is—as in the past—capital exports. This is often supported by several other factors like strategic innovations, preferential treatment, economies of scale, etc. In the first half of the 1980s some 10.000 companies have controlled 90.000 undertakings abroad. The most powerful 500 of these control 80 per cent of all foreign capital investments. The changes in direct foreign capital investments reflect the changes in the positions achieved in the course of competition (Table 15).

The factors which are the source of the strength of the transnational corporations in the system of international economic relations—i.e. the easy availability of capital resources, the quasi monopolistic or oligopolistic control of the international source and the transfer network of research and development, the purchasing of the necessary materials under favourable conditions, the broad international basis or marketing opportunities, etc.—have given special advantages to the transnational corporations even under the difficult world economic circumstances of the 1980s. At the beginning of 1984 these corporations disposed of about $ 600 billion of foreign capital investment, and their turnover abroad was more than $ 2,400 billion in 1983, i.e. they surpassed the value of total world exports by about 30 per cent.

The differences in the situation of the countries where these corporations have their headquarters, the development of their international mergers and specialization as well as changes in other conditions (e.g. support by or restricting rules of the governments) are all important from the point of view of the trends in competition and the changes in the balance of power. The displacement of a number of American

Table 15.
Ownership of Direct Investments Abroad (per cent)*

	1960	1967	1973	1980	1985
USA	49	49.2	47.5	40.0	35.1
United Kingdom	16	15.2	12.6	14.8	14.7
FRG	1.2	3	6	7.8	8.4
Japan	1	1.3	5	6.6	11.7
France	6	5.2	4	3.8	3
Switzerland	3	3.2	4.8	7	6.4
Canada	3.8	3.2	3.7	3.9	5.1
Netherlands	10.6	9.6	7.2	7.6	6.1

* *International Direct Investments,* US Department of Commerce, Washington, 1984, p. 45, Book values.
U.N. Centre on Transnational Corporations: *Transnational Corporations in World
Development.* New York. 1988. p. 24.

corporations from their leading positions, the surging ahead of Japanese, West
German and Italian giant enterprises are the results of these factors. Nevertheless, the
American corporations are still ranking first in spite of the changes. According to the
statistics of the UN Transnational Centre, 47 per cent of the 380 major world
corporations registered by the Centre had their seats in America. (In 1970 this
percentage had been 51 per cent, in 1960 60 per cent.) Of the 50 biggest transnational
corporations of the capitalist world in 1960 42 were American, whereas in 1985 only 19
were.

The transnational corporations, too, are different. As regards decision-making and
power relations, two basic types have emerged: internationally controlled global
corporations and nationally owned global firms. In the first type of the transnational
corporations ownership is spread over several countries, it is gradually internationalized and thus, on the basis of the interest structure, these firms are more
globally oriented in their strategies.

The other type is represented by enterprises which are international according to
their activities but as regards ownership are linked to only one country. However, they
cannot be regarded as simple extensions of the national enterprises either. Since they
operate simultaneously, in more than one country, their interest can clash with those of
the countries where their shareholders are. Their decisions are also guided by
international business interests. Thus the laws of the United States are in the last resort
of binding force for all the foreign ventures of transnational corporations with
headquarters in America. However, particularly in vital strategic questions, the
majority of such corporations set out from their own business interests, and if
government decisions and regulations tend to seriously interfere with their activities,
they often try to "circumvent" or doublecross them. Transnational corporations,
therefore, are in many respects independent factors in the international microsphere,
linked in various ways and organically to the macrosphere. If necessary, they have
recourse to the macrosphere, ask for guarantees, expect (and generally get) sanctions
from the state if their positions are threatened or jeopardized at any point in the world.
At the same time, they try to evade the control of their own and other governments.

Naturally this means that they could get into conflicts with the governments of more than one country at a time if those tried to enforce their economic power on them: they protect their economic interests and resources.

Thus, the transnational corporations are able to restrict the governments in the exercise of their economic power but can also serve as a means of economic power. The activity of the transnational corporations within the system of international relations is of great importance also because—as owners of capital in the given countries which nevertheless transcend national frontiers—they might get into direct connection with foreign policy or the policy of the host countries, and also with international power struggles and conflict areas. In principle it is naturally understood that they should maintain—as often stressed—their "neutrality". Practical experience, however, indicates that they were often driven by interests which linked their activities to certain foreign political aspirations. They were frequent participants or even initiators of destabilizing efforts aimed against the progressive regimes of the developing world. Sometimes, however, they can tolerate and even promote these governments, supporting the policy of détente and cooperation in the relations between the states of the two systems, and taking a stand against restrictions and discriminations.

4. Economic Power and International Economic Policies

World economic processes are influenced in various ways by changes in economic power relations. Conflicts among states, interstate struggles for markets and for their redistribution or for conquering new markets are sharpened by such changes. From cartel agreements to government subsidies or old and new forms of protectionism the most diversified traditional and new means are made use of by the individual countries in the course of this struggle. New economic power coalitions are founded on common interests. Such conflicts disintegrate and break up organizations which had been called into being in a previous era to further international cooperation, and impede the work not only of global but also of regional organizations. Thus, the GATT has been more than once paralysed in recent years as a result of debates among the member countries of the Common Market. The development of the Common Market, too, has slackened, its efficiency has suffered during the past decades.

Interdependence, as well as political and military interests, tends the prevent to sharpening of conflicts, moreover it stimulates compromise and the search for common solutions even during periods when the conditions of economic development are less advantageous. Actually the price Western nations would pay for economic warfare or for the collapse of the economic foundations of the system would be much higher than ever before. These factors upgrade international economic policies.

International economic policy is the branch of economic policy through which a government wishes to enforce the national interests and objectives of a country in the international sphere and also strives to influence, control and regulate the activities of the participants of the international economic life in the sphere of trade, finances, capital exports, tourism, etc. It also endeavours to assert different international influences in the interest of the given countries (e.g. more favourable competitive conditions) and to neutralize, moderate or control such external effects from the world economy. Thus, international economic policy is the means of expansive assertion of economic power by countries which are capable of doing so and at the same time it also serves defensive objectives and is destined to defend the security of the country in question.

Political security highlights first of all social, psychological and military problems in each and any country but involves, of course, vital economic problems as well. Military security has been defined traditionally as a situation in which there is no armed threat.

Even in the past and in the case of the larger countries national political and military security always included a very important economic component: the economic potential of a given country to maintain its military (defence) capabilities. The significance of the economic component of military security was different in peaceful periods, when national resources could be supplemented by external sources, from that of the period of war, when countries had to rely completely or predominantly on their national resources. The greater economic potential of the allied forces in World War II was an important factor in their victory. Economic potential includes human resources, technological levels, organizational capabilities, the size and structure of industry and agriculture, the performance of the infrastructure and the natural endowment. Economic vulnerability is an important military liability for any country.

The importance of economic security with different implications as a component of over all security has substantially increased in the present world system in general and not only in the development of the smaller countries.

i) National economic stability in a modern socio-economic structure depends greatly on the economic positions and social security of the individuals. In the smaller countries, international economic conditions influence the individual stronger and faster. They may cause more unemployment, more rapidly decreasing social programs, greater cuts in educational expenditure, etc. Therefore they have a much greater destabilizing effect. This was clearly reflected during the first half of the 1980s.

The struggle of individuals to increase their security within those countries tied the problems of individual security to national policies of welfare, education, health and human rights. National social and economic institutions became basic instruments to achieve the goals of individuals and thus the security of the individuals became a highly politicised issue within the countries, involving directly such important aspects of economic life as income distribution and redistribution, efficiency, or state intervention.

ii) The increasing importance of international economic relations for growth, existence or survival in the great majority of the 170 countries of today (and not only in the smaller countries), added new factors to those on which economic security on a national level was formed. National economic security policies became highly internationalized. In most of the less developed countries national economic security was directly influenced through their international economic relations from the very beginning of their independent existence. Weak bargaining power, dependence on one or two raw materials in their exports and on a whole range of goods in their imports, exposure to the fluctuations of the world market and to the policies of more developed countries became the most important sources of their economic insecurity. In some cases, special arrangements with certain developed countries reduced the level of insecurity. Industrialization policies were also aimed at the reduction of international vulnerability. This however was achieved with varied success. Similar problems emerged also in certain socialist countries in a different context.

Among the longer term structural changes, in the larger developed industrial countries, several authors have found the roots of the increasing importance of the economic component of national security in the progress of international interdependence. Interdependence, as a more developed stage of internationalization of the economic, technological and institutional life of the countries, from the point of view of an individual country is certainly a source of insecurity, though at the same time, under certain conditions, it could increase the security of all nations. Interstate economic relations could develop simultaneously with the system of political interests. The relations between states as a result of interdependence may become more stable. In the present international system, however, the process of interdependence is expanding in a framework full of inequalities and conflicts of a different nature. Interdependence is a highly asymmetrical process for the smaller and weaker countries of the international system and mutuality may be completely absent in many cases. Different intensity and forms of unilateral dependencies are keeping the majority of the countries in an insecure and vulnerable position and even the industrially developed countries may have great limitations in their ability to influence their international economic environment. The majority of the countries are forced to adjust to the changing environment. A country may of course substantially increase its economic security by properly selected adjustment strategies through unilateral actions. Adjustment however involves costs in different forms; these may include inflation, unemployment, bankruptcies or major losses of output. The social costs, mentioned above, may be prohibitively high. In the world economy of the 1980s, therefore, many countries had to face important dilemmas.

Substantial adjusment efforts may require fundamental restructuring of economic relationships. This may involve substantial and sometimes violent changes in a political system as well.

Corrective actions also require a supportive international environment. During the period of stronger growth in the world economy it is easier to implement even larger adjustment measures. Severe difficulties, contraction or slow world trade growth represent a "hostile" and "insecure" international background and the costs of adjustment for the national economies are much higher.

The feasibility, objectives and means of international economic policy depend on the character of the economy of a country and also on its position in the system of international economic relations. International economic policy, therefore, is closely associated with national economic policy on the one hand, and is linked to foreign policy on the other. The significance of international economic policy in the life of all countries has been upgraded as a result of the increased importance of international economic cooperation in the past decades, whereas the strengthening of interdependence among the states has brought about rather difficult conditions for the assertion of the autonomous objectives of international economic policy even for larger countries. Conditions have become even more serious for smaller, weaker nations. In countries with strong economies the objectives and means of international economic policy often represent a more complex and frequently more contradictory sphere than in smaller countries. The different groups and their interests in the background of international economic policy are also of a more complex character.

According to the character of relations, the international economic policy of states can be bilateral or multilateral. The two are not independent of each other, moreover there is often some overlapping, but as regards the means used for attaining the objectives they represent different forms.

National aims and objectives related to the global system of international economic relations are generally intertwined in the international economic policies of the major Western industrial countries. Global agreements related to the international monetary system and to trade policies, the control of seas and oceans, and capital flows naturally have a considerable influence on the possibilities and interests of such countries: they try to shape the conditions so that these assist their international targets.

The United States is a characteristic example, of a dominating power that tried to subordinate the newly founded international economic institutions to its own objectives following World War II. At the same time it is still a hotly debated question—particularly among the Marxist political economists of the West—whether the "free enterprise system" which the United States attempted to force upon the Western world were merely the consequence of American supremacy or a policy dictated by the necessities of the internationalization of capitalist accumulation.[60]

The liberal slogans and institutions have probably developed as a result of the specific mixture of compromises of American supremacy and the general Western interests. As the most powerful state of the postwar world the United States succeeded in raising its economic supremacy to the status of official foreign policy.

Relations established in 1945—and prevalent practically until the 1960s—were founded on some fundamental conditions.

First, leading circles in the United States and Western Europe set out from the principle that the main aim of their policy was to defend the region against the spread of communism and to stabilize the positions of the capitalist order in Western Europe. This resulted in a peculiar and lasting community of interests among them. The Marshall Plan had an outstanding part in laying the foundations of this.

Second, the United States took a leading part in the emerging Atlantic system (in the fields of military, economic and foreign political affairs alike). The organizational structure of the Atlantic systems was shaped on this basis from the very beginning. The American policy set the aim of establishing a unified Western Europe organized on the American pattern and serving as a free and secure buyer's market for American industrial products and at the same time, as the recipient of American capital investments. The sometimes similarly defined conceptions have often been interpreted, differently, however, by the leading circles in Western Europe, who regarded the restoration of their independent power positions as their chief objective.

Third, the United States tried to establish—together with the countries of Western Europe and associated with Japan—a global, liberal, "self-regulating" free trade and monetary system the pivot of which would have been the economic supremacy of America. However, from the very outset there were some divergences of opinion among the states concerning the definition and interpretation of objectives.

Fourth, the leading circles of the United States counted upon the gradual disintegration of the system of the colonial empires, and also furthered this process hoping that the collapse of these empires would open up for them the road to the commodity markets and raw material resources of the former colonies. It was thought that the emerging and fractionalized new world dependent upon them would serve as a secure raw material exporter and finished goods market for a long time to come. It was also regarded as a matter of fact that within the system of subordination the United States would have a dominant part in both military and economic matters while the former colonial powers forced into the position of the weaker partners would themselves become parts of the new American global empire. The former colonial powers, in turn, tried to stabilize their own positions with the help of the United States.

Fifth, the participation of the socialist countries—first and foremost the Soviet Union—was never really counted upon as an economic partner in this global system. The perception of the Soviet danger, however, would have served as the main cohesive element of the global world political and economic structure facilitating the maintenance of strategic unity and the realization of strategic plans aimed against the Soviet Union and the socialist countries.

Neither the American plans nor the objectives of the leading circles of Western Europe have been attained. More than one American strategic plan has failed in Western Europe since the 1950s, but neither has the course of events taken the turn expected by the leading circles of Western Europe.

Western Europe did not become "united" or a "third force" in world politics and the world economy. The states which have joined the integrated organization have developed under the influence of a peculiar unity of common interests and discord. As a result of this as well as of external changes, the situation and prospects of West European integration have changed. Neither the customs union nor other regulations in the course of the integration programme succeeded in changing the position of the member countries, as it had not changed when the former "Six" became "Ten". However, the external economic sensitivity and vulnerability of the individual countries was enhanced by the process of European integration and the active part played by the West European countries in the world economy. Under the world economy conditions of the late 1970s and the early 1980s, integration tended to serve as a means of joint protectionism aimed also against the United States.

In the leading Western countries—particularly in the Unites States—international economic policy is closely linked up with foreign policy and military-security interests. In the USA the connections are much closer and more direct than in the other leading capitalist countries. A well-known Republican economist closely associated with the Administration pointed out that influence and power in international relations have increasingly become dependent on economic capacity. The notion of national security ought to be broadened, he wrote, and together with military power and the policy of deterrents, economic power and stability, too, should be comprised in it. The costs of global policy are enormous. The critical precondition of the superpower status, therefore, is a strong national economy, at least in democratic countries. He stressed the point that economic problems have come to the fore not only because these are basically of great importance but also because actual international manoeuvrability is concentrated in this sector.[61]

Myer Rashish, a leading official of the American State Department, has defined even more unambiguously the correlation of international economy policy and foreign policy as regards the Soviet Union by stating that the international economic policy of the United States should further the changing of the military balance of power.[62] In his opinion the supply of any such equipment ought to be prohibited which could contribute significantly to the strengthening of the military potential of the Warsaw Pact countries. And since trade policy in this relation could not be separated from the general security problems of the USA, it should be subordinated to these problems.

The subordination of economic cooperation to the objectives of foreign policy is not a new phenomenon in international affairs. The backing up of economic dependence and/or vulnerability by financial, trade and other means, as well as prohibitions and restrictions, are not novel phenomena either in the history of international relations. The techniques of economic warfare, however, have been brought to perfection during the past 40 years.

The changes in economic power relations and the various degrees and forms of economic dependence (from one-sided political and economic dependence to the complex system of interdependence) have created new conditions for the introduction of economic weapons in interstate relations. Thus, the international aid programmes of the Western world have become typical and important means of furthering political objectives and economic advantages in the second half of the twentieth century.

The aim of the Marshall Plan or the economic aid granted to Japan was not merely to stabilize the existing social system but by means of it the United States wanted also to strengthen its own position. The military or economic aid granted to the developing countries or highly favourable interstate loans aimed to further the exports and capital investments of the donor country, too. At the same time, to reduce the influence of foreign competitors and to prevent their gaining ground was attempted. To stabilize the position of governments which have taken political, military and economic measures favourable to the donor country was frequently tried.

International aid, threatened withdrawal, or actual withdrawal of such aid was part and parcel of the arsenal of postwar Western policy. Particularly in the 1980s the political and military objectives of aid are emphasized unashamedly by the American Administration. The main recipients and beneficiaries of this aid policy are Israel, Egypt, Pakistan, Honduras, El Salvador and some other countries. One of the recent examples of a country sanctioned by the withdrawal of aid was Nicaragua, a country which had confronted the United States.

Among the economic leverages in foreign policy—particularly if these are aimed against the Soviet Union—the strategy of linkages is often mentioned in cases when the development of economic cooperation is linked not with general political conditions but with one or another concrete political demand. It may happen that some country does not meet the stipulated terms and as a consequence, the supply of some commodities or the payment of loans ceases or some trade-political favours are withdrawn as sanctions. This measure—which used to be one of Dr. Kissinger's favourites—is, however, hardly stimulating; it is simply an economic sanction which is set into operation when some given conditions come to pass. This represents a peculiar form of sanctions since it is open to bargaining. But traditional economic sanctions are unilateral measures in foreign policy, their aim being to undermine the economic security of the adversaries. Enforcing different sanctions, meant to achieve its political objectives and assert its claims in this way. The most extreme form of sanctions is the full economic blockade where military force, too, is involved. This, however, is applied only rarely. In recent decades the means of economic warfare were, among others, the following: ban on transport, quotas, special tariffs and other discriminative measures, special export control, control regulations relating to specific single transactions, artificial bidding of prices, recall of experts, denial of supply of spare parts, the calling in of loans prior to maturity, a credit embargo, seizure of the adversary's property, refusal of use of ports and airports, disruption of scientific relations, interruption of the flow of valuable technological information.

The West German review *Europa Archiv*[63] highlighted the following general aims of economic sanctions brought against socialist countries:
—destabilization of the social system;
—impeding the international activities of the Soviet Union;
—isolation of the socialist countries;
—influencing certain decisions.

An American research institute has documented 99 cases of economic sanctions with foreign political objectives since World War I. Two thirds of these sanctions were initiated by the United States against its adversaries.[64] In 18 instances in was Great Britain that applied economic sanctions motivated by objectives of foreign policy. The subsequent governments of the United States resorted to economic bans or restrictive measures for different reasons. According to American presumptions, the industrialized countries of the Western world and the economy of the USA are less jeopardized by restrictions than their adversaries. Actually, however, some foreign trade restrictions declared by the USA against the socialist countries, first and foremost against the Soviet Union, and which the USA persuaded them to accept have plunged a number of Western countries into serious difficulties since they endangered significant transactions. As regards, however, the economy of the United States, the adverse effects were much weaker.

The frequent resort to restrictions and bans were related to domestic policy, too. Since the use of military force would have been more dangerous and costly, the government of the United States reacted with such restrictions to measures—deemed unfriendly—taken by its adversaries in the field of foreign policy. In certain cases the American government has applied economic sanctions combined with measures of foreign policy (e.g. internal subversion, military actions, blockade, etc.). Economic means are given priority by the USA because these are more easily accepted by the general public.

Woodrow Wilson, a former president of the United States, in 1919 supported the economic boycott as a means of foreign policy with the following arguments. The country boycotted readily capitulates. If this peaceful, quiet and deadly effective economic remedy is applied, there is no need for military force. It is an appalling cure: it does not demand human sacrifices in the boycotted country but exerts such a pressure that no nation is able to resist.[65]

Some weapons of the arsenal of economic warfare have been applied by other countries as well. Following World War I, Great Britain applied between 1918 and 1919 a series of economic sanctions against the Soviet Union in order to destabilize its economy. Collective economic sanctions were declared and/or applied by the League of Nations, among others, against Bolivia, Greece and Italy.

It should be regarded as a collective sanction that on the initiative of the United States various export embargo lists were drawn up, and special control commissions were set up to enforce these prohibitions. The observance of the prohibitions aimed against the European socialist countries is controlled by the COCOM, whereas that aimed against the Chinese People's Republic is organized by the CHICOM. The economic boycott against Israel was also collectively decided upon by the Arab countries. Collective economic steps were taken by the United Nations Organization against the racist South African regime in 1962, and against the Rhodesian government between 1965 and 1979.

Under the present international economic and power conditions the expected results were rarely achieved by the means of economic warfare applied in the interest of attaining objectives of foreign policy. The reason for this was, among others, that even so-called collective agreements supported by a number of countries were not adhered to. Countries against which foreign trade embargoes or other measures were declared generally had supporters, occasionally even strong allies. Thus, the United States, Israel and a number of other countries upheld relations with the Republic of South Africa even after the coming into force of the collective measures.

It often happened that it was the enterprises of the countries which had enforced the restrictions that took a stand against the restrictive measures since these afflicted both their direct business interests and their international competitiveness. All things considered, the American economic restrictions aimed against the Soviet Union have proved ineffective. Naturally the fact that some countries were ready to sell the embargoed technology or commodities because of their business or other interests had a considerable part in this turn of events.

The economic strength and technological development of the Soviet Union have in the long run in strategic areas neutralized those means of economic warfare which the United States and other Western countries tried to apply against it. It was proved that such means were ineffective against an adversary of similar strength. They could not prevent the growth of the military power of the Soviet Union, the establishment of a military balance of power, and the attempts to "crush" the economy of the Soviet Union failed, too. The policy of embargo adopted against the other socialist countries at the end of 1940 resulted in the development of the mechanisms of joint defence.

Economic warfare naturally caused harm to those countries to which it was applied, but occasionally it caused serious losses in the economy of the initiating country as well. An extreme example was the grain embargo ordered by President Carter against the Soviet Union. The grain embargo resulted in $ 2 to 2.2 billion direct losses to the American farmers, moreover the buying up and storing of grain burdened the American budget by $ 600 million.[66] The loss to the Soviet Union—according to American estimates—was $ 525 million, i.e. much less than that of the country ordering the restrictions.

The economy of Poland, however, suffered serious losses as a result of the restrictions enforced by the government of the United States following the proclamation of the emergency. Nevertheless, the result desired was not attained because the domestic circumstances of the country and the support rendered by the socialist countries—first of all by the Soviet Union—made it possible to neutralize a number of consequences of the American restrictions. Moreover, the Western banks and companies concerned also suffered losses.

Thus, it is a noteworthy fact that while the significance of economic strength and power has considerably grown in the world economy, using it as a means of achieving the objectives of foreign policy has not led to the results expected neither in its form of economic or military aid, nor as restrictions. The reasons of failure can be traced to the characteristics of the present-day world order. Aid, for instance, was unable to counterbalance the tensions resulting from the serious inequalities of the world and from the nature of economic relations within the Western world, moreover—since the preservation of the internal conditions of the countries in question was attempted— such aid did not help but rather hindered the solution of internal problems.

In a world where no single state or group of states has a full monopoly and alternative sources are always available, economic restrictions can be effective only under certain circumstances: if dependence on the country applying economic sanctions is overwhelming, if the country against which such measures are taken is extremely isolated, if its internal socio-economic structure is weak, political tensions are great and the state power is unpopular. However, the simultaneous presence of all these specific conditions is a very rare occurrence within a country.

It also follows from the nature of the present world order that it is rather the development of cooperation, the establishing of more harmonious relations which seems to be the future course of the world. The common interests of the countries have already contributed to the development of certain institutional forms. Global concerns and tensions, which could take the form of dangerous crises and jeopardize mankind as a whole, would demand such a policy even more. Using economic power in the interest of cooperation would also be a possibility or even a necessity, since the world economy could function successfully only if institutions established in the interest of general stability and development as well as with the objective of the democratization of the world economy, were supported by its major participants.

5. The Socialist Countries in the Changing Global Power Structure

To what extent are the European socialist countries, their world economic position and role influenced by changes in the global power structure? The European CMEA countries have a specific position in the system of international economic power relations. As pointed out, the Soviet Union as one of the most powerful countries in the military field of today, has a considerable influence on international political relations which cannot be viewed independently of economic relations. The relationship of the Soviet Union with the Western world has an effect on the world economy not only through the political conflicts and the arms race but also through international economic cooperation and through its political consequences.

The changes which have taken place in the comparative economic potential of the European CMEA countries are principally of a defensive nature from a geostrategical point of view. First of all, as compared to postwar conditions there have been changes within the system of international economic relations, in so far as by developing their economies and transforming their structures, as well as by cooperation, they have become capable of parrying economic attacks aimed against them and have also developed the basis of up-to-date national defences. True, their dependence on international relations has increased and has strengthened particularly through their trade relations with non-CMEA countries, i.e. with developed Western nations. In the case of some countries the growth of their indebtedness and their dependence on imported technology, component parts and equipment have linked them to other parts of the world economy from a new point of view. Their dependence, however, is not of a strategic character and significance. As was already mentioned, certain elements of interdependence, too, have developed in East-West relations (e.g. the relationship of debtor and creditor or the natural gas deliveries by the Soviet Union).

The changes in the position of the European socialist countries were reflected also by the fact that they offer an alternative possibility to the developing countries as regards the supply of capital, technology, and various important commodities as well as arms. Thus, they exerted a considerable influence especially in the 1960s and 1970s, on improving the bargaining positions of the developing countries. The socialist countries intensified their participation in the cooperation in international organizations and have an influence on the norms and conditions of such cooperation. This, however, still has not a significant effect on the functioning of those international organizations the norms and standards of which are determined by the general system of terms and the balance of power on the world market. As reflected in Table 16, the share of the European CMEA countries has considerably increased in the world production of some commodities.

As compared to the beginning of the 1950s the share of the European member countries of the CMEA has also increased in the gross national product of the world by the early 1980s. The growth of the share of the CMEA countries had been considerably faster in the 1950s and 1960s whereas the increase came to a standstill in the second half of the 1970s. Their domestic economic difficulties coincided with the worsening of world economic conditions. The smaller East European countries were affected by both of these factors to a much greater extent than the Soviet Union.

The share of the European CMEA countries in world trade is less than that in world production. The world trade proportion relating to the CMEA region reflects by and large the ratio of the Soviet Union. As concerns the other CMEA countries, the share in world trade is nearer to that in world production (though it tends to lag behind that somewhat). The smaller share of the CMEA region in world trade is explained to a certain extent by the fact that in all of the European CMEA countries the economic policy has had a limiting effect on international cooperation in economic growth for several decades. The system of economic management has not had a favourable effect on the development of external economic relations either. Moreover, an inward looking policy was encouraged—particularly in the years of the cold war—by the power relations on the world market and by the various restrictive measures against the CMEA countries. The industrial development of the CMEA countries took place

Table 16.
**Share of the CMEA Countries in the World Output of
Some Products (per cent)***

Product	1950–1952	1978–1980
Steel	19	27
Coal	23	31
Mineral oil	8	20
Electric energy	14	22
Natural gas	5	30
Cement	14	26
Fertilizers	21	37
Trucks	12.2**	27
Passenger cars	2.1**	6
Synthetics	7.8**	13
Paper	7.7**	10
Sugar	16	17
Textiles	14.6**	19

* Calculations of the author on the basis of U.N. and national statistics
** 1960

to a great extent despite world market conditions and by limiting their effects on domestic markets. Some other, often individual factors (e.g. problems of the balance of payments) have contributed to the stimulation of an autarkic economic policy in some of the countries and in certain periods.

Taking all this into account, it seems obvious that the share of the European CMEA countries is in general small and the trends are diverse. This is reflected by the export ratios (Table 17).

As it is seen from the data, the share of the Soviet Union in the total exports of the CMEA countries has considerably increased (while it has remained almost unchanged in world exports). Soviet exports have increased almost twice as fast as the growth of national income in the 1970s. Trends and price conditions in the 1970s were exceptionally favourable to the Soviet Union since the percentage of fuel and raw materials in its exports are very high (about 50 per cent), and conditions on the gold markets, too, proved to be rather advantageous.

Nevertheless, with the exception of some commodities (raw materials and basic materials) world market conditions and the terms of competition are not directly influenced by the Soviet Union. This is even more so as regards the smaller CMEA countries.

The possibilities of the socialist countries within the system of inernational economic power relations are rather limited in shaping world economic conditions, and as a rule they are obliged to adapt themselves to these conditions. Under the circumstances of the given type of growth and economic mechanism, the objectives of the international economic policies of the smaller socialist countries are linked very closely to the concrete necessities of their national development. Of the factors determining the success or failure of adapting to world economic changes the efficiency of cooperation within the framework of the CMEA is of outstanding importance.

Table 17.
Share of the European Socialist Countries in World Exports
(per cent)

	1948	1955	1960	1970	1980	1985
Total of the European CMEA countries	5.5	8.3	10.1	9.7	7.7	9.4
of this:						
Soviet Union	2.0	3.5	4.3	4.0	3.8	4.5

Source: U.N. Yearbook of International Trade Statistics, various volumes.

Of all the socialist countries it is the Soviet Union whose international economic policy is most significant in the world economy and the system of power relations.

The objectives and means of the international economic policy of the Soviet Union naturally tend to reflect different aims from those of the developed Western countries, and their characteristics are shaped also by the fact that—as mentioned above—international economic relations are less important in the economy of the Soviet Union, than in the small European socialist countries. The development of the socialist world system and the achievement of independence of the former colonial countries has of course brought about considerable changes in the external conditions of the international economic policy of the Soviet Union. Contrary to the pre-second World War conditions, representing a mainly hostile environment, a basically friendly external economic and political background emerged in the given segment of the world economy and the role of the USSR increased substantially as a source of raw materials, technology, loans and as a market for different goods. Though Soviet objectives and foreign economic policy instruments have been widened following the changes of external political and economic conditions the economic mechanism in implementing international economic policy basically remained unchanged, which often hampered the realization of objectives.

Among the chief objectives of Soviet international economic policy the defence and strengthening of the economic security of the country continues to be of outstanding significance and it is closely interwoven with the objectives aimed at increasing the joint economic security of the CMEA countries. The CMEA countries wanted to achieve regional collective security since the late 1940s. They wanted to reduce economic vulnerability and wanted to create conditions which secured their economic and social progress based on the system of values which they shared. The realization of such aims have proved, however, to be an extremely difficult task. This seems quite obvious if the situation of the socialist countries is examined on a global scale and by taking into consideration the changing world economic circumstances and the balance of power, which in my view, is the only feasible approach on the long term. It became also clear—both in a positive and a negative sense—by the example of the socialist countries that the value of statically interpreted short-term security and collective security deriving from the strengthening of the economic foundations and from economic growth is greatly different, and also that the mechanism necessary to achieve a greater degree of higher level collective economic security is not similar to the mechanism for attaining a narrowly defined economic security.

Under the circumstances prevailing in the second half of the twentieth century, economic security cannot be separated from the efficiency of production and neither can it be improved lastingly without the acceleration of technological development. Increasing efficiency also demands international cooperation, actively joining in the international division of labour. The solution of the tasks of increasing internal efficiency and participating more actively in international cooperation cannot be separated from the radical improvement of the internal system of planning and management: the mechanism of the economy, including the mechanism of international economic cooperation.

Economic cooperation with the developed Western industrial countries and the developing nations has always been regarded by the Soviet Union—beyond the achievement of short-run economic advantages—as significant for political reasons as a form of assistance in the interest of eliminating the consequences of the colonial system and of the successful struggle for economic and social modernization.

The standpoint of the Soviet Union and its interest in the extension of multilateral international cooperation are defined to a great extent by the above mentioned objectives.

The increasing role of international cooperation as an important condition for the intensification of economic development is well understood by the CMEA countries. Accordingly, the role of international economic policies is on the increase.

The common elements of the principles guiding the international economic policy of the CMEA countries are pointed out in the document adopted at the high-level meeting of member countries in June 1984. The following points were stressed:[67]

a) All methods of economic aggression such as embargo, boycott, the adoption of and/or the threatening with trade, credit and technological blockade are to be excluded from the practice of international relations.

b) In the economic relations of all countries national independence and sovereignty are to be respected, non-intervention into internal affairs is to be honoured fully and completely, the adoption of force and threats is to be abjured. Full equality of rights and national interests should be respected as well as the right of all peoples to dispose of their own destiny taking into consideration mutual advantages, abstaining from discrimination and the assertion of the most favoured nation clause.

c) It is the firm intention of the CMEA countries to develop fruitful trade, economic and scientific as well as technological relations with all and any socialist, developing and developed capitalist countries which announce their readiness to adhere to such a policy. The CMEA countries deem it expedient to extend such relations first and foremost on the basis of long-term programmes and agreements, to adopt various mutually advantageous forms of cooperation inclusive of joint participation in installing and setting up certain technological projects, industrial cooperation, the joint solution of scientific-technological problems, and so forth.

d) The CMEA member countries support the establishment of mutually advantageous relations between the Council for Mutual Economic Aid and the economic organizations of the developed capitalist countries as well as the developing countries. In this connection it is pointed out once again that they are ready to conclude an adequate agreement between the CMEA and the EEC keeping in view the promotion of further developments in trade and economic relations among the member states of the organizations in question.

e) The leaders of the communist and workers' parties of the CMEA countries as well as the heads of state and premiers of these countries consider it as highly urgent to reorganize international economic relations in a just and democratic way, and to proceed more actively with the establishment of a new economic world order.

Naturally this would need considerable changes in economic policy, organization and mechanism in the countries of this region. It is of course an open question to what extent certain circles of the Western countries which have a major part in the world economy, would regard such changes as desirable or not.

All these indicate, that the increased participation of the CMEA countries in global economic cooperation is not only a question of their policy preferences. It is a function of different factors and it is also influenced by the international economic power structures of the given era. The CMEA countries have great economic potential to increase their role in the global system. The quality of the labour force, the industrial foundations, research and development infrastructure and other assets can be utilized however by improving the incentives, the innovative capabilities and the efficiency of labour and capital utilization only and by making the economies more flexible and reactive to domestic and global changes.

Part Three

Technology in the Global Economic System

Throughout the history of human civilizations, great, revolutionary changes in technology have always affected the different societies. The socio-economic impact of major inventions, which laid the foundation of basic technological transformations became especially strong during the Industrial Revolution which marked the transition from a basically agricultural economy to a modern industrial one. Leading innovations influenced not only national economies but also their relative position in the international division of labour. The revolutionary changes undermined traditional monopolies, created major shifts in cost structures, consumption patterns and production capacities. The "regulating role" of major technological changes in the world economy in the last part of the twentieth century is closely tied to progress in micro-electronics, which is the technological foundation of the information revolution in bio-technology (facilitating major advances in genetic engineering, neurology, etc.), to the new "material revolution" and to innovations in the energy economy. Those countries which were able to generate and introduce them in a comprehensive way in various sectors of their economy at the fastest rate and maintained (or obtained) the capability to remain in the forefront of the changes in the world market, obtained especially advantageous positions. Innovations in the traditional sectors are also based on high technology introduced at an increasing scale.

1. Economic Sciences and the Role of New Technology

It has become almost a truism of economic sciences that technological development is a decisive factor of growth and plays a prominent role in increasing production, productivity and effectiveness.

Though the correlation between research and development and economic growth is frequently highlighted since World War II, there are a number of blank spots in the exploration of the actual connections between these two processes. This can be explained by the highly complex character of such interrelations. Economic development is influenced by technological innovations in many direct and indirect ways. The effects can be felt only after a long period of time and are generally combined with a number of developments which are independent of the process but coinciding with it in time.

Primarily, economic theory explores the most general correlations between the two processes. On a global scale, the differences between the various "technological regimes" as well as the structural problems of transition from one regime to the other, were investigated. On the level of national economies investigating the causes and consequences of the growth of factor productivity as well as the national differences in it, economists attempted to find out to what extent the different rates of growth could be explained by the differing roles of science and technology. They also attempted to find an explanation for the technological gap between individual countries in world trade and the dynamic exploitation of comparative advantages. Though researches proved unable actually to throw much light on the complex correlations, the "science policies" of the government were seen in a new light. It was emphasized that science policy could not be an isolated branch of economic policy or cultural policy.

In recent decades new ideas have been formulated on the new role of science in economic growth in the scientific and technological revolution: research activities have been greatly extended. The following problems came into the limelight: on what does the innovative capacity of a given economy (society) depend and how can it be further developed in an interdependent world; can the negative socio-economic consequences of the new technology be absorbed by the society within itself and, on international scale, can scientific and technological development be made to serve major global objectives and under what political, economic or institutional conditions? A new dimension in the role of science and technology in economic growth was opened up after the collapse of the colonial system and the emergence of the developing countries. The problems of technological development, too, gained a new aspect under these conditions. Previous analyses on a macro level had mainly dealt with the questions of the advantages of the late-comers and the technological and economic conditions of "catching up and outstripping". Under the circumstances of the late twentieth century the investigation of the problems of technological dependence tended to stress the "technological" aspects of the great inequalities of world economic relations emphasizing the necessity of diminishing such disparities. Technological protectionism influencing both exports and imports became an important part of trade policies. The problem of the internal or international spread of the new technology has become an important problem of economic strategy.

The contribution of science to economic development, the effectiveness of research and development input and the possibility of measuring such outlays have raised a number of questions as well. A significant restrictive factor is seen in the fact that it is the use of achievements of research and development input and not the input itself which has an effect on development. The effectiveness of financing the alternative sources of R & D is, therefore difficult to define.

The need to combine macro and micro-economic implications in research is stressed more than ever by the important part technological development plays in international competition. Technological development has gained vital importance in the arms race.

In the early 1980s about 30–33 per cent of global research expenditure was spent on non-civilian projects. Many of the important breakthroughs in natural sciences led first to a military application of the technology based on them. Military application united several important innovations in different new weapon systems which resulted in revolutionary changes in the arms race. The "traditional" or conventional weapons were also substantially refined and modernized with the help of new technologies.

The interaction between civilian and military research and technology became more intensive. National security considerations had a great impact not only on the research and development of individual countries but also on international cooperation.

The American strategic defence initiative is the most recent example of military research and development projects which integrate such different areas as aerospace, energy resources, computers, telecommunication optics, biotechnology etc., which also play an individually important role in the arms race of the late twentieth century.

The changes in the conditions of economic growth, the emergence of new economic and power centres made it imperative to study the national economic and international correlations of technological development from the point of view of competition on the world market. The relative international competitiveness of the states is defined by the correlation of a number of factors the most important of which are the following:
— quality and quantity of human resources;
— the efficiency of economic policy and the innovative capacity;
— the character of the infrastructure;
— orientation of the leadership, correct or incorrect judgement of international conditions and prospects;
— internal socio-political consensus and stability;
— the volume and the possibility of mobilization of the raw material and energy basis.

The above factors are correlated and their rating changes from time to time.

The volume and availability of natural resources (minerals, fuel, agriculture, forests, waters, etc.) for example was considered of secondary importance, at the time of low raw material and energy prices (but in the 1970s it has become important again). The importance of the effectiveness of fixed assets, the volume and structure of investment in capital machinery and equipment, plant and economic infrastructure, road and railway networks, telecommunications, and public utilities were temporarily overshadowed in some developed Western countries under the slogan of the "post-industrial society" in the postwar years. In the 1980s, however, under the circumstances of bitter world market competition the significance of these factors came up with increased vigour.

In the postwar period the importance of the accumulated and useful technological-scientific knowledge, production and organizational experience has been outstandingly important since these constitute the "intellectual capital", the most mobile component of a given society. Moreover, the "technological factor" has become a decisive element in international competition, too, as a result of the scientific and technological revolution. The positions of the various nations in this respect, and how these positions change in the light of the resources mentioned, can only be estimated approximately.

"Capital ratings", highly important from the point of wiew of technological development, i.e. the relative volume of capital invested have changed in the major Western countries. See Table 18 for the percentage shares in total global capital invested of some leading Western countries.

Table 18.
**Share of Some Leading Western Countries in
Global Capital Stock (per cent)**

	First half of the 1960s	Second half of the 1970s
USA	42	33
Japan	7	15
FRG	9	8
United Kingdom	6	8
France	7	8

Source: Report of the President on US, Competitiveness, Washington, D.C. p. 9.

The five countries mentioned in Table 18 have declined only by 2 per cent in the light of the above index, whereas the share of the Federal Republic of Germany, Great Britain and France has remained almost unchanged, and the position of Japan has considerably improved.

The global distribution of accumulated intellectual capital shows even more unevennesss. Examining only the distribution of highly qualified technological-scientific experts it can be stated that their concentration lags only minimally behind of that of the capital invested.

Regarding the international distribution of highly qualified manpower the changes in proportion—on the basis of calculations according to data from sources in Table 18—were as follows: the share of the USA has dropped in the two decades mentioned from 29 to 26 per cent, that of the Federal Republic of Germany from 7 to 6 per cent, whereas that of Japan has risen from 7 to 9 per cent. Virtually nothing has changed in the positions of Great Britain and France.

The cumulative technological culture of any society is of great importance. This is rather a complex term difficult to define, comprising—among others—the following main elements:

a) specific technological knowledge embodied in materials, products, processes and organizational systems of production, developing continuously but only over a long period of time;

b) ideas, knowledge and initiatives evolving in the broad masses of the people with the aim to develop materials available, product, processes and systems of production;

c) the cumulated individual experiences and skills, positive and negative inferences providing adequate adaptability, flexibility of the society and its members;

d) the technological infrastructure: vocational and higher educational institutions, research institutes, technological information, the system of enterprises specialized in research;

e) capacity and experience of the establishment in technological development which—as a result of the part the state plays in furthering technological development—have accumulated under the influence of various factors (wars, crises, competition, internal tensions, etc.).

As is well known, the countries of the world can be divided into three categories according to the level of their scientific and technological development: *"innovative" countries,* where products regarded as new on the world scale are elaborated (and where new sectors of industries emerge); *"follower" countries,* which adopt—without any changes or with certain modifications—the new technology after a shorter or longer time-lag; the so-called *"technological wasteland",* where not even the preconditions of following the most up-to-date technology are given.

Naturally this categorization cannot and should not be regarded as an absolute standard since there are no rigid dividing lines between the "innovative" and the follower countries, and with considerable efforts, even in the so-called "technological wasteland", some preconditions of introducing and adopting modern technology can be brought about. In the contemporary world economy there are significant differences even within a single country regarding technological levels. The proportion of exclusively "high tech" sectors or industries is relatively small even in the most developed Western industrial countries. The domestic spread of the newest technology is also uneven. Countries are not categorized as innovative or follow-up ones according to where the invention resulting in a new product or production process has been born but according to where it has first been put into production or from which economic utilization has spread all over the world. A number of inventions which were made in Europe were first utilized in the USA and spread all over the world from there.

Statistically the basis of categorization is the technological balance of payments resulting from expenditure and revenue originating from new technology in the various countries. This method of measuring, however, uses too comprehensive categories and does not throw a light on the complexity of the situation in the innovative or follow-up countries. The innovative capacity is not a notion characterizing scientific abilities. It is basically a combination of socio-economic and techno-economic factors. It comprises those skills which make it possible for a given country to elevate its inventions and scientific achievements to the level of technological-economic results and to make use of them in the economic sense of the term. Thus, it might happen that there are many outstanding scientists living in a country which is lacking entrepreneurs, capital and an innovation oriented technical labour force. The individual factors develop under the effect of different incentives and, under the present conditions, the innovative capacity of any country also depends considerably on how it is able to synchronize the factors often moving under the influence of differing incentives with its economic objectives within the scope of its scientific and development policy, and to concentrate them into a single logical system.

Numerous attempts have been made by a great many countries to formulate a technological development policy coordinated with the objectives of economic policy. The definition of and the changes in the objectives of a technological development policy depended generally on the economic and technological-scientific development level of the given countries, on their economic possibilities, their position in the international division of labour, on the social system and partly on the role the country is playing in international affairs.

The technological development policy of the United States' government, for instance, was decisively influenced by objectives related to an increase in military potential after World War II. Such objectives had a vital part in almost every significant innovation, from computers to the nuclear or space research programmes.

This was also the main motivation of government control on international technological cooperation.

Of the West European capitalist countries, in the United Kingdom and France technological development policies were also highly influenced by strategic objectives. In the Federal Republic of Germany and some minor West European countries, as well as in Japan, it was the strengthening of the international competitiveness of industry which tended to be the central aim of technological development policies.

In the Third World countries the development of the basis of the national economy and innovative capacities, the more efficient assimilation of foreign technology, and strengthening of the countries' bargaining positions were the most frequently voiced objectives of technological development policy.

Such objectives—the general and sectoral strengthening of the innovative potentials, catching up with international standards, the elimination of the bottlenecks of economic progress, the improvement of the efficiency of technological development and technological transfer—were stressed mainly in the technological development policies of the socialist countries. In the Soviet Union objectives related to the strengthening of the technological basis of national defence are highly important in addition to the above mentioned aims.

Significant differences have evolved as regards the instruments of technological development policies as well.

The economic policies of the countries are characterized in practice by a combination of direct and indirect instruments, and specific and general measures—both as regards character and effects—realized from the aspects of input and demand. These measures are often formulated in the framework of special national or international programs. The most general instruments of technological development policy are the following: public research and development expenditure, subsidies, special credits, public subvention with the aim of diminishing or sharing risks, investments, fiscal incentives (tax reduction, tax refunding, accelerated depreciation allowances), public purchases. In the five leading Western countries (USA, Great Britain, France, the FRG, Japan) 55–60 per cent of all research and development expenditure was financed out of public funds between 1960 and 1983.

The state and the armed forces are the greatest individual purchasers in the USA in a number of industries that are important from the point of view of modern technology. And the research and development support rendered to private corporations manifested itself also in the high prices paid for the goods and services.

In addition to substantial government contracts, the French government grants considerable financial assistance to enterprises which have successfully finished the development stage of new technological achievements (prototypes or pilot plants). This is done in order to promote the commencement of marketing of new products.

In the Federal Republic of Germany industrial enterprises can occasionally receive direct assistance or favourable loans for similar purposes. In all developed capitalist countries industrial companies get considerable tax reductions, too, as support for research and development activities. This amounted to 10–25 per cent in the first half of the 1980s.

Support for the educational system to facilitate university research, the founding and operation of public research institutes and laboratories, and the handing over of research results on favourable terms to private firms—all these are of outstanding importance as instruments of technological development policies in addition to direct financial support. In many countries the establishment of public data banks and dissemination of scientific information have become important functions of the state.

Government assistance to the research and development activities of small and medium-size firms is highly important in almost all industrially developed capitalist countries as these enterprises play a special part in the innovation process. It should be emphasized, however, that this method is adopted chiefly in major countries, while in the smaller Western industrial countries it is rather the bigger enterprises and those ranking high in technological progress which get special benefits and support.

Utilizing the "international" character of science and technology properly is an important practical condition for successful technological development strategies. Every new scientific and technological achievement in any country is based on the cumulative experience of previous ages and other countries. It has been shown from experience of scientific development that as a result of independent research and development activities similar achievements make their appearance in a number of countries of the world at different times in history but these inventions increasingly occur simultaneously. The mutual influence of research and development activities, their "enriching" character could be an important source of national innovative activities, too.

International cooperation occupies a central place in the technology policies of the smaller countries. It helps to overcome some of the constraints which are inherent consequences of the "smallness".

Small countries can participate in such areas as space science and technology, oceanography and marine exploration technology and in other similar areas which require very expensive research efforts and costly equipment through international projects. They cannot follow the trends in scientific and technological progress which require large investments and continuous support for an increasing number of sub-disciplines in sciences. They have to choose the most appropriate field for themselves and rely on cooperation in other areas. The constraints of size are also evident in the commercial development and marketing operations, which are expensive and difficult, especially when new industries are started up. The only feasible and potentially efficient policy in small countries is specialization, cooperation and internationalization, by various schemes, among them multinational projects.

International or multinational research and development projects, like the Eureka program of the Western European countries or the General Agreement on Multilateral Technological Cooperation of the CMEA countries represent an increasingly important form for the utilization of the international character of technological development.

These projects or programs have several advantages. The first is the scale. The countries participating in the work by pooling their resources can achieve goals at a scale which would not be possible for the individual countries. As a second advantage, they can use their resources more efficiently by avoiding duplication and thus they can save time and money. Thirdly, they could cater for the demands of more than one country thus finding larger markets which are standardized from the very beginning.

Their projects may also increase the competitiveness of those countries on an international scale.

There are, of course, important conditions for the implementation of international projects. Financial resources must be readily available from the budget of the national participants or from international borrowing covering research and development costs. The forms of risk-taking as well as the dissemination of the results must be well planned, which requires not only the precise evaluation of input and output but also the establishment of the institutional framework to deal with such details as the rights of publication, patenting, the exploitation of patents, scientific norms, reference materials, information flows etc. The multinational projects must also be supported by well coordinated national policies, joint assessment of the technological changes and priorities. The equality of the partners must be achieved through different mechanisms securing the mutual advantages, and clear benefits.

Influencing international technology transfer and improving its effectiveness also plays an outstanding part in national technological development policies.

As a "follower" and relatively small country, Hungary for example is traditionally interested in international technology imports. Hungarian technological development policy therefore, ought to pay special attention to such issues as the relation of technology imports, the development of domestic innovative capacity, the proper selection of scaled-down areas of development, etc. Before World War II the overwhelming majority of new products and methods of production introduced in the country were of foreign origin. Imported technology almost without exception came from countries more developed in the fields of both technology and economies than Hungary. For any agrarian country from the lower ranks of middle level countries advanced foreign technology had constituted an island both in industry and agriculture.

After World War II a new situation took shape in the Hungarian economy both as regards the internal conditions of innovation and those of international scientific technological cooperation. Industrialization and extensive economic development brought about the establishment of new industries, the introduction of new manufacturing processes and products as well as new organizational forms. Owing to an international embargo measures and self-imposed constraints, the criteria of quality effectiveness and up-to-dateness were often disregarded. Many of the new products and technologies introduced lagged far behind the high-quality products of the more developed world.

The necessity and possibility of scientific-technological cooperation and the import of more developed technology emerged in the economic policy under the new conditions of the 1960s. Increasing economic effectiveness, faster growth in productivity, the realization of inevitable social and economic changes was possible only by the substantial acceleration of technological progress. This, in turn, required the improvement of internal innovative activity and closer cooperation with the centres of global technological progress.

New conditions have been created for all these tasks in Hungary. Under the influence of changes since World War II the country entered the upper group of middle level countries. A strong industrial basis was established capable of solving rather difficult technological and production tasks, and some industries have developed technologies and products conforming to world standards. Technological development in agriculture was also substantial. Stepping up the pace of technological development and increasing its effectiveness in that stage rendered international cooperation important in general, too, but especially in the sphere of science and technology. Potentials today as far as absorptive capacity and adaptation is concerned are much more favourable in this respect than in the postwar period.

Hungary has a substantial research infrastructure and in some areas has become an exporter of new technology. In territory Hungary ranks 104th in the world (on the basis of 1980 data), by population 55th, by per capita gross national product 36th, by volume of per capita industrial production 28th and by specific human and material resources allotted to research 17th. In the course of the twentieth century quite a few remarkable technological inventions were born in Hungary. The number of new inventions is, however, on the decrease, as a result of the shortcomings in policies in the field of science and technology and in the whole economy.

Thus the example of Hungry reflects the complex nature of problems in the relationship between technology imports and national innovative potentials and policies.

2. Main Trends of the Technology Market in the 1980s

The world market is the sum total of the markets of internationally sold raw materials, finished goods, money, services, information and so forth. The world market for technology is the international turnover of very special products which can appear in a number of categories simultaneously. This market is markedly more complex and heterogeneous than that for many other goods.

Technology as a world market commodity is bought and sold in various forms:

a) capital goods necessary for investment, and the necessary know-how.

b) human labour, first of all highly qualified and specialized labour force capable of adequately using and handling equipment and technology and solving problems on a high level;

c) technological or commercial information gathered in the market and kept secret as a monopolistic strategy;

d) technological or economic organizational services;

e) embodied in different products for civilian or military use.

World markets of every commodity have specific participants: the buyers, the sellers and their various organizations: (national and international institutions). Participants in the world market for technology are rather a heterogeneous group:

— the market for new technology is dominated—more than any other commodity markets—by the transnational corporations determining its conditions and norms;

— small and medium-size enterprises, too, have a considerable role—often as independent entities but sometimes linking up with transnational corporations;

— enterprises of all types (public and privately owned, small, medium and big ones) are to be found among the buyers and sellers;

— enterprises specialized exclusively for new technologies, technological expert services, advisory services or organization have been called into life;

— among the participants in the market for technology there are universities and research institutes, too, which occasionally market the results of their activities directly;

— from time to time governments, and various state institutions (e.g. the army), appear as participants in international trade in new technology.

— inter-state organizations, institutions founded for bringing together and putting into effect different agreements, such as WIPO (World Intellectual Property Organization), UNIDO, UNCTAD and others may also be considered as actors of the market.

Naturally the significance of the participants varies considerably, and their possibilities to influence market conditions are different, too. The international market in technology is a hierarchical structure reflecting global power relations from the very outset. The international flow of technologies is at the same time a multichannel process where differences between the forms of flow and their variations are significant (as will be seen later on).

Many attempts were made in the past decade to define the world turnover of technology but all of them produced only partial results. This cannot be explained by the deficiencies of the experts or the methods adopted. No definition relating to a complex process can be regarded in itself as "exact" or "adequate".

·The actual content of the definition was analysed in the United States chiefly in the course of examining competitiveness, and a number of approaches were elaborated. By one method a definition of the sequence of research intensity of commodity groups entering world trade on the basis of R & D input in the different industries was attempted; another method focused on the individual products, categorizing them according to their direct R & D content. The adherents of both methods tried to translate the result of their investigations into SITC language, the nomenclature for foreign trade standards adopted by UN agencies. An input-output balance of R & D was elaborated in a third approach trying to define the index of research intensity for the individual product groups.[68] The fact that technology influences not only a single branch of industry but comprises all industries adopting the technology in question was taken into consideration by the latter approach. Accordingly, total national economic effects ought to be examined not only for a single technology but for every new technology adopted in the industries in question. And finally, all technological innovations developed in the national economy as a whole could and should be analysed. Total national economic effects, however, should be analyzed not only for a given year but for the whole life-span of the operation of the technology (technologies) in question since it is not exclusively related to the current year.

The international turnover of technologies can be defined quantitatively but comprises also qualitative—i.e. directly unmeasurable—elements as well (e.g. knowledge, information, experience embodied in materials, machines, equipment). Even in the case of a small country such as Hungary it seems impossible to define exactly how much of technology introduced at a given period is of foreign origin. There can also be other approaches. One of them is the method of measuring the new products according to their origin. In the early 1980s about 8 per cent of new products introduced (incidentally such products were not very numerous) were produced on the basis of foreign licences. The share of new products developed by enterprises independently was 89 per cent. The above data cannot be interpreted exactly since research institutes, too, have participated in development work, and it is also fairly clear that even in this part of the work there had been some "foreign" elements the percentage of which is unknown. Moreover, technology received by informal, i.e. non-commercial, channels was represented among their sources as well. The relatively small remaining percentage came from the research institutes but since their activities play a considerable part in the internal development work of the enterprises as well, their contribution to product innovation tends to be greater than can be traced directly.

The part of the world turnover of technology which finds its way somehow into the international trade statistics can be measured most easily. In the nomenclature of international trade adopted in the UN statistics (SITC), it is mainly Commodity Group 7 (machines and means of transport) and Commodity Group 8 (different measuring and control instruments, optical goods, photo equipment, clocks and clockworks) that can be classified as goods embodying "operating technologies". The main sources of the world exports of these goods have changed between 1970 and 1980 as demonstrated by Table 19.

The leading importer countries and regions, respectively, of the world are listed in Table 20 (as a percentage of world imports).

Goods embodying "measurable" technology exports made up 25 per cent of world exports in the 1980s. Within that, high technology had a relatively small share. The decisive part of world turnover consisted of goods embodying the average technology of the period in question. Another approach is to measure imported machinery and equipment in new investment, bringing more developed technology to the country. In the case of Hungary the proportions of imported machinery from more developed sources was about 25 per cent of the total during the 1970s.

"High-tech", i.e. the most advanced, "pioneering" technology, has no universally agreed definition. There tends to be a general consensus that high research intensity is the most important criterion.

On this basis, there is a more or less general international consensus about the following product groups as representatives of high technology in statistical analysis:
— guided missiles and space craft
— communication equipment and electronic components
— aircrafts and parts
— office computing and accounting machines
— ordnance and accessories
— drugs and medicines
— industrial inorganic chemicals
— professional and scientific instruments
— turbines and parts
— plastic materials and synthetic resins, rubber and fibres.

A singificant indicator in this respect is the fact that the share of research and development input in the sales price is higher than the national average. However, there is no general consensus as to what should be regarded as research and development input, and methods of price calculations are different, too.

Table 19.
Sources of World Exports in Engineering (per cent)

	1970	1980
USA	20.0	16.7
FRG	17.7	17.2
Japan	8.8	15.3
United Kingdom	8.9	8.0
France	6.6	7.4
Canada	5.9	3.4
Italy	5.4	5.0
Netherlands	2.6	2.5
Belgium-Luxembourg	2.7	2.8
Soviet Union	3.2	2.5
GDR	2.5	1.7
Czechoslovakia	2.1	1.5
Poland	1.5	1.4
Hungary	0.8	0.6
Bulgaria	0.7	0.8
Romania	0.5	0.7

Source: Bulletin of Statistics on World Trade in Engineering Products. U.N. 1982, New York.

Table 20.
The Leading Importers of
Engineering Products (per cent)

	1970	1980
USA	12.8	11.9
Canada	6.5	4.4
FRG	6.5	6.6
France	5.1	6.2
United Kingdom	3.7	5.0
Belgium–Luxembourg	3.6	3.4
Netherlands	3.8	3.2
Japan	2.0	1.3
Africa	6.9	7.6
Middle East	2.7	6.5
Far East	6.6	8.9
Latin America	7.5	7.7
Soviet Union	4.8	4.1
GDR	1.3	0.7
Czechoslovakia	1.2	0.8
Poland	1.2	1.1
Hungary	0.8	0.7
Romania	0.7	0.5
Bulgaria	0.8	0.6

Source: Bulletin of Statistics on World Trade in Engineering Products. U.N. New York, 1982.

Table 21.
**Industrial Research Expenditures as the Percentages of
Net Sales in U. S. Manufacturing**

	1976	1983
Total manufacturing	3.1	3.9
All high-tech industries	6.4	7.8
Chemicals and allied products	3.5	4.3
Nonelectrical machinery	4.9	5.8
Electrical equipment	6.7	8.6
Aircrafts and missiles	12.6	15.8
Professional and scientific instruments	6.2	9.3
All other industries	1.2	1.3
Share of high-tech industries in manufacturing	36.2	37.9
Share of high-tech industrial research in total industrial research	73.3	75.4

Source: National Science Board Science Indicators. Washington 1985. The 1985 Report, p. 254, 257.

Another index is the share of direct research and development input in the value added. In the USA, which has a leading position in technological development, the share of the most research intensive product groups or industries in 1980 was as shown im Table 21.

The high technology products were nevertheless defined somewhat differently from the point of view of East-West trade by the United States Department of Commerce, International Trade Administration. This category partly comprises products which embody the "top quality" on an international scale and partly contributes (relatively to a great degree) to the development and technological capacity of the importer countries.[69]

According to the above definition—for example—the following products have been classified as high technology goods on the basis of the SITC standards:
SITC No.

71142 Jet and gas turbines to be installed in aircraft
7117 Nuclear reactors
7142 Calculating machines (including electronic computers)
7143 Statistical machines (punch card or tape)
71492 Parts of Office Machinery (including computer parts)
7151 Machine tools for metals
71852 Glass-working machinery
7192 Pumps and centrifuges
71954 Parts and accessories for machine tools
7197 Ball, roller or needle roller bearings
71992 Cocks, valves etc.
7249 Telecommunication equipment (excluding TV and radio receivers)
7262 X-ray equipments
72911 Primary batteries and cells
7293 Tubes, transistors, photocells etc.

72952 Electrical measuring and control instruments
7297 Electron and proton accelerators
7299 Electrical machinery
7341 Aircraft, heavier than air
73492 Aircraft parts
7351 Warships
73592 Special purpose vessels (submarines incl.)
8611 Optical elements
8613 Optical instruments
86161 Image projectors (might include holographs)
8619 Measuring and control instruments n.e.s.
8624 Photographic films
89111 Gramophones, tape recorders (videorecorders)

While the majority of the above products are really important from the point of view of scientific and technological development, some of them are exported also by the socialist countries to the West. The goods in the above groups do not necessarily represent the latest technological achievements. It is also important from the aspect of the evolution of the global technological revolution—and this is not reflected by statistical data—that the significance of the exports of technological systems has greatly increased.

As compared to products representing earlier technologies, the factors of international competitiveness in high-tech industries have broadened and changed. Certain factors have gained greater importance, such as:

— the economic atmosphere favourable to research, development and investment as well as government policy supporting directly investment and research input;
— financing sources directly aiding entrepreneurial capacity, as well as favourable conditions for venture capital;
— business activity linked with specific government programmes supporting research aiming at establishing high-tech;
— availability of an adequate staff of experts;
— an industrial and trade policy furthering structural changes;
— a system of international relations which creates favourable conditions for the export of developed high-tech.

Various combinations of the factors mentioned above have developed in the individual countries and industries in the past fifteen years. Accordingly, the world economic changes in the 1970s and 1980s has affected the international flow of technology in many ways: through a new division of labour, increasing competition, etc.

The rapid evolution of new trends in technological development has continued, indeed accelerated in the recession period of the 1980s as a result of the long-term objectives defined and set in almost all developed industrial Western countries. Instances of these are the increase of productivity and effectiveness; the elimination of the consequences of the stagnation of infrastructural and technological development characteristic of the 1970s; development of energy and material saving technology; fast technological and structural updating of industries and services having a decisive part in international competition (by means of the complex utilization of the latest technologies); and finally, the rapid introduction of the latest achievements of military technologies in the strategical and tactical weapon systems. In the developed Western countries where structural transformation is the fastest and the most intensive, some important new trends have emerged. New technology, especially microelectronics, rapidly entered into different areas of production and service. Technological progress required the combined utilization of microelectronics new materials and energy sources in many cases. The biological achievements like genetical engineering became viable only as a result of progress in microelectronics. The acceleration of technological change opened new markets rapidly but fast saturation could also be observed.

The reconstruction of enterprises was also speeded up. The changes are characterized by the mergers and joint research and development ventures in the USA, France, the FRG and Italy. Leading firms in Western Europe, e.g. Philips and Siemens, in microelectronics established "strategic alliances" which are basically joint research groups for the research of semiconductor materials and the development of integrated circuits. All large firms try to get rid of business activities which are less profitable either by selling them, discontinuing their operations or by considerable modernization of their plants. Problems were more easily solved by international concerns well supplied with capital and having global strategies of technological development, production and marketing. Such firms were able to bring about and coordinate structural changes on an international scale within the single branches of industry and production sectors. Naturally there are some exceptions, too, but the failures were mainly due to hesitancy in management. For this reason strategic planning has be come paramount once again in the big enterprises.

Specific conditions have evolved for small and medium enterprises. The rapid development of microelectronics, the miniaturization of microprocessors and the fast decrease of production costs in the 1970s and 1980s have resulted in a generation of high-capacity but small-size machines which can be used remarkably well in small plants. A small enterprise sector emerged for the development of the latest achievements in technology. *Rapid technological development demands huge amounts of venture capital willing to take risks.* Generally, however, it is mostly the larger countries with plenty of capital which are able to raise such huge sums of money. These countries are also in a position to meet the immense and increasing costs of developing high-tech. And it is these countries, too, which dispose of the most developed marketing structure.

The scientific and technological developments gaining ground in the late twentieth century have also created new conditions in the system of world economic relations. *The advantage of the leading industrial countries has further increased.* This is reflected in the fact that as a rule it is the most developed Western countries which are capable of utilizing and exporting the most advanced technological achievements, and it is the very same countries which were previously, in a leading position in the branches of technology in question. The changes are also characterized by the fact that in all other countries it is much more difficult to introduce and establish the latest technology than was the case with earlier technologies since the composition of the labour force and the structural conditions of the industry represent qualitatively new requirements. The further development of high-tech is also considerably more difficult in these countries.

The content of such an important category as "the advantage of the latecomers", too, has undergone modification as a result of the latest technological development. When the development of the new technology did not demand a vast scientific basis and no large scale marketing system was needed for the introduction of new products or production methods, it was relatively easy for newcomers to catch up with the previously industrialized countries. The more difficult and costly, the more rapid and continuous innovations have become in the top-ranking countries as regards technology, the more significant the research, development and industrial basis has become there, the more difficult the position of the latecomers has become; the number of the countries which were able to realize the advantages resulting from a more recent start in the technology of the period has decreased. The great differences in the level of development among the countries are a marked characteristic of technological development in the present-day world economy, and considerably restrict the circle of countries and branches of industries which could benefit from "the advantages of the latecomers". Therefore the less developed latecomers are able to compete mostly with the branches of industries using traditional technology—becoming obsolete—of the advanced industrial countries. (In some cases they are remarkably successful in doing so.)

Changes have taken place among the leading countries as regards trade in advanced technology, too. The most important factor was the weakening of the hegemony of the United States—though its leading position remained untouched. Under these circumstances the role of Japan has become more important. The share of the Common Market countries taken together declined too, and the proportion of the newly industrialized countries increased between 1970 and 1985. As far as the sources of major innovations were concerned the trends were also similar.

Between the end of World War II and the early 1970s 80 per cent of the most important 500 innovations in the world were introduced first and adopted on a mass scale in the United States. The dominance of the USA in the introduction of such innovations dropped to 67 per cent between 1933 and 1958, to 57 per cent between 1965 and 1973, and diminished to less than 50 per cent by the end of the 1960s. According to calculations by the American scholar on the history of science, Derek Price, the share of the United States in the global scientific and developmental potential will drop to 25 per cent by the end of this decade.[70]

Nevertheless, until the present day American science has remained in the forefront: in a number of industries important innovations were introduced, and an adequate volume of venture capital has been available for the acceleration of technological development.

The two main driving forces of technological development in the sphere of electronics are the decline of the capacity unit costs of computers (in the United States the decrease in cost of computers was by 50 per cent every two and half years) and the spread of the utilization of microprocessors in the most diverse range of new products. The spead of computer aided design, computer aided manufacturing in the manufacturing industry and the adoption of industrial robots has an outstanding part in both of these tendencies.

In the wake of the linking of computer aided design with computer aided manufacturing (CAD–CAM), the computer integrated manufacturing (CIM), emerged, i.e. the system of manufacturing integrated by means of computers.

As regards CAD, the United States undoubtedly has an advantage on the world market. It is characteristic that 80 per cent of CAD technology marketed in Japan was imported from the United States in the first half of the 1980s.[71]

The spread of CAM virtually depends on to what extent it is possible to provide the single machines with independently programmed but centrally controlled and interlinked computers.

The dwindling of the unit cost of computer technology and the mass adoption of cheap computers are the basis of the spread of CAM. The Japanese have overtaken the United States in the field of CAM for the time being, but the USA has a better chance in the joint adoption of CAD and CAM. The elaboration of the integrated system by the aircraft and rocket industries was started with considerable government support in the late 1970s. (As a matter of fact, the CAD–CAM system is of outstanding importance for industrial mobilization, too, and private capital can reckon therefore with substantial public aid when introducing the system.)

The United States also has a strong position with regards to the latest trends in computer technology, optical computers included, which operate on the basis of visible pictures (i.e. not by means of digital coding) as well as super-computers which will be many times faster than the greatest capacity models of today, and the new microprocessors the capacity of which is also considerably higher than that of their predecessors.

In the field of the so-called material sciences, too, which are of exceptional importance for the remaining years of the twentieth century, the advantage of the United States is quite significant. Considerable results were achieved in developing conductive polymers, in testing metal substituting ceramic materials, in developing combinable metal powders suitable for alloys unknown until recently, in producing non-oil derivate plastic materials and new fabrics.

The United States has a strong position in energy research and biology too, and is considerably ahead of all the other Western countries in research into genetic engineering and cell and tissue cultures. Japan, on the other hand strives mainly to make commercial use of biotechnology as soon as possible; for this purpose they are strengthening the scientific base. As an example, a special research and production syndicate was founded by Japanese chemical corporations. Simultaneously mutual technology transfer agreements were reached with American corporations. As compared with some of its chief rivals, the advantage of the USA diminished in the fields of fibre optics, chemicals, pharmaceuticals and civilian aircraft. Moreover, its rivals try to defend their domestic markets by greater efficiency.

Of the 12 biggest corporations of the global pharmaceutical industry, 9 were American, in the early 1960s, whereas at the beginning of the 1980s their number decreased to 6. Of the turnover of the 12 biggest corporations American firms had a share of 61.6 per cent in the early 1960s while in 1978 their share dropped to 3.5 per cent. Similar tendencies are observed in the production of civilian aircraft.

In the pharmaceutical industry—one of the sectors which has the brightest prospects for adopting high-tech processes—the United States had a dominant position on the market between the 1940s and the 1960s; the decisive part of the most important drugs and medicines originated from the United States at that time. The USA up to the 1960s had the strongest pharmaceutical research basis in the world; nevertheless, while two-thirds of global pharmaceutical research was concentrated in the USA in the early 1960s, this percentage dropped to a mere one-third by the beginning of the 1980s. Pharmaceutical research expenditures rose fastest in Japan, in the Federal Republic of Germany and Great Britain. As compared with the 1950s, the number of new products has decreased while the input needed to test a significant innovation has sharply risen coming up to $54 million in the early 1980s. This is to be explained primarily by the increasing costs of clinical tests and marketing activities. As a result of increasing expenses the share of the big corporations in industry has continued to grow. Pharmaceutical production in the USA has expanded by an annual 5 per cent between 1960 and 1980, and by 15 per cent in the main rival countries.

The United States continues to have a decisive role in the production of military aircraft and in the technological development of such aircraft; however, in the market for civilian aeroplanes it has lost its former advantageous position. While in 1975 American companies had 75 per cent of all contracts for civilian aircraft, the airbus developed by the European corporations gained 26 per cent of the market of turbojet aircraft. The leading competitors of the American companies got substantial government support for research and development while in the USA R & D input has relatively diminished (government support for such research and development in this field was lower by 32 per cent in the 1970s than it had been in the 1960s). On a global scale the volume of airbus contracts was rated second behind the Boeing in 1979 and outstripped the total orders on hand of Douglas and Lockheed. The members of the airbus syndicate are French, British, West German and Spanish companies (all of them, with the exception of one, state-owned enterprises). The French and the West German governments took a leading part in financing the production of airbuses. By 1985 the government of the FRG had invested $1.1 billion in the programme whereas the French government, which had invested about $ 1 billion up to 1980, has taken on the obligation to invest a further $ 1.2 billion up to 1985.

Japan is also an important factor in the market for aircraft engines and components. Through establishing joint companies with European and American firms in the first half of the 1980s, Japanese experts have acquired the technological know-how needed for consolidating Japan's position on the international aircraft market.

The volume of research and development expenditures of the United States still surpasses the total input of the Federal Republic of Germany, Japan and France. The proportion of research expenditures, however, has declined in the 1970s in the gross national product of the United States and has begun to increase again from the end of that decade, owing to the increase of military expenditures. Within total research expenditures the share of civilian outlays has diminished. On the basis of strictly defined industrial R & D expenses—taking those of the USA as 100—the ratio of expenditures in Japan had been 4.2, in the FRG 7.2, in France 6.8 in 1964, whereas in 1979 the ratio of these expenditures grew to 25.1, 19.9 and 12.3 in these three countries. Thus, taken together, they have reached 57.3 per cent of the United States as against their 18.3 per cent in 1964 (OECD data). In the research intensive branches of the economy the exports of those capitalist countries increased most dynamically where the ratio of civil research and development was highest in the GNP. The R & D content of the total exports from the OECD countries (i.e. the volume of research and development input as against the value of exports) increased from 2.5 per cent to 2.6

Table 22.
The Share of High Technology Goods in Trade in Manufactures of Selected Countries, 1983.

	Percentage of exports	Increase in exports[1]	Percentage of imports	Increase in imports[1]
USA	42.6	11.1	25.0	11.8
Japan	32.1	11.2	28.2	3.7
Common Market	25.0	4.3	26.6	5.7
Countries NICs	24.9		33.3	
World	26.2		26.2	

[1] Annual average, 1975–83.

Source: CEPI, *Economic Prospective Internationale,* Paris, 1985, No. 23, p. 23, and OECD. *Science and Technology,* Paris No. 8. 1988.

per cent between 1970 and 1980, whereas the same percentage dropped from 3.7 to 3.6 per cent in the exports of the USA.[72] The OECD countries exported in 1980 nearly $274 billion worth of highly research intensive commodities (21 per cent of their industrial exports). Of these exports 87 per cent came from the USA, the Common Market countries and Japan; half of the total trade took place among the OECD countries themselves. The USA had a share of 29 per cent in the research intensive exports of the OECD countries in 1960, whereas by 1980 this dropped to 24 per cent. The Common Market countries had a prominent share in the global trade of these commodities. The share of goods embodying high R & D costs in the foreign trade of the major developed capitalist countries can be seen in Table 22.

Trade in research intensive commodities among the OECD countries themselves and with other regions is noteworthy. In contrast to Japan the trade balance of the USA in such goods has been negative ever since 1970, and indeed since 1977 the deficit has been increasing. On the other hand, the USA has a significant export surplus in its trade with the Common Market countries. Only 1 per cent of the research intensive exports of member states of the European Common Market flows to Japan. These countries also have difficulties in opening up the American market, and this is particularly true for high research and development intensive industries. A mere 6 per cent of their exports goes to the USA. Growth in this respect is rather slow and uneven.

Despite the fact that 50 per cent of the world trade in technology takes place among the developed Western countries themselves (and as regards advanced technology, this ratio is even higher), the significance of the developing countries—and to a lesser extent that of the socialist countries—as buyers' markets and exporters has grown in the 1970s.

The technology import embodied in machines and equipment, and particularly in turnkey plants, has been increased by the developing countries even in the highly research intensive sectors. About 30 per cent of the technology exports of the OECD countries was purchased by the Third World nations (within that the share of the OPEC countries amounted to two thirds of total purchases).

The developing and the socialist countries have also appeared as technology exporters on the market of new technologies though their share is still rather low particularly in the highly research intensive branches of the economy.

At the same time, the export of highly research and development intensive goods from the OECD region to other regions takes place under conditions of sharpening competition, and the positions of the major countries changing continuously. The chief markets of the United States are the Latin American countries and some Asian nations which buy 33 per cent of the highly research and development intensive American exports.

The USA, at the same time, imports a considerable amount of audio-visual equipment and semiconductors from some developing countries also. In order to improve its position against competitors, the USA has transferred certain industries to some developing countries (to Mexico, Brazil, Venezuela, Singapore, South Korea, Taiwan and Hong Kong). Trade between the socialist countries and the USA in research intensive goods rose rapidly in the 1970s. However, from the end of the 1970s this trend came to a standstill.

The research intensive exports of the Common Market countries are divided by and large evenly among the vast regions of the developing world, their main direction being to the Middle East and Africa. A third of the exports originating from the Common Market comes from the FRG. The Common Market countries are also main technology exporters to the CMEA region: 68 per cent of exports to the CMEA region comes from these countries. Within that, 40 per cent of total exports comes from the Federal Republic of Germany.

Japan had increased her trade with other regions in the 1970s. The share of the USA in the highly research intensive exports of Japan diminished from 60 per cent in 1970 to 40 per cent in 1980 (in 1980 40 per cent of Japanese exports were directed towards Third World countries). Socialist countries have purchased 6.5 per cent of highly research intensive Japanese exports. Incidentally, within the framework of research intensive economic sectors Japan developed rather diverse technology and thus—considering the level of development—she was able to meet diverse demands. In 1983 about 3 per cent of the machinery invested in the OECD countries came from the developing countries and 0.23 per cent of it from the socialist countries.

The importance of political factors in the world trade in highly research and development intensive commodities embodying *the new technology* has increased by the end of the 1970s. Following World War II militarily strategic factors have gained ground on the international market for new technology and have become particularly prominent in the 1980s. In the branches of the American economy developing and adopting the most up-to-date technology the proportion of research expenditure serving military objectives has grown considerably. Strategic considerations affected particularly the markets for semiconductors, integrated circuits, computers, nuclear equipment and machinery, as well as certain types of aircraft. These tendencies made themselves felt not only in the economic relations of America with its adversaries but also in those with its allies. The government of the United States denied, for instance, an export licence for a special computer for the French Atomic Energy Commission (this refusal actually became one of the main stimulants of the independent development of French computers).

The role of military factors in the market for modern technology manifested itself in a particularly direct way in the international arms trade. At the same time, the interests and objectives of "national security" or "strategy" have become specific, independent factors in the international trade in technology between the countries of the two social systems, first of all as a result of the policy on East-West trade of the government of the United States.

From the point of view of economic relations "the importance of military factors", the "strategic significance", the "military usefulness" or the interpretation of strategic risks have changed many times since the end of World War II. The embargo list was particularly long—alluding to "indirect strategic importance" in the cold war period of the 1950s. In the period of the *détente* restrictions were eased because—as was stated—the economic and political advantages of *détente* were more important than the military risks related to selling advanced technology. However, the United States has gradually modified this standpoint ever since 1976. Exports were restricted for reasons of national security by the government of the United States prior to 1949; the Export Control Act of 1949 was actually promulgated in connection with the cold war. This Act was replaced by the so-called Export Administration Act in 1969 reflecting the mitigation of strategic restrictions. The Act was amended three times (in 1972, 1974 and 1977) emphasizing increasingly the need for a moderate tightening of export controls. A significant change was brought about in 1979 when a comprehensive system of control and licensing was introduced.

On the strength of the complex evaluation of conditions some American strategists stress the point that the import of new technology has gained considerably in importance for the development of the Soviet Union since such technology could increasingly serve dual, i.e. both civilian and military, purposes. As regards economic warfare or strategic solutions it was further argued that the socialist countries—among them the Soviet Union—had bought such Western equipment for which the spare-part supply and repair seemed impossible.

On the initiative of leading military circles taking a decisive part in strategic decision making in the United States definite steps were taken in the early 1980s—in the course of introducing the control system of 1979—to subordinate American relations with the socialist countries and to a certain extent with the developing nations to a greater degree to their strategic objectives. Several measures were taken to conform to this policy.

a) The range of commodities belonging to the so-called "critical technology" was redefined and broadened. Products, processes, patents and licences which according to their views could strengthen the military potential of the socialist countries came under this category. Furthermore, the rules and procedures for licensing the export of advanced technology to the member countries of the CMEA, or to any country which would be able to re-export such technology to the CMEA region, were tightened up.

b) The American Department of Defense and the National Security Council were put in charge of the systematic control of such technology and instructed to systematically develop its definition accordingly.

c) The range of military and civilian technology was re-evaluated and an attempt was made to draw a clearer line between the two. Similar efforts were made in all the other member countries of the NATO as well. The control of strategic technological exports to NATO countries was tightened at the same time. In addition, the export of data and know-how to socialist countries which—though otherwise not falling under embargo—could facilitate local production, were restricted as well.

Despite the efforts of the Reagan Administration, there is no consensus either within American political or business circles regarding the programme suggested. Besides, other developed Western countries do not follow the lead of the USA unconditionally.

The extension of strategic restrictions is opposed by important enterprises in some of the Western countries since cooperation with socialist countries is regarded as advantageous both for the economy and for technology. Nevertheless uncertainty and fear was enhanced in business circles by American efforts to emphasize political considerations. Naturally, socialist countries also attempt to strengthen their self-sufficiency, bearing in mind the increased security of their technological development, and try to channel their purchases to reliable partners who are willing to guarantee the delivery of the machines and equipment ordered.

Technological-scientific cooperation demands a higher degree of stability in economic relations than traditional foreign trade, and continuity and mutual trust among the partners is needed for such relations. Naturally this does not preclude a divergence of political interests.

Technological-scientific cooperation is more efficient in the relations between the Western European and the Eastern European countries than in the relations between Eastern Europe and the United States. This is also partly due to traditions.

As regards the future, this branch of East-West relations is treated by the West European countries mainly from the point of view of strengthening their own world economic and technological positions and, according to some perspective, cooperation with the socialist countries could greatly strengthen the technological-scientific autonomy of Western Europe. It could expand their markets and furthermore the scientific potential of the socialist countries could be made use of as regards certain aspects. In the recent past such views have been formulated not only by businessmen or exporters but also by the documents of the Council of Europe and the European Parliament.

3. The Problems of International Technology Transfer

Technology transfer on an international scale is quantitatively of a greater volume and qualitatively more complex than technology traded through the world market. International transfer includes technology which is not channelled by means of trade. For this reason the notion of "technology transfer" is a highly debated issue among experts. Besides the problem of what to consider as 'technology' and actually what is meant by the term 'transfer', there are a number of further questions involved in the debate. Since both notions have many dimensions they are open to different interpretations.

International debates on the definition of technology transfer are centred around important practical issues. These issues include such important notions as the information available about the new technologies (technological awareness) which is the beginning of the transfer process and the conditions for the efficient use of the imported technology (the final stage of the transfer deal.) The developing countries particularly are trying to change the present market relations and would like to render technology transfer practically free of charge or at least much less business-centred than today. In their opinion the experience and knowledge of different ages and countries of the world is accumulated in the technology; therefore, its achievements ought to be accessible free of charge.

For other reasons, similar ideas were formed as regards technology transfer among the socialist countries in the early period of CMEA cooperation. In practice, however, the only technology which was transferred free of charge by the individual countries was the middle level or even less advanced technology from the point of view of the technological standards of production. It was for this reason that later on the conditions of international transfer of new technologies were established on a commercial basis.

The notion of international technology transfer was more than once defined by different authors and by the studies compiled by international organizations in recent decades. These definitions are rather similar—all of them set off from a broader interpretation of technology and usually the following main factors are emphasized:

a) International technology transfer is a process related to economic activities.

b) Since technology is developing continuously everywhere, new products and production procedures are brought about in different countries of the world—mainly in those ones which are highly developed industrially—and therefore, international technology transfer has become a stable element of development in international production.

c) As a process the transfer happens by stages, one being the transfer of accumulated knowledge, the other the handing over of various rights.

d) International technology transfer is "multichannelled", comprised of a number of concrete forms.

One of the most recent definitions of international technology transfer (actually the most significant one from the point of view of economic relations in the 1980s) has been made by UNCTAD, the United Nations Conference on Trade and Development, more precisely by one of its important workgroups. Within UNCTAD the elaboration of a Code of Conduct as regards technology transfer is under way.

Partners of different character come to establish relations in the course of transfer, and both commercial and non-commercial relations can be established between them. "Non-commercial" transfer occurs mainly among governments, various international organizations as well as so-called non-profit institutions. "Commercial" technology transfer is brought about as a rule in some kind of an agreement. The non-commercial form, too, can be effected as an agreement but these are generally concluded not with the aim of making profits (e.g. it can be an inter-governmental aid agreement or a private grant). So-called "informal" methods are of outstanding importance as regards non-commercial or non-contractual transfer. As one can see from the following analysis, the different forms of transfer are often interrelated.

Informal Methods of
International Technology Transfer

Though commercial methods dominate the field of international technology transfer, "informal" channels, too, have a significant part. As a matter of fact, non-commercial methods are confined to information and the technology transfer embodied in these.

a) *Professional visits of experts, engineers, scientists, businessmen and managers, professors and students.* These are the sources of an immense amount of up-to-date information, therefore their significance is invaluable. Information coming from this source has been collected, processed and stored most consistently by Japan. Recently some other countries, too, established organizations similar to the Japanese ones, to process such information centrally; however, these work less efficiently than their Japanese counterparts. Generally the majority of information remains with the individuals or the institutions, and its utilization is rather erratic depending on the general innovative atmosphere and possibilities. In Hungary the organized and comprehensive collection, processing and dissemination of different scientific and technological information coming from the sources mentioned above have been organized so far only on a very small scale. Emigration or immigration has a peculiar part in the transfer of knowledge embodied by the experiences of experts which could give considerable advantages to the recipient countries. Thus the emigration of their experts is regarded as a "reverse transfer" by the developing countries.

b) *The utilization of non-classified published technological data, books and patents.* This, too, is a source of outstanding importance. Information acquired in this way can be used systematically and in quantity only of it is collected, processed by reliable data banks, documentation centres, etc., and forwarded to organizations which are able to utilize it in the most expedient way. An overview of the vast technological and technical literature is almost inconceivable in any other way since smaller institutions interested in certain data could acquire only a fraction of those. The most efficient technological data bank services have been organized by the United States and Japan. (In the early 1980s one of the embargo policies of the American Administration was the prohibition of the transfer of certain processed technological information to the member countries of the Warsaw Treaty.)

c) *Attendance of international seminaries, symposia, conferences* organized by national and international organizations, enterprises, etc. on scientific and technological problems. In this way an immense amount of technological and scientific information is exchanged contributing to international transfer. To discern and register the character, significance and effects of technological achievements and scientific results this method is of utmost importance, having an effect on individual prestige, too, since much valuable and essential information could become accessible. Probably for this reason attendance at conferences by experts of the socialist countries was limited by some Western countries.

d) *Participation in fairs and exhibitions.* This method provides ample opportunity to gain direct experience of new products and production processes, and is generally an important basis of commercial transfer.

e) *Technological-scientific intelligence work is a specific transition* between the commercial and informal methods of technology transfer. In the second half of the twentieth century the extension of "secrecy" to the spheres of research, development and some important phases of production has become an essential characteristic of technological development. There were always technological-scientific and business "secrets" and guarding them was an essential part of competition. Under the present international circumstances as a result of the increased technological-scientific potential of the socialist countries, principally of the Soviet Union, new fields of technological development have gained strategic significance.

The importance of the rapid adoption of new technology and innovations has become an outstanding feature of competition among the enterprises of the capitalist countries, too. Though state secrets and business secrets are not necessarily identical notions, they often coincide. The dividing lines between traditional industrial intelligence and international scientific and technological intelligence have become blurred also. Almost all the countries of the world—and a number of big companies— have established their own industrial-technological intelligence and counter-intelligence organizations. Within the framework of this method secret commercial transactions can also be effected when information, instruments and documents about production are exchanged. There are no estimates of the volume of technology which flows in this form. Usually only attempts which failed are revealed, whereas information about successful transactions becomes available very rarely and belatedly. It is a well-known fact that, for instance, Japanese firms acquired highly important information by this method of "transfer" and have operated a ramified intelligence network up to this very date. The methods of industrial intelligence and technological-scientific intelligence work are highly diverse. As regards competition among the big corporations of the Western countries, frequently an employee of these enterprises will sell scientific achievements, information on technological development, documents, or blueprints classified as "business secrets" to rival domestic or foreign corporations. Countries opposing each other strive to obtain illegally scientific and/or technological achievements which are not exchanged under the conditions of normal trade. One form of this is an "illegal export" arranged by the producer himself or another firm specialized for this task to get round the laws of the country in question.

The category of technological-scientific intelligence work has been extended by some countries—under present conditions for instance by the United States—to the so-called "informal" channels of technology transfer based on the fact that informal relations are in fact highly important for science. Such policies of the government of the United States in the 1980s seriously jeopardize the informal methods of scientific and technological information flow and not only as regards the USA but even more broadly. At a scientific meeting in January 1982 the deputy director at that time of the American Central Intelligence Agency (CIA), Admiral Inman, expounded in his lecture his view that the Administration would intensify its control over science if it did not to gain the help of the scientists to prevent the technological "loss of blood" of the country. A heated debate developed between the representatives of the Administration and the scientists. This argument, too, contributed to the agreement in 1982 between the Pentagon and the American National Research Council as a result of which an interim commission was charged to investigate the problem (Corson Commission). In the report of the commission it was pointed out that the charges according to which the leakage of scientific information had harmed the security interests of the United States were unjustified. Incidentally, it is not the publication of research results which could cause harm but the description of the know-how, the technological specification and the operational principles. Five kinds of control mechanism were examined by the commission: the method of declaring certain studies classified material; measures of export control; the checking of foreign visitors; restrictions relating to public contracts; authorization of scientific papers prior to publication.

On the basis of extensive consultations the committee came to the conclusion that instead of comprehensive controls and restrictions "a high fence ought to be built in a narrow area" in cases when the following four factors obtain simultaneously:

a) Technological development is rapid and the period between basic research and and adoption is necessarily short.

b) The technology in question can be utilized for military purposes too, or—in case of dual utilization—comprises know-how related to the organization of the production process.

c) By acquiring the information about the given technology the Soviet Union would gain significant and immediate military advantages.

d) The only source of information is the United States or those Western countries in which this information is guarded as strictly as in the USA.

The American scientists strove, therefore, to limit the control and restrictions to fields of truly strategic importance, and in such a way as not to harm scientific relations.

Before the competent government authority, i.e. the Office of Science and Technology Policy, could make its decision regarding the suggestions of the committee (no decision was made by the end of 1984) a so-called "Joint Committee of Technology Transfer" had been established within the Pentagon which elaborated a great number of recommendations on contracts, visa control, scientific conferences and publications. On the basis of these suggestions it was stipulated by the Defense Authorization Act of 1984 that even the publication of non-classified scientific papers could be prohibited by the Department of Defense. It was also decreed that any scientific publications could be rated as classified if any doubts arose as to whether it was or was not classified material, including documents which had previously been rated non-classified. Quite a few embargo lists were compiled regarding branches of production which were considered of military importance by the Pentagon. Among them is the "Projected List of New Technologies of Potentially Military Significance" which could cause the most serious harm to future international scientific links. This list refers to technologies which are still under development (and thus their strategic importance is not proved) but nevertheless the Pentagon wishes to restrict the leakage of such relevant information. *Science,* the journal of the American Society for Promoting the Development of Science, correctly stated in its May 4, 1984 issue that by enforcing these measures the United States is risking its best hopes in the long run to bring about the security of the country, believing that control is necessary in order to safeguard certain short-term strategic advantages.

Commercial Methods of
International Technology Transfer

It is generally within the scope of some form of commercial agreement that a new technology as an object is transferred to the recipient country.

The most frequent of such methods are *export and import transactions*. Within the scope of these it is the turnkey export of enterprises, equipment and plants or the transfer of the utilization of technology embodied by them which is most important. (Because of its unique character this transaction is not regarded by some international organizations in recent documents as a form of technology transfer though it represents an important way of acquiring new technologies.) As regards turnkey plants, the new products and the new production processes appear simultaneously in the country which had purchased them. Turnkey projects play an important part— particularly at the time of extensive development—in the technology imports of the developing and middle-level countries. In practice technology purchasing and establishing turnkey plants can take various forms. One of them is the "supervisory undertaking" when a so-called supervisory undertaking is entrusted by the importer with technological planning, choosing a production process, control of investment, training of local experts and organization of production. The enterprise is taken over by the importer only when the plant has reached an adequate degree of technological competence. Naturally the turnkey form can be combined with the transfer of various licences and know-how, the training of experts working in the new enterprise as well as with the initiation of the technological planning and development potential originating from the importing country. Thus long-term and mutual interest can develop between the technological planning and innovation activities of the contracting parties. In practice, however, the party exporting technologies is seldom interested in such cooperation particularly if certain elements of the turnkey enterprise had to be purchased by himself from other sources. An analysis of the cases under survey indicates the fact that both quantity and quality of the technology imported in that way depends to a great extent on the possibility of choice, as well as prudence and far-sightedness of the importer.

The most important factors influencing the bargaining position of the importer are the following:

— To what an extent he is in the position to pay in cash and to what degree he is compelled to sign compensation agreements (the repurchase of products of the new project or offering other goods).
— What kind of supporting industry is available to produce machinery, equipment, components, materials for the plant in question (to what extent the importer is dependent on foreign partners in the course of running the enterprise).
— How much experience the experts of the importer country have to judge a given technology, to choose alternatives, to purchase, operate and repair adequate technologies and equipment.
— The technological development policy of the importer country and its capacity to integrate the technology imported.

The commercial form of transactions comprises also the importing of machinery, equipment and components for operating plants. The significance of importing new processes is conspicuous particularly at the higher stages of technological development.

Since there are significant differences in the technological levels of the individual branches and/or enterprises, the two methods mentioned can be realized in rather different ways in the various industries.

Technology supply is generally more abundant for countries in the initial stages of their development buying technology which has been on the market for a long time and represents an actual standard, i.e. which is low priced and can be purchased cheaply and in many variants. On a higher level of development countries encounter to a greater extent conditions influencing the market of more complex technologies and therefore, imported technology becomes more expensive and its conditions are more complex, too.

The more complex technology can be purchased, usually, from only a few companies. Firms disposing of most up-to-date technology are generally willing to sell these only with constraints and conditions which are usually difficult ones from the point of view of the importers. One of the striking consequences of this is that certain countries are capable of importing modern technology en masse and adopting it efficiently only if they participate actively in the global industrial division of labour. It also becomes an absolute necessity for them to strengthen the innovative capacity of their economies and to bring about conditions most suited for the implementation of the technology needed in the current situation of their countries.

This stage of development is characterized generally by the strengthening of mutual dependence, and it is an essential question to what extent the given country is capable of being simultaneously the recipient and exporter of technology, or at least to what extent it is able to counterbalance its higher-level technological imports with a commodity export considerably more valuable than previously so as to permanently further the inflow of new technologies. In the present phase of development these problems are of primary and marked importance for the socialist countries. It should be noted, however, that developed Western countries, too, have gone through this phase of development.

A further serious problem is what kind of new domestic and international conditions should be established e.g. in the socialist countries or in cooperation among the socialist countries to enable them to ensure rapid and efficient technological development and the adoption of new technology on a mass scale. This undoubtedly requires considerable institutional change both in the economies of the socialist countries and in international cooperation.

This is also important because in this new phase the conditions of the international technology market influence to an increasing extent trade among the socialist countries themselves particularly in areas embodying more advanced technology.

From the point of view of this form of technology transfer the proper choice of partners is of outstanding importance. As regards East-West relations the socialist countries have to face some objective conditions in this field. Concerning technology imports of the socialist countries, those Western firms proved to be most successful and won most contracts which:

— were able to draft, implement or introduce relatively developed technology—even though it was already operating in other countries—of proven efficiency (occasionally as parts of complex production facilities),

— were able to work out detailed and thorough technological and commercial offers within a relatively short time,

— were willing to modify their suggestions in the course of the long period of time prior to signing the agreement (this was generally twice as long as that in Western countries) and were capable fo keeping the protracted negotiations going,

— mere willing to accept the products of the East European country in question in compensation for their deliveries,

— operated in countries governments of which did not hinder (at least not actively) credits and technology transfer to socialist countries.

Of the methods of international technology transfer—particularly in the relations of developed capitalist countries—*direct capital investments, joint ventures and various forms of industrial cooperations* have an outstanding part. In the past particularly United States' and United Kingdom companies which gave preference to direct capital investments in their technology export:

— because of the complex character of the technology exported,

— in order to strengthen their direct control of the market,

— to intensify their monopolistic positions,

— to keep a safe hold on the productive process exported,

— in order to integrate research and development activities with the enterprise system in question.

Direct investment was effected by other countries, too, to further not only technology exports but technology imports as well. Thus enterprises were founded by Japan and some minor West European countries for instance in the United States to acquire most advanced technology, to train experts on the spot and to master American organizational and marketing experience.

Under the conditions of the early 1980s all developed Western countries strove to strengthen their world economic positions (particularly on the world market for new technology) by means of direct capital investment abroad.

As already mentioned, the book value of direct foreign capital investment originating from developed capitalist countries reached the sum of $ 700 billion by the mid-1980s. (Of this, however, only approximately 40 per cent went into the processing industry resulting in about $ 1200 billion worth of production annually.) Half of all foreign capital investment was in American possession. Two-thirds of the direct capital investment of the developed Western countries was effected in other advanced industrial countries, the remaining part was directed to Third World nations. (The ratio of such investments in socialist countries—joint ventures included—was much below 1 per cent.)

Technology imported as foreign capital investment is in itself not measurable. However, information related to conditions and problems indicate that, particularly in the range of imported latest technology, this is a highly important method. Considering this form of technology transfer naturally it should be taken into account that the objectives of direct capital export (or import) are broader than those of technology transfer. In the case of direct foreign capital investment technology exports or imports are only secondary or tertiary factors, and under certain circumstances capital exports have quite a different aim. This is also indicated in surveys made for some leading capitalist countries in this respect.

The main objective of Japanese capital exports is to open up new possibilities for markets, whereas in America the aim is the substitution of domestic production as well as making monopolistic market positions permanent. Japan sometimes invests abroad in branches of industry where it has comparative disadvantages and thus is able to acquire technologies with the help of which production at home can be made cheaper and markets can be expanded.

One of the primary objectives of American industrial investments abroad is to expand production there with a cheaper labour force, sometimes even in industries which have American internal resources as well. It is also an important objective— mainly in more developed countries—to extend the technological monopoly of the USA in certain industries. The exporters of working capital try to control the technological conditions of one or another product or productive process through foreign investment as long as possible—adapting itself to the life-cycle of the product. Thus, such exporters are able to obtain monopolistic rents. In some places, however, this attempt fails and the monopolistic position of the exporter is weakened.

The new producers entering competition are stimulated by the high profits the exporting enterprises had achieved to force their way into the market as soon as possible. If the technology in question can be imitated or copied only under considerable difficulties or if the patent rights are guarded very strictly, it can take a long period of time for new companies to enter the market. Under present conditions there is hardly any technology which is so complex that copying or imitation could be almost completely prevented. Capital exports themselves bring about imitation in the recipient country particularly if the recipient is a developed industrial country. Incidentally, monopolistic rent decreases considerably whenever new competitors force their way into the market.

Regarding this method it is true, too, that with the obsolescence of an innovation the structure of the market changes on the demand side as well, due to copying and imitation. Initially the market is monopolized but the moment the competing companies enter the market with some substituting technology the monopoly slackens and to an increasing degree a competitive market structure develops. However, certain counterforces function, too, working contrary to this trend. Capital exporting transnational corporations gain great advantages as a result of the scale or differentiated character of their production. Such corporations often succeed in their efforts to maintain their monopoly of technology even in the later stages of their product-cycles. Within their international system they try to continue developing the original innovation, thus bringing about substitutes for the technology they had developed. They are also better able to manipulate prices in order to maintain their own monopoly, "restricted prices" are developed taking into account the position and strength of the competitors. Such restricted prices actually mean that further innovations are not profitable for the producer at a time when he had already made considerable profits out of the original innovation. In practice, however, the capital exporting companies are diversified enough—they deal not with a single product but with whole product lines. Thus, they are able to solidify their positions. Technology adopted in foreign ventures and particularly in enterprises in developed industrial countries usually originates only partly from the exporting country and is in fact "collected" from all over the world. This "world wide sourcing" holds true also for the introduction of new products and processes. This is most spectacular in the activities and operations of the biggest corporations.

The chances of technology exporters are more limited in the developing countries where usually even rather obsolete imported technology is rated as a novelty and the internal assimilation of foreign technology and capital is more difficult. For this reason the technological and economic control of direct foreign capital investment and the regulation of the behaviour of enterprises in foreign ownership is particularly important in these countries. There are two influencing factors in this connection: one is the price to be paid for the imported technology, the other the extent to which such imported technology or production processes could be promulgated in other enterprises or sectors in the recipient countries.

The owners of direct foreign capital investments attempt to make profits from exported technology under various pretexts. They try to maximize the direct profits of the enterprise in so far as

— special rates are charged for know-how and for licences;
— materials, machinery, and equipment needed for production are sold by them (as exclusive deliveries) at very high prices.

It is a characteristic of the business strategy of transnational corporations that decisions on development, the distribution of resources and investment are all made with the aim of maximizing profits and maintaining control. This strategy of transnational corporations often encounters bitter opposition from the governments of the recipient countries. On the basis that it runs counter to their national interests almost every country has introduced some measures to regulate the activities of transnational corporations and to control technology transfer. Such regulating activities, however, seldom achieve the desired results. It is not just because the national control of technology transfer and productive processes can be evaded in variety of ways by foreign firms, but because the need to attract foreign capital and technology is often stronger. This is especially true in those cases in which the profitability of the venture is not sufficiently stimulating for the foreign investors.

As regards technology transfer related to direct foreign investment, it is also important how much the internal spread of imported technology is furthered by this transfer. Experience shows that this is often hindered by restrictions ordained by the conditions laid down by the foreign firm exporting the technology in question. The internal spread of technology is usually restricted by contracts, so that enterprises in national ownership wishing to obtain technology already used by foreign owned firms in their country and wanting to purchase the new technology directly from the original foreign sources and not from the local affiliate of the foreign firm are not allowed to do so.

Another method of direct foreign investment is the joint venture. Experiences and a great number of case studies indicate that this form is adopted by the owners of technology—only if special advantages are offered. Firms which own technology that is difficult to access seldom initiate joint ventures with local partners. This method however, is frequently preferred by the importers of technology. More often than not a special share in the capital is granted to the exporters in exchange for their new technology. Many West European countries attempt, for instance, to establish partnership relations with American or Japanese enterprises to strengthen their competitive positions in the field of microelectronics. By the end of 1988 of about 200 joint ventures in Hungary, 30 or 35 were directly involved in technology transfer.

Industrial cooperation represents a specific transitional form between full or partial ownership by foreign firms and simple licence purchases. This is a particularly frequent method employed by socialist countries. It is not the aim of this study to treat in detail the various methods of cooperation and the international experience which have been gained. This method is touched upon only in connection with technology transfer.

There was a widespread view in socialist countries that industrial cooperation was considered to be the most effective way of importing technology from Western companies. This view was supported by projects based on long-term relationships between the partners, a continuous flow of technology (not limited to a single transaction), and the technological level of both partners participating in the cooperation being high. Industrial cooperation of this kind is generally regarded as a more efficient form than the purchase of turnkey plants or just licences. According to such assumptions, Western partners are interested to a greater extent in promoting successful assimilation of the technology imported by socialist countries and their continuous further development.

Industrial cooperation can indeed be a suitable mechanism for the furthering of technology transfer. The lack of lasting and intensive industrial cooperation could limit the scope and efficiency of the transfer.

Cooperation conditions are different in the case of product and process technology. As regards product technology (new products) there is little possibility of substitution. Though a new product may require an entirely new production process, too, in the majority of cases such new products can be introduced by simple changes or adaptions in the production process. The advantage for the transferring company generally originates from the fact that this firm is the owner of the technology embodied in the new product. Corporations concentrating on developing special new products or entering the market with such products generally strive more than other firms to effect the transfer of technology within the scope of the enterprises owned by them, since firms developing new products as a rule employ a highly qualified labour force and use special equipment. Thus, research and development input is generally a high priority for the managers. Besides, the development of new products is a risky operation. Research and development costs can be recouped by the enterprise only in the form of successful products. It is for this reason that the firm tries to monopolize the production of such products for as long as possible. Innovations connected with production processes, on the other hand, are usually less expensive and therefore, their transfer involves less risk.

The calculation of prices may be complicated by the special character of new products, particularly if the production rights are sold abroad. It is uncertain whether an adequate substitute commodity for the new product exists and its components may not have alternative uses. Accordingly, there is no fixed market price which could serve as a basis for international transfer between enterprises. For innovations within the scope of a given process, at least one substitute procedure usually exists (e.g. the technology of the product in question had been made with previously), and if it is not an entirely special product, several kinds of technology could be available. The setting of prices for intermediate products is facilitated by alternative technology and the component and spare part maket.

The innovating company draws monopolistic profits from the ownership of the product thus offsetting the considerable research and development expenses. At the same time, the production technology can be regarded as the capacity of a certain form to produce or market the product in question. A company has an advantage over its competitors if it turns out the same product cheaper and in superior quality or a product of superior quality for the same price.

Every company tries hard to innovate in the fields of product design and production technology in order to strengthen its competitiveness. The differences between the branches of industry and even within the industries are still very significant as regards what proportion of the resources of the enterprises are made use of for one purpose or other. In some industries competition is entirely on the basis of new products whereas in others competition is related to production processes aiming at the reduction of production costs, better marketing and occasionally product differentiation. Companies participating in competition with new products are generally centralized, vertically integrated, and do not strive to transfer the new technology even if there is some measure of industrial cooperation. Such firms are not easy partners in East-West industrial cooperation either. On the other hand, firms participating in competition in the field of production technology are usually decentralized, horizontally integrated and are more ready to perform technology transfer than the above mentioned ones.

The pharmaceutical industry, for instance—since it produces an end product which is often very specialized and product oriented, at the same time it attempts to realize maximum profits from such products—rarely commits itself to technology transfer either in the form of joint ventures or industrial cooperation. Research and development take a very high proportion of total costs in the pharmaceutical industry, and there are relatively few really successful products as compared to research outlays. Pharmaceutical enterprises are therefore stimulated and compelled to try to amortize their research and development expenditures by highly successful products. Engineering and some other industries where the degree of cooperation is of decisive importance and the end product is part of a given process in the production system are much more open to joint ventures; the majority of industrial cooperation, too, is concentrated in these industries.

Industrial cooperation agreements have an important part in Hungarian technology imports, too. According to data of the UN Economic Commission for Europe on 1981, 41 per cent of cooperation agreements of the Western countries with the CMEA countries were signed with the Soviet Union, 24 per cent with Hungary, 17.2 per cent with Poland and 8.9 per cent with Romania. The remaining part went to the GDR, Czechoslovakia and Bulgaria (2.2, 2.9 and 3.5 per cent). Thus, Hungary ranks second in this respect. Hungarian experience with this method of technology transfer does not considerably differ from international experience.

Technology received—though it was regarded as new in the Hungarian economy— was in the majority of cases more than 5–7 years old and the share of technology "younger" than 5 years represented only a relatively small ratio, i.e. 10–15 per cent.

From the aspect of technology transfer industrial cooperation was really successful if the contribution of the Hungarian partner, too, was significant. Owing to serious passivity as regards technological development and deficiencies in its research activity, the Hungarian partner firms have proved unable to make reasonable profits out of technology imported within the framework of industrial cooperation.

Many industrial cooperation projects are tied to the purchase of licences. Neither is it a rare practice in international business life—but it is not made clear that the purchase of licences is a specific independent form of cooperation though this is exactly what it is.

The most important sphere of the market in new technologies is *the international trading of patents, licences and know-how*. This is the most unambiguous and most directly perceptible form of international circulation of innovations. However, it is this very form which demands the utmost scientific and development capability (or at least the adequate adaptive activity), organizing ability in the importer country, and well-planned development of its industrial background. The significance, conditions and effects of trade in licences is greatly influenced by the different development level of the various countries, the peculiarities of the branches of industry, the strategies of the companies in question and the characteristics and age of the technology (product or process) transferred.

Experience, shows that this form is often adopted in the relationships between international corporations, and in some branches cross licencing has become popular. Trade in licences is important within the transnational corporations, too, mainly in the field of technological relations between the parent company and its subsidiaries. Thus in 1981, 81 per cent of the incomes from the royalties of licences of American corporations and 40 per cent of those of the British corporations came from this source.[73]

Royalties from licences sold to developing or socialist countries amounted to only a relative small percentage of the total earnings of international corporations. Nevertheless these countries represent favourable markets for various reasons since international corporations:
— make additional profits out of technologies for which there is less demand in other countries;
— get a chance to penetrate markets where they could not be present (or only under unfavourable conditions) by means of foreign capital investments,
— get a chance (through adaptation) to utilize their technological development potential more fully;
— can become known in new countries and/or regions.

Different data are published on the magnitude of international trade in licences; according to my computations, directly paid royalties from licences come to 3–4 per cent of the value of annual world exports. Two-thirds of these royalties derive from the licence turnover between the developed capitalist countries. East-West licence sales are estimated as 7 to 8 per cent of the world trade in licences.

In Hungary royalties—in terms of expenditure of companies on technological development—amounted to 4.7 per cent in 1969, and to 7–8 per cent in 1986. This is quite negligible compared with other countries of the same development level. They were higher, however, than in the other Eastern European countries.

Investigations concerning technological imports of medium-developed countries indicate that about 45–49 per cent of new products and productive methods of foreign origin have come to these countries by means of licences. (The technology flow among the industrially developed Western countries is more diversified and the various forms of technology import are interwined more closely. In most of the developed smaller industrial countries the share of manufactured products based on licences was about 10–15 per cent.)

Licence purchase is preferred to all other forms by middle level countries. This is explained by the fact that usually their bargaining positions are weaker, and moreover their own development and marketing capacity is not strong enough. These countries also entertain hopes—by the purchase of licences—of reaching the quality parameters with their products which are demanded on the markets of the developed countries, and so improving their marketing possibilities. (Licence purchases by developed industrial countries in turn are motivated by their endeavour to diversify their production profiles, extend the marketing horizon of their companies and to widen their choice among the new technologies marketed, and—since they dispose of excellent innovating and development capacities—easily to adapt and occasionally further develop the licences purchased.)

Licence purchasing is of such a great volume in the technology imports of many middle-level countries that they can stimulate local autonomous innovating activities only in case of the creation of adequate conditions. If licence purchasing is not combined with deliberate and well defined objectives of technological development, and if an adequate domestic research and development basis is lacking, then innovations could be impeded, and direct and indirect technological dependence could even be turned into a permanent characteristic. Direct dependence means various constraints prescribed by the licence contract (geographical limitation of marketing, strict control of the trade mark and its advertisement, fixing the exact time-span of sales, exact definition of the sum of licence royalties and the ways of paying them, etc.). Indirect dependence is reflected in the additional import needs made absolutely necessary for production by a given specification which cannot be produced by the country in question, further it can be felt in bringing about relationships under which the development of products or processes is linked to restrictive conditions. A still more important problem is the fact that as an exporter of technology the owner of licences has practically a monopolistic position and tries to maximize his profits derived from the technology in question. His monopoly could comprise not only the production technology itself but the machinery, equipment, materials needed for production and, frequently, even the sale of the product.

Under certain conditions, e.g. strong supporting industry, adequate technological development policy and innovating capacity, even leaps of up to 7–8 years in technological development are made possible by licence purchasing.

Additional purchases and expenses related to technological imports often represent 30 per cent of the value of the technology in question. Hungarian experience supports this opinion. The deficiencies of the supporting industry are mainly responsible in the majority of cases.

In the case of technology imports and machinery, equipment, spare parts and material imports the transfer-price mechanism established between the parent company and its subsidiaries (which has nothing to do with real prices) allows prices to be set much higher than those of the supplementary inputs needed for the products. Such so-called indirect costs represent a further problem since they are embodied in remitted profits or other similar payments. In the licence purchases of middle level countries two-thirds of imported machinery, equipment and component parts came from the sellers of the licences. The economic difficulties of Poland, for instance, were partly due to the fact that in the second half of the 1970s the expenditure on imports needed for production based on licences made up many times the sum of the royalties. Direct investment needs amounted to six times the annual sum of royalties while imports needed for production came to five times the royalties. Similar ratios were characteristic of Czechoslovakia.[74] Products manufactured under licence did not contribute proportionately to the increase of exports.

The purchasing of licences and know-how connected with it is advantageous in so far as it facilitates the organization of technological development experience, helps to give a better knowledge of market conditions, and improves technological "disciplines". Without the development of an autonomous research and development basis and the simultaneous adoption of other forms of technology imports, however, the advantages of licence purchasing become doubtful and they become too expensive. This is borne out by Hungarian experience, too. Many firms, mainly in the engineering industry, did not have the necessary research and development background and the further development of the products therefore remained in the hands of the seller of the licences. But there are also some favourable examples. In certain cases the purchasing of licences stimulated the development of domestic research and development activities.

A major requirement as regards the purchasing of foreign licences is that the product may be exported more easily to the world market and that markets which previously had been closed for the commodities of the country in question may be opened up. However, more often than not this hope is not realized, partly because of the various restrictions on technology exports, and partly because products are often transferred to the importing countries at a time when demand slackens and so the new producers can only share the market if production is curbed to a certain extent by the old producers. However, this can be expected only under favourable world economic conditions.

Efforts to Control the Transfer of Technology: "Appropriate Technology" and Conditions

The problem of technological transfer has been heatedly debated in international organizations ever since the 1960s. Two major subject groups have emerged in the course of this debate: one is the selection of the so-called "appropriate technology", the other the changing of the conditions under which technology is transferred to the developing countries. Both subject matters touch upon the characteristics and structure of the market for technology exported through commercial channels.

"Appropriate technology" does not mean some special type of technology. Neither does it mean that technology should not be new or of a sophisticated nature. It only means that the technology imported should be selected with the view to being most expedient in promoting the development targets of a country. "Appropriate technology" could mean the selection of cheap energy sources, suitable industrial and agricultural machines, lower capital intensive construction, service and production processes, small-sized plants rendering it possible to decentralize industrial activities. Countries lacking capital but having at their disposal a considerable amount of free labour resources are well advised not to import capital intensive technologies or even less capital intensive industries. There are, however, industries where capital intensity is inavoidably high by reason of the very character of the technology. Thus, when introducing and establishing an up-to-date chemical industry the less developed country has no choice. On the other hand, the increase of employment as an objective of industrial development demands the introduction of industries which are dominated by labour intensive processes. When importing research-intensive industrial technology (where technological processes are of an extremely complex nature), it must be taken into account that in further development and servicing of this technology the recipient party will become dependent over a long period of time on the exporting country.

The output of new products by means of technology imports offers different possibilities in each industrial branch. Complex products (the turning out of which is rather complex, too) usually demand very costly maintenance and servicing networks which are difficult to establish in less developed countries. The continuous development of products demands a considerable research and development basis in industries where product innovation is an essential factor of competitiveness. The conditions under which technology is imported are generally rather unfavourable for the recipient countries in such industries.

From the point of view of "appropriateness" the growth potential of the industries in question as well as their share in the foreign trade of the technology exporting country is an essential point. Incidentally, developed countries are more willing to transfer products for which the growth potential is low and which are therefore more difficult to export.

In developing countries "appropriate" technology has often helped to cure diseases or eliminate parasites or pests that are unknown in developed industrial countries. Further, they have promoted the introduction of production processes which would facilitate import saving and a lower specific material consumption. Appropriate technology also means the use of such machinery, equipment and products which take into account the standards of professional training and qualifications available in the developing countries and also the conditions of management and organization.

"Consumer" technology has to reckon, in turn, with the local income level, habits and objectives. The latter can be set only by the Third World countries themselves but they need adequate assistance through international cooperation.

In general international corporations carry on research and development activities in branches promising the potentially greatest profits. However, they have to promote research and development which are unambiguously favourable to developing countries also: machinery, equipment and production processes must be suitably adapted. About 1 per cent of the research activities of the developed capitalist countries fall in line with such objectives, while only 5 per cent of global research and development expenditure is concentrated in the Third World countries.

The selection of appropriate technology is, of course, not only the problem of the developing countries—it is a vital question in the socialist countries and in the developed Western countries as well. It has been shown by the experience gained in technology transfer deals that the operating effectiveness of imported technology is often lower by 40–50 per cent than in the exporting country. This is mostly due to the lack of a well-conceived research and technological development policy which should take into account the development level, the possibilities, management and organizational abilities. Some socialist countries often import inconsistent technology implying heavy burdens. However, the socialist countries in principle have a good chance of formulating a reasonable and comprehensive technological development policy (professional competence, organization, etc.). It is first and foremost the deficiencies in economic management and the system of incentives which are responsible for the fact that no proper conditions have been brought about for the selection of "appropriate" technology. Nevertheless, the selection of "appropriate" technology is not an easy task in the developed Western countries either, though the conditions for selection on a company level are usually more favourable, even if the problems of environmental protection, social and employment questions are less emphasized there.

In both socialist and developed capitalist countries domestic institutions are capable of solving the task of selecting the appropriate technology. As regards the developing countries, however, international cooperation is of vital importance. They are supported in this regard by the studies and consultants of the UNIDO, the World Bank and other institutions. But actual needs are not fully met by such aid.

The demand of the developing countries was formulated by the declaration on the New International Economic Order adopted at the Seventh Special Session of the UN General Assembly. According to this declaration the developed and developing countries should cooperate in establishing, developing and strengthening the scientific and technological infrastructure of the developing nations. Cooperation is also needed among the states in elaborating an international Code of Conduct as regards technology transfer taking into consideration the specific needs of the developing countries. The declaration emphasizes the task of revising and modifying the agreements on international patents and trade-marks in order that such agreements should aid the developing countries more than they do today in the field of technology transfer. It is also suggested that the developed countries should make it possible for the Third World countries to acquire freely completely new technologies wherever this does not depend on private decisions. Finally, it is stressed by the declaration that the developed countries ought to improve the transparency of the international market in intellectual property, thus rendering it easier for the developing countries to select "appropriate" technologies.[75]

The international convention on the regulation of one of the elements of technology transfer, the trade in patents (the so-called Paris Convention), was signed almost hundred years ago. The paragraphs of this convention have been modified several times. A characteristic feature of the Paris Convention is the fact that primarily it defends the owners of patents while little attention is paid to the interests of the users, though pressure has increased since the 1970s to bring about changes in this one-sided approach.

International negotiations for the establishment of an international "Code of Conduct" have been going on for years on the initiative of UNCTAD. Other international organizations, too, have participated in the elaboration of the details (UN Center of Transnational Corporations, UNIDO, ILO as well as the World Intellectually Property Organization).

As regards the Code of Conduct a compromise was reached which makes it doubtful whether such a codex could function efficiently. As a matter of fact, the Code is not a collection of recommendations of binding force. International norms and rules so far agreed upon serve only as recommendations for the developing nations and their regional organizations regarding the conditions for technology imports. Most important of these are the recommendations on preventive clauses relating to developing countries.

The following restrictions were particularly objected to by the developing countries:
— the prohibition of an alternative use for the imported technology;
— the ban on obtaining technology which would compete with the imported ones;
— the enforcement of the prohibition in the sphere of utilization of the imported technology;
— the prohibition on the marketing of licences within the importer countries or in international markets (sub-licensing);
— the practice of the so-called "licence package" the (stipulation of highly important import obligations as regards equipment to be purchased, thus shifting additional burdens to the developing nations);
—"tied purchases" (it is stipulated where the purchaser has to buy raw materials, machines or equipment from, in principle aiming at quality protection; actually, however, this clause tries to compel the buying country to make additional purchases);
— quality standards, shifting an exorbitantly heavy burden to the developing countries.

The problem of guarantees regarding the elimination of discrimination has been emphasized repeatedly by both the developing and the socialist countries.

As regards its content, the Code of Conduct has four main parts. The first part contains the definition of international technology transfer (as cited in Chapter 3), and also defines the notions "technology importer" and "technology exporter". The relationship of the codex and national regulations is also clarified in this part.

In the second part the scope of national regulations relating to technology transfer is defined. The necessity for a special treatment of developing countries is emphasized as well, and the problems of international cooperation are dealt with. The right of governments to control technology transfer in a sovereign way is recognized and they are entitled—on the basis of their legislation—to reconsider or renegotiate all agreements concluded on technology imports up to that date. It is also stipulated that governments have to respect the rules on the protection of intellectual property and all relevant international obligations. As regards the developed countries, three important obligations are prescribed by the code: in order to develop technology needed by the developing countries, the scientific and technological development capacity of these countries must be strengthened and assisted, institutions furthering the adaptive capacity of science and technology must be established, and private companies must be stimulated.

The third part of the code takes a stand against the following stipulations of previously signed agreements on technology transfer:

— the free transfer of local contributions to the improvement of the quality of imported technologies to the owner of the licence;
— provisions facilitating the contest of the validity of the agreement at a later date;
— provisions on exclusive transactions;
— restrictions on research;
— limitations connected with the utilization of manpower;
— limitations on the setting of prices;
— stipulations preventing adaptation;
— paragraphs relating to exclusive marketing or representation;
— linkages in sales;
— export restrictions;
— stipulations on patent pools and cross licensing;
— secrecy clauses;
— financial obligations after the expiry of the agreement as well as other restrictions.

The vaguest elements of that part of the code are the stipulations on technology transfer between the parent companies and its subsidiaries.

The fourth part comprises the conditions for the solution of litigated issues and the selection of courts of arbitration and clarifies which countries' laws should be regarded as binding by the contracting parties.

Finally, the establishment of a special international body within the framework of UNCTAD (linked up with the Trade and Development Board of that agency) is suggested, to deal with the problems and conditions of international trade in technology.

This organization should have the following tasks:

— to provide a forum for inter-state consultations (primarily as regards the adoption of the code);
— drafting documents about the utilization of the code;
— elaboration of reports and recommendations;
— organization of symposia and sessions of working groups;
— presentation of an annual report to the Trade and Development Board of UNCTAD.

The above international body could have additional functions as well and, if necessary, could serve as an arbitration forum, too.

Many vital problems of the Code of Conduct could not be agreed upon until the mid 1980s. The debates (even in the case of actual agreements) show the potential (built in) limitations of the Code if adopted. Such an undecided question was, for instance, which country's law should be used on matters in dispute. According to the view of developed Western countries, the contracting parties themselves have to decide which country's legal system and courts should be chosen to solve a disputed question (provided both partner countries have "de merito connections" with the legal system and country selected). According to the view of the socialist countries, the contracting parties have to decide this problem by taking into consideration "the rulings formulated by their national legislations". The developing countries, in turn, insist on adopting the laws of the recipient countries.

There was no agreement on some problems related to restrictions, e.g. on the basis of what criteria should the notions "acceptable", "unacceptable", "unjustifiable" or "unreasonable" be defined in practice.

All of these problems touch upon the applicability of the Code of Conduct. No unambiguous settlement could be reached on the question of whether the following could be categorized as restrictions defined by the exporter of the technology (and considered unjustifiable) or how these problems could be interpreted:
— provisions related to the volume of production;
— methods indicated as regards quality control;
— obligations connected with trade-marks;
— requirements related to equity participation and/or participation in management;
— The exorbitantly long validity of agreements;
— Restrictions on the utilization of imported technologies.

Naturally it is rather difficult to foresee the significance of the code beyond its "guiding" character—even if it is adopted at all by the interested countries. Presumably the role of the governments, not only of the technology importing countries but of the technology exporting countries, too, will be enhanced if important transactions are taking place. It would not be out of the question for governments to attempt to sign bilateral agreements with their major partners on the interpretations and adoption of the rules.

The acceptance of the code could to a certain extent confine the conditions of the transnational corporations within limits on the following points:
— the volume of profits, patent and licence royalties;
— the character and scale of restrictions ordained for the importer of technology;
— the definition of technology exported and additional exports;
— issues of extending and defining the "performance requirement" connected with the technologies purchased, from the point of view of the government of the recipient country (e.g. recognition of obligations by the technology exporter to further exports).

No changes will be brought about by the code in the inequalities characterizing the present-day world economy as well as in the development and research, organizational and marketing conditions which are the main pillars of the large firms of developed industrial countries.

National legislation was passed on technology transfer by a number of developing countries in the 1970s. The aim of these laws was to establish a system of national licensing, the creation of a national "filter" by means of which the governments were able to realize the priorities of their economic policies or technological development policies. These laws, however, could achieve their goals only to a very limited degree.

4. Internal Conditions for the Efficient
Use of Imported Technology

As a consequence of the large volume of technology flows in the world economy, the economic efficiency of imported technology became an important issue. The countries in the "followers" category become especially aware of the problems and conditions of efficiency in the use of technology purchased from abroad: to counter balance the high costs with appropriate benefits.

In technology imports, too, efficiency consists of quantitative, i.e. measurable, and qualitative effects. These latter can only be estimated as far as the effects are concerned. An increase of production by means of imported technology, for instance, or an increase in productivity is measurable quantitatively. Indirect effects achieved with the help of imported new technology introduced into an already operating production system are measurable, too. Such indicators can be balanced with the direct and indirect costs of imported technology. The export-increasing effects of imported technology can also be directly defined by these cost factors since such costs can be compared with the additional import requirements of technology imports (materials, spare parts, experts, etc.).

Effects such as the degree of absorption of imported new technology in the national industry (or certain branches of it) or achievements in the reduction of production costs and improvement of productivity can be evaluated only be means of various complex investigations since these factors are of a qualitative character.

Certain other effects can also be considered from the point of view of the efficiency of technology imports. Such effects are, for instance, the possibilities of local upgrading linking imported technology with the national research and development potential or the stimulating effects of technological imports on the local research and development sphere as well as on the opening up of new markets. From the point of view of efficiency the possibilities of the internal spread of imported new technologies are highly significant, and not only as regards machines, equipment and processes but also experience gained in organization, management, marketing, etc. as well.

It is a well-known fact that the innovative capacity of a country is not merely the aggregate of natural, physical and human resources but also depends very much on its socio-economic organization. This plays a major part in defining the influence of the technology imports of a country on its research and development capacity, on the quality of its labour force and its professional standards, on the distribution of resources and the efficiency of the innovative process. Nor are the effects of technology transfer on the volume of foreign trade of a country whether it increases exports independent of social organizational and guiding conditions. Thus, international technology transfer is not a "neutral" activity from the point of view of social conditions but reflects the values and interests of the different participants of the world economy. Some highly interesting conclusions can be drawn from the practice of technology transfer regarding the interrelationship of the spheres of technology and socio-economic conditions.

a) *Any significant technological change brings about new conditions for successful technology transfer as well*. Thus, the greater the interrelationship between the isolated innovations in the applications the more conspicuous the fact is that the technological level cannot be raised by the import of the individual elements of the new technology itself. It could bring about serious production difficulties if the connected technological innovations are missing or inadequate. Because of the considerable differences among the countries and the discrepancies of technological-economic development it is important to decide prudently and in advance what kind of technology should be imported by a country, at what time and in which branches of production.

b) *Efficient use of imported technology* (and also its adaption) *demands from the recipient country high standards of general education, technological competence and a readiness to take risks.* It is not by chance that in the nineteenth and twentieth centuries in countries which proved most successful in adopting foreign technology a relatively highly educated and trained labour force was available and the increase of international experience of their highly qualified manpower was encouraged in many ways. Today demands are even higher in this respect.

c) *Technology has to be interpreted not only as knowledge embodied in material resources.* Imported technology enters a given social medium, and has precisely defined social parameters in the recipient country, and the degree of its usefulness depends on management qualities and the functioning of incentive systems. The social medium is particularly important today from the point of view of the capacity to develop the technology further, to replace old technology and continuously to introduce new technology. Competition as a compelling force is essential in this respect, too, though it cannot be narrowed down to competition in the market but has to be interpreted in a broader sense of the term, i.e. as competition and rivalry between the different societies. This latter factor, however, can influence the compulsion to innovate only indirectly through the macro-sphere.

d) International comparisons prove the primary importance of entrepreneurship, the capacity to innovate, and to switch over from one product line to another and to adjust. Countries (companies) that *are able to make use of the greatest financial resources (in absolute values) and to employ the greatest number of researchers* have an advantage over all their competitors in this respect. The importance of the financing and research basis in the second half of the twentieth century is highlighted by the nature of technological development. The "entrance fee" is often taken upon itself by the state in rendering financial support to the financing of research, testing, development or marketing activities. Japan is frequently cited in the professional literature as it is the country which has achieved the best results in the Western world in this field since the end of World War II. In addition to historical experience, Japan was aided in this respect first and foremost by the close cooperation and dialogue between government and industry. Much less is written, however, about the experience of smaller countries, which, owing to their position in the world, are generally at a disadvantage compared to the major economies.

Even if much is spent—from limited resources—on scientific and technological research (in percentage of the gross national product) by small countries, because of the high "entrance fee" in research intensive industries they are not in the position to participate in the broad range of technological development so as to compete for leadership. In the sphere of enterprises, however, they were able to achieve even leading positions in one industry or another by means of adequate concentration and bold business policy. It is a well-known fact that some small West European countries—such as Sweden, Switzerland or the Netherlands—could raise their share even in the trade of research intensive products because they specialized in turning out a relatively small number of extremely complex exportable products. The relative successes of some other small countries could be attributed to the fact that they quickly adopted technological innovations of foreign origins in industries where, owing to their research facilities or traditional specialization, they were in favourable positions. Thus the Swedish corporation Ericson has undergone a radical transformation in the 1970s in its earlier production profile of small electronic systems: by means of strategic innovations its small-capacity telephone system was transformed into one based on modular technology. The majority of Swiss research and development resources have been concentrated in the pharmaceutical industry as well as on the production of scientific and precision instruments, and Switzerland has been in the forefront of these rather research intensive industries for decades; moreover, the technological balance of payments of Switzerland is positive. The Netherlands, in turn, has combined domestic and international innovations in her electronics industries. Her position has weakened somewhat in this field, but basically her front-rank situation has remained intact. As regards small countries, those industrial policies are primarily significant which integrate to a high degree the support of innovative processes with the stimulation of a structural switch-over as well as strategies aiming at strengthening international technological and economic competitiveness.

e) *The effectiveness of technological imports* has taken a different turn in countries where technology originating from foreign countries have not represented an "alien body" and could therefore be adopted easily. Accordingly, such countries have relatively easily achieved similar (or, occasionally, even better) results to those of the exporting countries. The utilization of imported technology has developed differently in countries where conditions have been unfavourable.

Importer countries usually buy production processes the technology of which is more capital intensive than those already in operation. As a result, the effects on employment and capital efficiency are often negative. Neither can the sudden increase in demands in the wake of imported technology always be met. Initially imported technology is frequently used by the less developed countries with a lower grade of efficiency than by the exporting countries; in the beginning they usually are unable to reach quality parameters and therefore, their competitiveness in international markets does not always increase in proportion to their technology imports. When importing new products the significance of needs met in a novel way or of a qualitatively new character is very different depending on the field of utilization. Dependence on the external economy is often enhanced by technological imports not adequately compensating the importer. (The problem of how imported capital-intensive technology aids or hinders the increase of employment in the developing countries cannot be dealt with in detail here.) By adopting an adequate technological development policy such problems can be avoided or the disadvantagous effects can be reduced.

f) *The effects of technology imports on economic development depend on economic policy and within that on the technological development policy* as well as on the so-called "follow-up strategy". If a certain technology is adopted without any changes (imitation) the favourable effects on economic development are inevitably more moderate than when an improving, "creative" follow-up (adaptation) is made, since potential profits are increased by the contribution of the recipient country to the further development of imported technology.

If the initation of a novel type of domestic production is furthered by technological development policy in order to meet the needs of the domestic market then technology imports generally take place under different conditions and in other branches of industry than when the establishment of an export basis is aspired to. Irrespective of actual strategic objectives, the situation of the individual sectors (and within them that of the various branches) differs greatly with respect to innovations and technology transfer. The difference is particularly significant between industry and agriculture, as borne out by Hungarian experience. The importance of imported systems of technology organization is greater in agriculture than in industry. The position of services and productive sectors differs, too, in this respect since the internal diffusion of new technologies takes place by different mechanisms. From the point of view of innovations and international technology transfer the public health service has a specific position among the service sectors. In this sector the interrelations and conditions of organizational and technological innovations are particularly closely interwoven. In the productive sector—and particularly in industry—the relationships and conditions of innovation, internal diffusion and technology transfer are rather different. In industry the conditions influencing technological development policy and decisions made in the sphere of companies depend on the development of demand and supply. From the point of view of international technology transfer quantitative and qualitative changes in the demand and supply relations of the individual countries as well as the supply in capital goods sometimes do not comply with the concrete economic targets set originally.

g) *Organizing the introduction and managing the effects of the new technology characteristic of the new stage of the scientific and technological revolution encounters many a difficulty* on the level of the firms too, and managers have to face quite a few new tasks. In addition to strategic questions such as what new products and processes should be introduced, when and how transition from one technology to another should be organized, the problem—causing a considerable headache even to the biggest corporations—of strengthening internal and international cooperation and specialization has to be tackled as well. Under the circumstances of extremely sharp international competition changes and switch-overs in products have to be accomplished very quickly which is not an easy task because of the differences between the existing and the new technology.

The firms are vitally important actors in the fight waged by the leading innovating countries for the monopolized ownership of "high-tech", the hegemony in the field of technology. An important element in strengthening the risk-taking capacity is the establishment of an organization capable of reducing company risks. Technological risks—in the strict sense of the term—are smaller than market risks. It is much more likely that a company will reach its technological objectives with a new product or process than that it will also achieve its market aims.

Since a considerable percentage of innovations is obtained by companies from outside, i.e. these are not the results of their own research and development, it is also very important that managers should have full knowledge of innovations realized in their field of activity.

International openness, integration with centres important in the field of new technology and technology imports demand the elaboration of adequate strategies of innovation and marketing from the importer countries. To pursue an offensive strategy in the global market of today (the aim of such a strategy being unambiguously to achieve a dominant global position) seems generally impossible for follower countries. The success of such a strategy in regional or closed markets naturally cannot be excluded if the company in question is able to establish adequate relationships with the leading technological centres and itself disposes of a considerable innovative basis and supporting industry. This system has been important in Hungary, for instance, when marketing productive systems as innovations internationally. So-called "defensive" innovating and marketing strategies, too, need independent research and development bases, but with the help of such strategies the risk which is involved for the firms that were the first sellers on the market can be considerably reduced. Companies adopting such a strategy can benefit in international competition from the market-creating and market-exploring costs of the first innovators and technology exporters, too. Defensive strategy does not equal "imitation" since a company adopting this strategy is itself an innovator modifying products and, if it relies on licences these are regarded not as ultimate objects but merely as stepping-stones. Defensive strategy demands a highly developed marketing system since it has to compete in the market with leading corporations adopting offensive strategies.

h) *An important task for all great companies is the tracing and forecasting of technological development abroad* in all sectors which are somehow related to their own activities (production input, technology, finished goods). Representative surveys of 508 American companies have led to significant conclusions. In 58 per cent of these firms special managers keep track of foreign developments (in major corporations such work is controlled by one of the vicepresidents). In smaller companies the keeping track of foreign technological development is usually the task of those persons who are in charge of R & D activities.[76]

i) *The situation of workers and trade unions is generally affected adversely by structural problems in the developed Western countries.* In industries producing traditional basic material (e.g. in the iron and steel industry), automation has been developed to the limit and output concentrated on quality products which need less labour. Most branches of the processing industry have used the years of recession to modernize production processes. It was not only the practice of labour-hoarding within the plant—a characteristic feature of the past—which was terminated. The number of automatons and robots has increased everywhere as a result of rationalization, and many big companies regard the number of staff "frozen" at a low level as decisive even when a boom in expected.

An instructive example of rapid rationalization is the Italian corporation, Fiat. Prior to the recession Fiat had turned out and sold an annual volume of 1.5 million cars to guarantee expected profits. This volume was reduced to 1.14 million units by automation and reorganization, moreover it was further reduced to 1 million in 1985. Productivity rose by 40 per cent within three years, and a further average rise of 6–7 per cent is expected annually in the years to follow. As a significant element of reorganization 20 per cent of the production of component parts was "transferred" to subcontractors.

Automatation of office work and services, too, has been considerably stepped up. The demands of technological development are also felt by the management and administrative staff of companies. Automation of office work and revolutionary developments in the field of informatics have made a considerable number of second-level managers superfluous. This stratum has been ousted both from production and management by the possibility of directly programming production, whereas in the field of marketing their position has remained by and large unchanged. These facts indicate that structural unemployment is going to remain a relatively lasting phenomenon.

Recent calculations indicate as characteristic of the United States and the developed Western world in general that in direct proportion to the introduction of the new technology (e.g. adoption of robots) in the various industries part of the unskilled and/or semi-skilled manpower becomes redundant, while at the same time, new jobs demanding a highly qualified working force appear. Every new industrial robot put to work makes the job of an unskilled or semi-skilled worker per shift redundant (e.g. a spot-welder or a painter). The number of workers employed in material handling has been drastically reduced, too. If the use of robots which can sense and react spreads, the semi-skilled workers on the assembly line will also be substituted for by such equipment. As regards the "creation" of jobs, this can be observed in four fields: in the production of robots, in the so-called supporting plants of robot-producing firms, in the engineering offices designing robot systems, and in services. Nowadays a worker producing robots turns out 1.3 robots annually, but presumably this will increase to 1.6 by 1990. Each robot-producing workplace needs 0.93 "supporting" workplaces, every 2.8 robots sold needs a systems engineer, every 5 robots a maintenance man. According to calculations made in the USA there will be 100.000 robots in operation by 1990. This would make 100–200.000 unskilled or semi-skilled workers redundant in the following 6–7 years, whereas it would open up 32–64.000 new jobs for highly qualified manpower. These, however, are only the direct effects. As a result of increased productivity actually much more manpower will become superfluous. Even under present conditions it can be observed that considerable problems crop up in the traditional industries because of the new trends of technological development, thus, for instance, in car and steel production and household electronics, but their influence will be felt also in other branches of production undergoing technological transformation. Not only will some of the manpower employed there become redundant but finding jobs for unskilled young people just starting on their working careers will become more difficult, too. Highly qualified manpower (engineers, technicians) is a rather small proportion of those entering production.[77]

Investigation of the direct effects and consequences of this are needed. New employment opportunities may be opened by increasing income. Service activities may expand. All opportunities, however, seem to be limited in the light of the changes. Most probably, society will be forced to introduce new methods, like job sharing, reduced working hours, etc.

How are all these problems dealt with in a smaller country with a middle level economy, like Hungary? Improving the internal conditions for technological development—and within that those for imported technology—has become an important problem in Hungary, too, since the 1970s.

Efforts were made to reform economic management so as to strengthen the innovative capacity of the economy, including social measures in employment and training. A considerable number of measures were taken in the field of organization at the level both of the national economy and firms. Though these could not be realized to the full and conditions require further important improvements, the stimulation of innovative activity has been more noticeable than before.

Certain measures had been taken in Hungary to improve the internal conditions for innovation.

a) The increasing autonomy of firms, more efficient material incentives, the introduction of regulations replacing the obligatory plan directives—all these have guaranteed in principle a higher degree of freedom of action and better chances for the enterprises to innovate, also. It happened, however, that in the 1980s this was insufficient and further complex incentives were needed to bring about more lasting and further reaching improvements in performance. Of particularly great importance—from the point of view of the development of innovation—have been and will be the improved recognition of highly qualified and creative technological and economic experts, and a better system of material incentives for them.

It has been emphasized that another important task is the coordination of the interests of the different organizations participating in the innovation-chain as well as the strengthening of the conditions of innovating compulsion with the help of the more consistent adoption of market relations. All these demand further institutional and economic changes.

b) The conditions of economic entrepreneurship have improved to a certain extent, and this is of primary importance for innovative activities. Statutory provisions for foundation and operation of "technological development" enterprises have been laid down, a number of research institutes have been transformed into engineering firms, and many subsidiaries and joint ventures have been called into existence with the aim of technological development. In 1985 there were some 40 technological development companies in Hungary. Entrepreneurial zest has been enhanced by more favourable financing and organizational possibilities. By raising various innovation funds the monetary sources aiding the economic utilization of Hungarian inventions have proliferated. The formation of enterprise funds supporting technological development at the national level has become more flexible, too. Bills passed on international joint ventures made it possible to call into being joint ventures of various types.

Naturally the improvement of conditions is not an automatic process. The rapid development and unfolding of new forms of enterprise was not facilitated either by the domestic economic situation or the world economic conditions in the first half of the 1980s. Such development would need more favourable financing possibilities, freer imports and a better economic atmosphere. The system of national economic decision-making (including the licensing of foreign activities) ought to be further simplified.

c) *Several measures were introduced to improve* the efficiency of research and development activities. Decisions on science policy have stipulated that:

— priority should be given to innovation oriented researches (within the scope of new-type ventures taking shape);

— the percentage of university research should be increased and its efficiency enhanced;

— the operational efficiency of scientific research institutes should be considerably enhanced and their activities combined increasingly with practice;

— basic research projects creating actually new ideas should be given absolute priority;

— organization and management of research should be transformed and modernized;

— a better system of stimulation should be developed serving as an incentive for research and development activities to produce concrete results and leading to the practical adoption of scientific achievements.

This opens up new prospects for changes in the practice still dominant in the mid-1980s. In scientific research, however, enhanced efficiency can be realized only in the long run due to the combined effect of personal, organizational and material obstacles. The importance of human conditions in the increase of the efficiency of scientific research is self-evident. The most suitable experts ought to be employed to do research work in institutes, at the universities, in industry and other places. To do this, however, it is not enough to improve their material conditions but also the practice of scientific training and selection must be improved: indeed, the quality of the system of education as a whole and particularly of higher education, ought to be raised, too. As regards the organization and management of research work the feed-back effect from application and marketing must be structurally integrated. In the interest of necessary change an adequate degree of flexibility must be provided. The establishment of interdisciplinary, complex research centres and other problem-oriented complex organizations should be encouraged.

Scientific international relations should be strengthened and regularized. The increased internationalization of research activity in Hungary is another highly significant task (e.g. agreements on specialization and cooperation, establishment of subcontractor firms). Strengthening international specialization and cooperation is necessary in other relations, too. The slow improvement of the internal conditions of the innovation process seems unable to neutralize the disadvantages deriving from the smallness of the country. The easing of such disadvantages is possible only by means of strengthening international cooperation and of increasingly integrating international technology trade and the major technology centres. As regards Hungary, the conditions of and possibilities for cooperation with the various developed Western countries and the member states of the CMEA are different.

In examining the world market for new technology and the mechanism of technology transfer we have dealt primarily with cooperation with the developed capitalist countries in the foregoing chapter. Let us now go more thoroughly into the situation and the role of the CMEA countries in this sphere of the economy.

5. The Markets for the New Technology and the Socialist Countries of Eastern Europe

The scientific and technological potential of any country or country group can be evaluated on the strength of its capacity to guarantee the technological conditions necessary for its own development as well as to what extent and of what level it is able to contribute to the technological development of the other regions of the world. The degree of international techno-economic vulnerability is also an important indication of its capacity. The problems of the European CMEA countries in the world trade in technology have increased in the first half of the 1980s. One of the most serious problems of the economic development of the member countries has been that the process of new courses and trends in technological development has not been rapid enough to reduce the backlog (as compared to the developed Western countries) and to strengthen their position in the international market for new technology. In the Hungarian economy, for example, new tasks have predominated: sources of manpower have been by and large exhausted at the present technological level; under the present conditions of development and efficiency increasing investment to the detriment of consumption would result in the further deterioration of the efficiency of funds and would trigger off internal tensions; the backwardness of the infrastructure has become a major obstacle to economic progress. In addition, the equipment of industrial plants established in the previous stage of development has to be renewed and, at the same time, as every CMEA country has to modernize technology and industrial structure. Without these it is impossible to considerably reduce material and energy consumption and to increase productivity at a greater rate. Under the present circumstances the strengthening of the innovative capacity of the economy and international technological cooperation has become more important than ever.

As mentioned before, the strengthening of the technological and scientific potential and the international relations of the European socialist countries was put on the agenda by the new conditions of world affairs and the new phase of the arms race. The questions were put in the West in the following way: to what extent are the socialist countries, first and foremost the Soviet Union, capable of meeting the requirements of their defence under the conditions of the new military technology, and simultaneously tackling the technological tasks facing the civilian economy? Has technological import not been upgraded in these countries and are they not ready to make some political concessions for this reason? Could they not be weakened in this way by restricting trade, and could they achieve highly important military and economic strategical advantages in that stage of development by means of technological imports?

Debates centring on the efficiency and expediency of the restrictions of technology transfer introduced by the United States and some Western countries also played a part in putting the problems of technological development and technology trade on the agenda.[78]

The need to step up technological development and strengthen international cooperation is a top-priority concern of experts in all CMEA countries. To study the conditions of the further development of relations both between East and West and in trade with the Third World countries is regarded as a highly important question.

As pointed out before, the part played by the European CMEA countries in the international (non-CMEA) market in new technology is smaller than desirable though the technological potential of the CMEA countries has increased considerably between 1950 and 1980. In the period under review a significant industrial, research and development basis was established by the CMEA countries, moreover their share in global industrial production surpassed 23 per cent in the early 1980s as compared to a mere 17–22 per cent around 1960. According to the official statistics of UNESCO almost 40 per cent of global scientific and technological manpower is concentrated in the European CMEA countries. Naturally this ratio in itself does not indicate the efficiency of manpower utilization. Efficiency—as is well-known—is highly dependent on the education and training of manpower, the organization of its activities, technological standards, practical experiences, etc. As regards efficiency, the socialist countries lag far behind the developed Western countries. In other fields, however, a favourable comparison can be drawn for some of the socialist countries. The great number of scientific and technological manpower is in itself an important asset sometimes even counterbalancing the insufficiencies of equipment. Nearly one third of patents applied for originate from the European socialist countries. The number of patents, of course, does not reveal the quality of these patents. Experience shows that some of the patents are obviously of negligible significance for technological development. Some patents are "inapplicable" and of a trivial nature. Despite this fact there are quite a few patents in the European CMEA countries which are of great importance or potentially significant.

A relatively high proportion of the national income of the European socialist countries (2–3 per cent) is spent on research and development. The ratio is higher in the Soviet Union, lower in the other CMEA countries. The share of the European CMEA countries in global research and development expenditures has been 28–9 per cent (Soviet Union 22 per cent, the other European CMEA countries 5–7 per cent).[79]

The international comparison of R & D data is naturally not exact and the ratios do not reflect the efficiency of utilization either. It is, however, undeniable that the CMEA countries represent a complex and significant scientific and technological potential. The technological development capacity of the Soviet Union is particularly significant. Its output could be higher with better organization and incentives, and with closer international relations.

a) The industries of the European CMEA countries are generally characterized by middle level technology. Within that, however, their technological progress is impeded by considerable inequalities. Some industries or companies have a high level of technology, and their product patterns, too, are rather similar to the average level of the developed industrial countries. Other industries in these countries, however, correspond to the average of the middle level countries both as regards character and quality as well as the technology applied.

b) The Soviet Union is the most complex country of the region as regards technological and scientific capacity. It has developed a high ratio of its technological-scientific achievements by itself, moreover the overwhelming part of its technological development is founded on internal resources. High-tech industry plays an important part, too, in its economy but such technology is distributed unevenly. The technological gap between the individual industries is relatively wide. There are some high-tech industries in the other European CMEA countries, too, but these are usually isolated from the other parts of the economy. Their spread in the other branches of the economy is hindered by a lack of funds, the weakness of the organizational, management and incentive systems of the economy as well as a shortage of specialists with adequate technological and organization experience. There is only occasional contact between production and research and development.

c) Foreign technology is imported by all European CMEA countries. The extent and character of dependence on technology imports differs, of course, within the individual countries and sectors of the economy. And since these are as a rule "follower" countries from the point of view of technology, the historically developed and very slowly changing technological development or follow-up strategy has a considerable influence on the degree of dependence. Thus, a powerful and manifold technological-scientific basis has been developed in the Soviet Union, nevertheless a mainly "imitating" strategy had been adopted (partly under the pressure of necessity) for decades, i.e. products already on the market have been acquired and, as a consequence, some branches of industry have fallen behind from the point of view of technology. Imitation but rarely improves the parameters of a product as compared to the original one. The production technology adopted is usually also more backward and less efficient. However, even this strategy resulted in favourable changes in the parameters of products introduced or it their production technology.

The significance of technology imports originating from spheres outside the CMEA has increased in the present stage of economic development (since the early 1970s), but not because in the CMEA countries new technology needed for the significant modernization of industry, agriculture and the services is insufficient both as regards quantity and quality or is lacking altogether. It is true that some sectors are facing such problems; however, increased dependence on technology imports is rather related to the fact that participation in global scientific-technological cooperation is unavoidable for further progress at the present development level of the CMEA countries.

The CMEA countries were unable to achieve scientific-technological autarky. At the previous—lower—level of development, however, branches of industry had been established, and products had been introduced the technology of which had been less complex and the development of which had not demanded such a vast research and industrial background as the high-tech industries of the late twentieth century. The modernization of these branches of industry is still impossible without technology imports. Changing the technological development policy is attended by many difficulties partly rooted in strategic causes. Internal development is stimulated by unfavourable experience relating to Western strategic restrictions. It is obvious that neither the Soviet Union nor the other CMEA countries can permanently depend on technology imports from the West in sectors of vital importance from the point of view of national defence. The fact that technological chauvinism still haunts the world constitutes a further problem. Even in non-strategic sectors the opinion crops up time and again that wherever possible everything ought to be researched independently and imports of technology ought to be avoided. This view is motivated by "capacity" and not by the costs of developing the new technology as compared to those of technology imports. Technological chauvinism is intensified by some unfavourable experience gained with technology imports. It actually happened in a number of countries that

Western technology was imported at a high price even in sectors where cheaper and better quality technology could have been produced. Many examples could be cited when imported technology was made use of inefficiently. In the latter cases, however, responsibility lay not with the sources but rather with the mechanism of utilization.

d) Currently the socialist countries are able to (and actually do) play an increasing role in the international technology market not only as importers but as the developers and exporters of new technologies as well. In their mutual foreign trade and their trade with the developing countries the share of research intensive products has increased. However, the share of such products is lower in their exports to the West though reciprocity could be greater even in East-West relations at the present level of their evolution. Today even their relations within the CMEA cannot be regarded as independent of global technological cooperation. Their relations established with the technologically more developed Western world and even those with other socialist countries cannot be successful and efficient without active participation in the international division of labour. Lacking such relations, their technological progress would be slower, moreover their backlog as compared to the advanced Western countries would grow at an even faster rate.

e) As regards the foreign trade of the European socialist countries, the majority of machines and equipment imported still originates from the CMEA region. The ratio of such imports is different in each country and branch of industry (it surpassed 70 per cent at the beginning of the 1980s). With its share of 23 per cent the GDR rates first among the intra-region suppliers. The share of the Soviet Union in intra-CMEA exports was 20 per cent, that of Czechoslovakia 18, of Poland 16 and of Hungary 10 per cent. The leading importer was the Soviet Union buying half of total exported supplies in the early 1980s. A considerable part of the technology trade within the CMEA represented—according to national statistics—medium technological standards. In intra-CMEA trade the following problems arose in the early 1980s.

— As a result of parallel development through East-West relations in the 1970s, the competitive character of the economies of the socialist countries in their mutual trade increased in the sectors using advanced technologies, and convertible currency imports embodied in the products introduced considerably increased. In general, the need to import from the West for production has increased in this way.

— Machinery, equipment and other products embodying new technology with a high Western import content are offered for sale in developed Western countries by the socialist countries, partly because it is difficult to get the convertible currency input in their mutual trade recognized.

— At the same time, the CMEA countries strive to get in exchange from each highly developed partner goods of great research intensity and comprising possibly much Western imports. Thus not only is actual cooperation impeded in the introduction of the new technology but, lacking convertibility, cooperation and also specialization is hindered until they are unable to gain enough hard currency.

In the interrelationship of the CMEA countries the conditions for selling advanced technology (i.e. technology marketable in any market and already operating) hardly differ from the general conditions characterizing the world market. At the same time, they prefer selling technology regarded as new by world standards, first of all to

Western corporations. Incidentally, such technology is often marketed through Western firms in other CMEA countries as well.

— Though informal relations among the scientific institutes of the CMEA countries continue to be of great importance, in some sectors they are not substantial enough to further economic development adequately.

f) Let us now examine East-West technological relations as reflected by machinery and equipment. New technology acquired by the European CMEA countries made up 28 per cent of their technology imports in the early 1980s. From the late 1960s on such imports played a highly important part in the progress of some industries as well as in the modernization of product patterns. Their share rose to 28 per cent by 1970 and to 41 per cent by 1975, whereas it has declined ever since.[80]

— 4–7 per cent of the total export volume of advanced technology of the West was bought by the CMEA countries in the early 1980s.

The share of individual countries in imports of advanced technology to the CMEA region was as follows in the 1970s (according to UN data and national statistics). (As a comparison the share in intra-CMEA technology imports in 1980, is given in percentages, in brackets.)

Soviet Union	44.9	(49.7)
Poland	15.7	(13.1)
Romania	15.6	(4.4)
Hungary	7.9	(5.2)
Czechoslovakia	7.7	(10.2)
GDR	4.5	(9.7)
Bulgaria	3.7	(7.7)

It should be noted that data relating to the GDR do not include technology imports from the FRG.

The main sources of Western technology exports directed to the socialist countries—as mentioned before—were the Federal Republic of Germany, Japan and France.

Since the beginning of the 1980s the increased import of new technology by the European socialist countries has slowed down and even decreased in some places. The following factors were instrumental in this:

— The deterioration of the international liquidity of certain socialist countries, the narrowing of their export possibilities, the high level debt-service and the considerable difficulties in getting new credits (inclusive of export credits);

— stricter strategic restrictions;

— the slowing down of economic development and the reduction or stagnation of investments;

— unfavourable experience as regards the effects and costs of imported Western technologies.

g) As exporters the European CMEA countries participate in rather a limited way in the markets of new technology outside the CMEA region; 5–7 per cent of technology exported to the developing countries came from CMEA countries between 1955 and 1980, and their share decreased in the 1970s. In 1985 it was 5 per cent.

The majority of technology exported by the CMEA countries consisted of turnkey plant, machines and equipment, transport vehicles, transfer of know-how and training of experts. The percentage of licences sold was much lower. The CMEA countries exported mainly medium level technology on favourable terms, and such technology complied with the possibilities and needs of the Third World countries. Of technology exported to developing countries by the CMEA countries 80–90 per cent went to twenty developing countries. The potential exports of the CMEA countries are actually better in this field, too, than their actual performance.

The volume of high-level technology exports from the CMEA countries to the developed Western countries is extremely small in physical terms and lags far behind their actual achievements. Technology exports to Western countries represent mainly highly valuable innovations, sometimes even of outstanding significance. American firms bought 125 licences from the Soviet Union in the 1970s, the value of which amounted to approximately $ 50 million. Japan, too, is an important buyer of licences and has mainly purchased innovations for her steel industry from the Soviet Union. France bought Soviet champagne licences. The soft contact lens originated from Czechoslovakia, and its patent and licence was bought by a great number of countries.[81]

Export was realized chiefly in the form of licences sold to Western companies, partly because the CMEA countries were hardly in the position to sell their products turned out for export on Western markets, partly by the restricted nature of independent development, and partly because they were unable to supply the necessary capital goods. Owing to the differences of standards or different technological design requirements, the CMEA countries frequently cannot meet the conditions necessary for marketing the product in the West and are therefore dependent on their Western partners. In addition to their domestic economic difficulties (or connected with them), the technology exports of the CMEA countries also suffer as a result of insufficient knowledge of Western market conditions; they have very few firms in Western markets which are capable of selling technology and operating locally; moreover, they have few experts familiar with technology marketing.

The restricted nature and the difficulties of exporting developed new technology react upon the technology imports of the CMEA countries rendering efficient cooperation in the field of high-tech industry difficult with Western firms.

h) Difficulties related to the internal spread of the new technology have an unfavourable effect on the position of the socialist countries in the international technology trade. The main factors of this are the following:
— a shortage of experts and funds which leads to the conservation of obsolete technologies;
— lack of readiness to take risks;
— lack of "innovation pressure" on the micro-level, the main reason being the monopolistic position of many enterprises;
— insufficiency of organizational forms capable of integrating the interests of enterprises with technological development;
— the restricted nature of technological communication among the enterprises;
— the relatively narrow scope of the diffusion of technological-economic information.

The fact that the defence sector operates in isolation from all the other industries also plays a part in the difficulties of the diffusion of the new technology. Though it was often pointed out by the leaders of the Soviet economy that it would be necessary to spread technological achievements brought about or operated by the defence industry into everyday civil life faster, these declared objectives have been realized only to a limited extent up to now.

i) The position of the socialist countries is made rather difficult by the stragetic embargo applied against them. The needs of the CMEA countries in the world trade in technology have become more diversified. At the same time, however, their capacities have improved, too, and they are now able to solve complex technological development tasks independently and even to export new technology.

It is evident that if the socialist countries do not receive the machines and equipment ordered because of the embargo this can cause harm to them until they are in the position to meet their requirements from other sources. If, however, they have to buy quickly, prices are higher. Certain losses may occur as a result of interrupted production, too. Yet, under present world market and technological conditions it is almost always possible to purchase similar products from other sources.

Since the technology adopted in the CMEA countries (and particularly in the Soviet Union) is mostly domestically produced and the intra-regional turnover of the region in imported technology is of a great volume, technology imports from the West constitute a relatively small ratio, though such imported technology is used in highly important sectors and is therefore, of great importance. The CMEA countries were often obliged in the past, too, to restructure their resources thereby stepping up the rate of scientific technological development in sectors in need of politically significant imports. This happened in the 1980s when a more intensive development of microelectronics became a matter of urgency. Though the reallotment of scarce internal funds can cause short-term difficulties, losses are compensated in the long run by an increased technological-economic potential.

The development of economic relations and the completion of transactions is slowed down and even throttled by the intricate procedure of checking and licensing combined with embargo measures, since risks and uncertainties are increased by them for both buyers and sellers. Such measures have negative effects on those Western companies involved which are ready to trade with socialist countries. Their rivals in other countries, however, skilfully exploit the newly revealed opportunities. (In such cases socialist countries prefer firms regarded as less risky partners.) Western companies retracting from agreements or backtracking because of risks of East-West trade suffer serious losses.

At the beginning of the 1980s the ratio of products under embargo was still relatively limited, affecting only a minor part of actual trade. Thus, the opinion that under present, peaceful conditions strategic restrictions have greater psychological than economic effect seems fully justified. Such limitations actually add to the deterioration of the general atmosphere and tend to declare magnify intentions.

6. International Relations and Future Changes in Science and Technology

The analysis of the changes and problems related to the new technological revolution indicate that the spread of the process has profound international consequences.

a) The hierarchical character of the international technology market will remain but with increasing competition in every segment of the hierarchy. The innovating countries at the top will increase their efforts to gain ground in the key areas, especially in computers, robots, telecommunication and biotechnology. They are going to increase their research and development potential by using more funds, more efficient national policies and international cooperation in their attempt to become more competitive. Developed countries on the lower level of the hierarchy will compete in a given segment of the technology market with methods similar of those above. They will try to achieve and maintain a leading position in one or another branch of advanced technology and at the same time maintain a high degree of integration with the major innovating countries through their transnational corporations and intergovernmental cooperation programs. Middle level Western countries are trying to find their place in the jig-saw of international specialization, utilizing their cheaper skilled labour forces, and the channels of the transnational corporations in the framework of carefully selected national projects. On this basis they will continue to rely on imports of technology but simultaneously strengthen their national innovative capabilities, in which product innovation will remain the most important field. These countries, will have to maintain especially strong adjustment abilities. Technological change will increasingly differentiate the international position of the developing countries. The technological capability of these countries is already highly unequal and the inequalities are going to grow. Some of the developing countries already have strong and globally important research and development potential in the modern sector of their economy (such as India, Brazil and Mexico), oriented basically to the local market. They will maintain strong contacts with the more developed world, sometimes offering access to their large domestic markets in exchange for advanced technology. They will continue to concentrate on the establishment and strengthening of indigenous research and development potentials. Some other developing countries will concentrate on the achievement of different cooperation agreements with the developed countries as suppliers of parts, components or offering assembly facilities for them in the global operations of the transnational corporations. Their competition for the use of global possibilities is increasing. The European socialist countries will continue their efforts to increase cooperation with the Western industrial countries in areas where it is possible, at the same time they plan to increase regional cooperation in advanced technology in the framework of international projects. The success of their efforts to upgrade their technological level will depend to a great extent on the improvement of internal conditions for innovation.

b) While the different areas of scientific and technological development offer great possibilities, it is highly questionable how and where they will be utilized, due to their different financial, organizational and problem solving characteristics. The revolution in the field of microelectronics offers for example a sharp decline in the cost of computation. Satellites offer dramatic improvements in the speed and costs of long distance communications and information. Computer-aided design and reprogrammable robots will permit small specialized production runs for various products. Improvements in transport, especially in air transport, will continue by such measures as all weather landing capacity, short take off, new engines etc. Progress in biotechnology is offering further improvement in yields, quicker crop rotations and more efficient drugs etc. Development in the materials sector is bringing a variety of new multifunctional composite materials, interpenetrating material structures, etc. which will facilitate the solution of many technical problems and increase durability, reducing the costs of manufacturing. The transformation of the energy sector and the efficient use of energy is offered by the new achievements in that area, bringing a higher degree of security in the world's energy economy. The utilization of all these and other potentials depends however on the flexibility of agents, business firms, governments and international organizations. The firms, especially the larger ones, will have to think and act within the framework of long-term strategy, which, by definition is more competitive than cooperative in the present world market structure.

Those aspects of competitiveness that are connected with the technological potentials will gain especially great importance. The response of the governments must accommodate this. This would imply increasing international openness in certain cases, better national adjustment policies in the field of employment, regional development, and environmental protection. Improvement in the conditions of international cooperation must also be a basic task of government policies, promoting the mobility of people, good funds and knowledge. International research and development projects must be encouraged.

It is highly doubtful whether those requirements will be fulfilled. Governments are also obliged to promote international competitiveness. They often try to solve problems emerging in the field of science and technology at the expense of other countries. They are, and will increasingly be, in conflict over the development and sales of advanced products, being afraid of the technology gaps and the loss of an alleged leading position. Technological nationalism will also remain a strong force creating new conflicts. Technological protectionism against political allies and adversaries may also increase. The danger of global technological anarchy is of course not isolated from other, economic and political problems. They do not represent independent variables. They may, however, increase the difficulties and tensions in the world economy.

Strategic restrictions in the international trade in technology can occasionally result in difficulties for the socialist countries since such restrictions tend to have long-range effects and afflict all the members of the Warsaw Pact. The effects of restrictions can be counterbalanced by intensifying cooperation among the CMEA countries but only if the functional mechanism of the CMEA is adequately developed further and the interests of the research institutes and firms of member states are better coordinated. If this aim is not achieved then a mechanism making more flexible and faster actions possible ought to be established at least in the high-tech industries.

c) A further important conclusion of international technology trade has been the realization that the efficient use of imported technology depends on the general technological and economic conditions of the recipient countries, the innovative capacity, flexibility and adaptive capacity of their economies. The factors determining such features are highly important from the point of view of operating technologies acquired through imports, internal diffusion of such technologies as well as a lasting integration with the world economy.

Technology imports themselves are not suitable for improving the situation of low-capacity and rigid economies, and occasionally can even worsen conditions.

From the point of view of the efficiency of technology imports an economic policy and/or a technological development policy taking into account the situation, the development chances and capacities of the country in question, as well as calling into existence adequate means for the realization of such a policy, is also of utmost importance.

d) International political factors do and will play very important role in the global changes brought about by science and technology. The most direct influence of the political factors is seen in the arms race in the framework of which weapon improvement and modernization together with the efforts to invent and introduce the new generation of weapon systems is a strong and permanent stimulative force. Military research and development has its special logic and reacts to driving forces which differ from civilian ones. They are interrelated with strategic doctrines, which provide general long-term guidance not only to economic, socio-political and psychological issues but also to technological development. New technological breakthroughs on the other hand often lead to changes in military doctrines. Military research and development is highly concentrated and mission oriented. The motivations for the increases always tend to achieve maximal rather than optimal results. They project the arms race into the future since the major innovations in the military field are always inducing the adversaries not only to introduce similar systems but also defence weapons which neutralize their impact. The spiral of offensive and defensive systems is a generating force which extends the cycle in the case of a major system to at least 10–15 years and in certain cases even longer. While technological changes did improve the chances of arms control agreements (like for example the progress in the technology allowing more accurate monitoring), in the political environment of the late twentieth century the probability of advanced technology being used for military purposes is extremely strong, even though it does not increase the security of those who initiate the new waves of the arms race. The potentially dual use of many components of the new scientific and technological revolution together with the role of technological capabilities in the arms race maintains a large part of the main innovations in strategic subordination.

Through the global spread of the arms race many developing countries have improved access to modern military technology. Production technology, know-how, licences and other facilities are offered by many industrial countries to them under competitive conditions.

In the transfer process, in many cases governments act on behalf of the arms industries and there are many examples of covert technology transfer operations.

e) The increasing role of national technology policies and intergovernmental relations in the field of science and technology opened up new branches of public administration and diplomacy. The importance of these government activities is on the increase. A new technological bureaucracy is emerging for policy making, promotion control and cooperation.

This bureaucracy differs from the traditional branches of governments not only in the skills required. They have to deal with the problem as a whole system and not in piecemeal fashion. Instead of using short-range policies, they have to work with long-range strategies which integrate socio-economic, scientific, engineering, industrial, political, national and international goals and means.

Different intergovernmental organizations were established for the regulation of certain issues, like intellectual property rights (WIPO) and the management of certain cooperation projects.

In the framework of the political or economic changes in the world of the late twentieth century the further progress of the new scientific and technological revolution will greatly influence the international system and pose new demands for international cooperation. The structural changes, problems and imbalances and efforts to solve them cross the boundaries of the present national decision-making centres and international organizations.

Part Four

Structural Disturbances in the World Economy and the Changing International Economic Relations in the Late Twentieth Century

1. Structural Interrelations between World Output and World Trade

As Disraeli said, the paradox of change is that it is constant. Structural disturbances, global or regional imbalances are permanent characteristic features of world economic development. They are closely related to the process of change. The intensity and significance of structural imbalances depend on their causes which may be connected with economic policy failures, mismanagement of national economies or adjustment problems. Their direct and indirect consequences may also greatly differ.

The structural disturbances of the late 1980s, which may well spread to the greater part of the next decade have many roots. The technological transformation, the changes in world output and consumption patterns, unequal and insufficient policy responses to the changes on a national and international level are the main factors of the structural problems which are often at a critical point.

In economics, too, structure is a complex notion. It can be defined in the broader sense of the term as the sum total of relations between the elements of the given system (production, consumption, national economy, world economy and so forth). And since there is an interrelationship of various types of elements in every economic unit which can be regarded as a system, the structure of the world economy, too, can be interpreted in several ways.

According to one of the interpretations the political structure and the network of political institutions of the world economy is the system of the relations within states and inter-state relationships. In this sense the changes in power relations and their consequences are of vital importance in the world economy (as emphasized in Part Two).

The microstructure of the world economy, the international market network, the international trade in commodities, money, capital and labour as well as the institutions established for the organization of markets represent another dimension of the structure and reflect other interconnections: all these are closely linked to production and consumption within the framework of the states.

Changes in the production and consumption of the states are increasingly connected by the new relationships between global production and trade and by the higher degree of international division of labour. The patterns of production and consumption within the states as well as relationships among the individual sectors and within these sectors are closely interlinked, internationally, too.

The development level of the structures is indicated by the proportion of modern, more efficient sectors as well as by the depth and intensity of inter-sectoral relations, virtually identical in countries with different social systems. The character of the structure depends, however, on the systemic values, too, since ultimately these have an effect on the actual circumstances shaping the structure. Countries with different structures coexist in the world economy of the late twentieth century. The majority of the world population lives in countries which have come into being on the ruins of the colonial system and this has resulted in a distorted, one-sided economy. It was on this basis that the so-called "dual structure" came into being in some of these countries. A relatively modern sector has developed, linked mainly or exclusively with the production process of the metropolitan country, more often than not by means of a mono-exporter (depending on one commodity only) and at the same time, agriculture based on traditional subsistence farming and a handicraft trade have survived, too. Certain connections among these sectors have come into being. These, however, have not developed into coherent, organic relations among the sectors in all the countries. The economies with distorted structures coexist in the world economy with some countries of complex, vertically and horizontally integrated structures which, in case of emergency, would be able to develop on a self-sufficient basis.

The production patterns are influenced by the scale of the countries (the domestic market), natural conditions and geographical position, as well.

It follows from the above that the notion "national economic complex" necessarily indicates highly different structures in the world economy of the late twentieth century. The actual forms of the self-sustaining structures also vary, depending on the specific conditions and circumstances of the states. Differences have been further increasing in the wake of the differentiation of structures in the past 20–25 years. This course of development did not always move, however, in the direction where the most efficient utilization of national resources could be achieved.

The economic structure of the developed industrial countries was generally characterized by an increasing international specialization within the branches of industry and by organic and intensive relations between the individual sectors and industries. The level of these structures is different and so is their specialization under the influence of actual conditions. The production and consumption of the countries as well as the structural changes within their economy are linked by the international division of labour.

The causes and consequences of the changes in production and consumption structures of the national economies are manifold. On a world economic scale the causes and consequences of structural changes are especially complex, because they are interrelated with political and power relations as well.

Of the driving forces of the structural changes in the economy, technological progress—the effects of which on the structure of production could be felt most directly as a result of industrial development—accurately reflects the complex nature of international factors. The concrete effects of this component are influenced by the national innovative capacity and international technology transfer as well as by market positions.

The changes based on other economic or political decisions, changes in the international division of labour (e.g. the extremely rapid expansion of the newly industrialized countries in certain industries) also have played an outstanding part in triggering structural changes. Naturally, these factors are closely interrelated. A series of chain reactions can be triggered in economic life by changes in one or another economic sector or industry. From this aspect the development of branches of industry which in their very scope of technological significance define the positions of other economic sectors (industries) are of vital importance. Thus microelectronics has transformed the situation of almost every branch of industry and was instrumental in shaping new structural conditions.

Structural changes are motivated by the natural and social conditions and factors of economic growth but their effects on the various economic sectors are highly dissimilar. The degree of divergence depends on the part played by the various factors in economic growth. The reasons for dissimilarities are manifold. They hang on international relations of dependence, resolutions of economic policy, factors of demand, technological and economic potentials, natural endowments and other factors. In the course of development structure becomes more flexible, its efficiency increases and the significance of sectors with higher productivity grows. Mechanisms take shape, stepping up the rate of structural changes in the desired direction, rendering it possible to diminish troubles resulting from the necessary changes. Such a mechanism for instance is, the institutionalized public support of inter-sectoral capital flows, the strengthening of labour mobility as well as direct or indirect influence on consumption.

Structural changes within the states take place in a system of interrelations between production and consumption. The vectors of such correlations, however, can be highly dissimilar as a result of specific conditions in the states involved.

The direct determinant of increased production and structural changes is obviously in demand. This reflects partly certain fundamental human needs (e.g. food, clothing, shelter) and partly indicates the effects of production, accumulation and external markets, and also expresses the social consequences of meeting demands, the character of society, its basic objectives and its scale of values.

As regards consumption, the world economy is as variegated as is production in the last fifteen years of the twentieth century. In many a developing countries the great mass of the population, living within the framework of a traditional subsistence economy consume the overwhelming part of their production themselves or hand it over to the state or the landlord in kind. Just as centuries ago, part of their products are exchanged for goods turned out by other producers. Wherever it is possible the producers attempt to sell a certain part of the products turned out by the subsistence economy sector in the market for cash. Thus increasingly they make contact with the market economy. Despite the disintegration of the subsistence economy a considerable part of the world population continues to live and work under such circumstances. A great part of their traditional means of production and consumer goods is produced by the households, the tribal or village communities. In the more developed countries of the world economy, production—in full accord with technological standards—has been extended incessantly whereas consumption has become rather diversified. In the internationally interlinked market of commodities and services, the range of goods almost doubles every decade. New products appear on the market and old ones are constantly being eliminated from production.

The relationship between production and consumption is rather complex when economic development has reached a high level. New demands are created by the development and structural differentiation of production which in turn serve as new incentives for the extension of production and the development of the product.

The appropriate correction of the main trends and pattern of consumption tends to be an independent socio-economic task. The level of income, the rational distribution and exchange of commodities and services among the countries as well as within the national economies, the price, income and consumption policies, the system of objectives and measures affecting the pattern of consumption—all these are highly important elements of public economic policies in our times.

International economic power relations are significant factors from the point of view of structural disturbances of global production and the utilization of goods produced. Eight countries turning out almost 75 per cent of global output (the United States, Canada, the Soviet Union, Japan, the Federal Republic of Germany, France, Great Britain and Italy) are of outstanding importance not only for their significance in international affairs but also because the various new trends—the main factors of structural changes—of technological progress and international division of labour have had their origins in their economies.

The most general characteristics of the structural changes, and transformation of the world economy are the changes in the ratios between the main branches of production and consumption. These are modified, as a rule, slower and therefore easier to evaluate.

According to global data—excluding financial, "public" and some other services not linked closely with production—in the 30 years between 1950 and 1980, the following major changes took place, as regards the proportions of the main sectors of production:
— The ratio of (extracting and processing) industrial output rose from 43 to 49 per cent.
— The share of the building industry increased from 8 to 9 per cent.
— The ratio of transport (all of its forms included) also rose, from 7 to 9 per cent.
— The proportion of agricultural production, however, considerably decreased (from 20 to 12 per cent).
— The share of wholesale and retail trade together diminished only slightly (from 22 to 21 per cent).[82]

The intensity of these structural changes has been rather different in each of the country groups and major regions, and the differences are even greater if services and material production are examined together (Gross Domestic Product) as the ratio of services has increased very rapidly in a number of countries.

Changes in the ratios between the major sectors are quite significant in the developed industrialized countries. The proportion of material production in the gross domestic product diminishes everywhere. The percentage of agriculture decrease from 12 to 3 per cent, that of the manufacturing industry from 28 to 23 per cent in the developed industrialized Western countries between 1960 and 1985. At the same time, the ratio of services increased from 48 to more than 60 per cent. The effects of these structural changes had been felt already prior to the 1960s and had influenced the economies of the developed Western countries. Thus the diminishing ratio of manufacturing industry restricted the increase of productivity (as regards the whole of the economy) since the growth of productivity and real incomes was lower in the non-industrial sectors of the leading Western countries. However, the effects of the fluctuations of industrial production had a weaker influence on economic development as well. Between 1973 and 1983 the growth rate of industrial production decreased to a greater extent than that of the gross domestic product in all the leading industrial Western countries (with the exception of Japan); this was a result of the moderating impact of the other sectors.

The change in the ratios of the major areas of consumption (personal consumption, public consumption, investments) was globally even slower in the past 30 years. Nevertheless, changes are very significant in some of the categories and regions.

The change in the pattern of world output and consumption has taken place in close interaction with the development of world trade.

In the period following World War II the significance of world trade increased constantly. The growth of world trade surpassed that of the world output: world production increased by an annual 5 per cent whereas world trade increased by 7.2 per cent between 1950 and 1973. While world exports came to only 10 per cent of world output in 1950, their proportion was more than 20 per cent in 1980. The cause and incentives of growth were different in the various periods and regions, and differences in the rate of growth, too, changed all the time. It was particularly in the developed Western countries that the ratio of imports to consumption increased spectacularly.

Intensified division of labour in industry, rapid economic growth, the acceleration of industrialization in the developing countries and the economic transformation in the CMEA region all served as incentives for the expansion of world trade. Under the effect of international capital flows, production, too, became internationalized serving as a further incentive for world trade.[83]

Under the effects of the two world-wide recessions of the 1970s and the 1980s, the growth of world trade slowed down and its volume then temporarily declined. There are, of course, long-term factors in the structural connections of world output and world trade which—despite all the problems—may stimulate the expansion of world trade. As regards the developed Western countries, the expansion of foreign trade is stimulated by the following factors.

— Beginning with the early 1960s intra-sectoral international trade considerably increased coming to an annual average increase of 10 per cent till the end of the 1970s. The multinational corporations were instrumental in this, since they were capable— within the scope of their systems—of organizing and locating their production and sourcing in the most cost-effective way. This process has been going on ever since. Another important incentive for the expansion of intra-industrial trade has been the scientific and technological revolution.

— Global specialization in engineering industries has increased. This continued even in the years of recession and stimulated the expansion of foreign trade. Its significance will not diminish in the future either.

— The demand of the oil-exporting countries for capital goods, war material, consumers' goods and food-products has considerably increased since the mid-1970s (the main suppliers of these were the developed capitalist countries of the Western world). Despite the drop in oil prices these countries will remain important markets in the future, too.

The increasing role of the industrial exporters from among the developing countries has also provided considerable opportunities for the developed Western countries. If the political and economic conditions are favourable the expansion of trade, made possible by an improvement in East-West relations, could also become a significant factor.

The proportion of services in world trade—and particularly in trade of the developed industrial countries—has increased. The importance of services in the exports of a country is determined by four factors: the size of the service sector, the shape of the service sector, the natural endowments of the country and comparative costs. Globally, the export of services nearly doubled between 1970 and 1980: it grew from $ 194.4 billion to $ 382.4 billion. The share of shipping was 14 per cent; of passenger transport 4 per cent; of other kinds of transportation, 12 per cent and of tourism 24 per cent in 1980.[84] The role of services in world trade continued to increase during the 1880s and it has become a central issue in trade policies.

The significance of foreign trade in relation to output has increased particularly fast for certain groups of developing countries since the 1970s.

— Under the effect of their high external earnings some of the oil-exporting countries started considerable development programmes the financing of which demanded the raising of their export incomes. The importance of exports also grew for structural reasons in countries which did not invest large amounts of money abroad. (Incomes derived from this source succeeded in balancing the drop of exports in some oil-exporting countries at the beginning of the 1980s; in the majority of the OPEC countries, however, this was not the case.)

— The internal evolution and model of industrialization of the rapidly industrializing countries and countries exporting industrial goods made it imperative for them to increase their exports.

For the decisive majority of developing countries with a monoculture or monoexporting structure, the stepping up of exports is—and will remain in the future—the basic source of their external foreign exchange income. The realization of their economic development programmes depends largely on this income.

— In highly indebted countries, the importance of exports has grown because of rising debt service burdens.

— The increased consumption of the oil-producing and oil-exporting countries functioned as an incentive to step up imports.

The importance of foreign trade for the socialist countries has also increased.

— In the East European CMEA countries efforts aimes at updating of industrial technology required considerable imports and as a result increased exports as well. As is well-known the importance of international cooperation has been growing for the economy of the Soviet Union, too, beyond the fact that the Soviet Union has become the leading raw material supplier as well as the main market of that region. Since the end of the 1960s, the intensification of the international division of labour and the heightening of its efficiency has become one of the main conditions of the transition to the intensive path of economic development. The new industries are also necessarily more international in the CMEA region.

— The increased imports of machines, equipment and—in some countries—food, required an adequate expansion of exports.

The worsening of the terms of trade in the 1970s has plunged some European socialist countries in to an extremely difficult situation. Serious internal and international imbalances resulted from the losses. Only increased efficiency can counterbalance such losses in the long run. A number of countries, however, have attempted to counter the price drop by stepping up the volume of exports.

— In some socialist countries also, indebtedness, enhanced the significance of exports in order to provide the foreign exchange needed to pay off the debts and interest. The increasing importance of exports and imports for the different groups of countries indicates only economic necessities which may be prevented by various means. Without major adjustment in output patterns in the most important countries, there will be no acceleration of world trade growth in relation to production growth in the coming decade.

The situation in the mid-1980s reflects the impact of slower growth and of structural disturbances on the relations between world output and trade (Table 23).

The declining demand for primary commodities, the growth of investment and personal consumption, the protectionist measures and the debt crisis were primarily responsible for the slowdown in the rate of growth of world imports. The decline of real import elasticities to output between 1977–85 in comparison to 1965–73 was the greatest in the energy importing developing countries (from 1.23 to 0.53) and in Japan (from 1.47 to 0.45) in the European Socialist countries the decline was also substantial (from 1.35 to 0.98). The Western industrialized countries also experienced a major decline (from 1.97 to 1.29).

The decline in the dynamism of world trade in the early 1980s was particularly serious for raw materials and fuels. Dynamism dropped to a lesser extent in the case of industrial products coming to 51–52 per cent of total trade and amounting to 65 per cent of trade among the developed capitalist countries. Global exports of finished goods grew by 11 per cent between 1963 and 1973, by 5 per cent between 1971 and 1980, and growth further slowed down in the early 1980s. This was due partly to diminishing demand and partly to growing protectionism. A considerable part of global trade in finished goods was affected by protectionism, particularly the car trade (amounting to 8 per cent of global industrial products trade), and trade in iron and steel (4 per cent of world trade). In some countries protectionist measures involved same advanced technology, too. (See Table 24.)

Data published on the years 1984-87, however, indicate that growth ratios between global output and world trade as they evolved in the period of recession tend to be only of a transitory nature. However, certain sectors of world production and the proliferation of production difficulties indicate that the international division of labour will sometimes be adversely affected by grave structural problems in the long run as well. Such unfavourable developments are government subsidies to sectors and industries which are lagging behind, the global strengthening of protectionist tendencies, import restrictions, exports subsidies, the possibility of overproduction in

Table 23.

Changes in World Production and World Exports (as a percentage of average annual growth or decrease)

	1970–1980	1975–1980	1981	1982	1981–85	1986	1987
World production (G.D.P.)	4.3	3.8	1.7	0.8	2.7	3.3	3.3
World exports (volume)	5.6	5.5	-0.8	-2.2	2.6	2.8	4.5

Source: U.N., World Economic Survey, New York, 1984, 1986, 1988.

Table 24.

Changes in the Volume of Exports (annual average)

	1960–69	1971–1981	1982	1983	1984	1985
Total exports	8.5	5.0	-3.0	0.7	9.5	3.5
Industrial products	10.5	6.5	-2.7	4.2	12.6	5.2
Oil (crude and refined)	—	0	-7.0	-6.5	3.0	-2.3
Minerals	6.5	2.5	-5.5*	1.5	2.0	-3.9

* Average value of the estimates of GATT and the World Bank 1980–83, 1987.
Sources: U.N. Monthly Bulletin of Statistics.—OECD—Quarterly Oil Statistics.—British Petroleum, Statistical Review of World Oil Industry.

some parts of the industry related to the new technology (e.g. microprocessors, integrated circuits, audio-visual equipment, etc.). The disturbances which occur in the international financial system add to the growing difficulties and structural problems which are naturally rather different in the various sectors of world production.

As for all the agricultural exporters, so the serious problems of the agricultural world market are also distressing for Hungary. It is a well-known fact that the structural disturbances of the world economy and world trade have a special effect on agriculture. This sector is also a typical example of the consequences of uncoordinated global growth. The problems begin with the fact, that the agricultural policies of the leading producers do not set compatible objectives. There are contradictions between major objectives such as
— security in food supplies (self-sufficiency within the framework of national units or on a regional basis),
— the introduction of a proportionate, balanced and acceptable income level in the national agrarian sectors,
— the stabilization of agrarian markets on national and international scales (the maintenance of acceptable and reasonable agricultural consumer's prices),
— the preservation of a regional balance between cities and villages,
— the creation of acceptable conditions for environmental protection and agrarian public health policy.

The difficulties in simultaneously realizing the above objectives resulted in the policy of agrarian protectionism in the developed Western countries, which—more than the climatic and organizational conditions distorted demand and supply relations, and resulted in considerable price fluctuations on rather unstable markets. Thus, the first half of the 1980s was once again characterized by an oversupply of temperate-zone agricultural produce resulting in a major decline in the prices.

Another characteristic feature of global agriculture and the demand in agricultural produce is the fact that while many important developing countries are as yet unable to establish permanent stable security of output and supply, the achievement of self sufficiency is not beyond their reach. The long-term trends in their supply and demand position are therefore highly uncertain. Their present internal shortages do not constitute an effective world market demand either, due to their limited purchasing power. Also the insecurity of the agricultural market is magnified by the fluctuating purchases of those countries—with sufficient purchasing power—which are unable to meet the demand of their growing population from domestic production for many years.

The agricultural sector is also influenced by major changes in technology, especially in biotechnology, which may lead to substantial increases in productivity and to greater integration between industry and agriculture. These will cause further major changes in global production patterns, and increasing competition.

2. The Problems of Agriculture at the End of the Century

The share of agriculture in world output and world trade is tending to decline. The growth of production is determined by specific conditions differing from those of other sectors. Agricultural production is supposed to meet first the basic nutrition requirements and in addition, it plays an important part in the supply of certain industrial raw materials, the development of incomes, the accumulation of capital, and exports, too, in a number of countries.

The surface of our planet is about 510 million square kilometres of which, however, more than two-thirds are covered by water. The land surface of the earth is about 149 million square kilometres. Of this 15 million square kilometres are under systematic cultivation, 30.5 million square kilometres are meadows and pastures, whereas 41.5 million square kilometres are forests. In 1970 807 million people—of the 1.551 million working people of the world—made their living directly from agriculture (52 per cent of all working people). Their proportion in the developing countries was 67 per cent, in the developed industrial countries 19 per cent.

In 1980 840 million of the world's working population of 1.827 million were employed in agriculture (their percentage thus dropped to 46 per cent though their absolute number increased). 13 per cent of the working population in the developed West and in the socialist countries lived on agriculture, whereas their proportion was 60 per cent in the developing countries.

According to the computations of FAO, by the year 2000 out of the total of 2.506 million working people of the world 852 million will find jobs in agriculture (34 per cent), i.e. numerically more than in 1980 (6 per cent in developed industrialized countries and 43 per cent in the developing countries).[85]

Thus, agriculture will continue to be of outstanding significance for mankind all through this century and not only from the point of view of the food supply of the world but also as regards the development of employment and incomes.

Agriculture is an important factor of economic growth both as a producing and a consuming sector. It is still the main source of meeting food requirements and at the same time it is both the raw material producer and a market for industry. Today almost one-third of the raw materials used by the industry are supplied by agriculture.

When defining the real importance of agriculture, all employed in the food industry, in agricultural transportation as well as commerce in agricultural products have to be categorized as related to the sector via their incomes. The possibilities of producing and marketing products in the auxillary sectors of agriculture are also determined by agriculture through means of intra-sectorial relations. For instance, 22 million people are working in agriculture and its auxillary sectors in the United States. Of these 4 million work in the fields, 11 million in auxillary industries, in the food industry and food transportation, 7 million have jobs in enterprises marketing agrarian produce and products as well as in agricultural administration (credit supply included) and agricultural research institutions. Their percentage—as compared to the sum total of people employed—came to 22 per cent in 1980.

The role of agricultural production combined is even higher in the economies of countries of a lower level of development where foodstuffs make up the greater part of the consumption of the population. The effect of the annual fluctuation in agricultural production is even stronger in these countries.

Agricultural Output
and World Trade in Agrarian Produce

World agricultural output rose by an annual average of 3.3 per cent in the 1950s, by 2.6 per cent in the 1960s and by 2.1 per cent in the 1970s. Later on, however, the recession grew stronger in a number of regions of the world as illustrated by the data in Table 25. It can be seen from these data that the subsequent slowing down of growth could be felt in quite a few areas of the world economy.

The expansion of world output has by and large kept abreast with the growth of population and has exceeded it to a small extent. The expansion of agricultural production was stimulated by an increase in the demand for valuable foodstuffs in the developed industrial Western countries. After 1980, however, the rate of growth of production was slowed down by a slower growth of population and the saturation of demand.

The agricultural production of the CMEA countries was increasing rather fast during the post-war reconstruction period. Later, however, under the effect of various factors (partly as a result of economic policy mistakes) it slackened considerably. The share of the main groups of countries in global agricultural production has changed. Between 1959–61 and 1984–86 the changes were as follows: developing countries from 54 per cent to 57 per cent, Western industrial countries from 32 per cent to 30 per cent and socialist countries in Europe from 14 per cent to 13 per cent.

Despite an unprecedentedly rapid growth of production a grave "food crisis" evolved in many developing countries as a result of the demographic explosion as well as the extremely low income level.

In the 1950s and 1960s the "golden age" of world economy characterized by rapid growth had a stimulating effect on the expansion of agricultural production, too; increasing incomes and better financing possibilities had a major part in this development. There were, however, differences in the growth rate of agricultural production in the individual regions. The differences were largely due to such factors as demand, natural endowment and technological factors. The differences in the rate of growth of production, were also influenced by the quality of soil and the availability of land as well as by some specific conditions rendering it possible for some countries to bring about more intensive production than others by public support or other means (e.g. irrigation, introduction of new plant species, chemicals). Differences in the efficiency of investment and incentives should also be mentioned among the reasons of different growth rates.

Differences in the growth rate of agricultural production are also connected with structural causes. The "backbone" of world food economy is made up of grain crops and oil-seeds. Two-thirds of foodstuffs consumed in the world consist of these products. In the majority of the countries of the world incomes are low, and the consumption of agrarian produce is not differentiated. The significance of grain crops and oil-seeds of high protein content remains unchanged since it is these products which supply also the basic fodder for the production of meat, milk and eggs. An increasing amount of grain crops and oil-seeds are used for fodder in the wake of structural changes. On a higher level of development, fruit and vegetables produced with up-to-date technologies take an increasingly higher share of agricultural production.

The share of agrarian produce (including raw materials) in world trade diminished from 32 per cent in 1955 to 14 per cent in 1983, whereas its volume increased considerably.

About 10 per cent of the 850 million tons of global feed grain grown, enters world trade, and of this 85–90 per cent originated from four countries (USA, Canada, Australia and Argentina) in the mid-1980s. World food grain output doubled between 1960 and 1985. In spite of this fact, many countries suffer major shortages. Food grain consumption increased by about 3.5 per cent annually during the mentioned period. Much of the increase of consumption was covered by domestic production. The most dramatic change in world food grain trade came in Western Europe.

Prior to World War II, Western Europe had been a significant importing region and it became a major exporter by the mid-1970s. The food grain output of the world totalled about 820 million metric tons in 1985–86. World trade in food grain surpassed 100 million tons in the first half of the 1980s; 57 per cent of production and about 70 per cent of trade is comprised of wheat. By 1980 there were two regions regarded as the chief wheat exporters: America and Argentina. Though there were some countries in all regions that were net exporters, only the four countries mentioned disposed of a considerable surplus of feed grain. Forty per cent of the mobilizable grain reserves of the world are concentrated in the USA and in Canada. In the first half of the 1980s 75 per cent of global grain imports, 50 per cent of cotton and sugar imports, 40 per cent of food grain imports and 20 per cent of soya imports consisted of purchases made by the developing and the socialist countries.

Problems in other sectors of the world economy are generally influenced by the increase of global agricultural output in a more indirect way with a certain time-lag. The effects of major structural disturbances of agricultural production, however, make themselves felt more rapidly and directly in the development of the individual countries and the world economy as a whole in the mid-1980s.

The world economic recession of the early 1980s affected agrarian producers in many ways. Demand for agricultural raw materials decreased as a consequence of industrial decline. Prices touched rock-bottom whereas credits grew more and more expensive which made it more difficult for farmers to purchase enough fertilizers, fodder mixtures and other basic ingredients needed for production. Global output and utilization of fertilizers decreased for the first time in 30 years. Agricultural investments were reduced. Thousands of agricultural enterprises went bankrupt in the developed industrial countries and unemployment rose in agriculture as well. The pressure on the governments grew to increase aid in order to protect domestic agriculture.

The situation of agriculture worsened particularly in the developing countries. The growth of agricultural production slowed down, per capita production diminished in many countries,[86] nevertheless global agricultural production taken as a whole, expanded even in the years of recession. Global agricultural output had increased at an annual average rate of 2.6 per cent between 1961 and 1985, which is a faster rate than that of global population. Of agricultural goods in world trade foodstuffs expanded while the volume of world trade was on the decline. The volume of agrarian foreign trade increased faster than global agricultural output in these years. However, these transitory growth ratios between agriculture and other sectors characterizing the years of recession do not modify long-term tendencies.

The reduction of the share of agriculture caused by two factors in the developed industrial countries in the past: first, the relatively slow growth in demand for agricultural produce and second, the restricted nature of advantages to be derived from the agricultural sector. Partly due to the expansion of the volume of agricultural production, the growth of per capita national income brought about a relatively greater demand for non-agricultural goods. As a consequence, increasing industrial production (for the domestic market, too) has become more profitable in a number of traditional agrarian countries as well. This was combined with growing imports of colonial foodstuffs made possible and profitable by the rapid development of transport and trade.

Under present conditions, however, the significance of agriculture has decreased in the developed Western countries and the reason for this should not be sought for in the fact that they import cheap foodstuffs and other agrarian products from the developing countries.

As compared to the period prior to and directly following World War II, the volume of agricultural production increased in the majority of developed Western countries (as illustrated by Table 25). The expansion of production—despite the shrinking of the percentage share of that sector—has been made possible by the process of technological "industrialization" of agriculture, the considerable increase of the organic composition of working capital in agriculture, being as a rule instrumental to the concentration of land ownership and changes in the distribution of land. Technological changes made themselves felt also in other spheres of agriculture.

Agriculture has been increasingly supplied with *machinery* by industry to meet a great variety of requirements.

A number of the traditional functions of agriculture have been taken up by industry. Industry has become to an ever greater degree the main supplier of agriculture even as regards products which had once belonged exclusively to the sphere of agricultural production (fertilizers, herbicides and pesticides). Nowadays the premix industry turns out products for animal feeding which extend the range of traditional agricultural fodder (e.g. fodder yeast). A number of labour processes (which had been the function of agriculture) following the harvest and preparing the produce for consumption (e.g. cleaning, husking, sorting) become industrial functions. It is an equally well-known fact that an ever growing percentage of agricultural produce reaches consumers preserved by industrial processing. Thus in the USA 80 per cent of foodstuff produced had been processed to some degree prior to consumer purchase. The corresponding percentage in the developing countries was 10 to 20 per cent in the early 1980s.

Under the influence of the "biological revolution", *biotechnology* has rapidly gained ground in agriculture.

Table 25.

Average Annual Growth of Agricultural World Production (per cent)

	Total production				Per capita production			
	1951–60	1961–70	1971–80	1979–85	1951–60	1961–70	1971–80	1979–85
World	3.3	2.6	2.1	2.0	1.3	0.6	0.3	0.6
Developed capitalist countries	2.5	1.9	1.8	1.0	1.3	0.8	1.0	0.4
North America	1.0	1.8	2.0	1.1	0.1	0.3	1.1	0.5
Western Europe	2.7	2.3	1.9	1.0	1.8	1.5	1.4	0.7
Japan	3.9	0.9	0.1	1.6	2.8	– 0.8	– 1.0	0.6
CMEA countries	4.4	2.9	2.1	1.6	2.9	1.8	1.3	1.0
East Europe	3.0	2.1	2.3	n.a.	2.0	1.4	1.6	0.9
Soviet Union	5.2	3.4	1.7	1.7	3.4	2.0	0.9	1.0
Developing countries	3.2	2.8	2.6	2.2	1.0	0.4	0.1	0.3
Africa	2.5	2.7	1.1	1.9	0.3	– 0.1	– 1.6	– 0.5
Latin America	3.5	3.0	3.4	1.8	0.8	0.8	0.8	– 0.1
Middle East	3.4	2.9	3.8	1.7	0.6	0.0	1.1	– 0.3
Far East	3.0	2.7	2.0	2.8	1.2	0.0	– 0.2	1.0
Chinese PR	n.a.	3.0	3.3	4.0	n.a.	1.1	1.8	3.3

Sources: F.A.O., World Bank and Statistics of the US Department of Agriculture.

a) It makes it possible to considerably improve the peculiarities and characteristics of plants (e.g. by genetical engineering rendering plants resistant to diseases or disadvantageous environmental effects, stimulating their growth and improving the efficiency of photosynthesis).

b) By genetical changes in micro-organisms it aids the fixing of nitrogen, brings about insecticide effects and prevents the diseases of plants while stimulating their growth.

c) As regards animal husbandry it facilitates efficient diagnosis, and prevents animal diseases, improves fodder utilization, accelerates the growth of animals and improves the genetic features of animal species.

Though there seems little possibility of developing plant and animal species with predetermined characteristics in the near future, man will possibly approach this goal in 10 to 15 years.

The development of agriculture points in the direction of further industrialization, yet it will preserve its sectorial independence for a long time to come. The future course of agriculture is influenced by the decreasing importance of natural factors, large-scale industrial animal husbandry utilizing the achievements of biology, "sea farming", the long-range possibilities of artifical photosynthesis. The present, however, seems less encouraging and the realization of technological possibilities is probably a rather difficult venture. Even the adoption of relatively simple technologies encounters many a difficulty in some regions of the world. Wood ploughs are still used in a great number of Third World countries. Of the total energy supply in the developing countries 70 per cent was human effort in 1980, 20 per cent was supplied by animal hauling power, and a mere 10 per cent of all energy used was of mechanical origin. Such ratios change only extremely slowly. Differences in utilization of fertilizers are also huge.

As a result of technological progress the productivity of agricultural labour has unprecedentedly increased in a number of Western countries, e.g. in the United States, Belgium and Denmark. In the United States the increase in the rate of productivity in agriculture—given a longer period of time—was quicker than in industry or in any other sector of the economy.

As a consequence of the considerable increase of production and productivity in the leading Western countries—first and foremost in the United States and in the Common Market countries—the agrarian surplus became a permanent feature resulting in the restriction of the growth of agricultural production and measures of public economic policy aimed at the stimulation of agrarian exports. The agrarian protectionism and export subsidizing policy of the Common Market brought about cut-throat competition with the other agrarian exporters. Hungarian agricultural exports, too, have been seriously affected.

The agriculture of the socialist countries set off from a lower level than that of the Western countries of Europe or the United States. There are significant differences between countries as regards the growth rates of agricultural production, and annual fluctuations, too, are quite considerable. The growth of agricultural production often lagged behind the plan targets. Partly due to economic policy mistakes, this occasionally resulted in great disequilibrium and had an adverse effect on economic development as a whole.

The migration of the agricultural labour force, too, was extremely fast and for a long time the technological development of agriculture did not keep abreast with these developments. Mainly the most efficient generations (from the point of view of labour) turned their back on rural districts. The mechanization of agriculture was not diversified enough, either. Agriculture did not receive adequate amounts of fertilizers, pesticides and insecticides for years on end, nor did it receive industrially produced animal feed. The material incentives of those employed in agriculture were not satisfactory either.

The expansion of agricultural production was hampered by these problems. Agricultural production growth of the European CMEA countries was extremely uneven. Between 1961 and 1970 it grew 20 per cent faster then world output. Between 1970 and 1980 the increase in agricultural production was by about one third slower than world output growth. In the second half of the 1970s the rate of growth of agriculture was about 40 per cent of the world output growth. In the first three years of the 1980s it has increased much faster than the global rate and in the mid-1980s it grew much more slowly again.

The utilization of reserves implied in the increase of yields must be the main source of agricultural development in the European socialist countries since—with the sole exception of the Soviet Union—cultivable land can hardly be expanded. In the interest of production, the transformation of low-quality land becomes a necessity occasionally (plough-land is turned into meadows, forests). As proved by statistical data, even in the Soviet Union, there are to be found far greater reserves in the more efficient utilization of land under cultivation than in the breaking up of virgin soil. The raising of efficiency, the increase of productivity of agricultural production continues to depend highly on investments and the improvement of technological conditions. It is, however, similarly obvious that economic means—adequate systems of marketing, management, control and incentives, measure of price policy, etc.—are also needed for the satisfactory utilization of developing technologies.

Naturally it should also be taken into consideration that in the CMEA countries climatic conditions for agricultural production are diverse and therefore agrotechnical (investment) requirements are different in each of these countries. Huge areas of the Soviet Union demand considerably greater investment to counterbalance unfavourable climatic conditions than for instance in the USA. It is also important from the point of view of the effectiveness of agricultural investment that the national economy will have to take great burdens because of the backwardness of the infrastructure necessary for the development of production, particularly taking into consideration the low ratio of such investments between 1950 and 1970. Another essential requirement for the progress of the pattern of agricultural production, is the broadening of animal husbandry and the increase of fruit and vegetable production. Incidentally, it seems quite clear that there are still considerable reserves to be tapped by further specialization among the countries. Yet, it is only by utilizing these reserves that the agriculture of the socialist countries can come abreast with the level of the developed industrial countries. The success of China in doubling its agricultural output within less than a decade proved that the role of incentives and new, more efficient forms of organization may bring major results in socialist countries. Further

Table 26.

World Population, Agricultural Production and Foreign Trade in Agricultural Products in 1985

Region	Distribution of world population	Total active agricultural population (in persons)	Share in world agricultural production (per cent)	Share in world agricultural*	
				Exports (per cent)	Imports (per cent)
Developed Western countries of these	17.0	32	30	63	62
North America	5.5	63	12	22	21
Western Europe	7.8	26	15	37	34
Others	3.7	25	3	4	7
Developing countries of these	75.0	4.7	57	33	33
Africa	9.3	3.5	4	4	4
Latin America	8.4	10.3	18	14	13
Middle East	5.0	7.2	4	2	3
Far East	28.4	4.1	15	9	10
Developing socialist countries	23.7	2.4	15	2	3
Others	0.2	4.0	1	1	—
European socialist countries	8.0	10.8	13	4	5
World total	4,836,960	4.6		265**	

* Agricultural, forestry and fishery products altogether.
** Billion U.S. $.

Sources: Calculated on the basis of F.A.O., World Food Report (1985), and FAO Production Yearbook. Vol. 39. 1985 Róma, 1986. World Bank, Economic Analysis and Projections Department, 1986.

results, however, will depend more on changes in productivity and efficiency based on new technologies in China.

Table 26 illustrates the position of different country groups in agriculture in 1985, indicating the inequalities reflecting per capita ratios between working and total populations, and in the range of agrarian exports and imports. It can be established on the strength of these data that global agricultural output in the last decades of the twentieth century is characterized by extreme inequalities and so is the foreign trade in agricultural produce. Differences in productivity, too, are reflected by the above data: thus, the ratio of the population to one person employed in agriculture is more than twenty times as high in the United States as in the developing countries.

On the basis of data of the late 1970s—given the production of the USA per capita of persons employed in agriculture as 100—the same index is 193 in Denmark, 47 in Great Britain, 37 in France, 23 in Italy and 23 in Japan. At the same time, the index of the production value per capita of those employed in agriculture in the developing countries came to but 4 to 7 per cent of that of the United States.[87] In the European socialist countries agricultural production per capita of agricultural earners has been 27–60 per cent of the similar index of the developed West European countries. Differences are relatively significant among the European socialist countries as regards productivity in agriculture (e.g. productivity in Hungary surpasses that of Bulgaria by 50 per cent).

On a global scale and in the long run the production of the main foodstuffs is by and large proportionate to the growth of population. As was pointed out, however, the territorial distribution is extremely uneven. In some parts of the world the problem is caused by agricultural overproduction whereas in other parts by underproduction. Overproduction, however, is combined with shortages in some of the monocultural countries.

At the end of the 1960s—on the subject of increased agricultural production and its place in the world economy—it was hotly debated in some industrially developed Western countries whether the growth of agricultural production was too fast or too slow compared to requirements. The source of the problems was the immoderately slow development of agriculture all over the world in the first half of the 1970s while difficulties had been caused by the rapid increase of production in the previous years.

World agricultural output ought to reach an annual growth rate of 2.6–2.8 per cent in order to meet world demands for food and agricultural raw materials. Some Western economists, e.g. the Australian Colin Clark, have voiced the view that the growth rate was too high in the past in relation to effective demand in the world economy. The prices of agrarian produce are too low on the world market. Even Colin Clark admitted the fact that if it were possible for India and other deficit countries to import more food so as to meet their needs by means of imports, this growth rate would probably, be too low.[88] He regarded an annual 2.3–2.4 per cent growth as more rational since—in his opinion—this would fit better with the increase of real incomes taking into account the coefficient of elasticity between agrarian consumption and incomes.

As regards world trade and effective demand, Colin Clark was right. However, he did not size up real needs. At least in the densely populated developing countries where the conditions for solving the food problems are worst, agricultural production ought to be increased first and foremost within the territory of the countries in question, and food demand adapted to the justified standards of consumption should be met from local production. It seems futile to expect these countries to be able to cover their food needs from imports. This was recognized both in China and in India. On the basis of the development of world market prices of agrarian products or the gap between world market prices of agricultural and industrial products, it cannot be said whether the growth rate in the world economy of agricultural production is too low or too high. Food continues to be the item of greatest volume in the consumption of the population.

The Demand for Foodstuffs and the World Market

The ratio of foodstuffs and related products to consumer expenditure in developed, industrialized Western countries was about 15–18 per cent whereas in the European socialist countries generally it was over 50 per cent in the early 1980s. Meeting food demands is still one of the most acute problems of world economy. About 500 million people are starving all over the world and nearly one billion people are undernourished. The global food problem is not simply the result of the "competition" between the different growth rates of the population and food production but also of the competition between food production and demand. Increased demand has two components, the growth of population and rising incomes. In the case of the rapid increase of incomes both demand and the population grows faster in many developing countries. The increased population of the world is concentrated in a few regions. Another very serious problem is the slow increase (or decrease) of employment and incomes. One of the most serious problems of global food economy at the end of the twentieth century is how to guarantee the food supply of the developing countries. The most important factors of this problem are the peculiarities of urbanization, the increasing number of landless rural families, the considerable regional inequalities of food production and the great dependence on climatic conditions. On average in the years 1984–86 the developing countries with 74 per cent of the world population produced 56 per cent of the global food output. The developed Western industrial countries with 17 per cent of the world population supplied 32 per cent of the global food production. (The respective proportions for the European socialist countries were 8.3 per cent and 12 per cent.)

The population of the world covers 56 per cent of its calory needs from grain crops, 7 per cent from roots and tubers, 10 per cent from fruit and vegetables, 7 per cent from sugar, 9 per cent from fats and oils, 11 per cent from animal products.[89] These ratios have changed very little during the past 30 years. It is still grain crops which have the predominant part in food consumption of the world's population. Grain or food produced from grain is either consumed directly by the world population or indirectly by means of feeding animals. Rice has continued to serve as the most important grain crop being the staple food of 56 per cent of global population.

Animal protein from livestock, poultry and animal products still constitutes rather a small percentage of the world population's consumption and in addition, distribution is highly disproportionate. One third of animal products are consumed by the population of the developing world (75 per cent of world population). Of total global protein production 25 per cent was consumed by the Third World countries in the 1970s. The decisive part of this came from grain crops. Thus, the population of India consumed an annual average of about 180 kilogrammes per capita—mainly directly— in the 1970s. Though grain is transformed overwhelmingly into animal protein in the industrially developed countries, per capita grain consumption has also remained high. (In the 1970s consumption came up to 700 kilogramme in the Soviet Union; 880 kilogrammes in the Federal Republic of Germany and France, and 900 kilogrammes in the United States.) "Exchange ratios" between grain crops and animal protein are well-known facts. In the United States 2 kilogrammes of grain are needed to produce 1 kilogramme of poultry meat, 3.5 kilogrammes of grain to produce 1 kilogramme of pork, and 6.5 kilogrammes of grain to produce 1 kilogramme of beef. Grain comsumption has been greatly increased by meat production (and not by population growth) in the industrially developed countries. The increase in grain consumption is slightly lower in the countries of the European Common Market and in Japan: partly because here other fodder is used in addition to cereals, and partly—especially in Japan—because direct meat imports are considerable, too.

Fish is a factor of increasing importance in the consumption of the world population. The total production of the four main sorts of meat (beef, mutton, pork and poultry) was 139 million tons in 1980, that of fish 75 million tons. Forty per cent of global fish production came from five countries (Japan, the Soviet Union, the People's Republic of China, the USA and Chile), and 90 per cent of total production is of maritime origin. Increasing fish consumption is of vital importance in the late twentieth century. This makes it imperative to introduce a reasonable system of fish farming and in some of the countries the stepping up of fresh-water fish-breeding.

On a global scale, from the point of view of global food supply security, the fundamental problem of the future is whether agriculture will be able to meet—both globally and regionally—the increasing demand of the population as regards food and fodder of agrarian origin. It seems to be an essential fact that the development in agriculture points towards strengthening self-sufficiency within national frameworks instead of a rational and intensive international division of labour. In order to achieve self-sufficiency many countries are subsidizing production, incomes and exports. There are of course countries which have proved unable to meet demands. Whether such a trend will result in famine or will manifest itself in the form of an effective import demand in the world market or whether it will lead to increasing prices and the strengthening of exporter countries as a result of growing demand, are significant problems having an effect on the development and cooperation of the CMEA countries, too.

As regards the future, there is another important question (and task): to what extent shall we succeed in building up global reserves? This will be of outstanding significance for the global population which will reach 6 billion by the year 2000.

From the aspect of global agricultural production and consumption it is the position of the developing countries which is highly problematical. Their demands and needs are determined first and foremost by the trend of their population growth. The various international projections are somewhat contradictory regarding the scale of population growth but there is one point on which they are in full agreement: the absolute number of the population will not "stabilize" for at least 40 years to come. Following from the high rate of population growth the age pattern of the population is continuously deteriorating: 35 per cent of the population will be under 14, and 5 per cent above 65 years, i.e. 40 per cent of the total population will mainly consume without, however, producing. The migration to the cities will continue, thus increasing market demand, and this could be met only by stepping up production, and by adequately widening the transport, storage and marketing network.

According to "moderate" growth forecasts there will be 6 billion people on earth by the year 2000, about 76–77 per cent of them in the developing countries, and of these more than 3 billion in but eight countries (China, India, Indonesia, Bangladesh, Brazil, Pakistan, Nigeria, Mexico). The share of the developing countries in global food output will reach 56–57 per cent by the end of this century.

The effective demand of the developing countries is influenced not only by population growth but also by the growth of personal real incomes. The annual average growth rate of this can be assumed to be potentially in general 2.0–2.5 per cent in the developing world.

The extremely low present-day level of consumption, too, should be taken into consideration when determining the future development of the food and other agrarian product needs of the developing countries. Per capita grain consumption in the developing countries as an average of the 1970s had been 30 per cent of that in the developed industrial countries, and that of meat consumption 12–14 per cent. The food elasticity of incomes in the developing countries is rather high though in the agrarian sector of many a developing country the traditional sector producing for direct consumption continues to have a significant part. The possibilities of raising internal production quickly depend on the bringing about of appropriate conditions.

Simultaneously with the changes there have cropped up a number of complex problems, too. Particularly in developing countries agriculture has sometimes been reduced—as the heritage of the colonial period—to the production of one or two products. A specific problem there is to what an extent and at what a rate could and should monocultures be eliminated and production be diversified. The answer will be different in the case of products experiencing a boom and those which render the economic situation depressed in one or another state. The conditions of the big and small countries are different. In the developing countries concerned the quality of the soil, the area of lands, production experiences, internal consumption, export demands, etc., should all be taken into account.

No substantial breakthrough can be expected in the 10–15 years to come as regards the expansion of agricultural production in the Third World countries. Though the results of the Green Revolution and the changes following in their wake are not at all negligible, they are of a restricted nature, and the basis of increased production is rather narrow even at places which can boast of considerable achievements. According to data on recent years, food shortages have grown rapidly in many developing countries. The situation has become particularly critical in Africa where 8–9 per cent of consumption is covered by imports.

The possibilities of food imports for developing countries are fundamentally determined by their export earnings. Since in all probability external sources will not increase considerably in the 1980s, the volume of imports of these countries will be less than 7 per cent of their total consumption (characteristic for the 1970s) coming to 3–4 per cent, and tendencies towards self-sufficiency will strengthen.

Changes in the developed industrial countries have been significant since the 1960s. Consumption of agricultural products of the temperate zone has increased at an annual average of 1.8–2 per cent whereas the ratio of imports has decreased from 6 to 4.2 per cent. The share of Western Europe in global agricultural imports dropped from 50 per cent in 1970 to 41 per cent by 1981 and at the same time, its share in world exports rose from 32 to 37 per cent. The share of the Western industrial countries in global food exports was 40 per cent at the end of the 1960s, it was 51 per cent in 1984–86 and by 2000 it will grow to 53–54 per cent according to the World Bank projections. Consumption of tropical food increased by an annual average of 1.5 per cent, the ratio of imports grew from 94 to 96 per cent. Consumption of protein fodder grew by an annual 5.0 per cent, imports dropped from 34 to 26 per cent. As regards future prospects, these tendencies will probably continue.

The food requirements of the developed Western countries will increase by an annual 1.0–1.3 per cent at the most until the turn of the century. The reason for this is the fact that their annual population growth rate will presumably not reach 1 per cent (according to the prediction of FAO it will be only 0.6 per cent) whereas the growth rate of per capita GDP will be—according to estimates—2 per cent and therefore the population is expected to spend a declining percentage of its income for food purchases. Owing to strengthening self-sufficiency, the ratios of food imports and food exports will evolve conversely to that of the developing countries. While exports covered only 70 per cent of imports in the early 1970s, this percentage rose to 87 per cent already by the end of the decade. It seems rather probable that the growth rate of imports of the developed Western countries will—as in the 1980s—not reach an annual 2 per cent whereas that of exports surpasses 3.0–3.5 per cent.

Demand reflects contradictions in the socialist countries, too. Serious disturbances were experienced in the agricultural production and food supply of the European socialist countries in the 1970s and the early 1980s. As compared to its industrial and overall economic development, meeting the demands of the population in this region tends to lag behind requirements and actual possibilities. In some of these countries the governments were compelled to introduce a rationing system which is an unprecedented step in peace time in countries of similar development. These problems stem from the insufficiencies of economic policy, particularly of agrarian policy, but are linked up with specific (e.g. climatic) temporary unfavourable conditions as well.

This has happened at a time when demand increased faster in the socialist countries than in the developed Western countries. The reason for this is not simply the fact that consumption of certain products (meat, milk, fish) falls behind that of the developed Western countries but also to do with the conditions determined by the income level of these countries. The situation is similar as regards consumption of tropical agrarian produce. In certain countries expansion of demand is also prompted by the growth of population (though this does not surpass an annual 1 per cent). In the CMEA countries the demand for foodstuffs is expected to increase by an annual 1.5–2.0 per cent till the end of the century.

In most of the countries the transformation of the physiologicaly unsuitable dietary pattern has been put on the agenda. The consumption of cereals and potatoes is too high. Demand will probably shift towards foodstuffs richer in protein (meat, milk, butter) as well as animal fodder in order to bring about an upsurge in domestic animal husbandry, to cover such needs.

Exports covered 53 per cent of the agricultural imports of the European CMEA countries between 1973 and 1975, whereas only a few years later this percentage dropped to 45 per cent, and to 33 per cent at the beginning of the 1980s. The share of the European CMEA countries in world imports rose from an annual 9 per cent in 1970 to 12 per cent in the course of the period under review but dropped from 6 to 4 per cent in global exports.

The corn production of the European CMEA countries increased by an annual 1.72 per cent in the 1970s (world average growth was at the same time 2.77 per cent). In these very same years their corn exports decreased by an annual average of 7 per cent whereas their imports increased by 6 per cent. The development of demand emphasizes the point that it is animal husbandry which has to be developed first of all. This, however, necessitates considerable yields of fodder. Even if according to plan targets these countries succeeded in increasing their agricultural production as regards certain produce (e.g. fodder of high protein content) faster than in other regions, they would need considerable amounts of agrarian imports. The volume of demand is so high that domestic output will not be able to satisfy within the region for about another ten years if the plans for animal husbandry reached the targets.

Assuming normal internal and international economic relations the majority of the socialist countries are importers mainly of corn fodder and other proteinaceous fodder. As indicated by our analyses on the possibilities of the development of the CMEA region, a considerably more rational division of labour could be established in food production as well as in the auxillary branches of agriculture. Incidentally, the Europe, by their efforts to strengthen food security and self-sufficiency and also the considerable technological development which is going to unfold in global agriculture in the wake of the biological revolution in the decade to follow.

All these changes, however, do not diminish the instability of agricultural markets, rather having the effect of increasing this very instability and precariousness. On the basis of further evolution the following problems seem predictable:

— The fluctuations in agricultural production and demand will not lessen considerably in the decades to come (the agrarian market tends to remain uncertain, famine and overproduction will remain simultaneous global phenomena). Competition is going to increase.
— The demand for processed food will grow faster than that for agricultural raw materials.
— Global demand for agricultural production systems, machines and equipment, agrotechnics, zootechnics, etc. will surpass the demand for agricultural produce.
— No considerable decrease can be expected in the regional imbalance of agricultural production and consumption in the following 10–15 years.

As evidenced by past experience, long-lasting advantages resulting from unstable markets are gained by neither exporters nor importers. Thus, it seems probable that in the more distant future both national and international efforts will strengthen to enhance the security of food supplies and to expand regional and global cooperation for this end.

3. Main Trends in Industrial Development and the Perspectives of Structural Changes in the World Economy at the End of the Twentieth Century

Industry has been and will remain the leading sector of the world economy in the decades to follow. The industrialization of our planet was sharply criticized in the 1970s particularly because of increasing environmental pollution and the exhaustion of raw material resources. The period after the 1960s has been declared to be the "post-industrial society" by many social researchers in the developed countries. Indeed, in many countries serious errors were committed in economic policy as regards industrial development. Disregarding actual conditions some industrial branches were selected for enhanced development, thus reducing considerably the efficiency of the economy as a whole. In spite of this, the globe will be even more industrialized in the next century than today and considerable changes will take place in the regional location and structure of industry. The role of industry will also change.

In the 1984 report of UNIDO entitled "Industry in the Changing World" it was pointed out that the expansion of global industrial capacity and the productive activity of industry have increased the differences in living standards of the nations. Changes to come in the global distribution of industry will affect the elaboration of industrial policies everywhere. Further, it was emphasized that changes in the industrial map of the world will influence the conditions of international trade, investment and technology transfer.[90]

The conditions of stepping up industrial development and increasing its efficiency once again came into the limelight in the 1980s in all these country groups.

The problems caused by the necessity for industrial development have come into prominence again particularly since the mid- 1970s because of the internal and international conditions affecting adversely industrial development in the highly developed Western countries (the sluggish growth of investment and consumer demand, the slower increase of profits or even their decline as well as uncertainty). Wide-ranging debates took place in some countries—particularly in the USA—on the need for reindustrialization.

However, the fundamental questions have not been clarified in the course of these debates as regards the relations between services and industrial development or the problems of re-industrialization. This was mainly due to the fact that services and material production were rigorously contrasted. Though services are sometimes considered as a sign of de-industrialization, their roles are highly different. Services linked up with material production which were separated from the development of production itself in the course of division of labour are of particularly great importance. Such are for example industrial maintenance, a great part of scientific research, and transport, as well as at the end of the twentieth century the "information industry".

Experts have classified services in the United States with regard to their relations to production in the early 1980s and established that 62 per cent of those employed in the services sector worked in services directly linked with production. For this very reason alone, the confrontation of material production and services seems incorrect. Moreover, a developed services sector can be "maintained" (i.e. supplied with the necessary material means) only by a highly developed and efficient material .production. The only exception is that of certain countries where the ratio of income of foreign origin is so high that a relationship can be developed between the various sectors on the basis of which services not based on local production are developed. According to historical experience, however, such a situation could only have a relatively short life. It is also possible that certain countries specialize in their international relations to a higher extent in exporting services. This, however, depends on the size, composition and stage of development as well as natural endowments of the services sector of the country in question. Contrary to some international organizations therefore, incomes originating from the export of direct productive capital are not defined by the author as incomes stemming from the export of services.

Such incomes actually flow from the material production of the productive sector of the recipient country to the exporter of capital. It seems that in the years to follow the importance in world exports of services connected with the development of the new trends of technological evolution will increase, and this is particularly true as regards exports pioneering in these fields.

Incidentally, the ratio of services has increased in the economies of both the developing and the socialist countries from the early 1960s to the late 1980s: their proportion grew in the gross domestic product of the developing countries from 42 per cent to 53 per cent and in that of the socialist countries from 17 to 40 per cent.[91] Statistical data, however, are not precise enough to determine the volume of services in any of these countries, and only suitable to indicate certain trends. The debate on re-industrialization, too, is connected to a certain extent with the problem of the service industries. Thus, the diminution of the international competitiveness of the USA is explained by some American experts overwhelmingly by the structural changes mentioned and/or by the relative set-back of industry.

In practice, however, even in the developed capitalist countries structural changes among the sectors were not followed by an absolute decline in industrial production. In the American economy, too, the volume of industrial production kept on growing: its share in gross production at the end of the 1980s was as high as in the late 1950s.

Industry—and particularly modern manufacturing—continues to be a fundamental factor in the growth of the world economy, the increase of its effectiveness and the internationalization of global development. The possibilities of enhancing the international division of labour arise from it far more than from natural endowments. The countries of the world are interconnected by industrial development despite of the fact that initially it tends to be of an import-substituting character in the less developed states.

It is also suggested by the analysis of global industrial development that the results of industrialization are enjoyed only in the long run—and not to an equal extent—by the industrializing countries. Industrial development has also triggered off serious world economic conflicts. The broadening of international trade was hampered often by "import-substituting" industrialization and protectionist tariff systems built around national industries. Incidentally, the limits set by national frontiers are quickly reached by import-substituting industrialization in the majority of the countries and the further development of industry makes export unavoidable. Thus, the existing system of division of labour changes permanently. Such changes are accompanied by serious international conflicts as well as by economic and commercial wars.

Struggles for the possession and monopoly of raw material resources and colonialization has been partly due to the characteristics of industrial development under capitalism. The developed capitalist countries strove to become "industrial suns" around which dozens of raw material producing "planets" could revolve.

Owing to the uneven development of technology, science and industry, some countries had managed to draw greater profits than others in the past, too. Industrial-technological monopoly was an important means of the expansion of the British firms in the nineteenth century. In a number of important branches of modern technology the leading position of the USA resulted in characteristic dependence as regards the industrially developed Western countries of the world. The industrialization of the developing countries—particularly the emergence of a group of newly industrialized countries—has become one of the most important problems of the world economy and international politics in the second half of the twentieth century as well as the cause of new conflicts in the world economy.

It is a well-known fact that industrialization has assumed a specific form in the life and development of the socialist countries. Socialism—contrary to the ideas of the founders of scientific socialism—has not come to power in the most developed countries. Thus the theory and practice of socialism had to face entirely new problems. The majority of the socialist countries had to pass through the difficult period of industrialization though actually industrialization is not one of the aims of socialism in the proper sense of the term being rather their precondition and starting point. It is also obvious that industrialization is not an end in itself for the socialist countries but an unavoidable stage in bringing about a technologically developed and materially rich society.

The various phases of conscious industrial development were relatively rapidly passed through by the European socialist countries, and—to some extents—the limits of intensive development were reached in the 1960s. It was at that point that increasing the effectiveness of investment and production as a whole became the growth factors of vital importance. The high concentration on intermediary products (steel, cement, etc.) was especially unfortunate during the stage which coincided with major technological changes in world industries. The necessary growth rates of industry are determined by complex demand factors and changes in the whole structure of the national economy. The quality of products is of vital importance. Both the positive and negative aspects and phenomena of the new phase in the European socialist countries indicate the fact that quality has to be improved, the intensity of structural interrelations between the industrial branches have to be enhanced both on the national and international scale, specialization has to be strengthened, and reserves inherent in economies of scale have to be exploited to a greater extent (as mentioned in Part One).

The development of services sectors is an increasing demand of intensification since it facilitates the solution of the tasks faced by industrial production and promotes increased effectiveness. Switching over to intensive industrial development tends to be a difficult problem in the socialist countries since it is not merely a problem within the enterprises. It equally effects economic policy, planning, economic management and the system of material incentives. The updating of the structure of industry and the improvement of the existing structure are of outstanding importance. The solving of these tasks is impeded not only by the force of inertia from the preceding stage of development but also by the fact that this has to be implemented in the phase of the new scientific and technological revolution when technological leaps assume ever greater dimensions.

The modernization of the industrial structure is taking place in economic policies and in the business policies of enterprises in the various countries for different motives and incentives, but all these are closely linked to technological progress. In the developed industrial countries the growing weight of certain branches of industry and production lines is accompanied by differences as regards increasing productivity; the growth process in the professional training and, qualification of the work-force is a major change and has a considerable part in all this. The development of the social division of labour is also reflected by the evolution of the industrial structure. The relationship between the extracting and processing industries, the ratio of materials and finished goods in manufacturing industry, the increased degree of the finishing of goods, the progressive changes in the industrial structure furthering the high-level processing of materials, and technological progress are all facts demonstrating growing differentiation and the better organization of production. As a rule, these changes result in an increased effectiveness of production. Naturally there can emerge new branches of industries, too, meeting the demands of new kinds of consumption, but the efficiency of production is not necessarily enhanced by them. New industries, emerging as a result of growing specialization and cooperation, however, tend to contribute to increased efficiency. Thus, added value stemming from the higher degree of processing, as related to one ton in metallurgy and manufacturing demonstrated the following (according to British data on the year 1975):

Iron ore	100
Pig iron	430
Ingot	692
Pre-rolled ingot	846
Hot-rolled steel	1.007
Cold-rolled steel	1.384
Engineering industry products	5.384

Source: Office of Technology Assessment. Washington. 1977.

The structure of production is greatly influenced by the new industries which have developed in the mainstream of the technological progress of our era as well as by the processes necessary for their implementation. Old industries are transformed, new ones are born and even within the individual industries there occur certain changes. The industries developing new technological processes are among the most dynamic ones. Their leading role in progress is reflected by the rapid expansion of their production, the increasing significance in world trade of the products turned out by them and the high ratio of investment in the field of development activity.

Owing to the character of the individual industries, the great number of products turned out and the differences in quality as well as the significant variances in branch groupings, the international comparison of the structure and structural changes of industrial production is an extremely difficult task. The broadening of the categories and the creation of more comprehensive groups facilitate this task; however, from the point of view of analysis the picture becomes inevitably blurred and important details are not given prominence.

Changes in the structure of industrial production are examined on two levels. First, changes in the ratios between extracting and manufacturing industries are analysed and, second, structural changes in manufacturing industry are studied.

As indicated by the analysis, the internal structure of the extracting and processing industries are undergoing a relatively rapid change; changes in their ratio as compared to each other as well as in their growth rate are much slower. This is borne out by the investigations of the American economist S. Kuznets on the present-day developed industrial capitalist countries for the first half of this century.[92] A considerable part in this has been the relatively slower decrease in the specific use of materials in the course of certain development phases of technology. The relationship and changing ratio of the extracting and manufacturing industries are fundamentally determined by the consequences of technological development, in the process of which the emerging new technology squeezes out old materials and introduces new ones or opens the way for the invention of qualitatively new materials. The degree of processing natural materials increases as a result of technological development absorbing an ever-increasing part of the labour of society. The introduction of synthetic materials and their growing significance renders the dependence on materials to be found in nature more indirect, at the same time bringing about new forms of dependence. For various economic and social reasons, their effect, however, is of different intensity.

The Raw Material Sector in the World Economy

The analysis of interrelations between technological and economic development and the use of materials indicates that a level of saturation is achieved in consumption in respect to certain materials due to increasing incomes and structural changes. Naturally, total consumption, the material requirements per unit of specific output and saturation are also influenced by the structure of the economy in the individual countries.

Owing to the techno-economic changes characteristic of the given periods, the trends in utilization are different and since the progress of such changes is uneven in the various countries, the differences between the states could be considerable. The slackening of utilization following saturation is especially significant in the case of iron, steel, aluminium and lead.

As a matter of fact, reaching the level of physical saturation can also result in improved specific utilization and the spread of substitute materials. The latter is closely linked also to the change and transformation of the structure of production and material consumption.

Changes in the composition of consumption are of vital importance for the development of the extracting industry. The extent to which the structure of the demand for materials is determined by the changes in the composition of the demand for the final products is a fundamental theoretical and practical problem. Changes in the input coefficients (e.g. material intensity) have a modifying effect on the structure of intermediate consumption even in the case of a similar structure of finished products. Competition among substituting materials has the same consequences. Data on the United States, as regards the material content of final consumption are available (see Table 27).

Demand for intermediary products can change under the effect of technological development even without a structural transformation of finished products and can, at the same time, bring about changes in the input coefficients as well. Such changes can

Table 27.
Changes in the "Material Content" of the Final Products in the USA, 1976

	Material content (per cent)	Share in total consumption of materials (per cent)
Consumption of the population	12	43
Investments	32	28
Exports	27	9
Military expenditures	17	9
Other public institutions	17	11

Source: Congress of the US Office of Technology Assessment, 1977.

be perceived by analysing the input-output balances of the individual countries. Making use of the input-output balances makes it possible to analyse in detail the causes resulting in structural changes of material consumption.

Recycling is an essential problem of the development of the extracting industry. The ratio of the utilization of new and recycled materials in production is determined partly by the technological potential and is partly the function of the relative cost relations. These latter are connected not merely with direct production but also for example with expenditures on environmental protection, emerging in the course of the storage or destruction of materials which cannot be recycled.

There are considerable differences in the various countries between potential and actual recycling. According to the computations of UN experts 55 per cent of materials used have the potential for recycling in theory, whereas in practice this percentage tends to be much lower.

About a hundred minerals are extracted and processed (in addition to fuels) which are traded internationally. In 1980 their value formed about 2.4–2.5 per cent of the total industrial world production. Together with the energy carriers the value of their production reached 12.5–13 per cent of global industrial production. Under the influence of relative price movements and fluctuations in the 1970s the weight of the extracting sectors has grown in global industrial production. Of the hundered minerals there are six which are of vital importance and a further ten are of considerable significance for modern economic development. These are an important element in world trade[93] since without them global industry and agriculture would practically come to a standstill.

The share of some important mineral raw materials in the production value of world mining—on the basis of the price level prior to the price explosion of the 1970s—was the following in the early 1970s (according to *Voprosi Ekonomiki,* No. 1, 1974):

Petroleum	41.4	Copper	7.5
Coal	21.4	Gold	3.1
Natural gas	3.9	Zinc	1.9
Iron ore	7.1	Lead	1.5
Manganese	1.2	Nickel	0.9

Tin	0.8	Phosphate	0.5
Silver	0.4	Rock-salt and	
Platinum	0.2	common salt	1.0
Uranium oxide		Diamonds	0.4
concentrate	1.8		

Since then those shares changed substantially. The changes in prices and in consumption patterns modified the relative proportions. There are no comparable data, but from the main trends the increase in the share of fuels has been the most important one.

In addition to the differing factor-intensity, changes in the composition of energy requirements of the various countries depend also on to what extent natural, traditional fuels are replaced by mineral fuels, on the volume of hydro energy available and the rate of improvement of efficiency of equipment used for the transformation of energy.

Important changes accompany the level of development, according to historical events in this century: dparting from the lower stages of economic development wood-burning, hydraulic-driven wheels, animal hauling power, wind-power are replaced by the use of mineral fuels. At a higher stage of economic development energy requirements are increased by leaps and bounds by the advance of communication and transport as well as industry, particularly heavy industry (later on, energy needs increase by and large proportionally to the growth of production).

In countries reaching a high standard of per capita income new energy needs are brought about by the widening range of services, the introduction of complex productive methods, a higher grade of product processing and the spread of labour-saving household devices (as a consequence of which the development of energy production is more rapid than that of any other productive activity).

Though former computations on global energy needs have been somewhat unreliable, they render some clues to the understanding of present-day conditions and also future problems.

The energy requirements of the world (calculated on the basis of coal equivalent) rose from 1 billion tons in 1900 to 1.5 billion by 1920. In the subsequent sixty years it has quadrupled, and according to the calculations of the Atomic Energy Commission of the United States, will reach 15 billion tons by the year 2000. The projected (World Bank) annual growth rates of global energy demand are 2.4 per cent between 1984–2000.

Significant changes have taken place in the use of fuels in our century. At the turn of the last century 37 per cent of all energy sources made use of originated from agriculture and sylviculture (16 per cent were agricultural waste materials and 21 per cent wood). The ratio of coal in fuel consumption reached its peak value in 1913 with 65 per cent; since then its share has diminished unceasingly and by 1985 it had declined to 31 per cent. The 1970s reflected a major turn in the energy economy towards the combination of different sources of energy in an efficient and rational framework in many industrial countries. Iron ore, phosphorus, bauxite, manganese, copper and chrome make up 95 per cent of global mining production (excluding fuels). The distribution of resources—both of fuels and minerals—is highly uneven. About half of the known and exploitable traditional fuels (coal, oil, natural gas) are to be found in the European socialist countries (overwhelmingly in the Soviet Union), 29 per cent of them in the developed Western countries (mainly in North America), and the remaining 20 per cent in the developing countries. The exploration of the resources of the Third World countries, however, is still in the initial phase.

Of the twenty most important other minerals 46 per cent of the resources are to be found in the industrialized Western countries, 20 per cent in the European socialist countries and 34 per cent in the developing countries. Almost 90 per cent of the resources of the industrialized West are concentrated in three countries (USA, Canada, South Africa), the decisive part of the resources of the socialist countries in the Soviet Union, whereas nearly half of the resources of the developing countries are concentrated in six countries. Western Europe, Japan, the East European socialist countries and the bulk of the Third World countries have only very limited raw material resources.[94] There is a close correlation between the level and structure of the given economy and the increase in the use of the various minerals (particularly metals). Taking the level in the United States in the 1970s as 100, per capita metal consumption was elsewhere as follows relatively according to data of the U. S. Bureau of Mines:

USA	100
Western Europe	60
Other industrialized capitalist countries	90
European CMEA countries	70
Latin America	15
Asia	4
Africa	2

The Western industrialized countries (representing 17 per cent of the population of the world) purchased 75 per cent of the world imports of metals and minerals in 1986. The country by country distribution of the mineral resources is very uneven, the rate of exhaustion is rather fast, which influences greatly the changes on the international raw material market.

However, since the end of the 1960s the situation of the extracting industry has not only been influenced by the growth problems of the developed Western countries. The production and utilization of raw materials and fuels were affected in many aspects by the unfolding of a new phase of world economic development. The three main aspects of raw material supply (development of natural needs, movement of raw material prices, political aspects of raw material problems) have all been influenced by the changes of the past one or two decades.

It is worth emphasizing some of these changes.

a) The growth of global population accompanied by relatively rapid industrial progress after World Warr II (particularly in the 1960s) raised the question of whether the world would be capable of meeting its growing raw material requirements.

b) More and more countries have become dependent on raw material imports, and at the same time the percentage of raw materials imported from developing countries has been diminishing.

c) Production and markets have been made increasingly unstable by the fluctuations of demand and prices.

d) The exporting countries made efforts to improve the degree of processing to be able to export processed materials instead of raw materials; this has changed the structure of international trade and raw material utilization.

e) Many developing countries wanted to strengthen their control over their raw material resources and intended to establish various organizations of producers (the most succesful of them has been of OPEC) thus bringing about new conditions in the relationship between enterprises and governments as within interstate relations.

f) The rapid progress of the material sciences rendered it possible to introduce new materials or combinations of materials, and to reduce the specific use of materials.

g) Environmental pollution has increased as a result of the quantitative growth of the extracting industries bringing about the resistance of society to activities that destroy the environment.

Four different views were held in the early 1970s regarding the problems of energy and raw materials (or more precisely: as regards the possibilities of increased utilization of raw materials and energy indispensable for economic progress).

One opinion was reflected by the views linked with the report of the Club of Rome "Limits of Growth". It was strongly emphasized by holders of this view that if economic growth characterizing the preceding period, i.e. the 1950s and 1960s, and the rate at which raw material and energy consumption continued to grow, the resources of the world would soon be exhausted and further economic growth would become impossible because of the shortage of raw materials by the end of the first half of the next century.

According to a second view, economic development will shift from material production towards the services in the highly developed countries and, as a result, raw material consumption will diminish.

The advocates of the third view stressed that mankind has always succeeded in avoiding a shortage of raw materials and therefore an exhaustion of raw material reserves is not a serious threat in our times either. (According to them the task is to exploit the traditional raw materials more efficiently, to reduce the material intensity of economic development, to seek for new natural and synthetic materials and to make use of and recycle the used materials in a more effective way.)

The adherents of the fourth view regarded the forces of the traditional market relations as sufficient in the future, too, and wished to restrict the intervention of state or inter-state organizations to a necessary minimum.

It was shown that the "limits of growth" school of thought—stripped of its sentimental and moralizing "garnish"—is nothing but a serious warning that the raw material reserves of our globe are finite. It is the unquestionably great merit of this school that by stimulating a great variety of research work, it was instrumental in a more scientific interpretation and better understanding of the problem of the "limits". The concept of sustainable economic growth was developed by scientists. This was achieved not by the strength of proof and evidence supplied by its theses, but through criticism of these views it was understood that a difference exists between renewable and non-renewable resources, and that in the case of the "finite" resources the problems will be caused more by the costs and possibilities of extraction than by the depletion of resources on our globe, for many years to come.

The continuation of the traditional methods of mining could devastate vast territories. The cost of rehabilitation is immense, where efforts aiming at the protection of the environment have increased. A great number of old deposits are in a state of exhaustion and therefore exploitation shifts to places with more difficult access or to lower efficiency resources. Thus specific costs become higher and higher.

Capital stock used for the exploitation of fuels and raw materials amounted to 1 per cent of the total capital stock in the developed industrial countries in 1970, to about 3 per cent in the European socialist states and nearly 4 per cent in the developing countries. By 1980 these figures had risen to 1.6, 5.3 and 5.1 per cent, respectively (according to computations based on UN statistics). Despite the progress in mining technology", costs kept on rising because of the increasing use of less efficient sources and also as a result of large infrastructural investment. Due to technological progress, however, society is able to reduce the material intensity of growth and, if necessary, to by changing its way of life. The new raw material and energy consumers (e.g. the industrializing Third World countries) are no exception to this rule. The truth of the above thesis is reflected in the peculiar conditions which have developed in global energy production and consumption in the 1970s and 1980s.

For the world as a whole in 1960 it was necessary to use 6.82 barrels of oil equivalent (BOE) commercial energy to produce US $ 1,000 thousand of GDP, in 1984 it required 5.78 barrels of oil equivalent. Deceleration was especially conspicuous in the developed Western countries (from 6.0 to 4.5 BOE) and in the European socialist states (from 13.6 to 11, BOE per US $ 1,000 GDP).

The slackening in the growth rate of energy consumption had a different cause in almost every country. In some countries it was brought about by the reduction of energy-intensive branches of industry, in others by the slackening of economic development.

Rising prices, too, had a part in the slowing down of consumption stimulating thereby conservation and the increase of productivity. Consumption, however, reacts relatively slowly to changing prices. The rate of deceleration depends partly also on the rate of replacement of energy-intensive devices, transport vehicles, etc. (in the case of cars this means ten years, for machinery 12–15 years).

The 1970s and the 1980s were extremely instructive as regards the relationship between economic development and energy production as well as energy supply, and also threw light on the economic possibilities connected with the above problems.

a) There are possibilities in all the countries of the world for further energy-saving economic development. Both energy transformation and utilization are of a much more energy-saving character today as compared to the dominant technology of the middle of the twentieth century. The prospects of the new technology have been enhanced particularly by the latest achievements of the scientific and technological revolution, first and foremost by the chances opened up by miniaturization and process regulation connected with microelectronics. Its application, however, demands the renewal and replacement of equipment produced prior to the 1960s. Thus, changes demand enormous investment, the amortization of which is very high and seems to be more profitable when higher energy prices rule. The oil price explosion has stimulated energy-conserving investment in the industrial countries ever since the 1970s. This process is also the source of significant structural transformations in their economies.

Predictions for energy consumption have been modified many times between 1973 and 1984, and without exception the new forecasts point in the direction of a more restrained growth rate.

b) Economic growth in the industrially developed Western countries was greatly helped by cheap oil in the era after World War II. It was oil which created the energy basis for the transformation of the way of life and the rapid development of a number of highly efficient industries. Even in the mid-1980s 41 per cent of global commercial energy consumption was oil-based coal provided 33 per cent, natural gas 22 per cent.

If the world is unable to secure inexpensive sources of energy in great volume then the uncertainty characterizing the 1970s will continue even if prices drop in the years to come, and the rise of consumption will slacken under the effect of economy measures or a slower rate of economic growth. This is true despite the fact that in theory global oil needs can be met securely for some decades, and that the leading industrial powers were in the position to declare once again in the middle of the 1980s that they reached the state of "energy security", i.e. they disposed of significant reserves and alternative sources under the condition of declining energy consumption intensities.

c) Despite the improved overall situation the individual countries—in proportion to their possibilities—try to diminish their dependence on one or two energy sources. A policy of energy production and supply is emerging which is based on the rational combination of different sources and takes into account the natural endowments and technological needs of the countries in question. There are three main trends in the various combinations:

— An increase of the share of power generation based on coal and nuclear energy.

— The expansion of production and an adequate combination of fossil energy sources (e.g. an increase of the production and utilization of oil and natural gas) by means of improving the efficiency of oil and natural gas exploitation or a more complex utilization of coal.

— The multiple utilization of renewable energy sources (e.g. solar energy and biomass) and at the same time, a considerable decentralization of energy transformation (e.g. application of individual solar elements in buildings rendering possible both heating, warm water supply and airconditioning, desalinization of brine and transformation of sea-water with the help of solar energy for consumption).

International raw material trade and its terms and conditions will remain an important factor for the majority of countries in the decades to follow.

While the presently prevailing tendencies in world trade, i.e. the decreasing ratio of raw materials, will probably continue, considerable further regional changes are expected as regards the production and consumption of raw materials, particularly of energy sources. The industrialization of the developing countries, too, will increase the growing dependence on raw material imports in the world economy. Of all energy sources made use of only 14 per cent had crossed national borders in 1925, whereas this ratio rose to 31 per cent in 1967 and to almost 36 per cent in 1982. Half of global industrial production depends on external raw material sources. Only a mere handful of states are able to meet their raw material and energy requirements from internal sources. Japan imports 99 per cent of her oil requirements, Western Europe (Great Britain excluded) 96 per cent. In Western Europe consumption considerably surpasses internal production as regards eleven basic and vital raw materials (bauxite, copper, lead, phosphate, zinc, chromium, manganese ore, magnesium, nickel, wolfram and tin). Copper, phosphate, tin, nickel, manganese and chromium used by industry are almost 100 per cent imported.

The United States, though relatively rich in raw materials was obliged in 1950 to meet the greater part of its needs by means of imports of four mineral substances: 64 per cent of aluminium, 88 per cent manganese ore, 94 per cent of nickel and 77 per cent of tin. By 1980, however, the USA imported already the greater part of its requirements of seven important raw materials. Admittedly, the increasing imports of certain materials and the stopping or reduction of domestic production can be explained partly by reasons of efficiency in the United States and to a certain extent in Western Europe, too. Raw material imports proved to be actually cheaper than the development of domestic production. On the other hand, in some countries, for instance in Japan, the import of raw materials remains the only possibility of meeting demands.[95]

The majority of the European socialist countries, too, have become highly dependent on imported raw materials and fuels. Their share of global non-fuel primary commodity imports increased from 9.7 per cent in 1969–71 to 13.4 per cent in 1984–86 and will increase to 15 per cent by 2000. Their industrial development was based to a great extent on Soviet sources. The slow improvement in the use of resources, in all the CMEA countries as well as difficulties in the development of the extractive sectors in the Soviet Union could cause increasingly serious problems in this region.

However, neither the increasing demand for raw materials, particularly for fuels, nor growing dependence on imports mean that in the foreseeable future (till the end of this century or the early decades of the next century) there would ensue a radical shortage of fuels or raw materials which would become a considerable obstacle to economic development. The instability of the markets may create problems. Production may decline because of the depressed prices which may lead to temporary shortages.

Rising costs, however, could be balanced by technological progress in the extracting branches and processing industry. Due to sharpening competition among the producers and an improvement in the possibilities of substitution, high prices cannot be sustained for a longer time.

The situation in the mid-1980s reflected the great problems dominating the raw material sector in the world economy. The ratio of aggregate minerals and metals consumption to industrial output declined by 9 per cent between 1979–84 in the Western industrial countries (by an average 1.8 per cent year compared by 0.9 per cent during the 1970s). This was compounded by an aggregate price decline of 27 per cent. From

Table 28.
Long-term Changes in Consumption and Imports of
Western Industrial Countries in Certain Commodity Groups
(1979–81 prices in percentages)

	1969–71 C	1979–81 I	1979–81 C	1984–86 I	1984–86 C	2000 I
Food	1.13	2.05	0.84	1.56	1.56	1.90
Agricultural raw materials	−0.62	0.02	−2.15	−1.56	−0.19	0.10
Metals and minerals	1.64	2.30	−0.74	0.63	0.39	0.96

C—consumption
I—imports
Source: World Bank. Economic Analysis and Projections Department, 1986.

1982 the output of these products has been practically stopped in some enterprises of a number of countries. A great number of mines, ore dressing plants and ironworks were closed down in the copper and aluminium industries of the developed industrial countries. Beyond these enterprises, which had to face serious difficulties, the problems of developing countries which depended on the sale of one or two minerals or metals grew very fast.

The loss of income of mineral and metal exporting developing countries amounted to more than $ 100 billion (more than the half of the total value of their annual production).

Of the 110 developing countries which can be analysed statistically 56 earn as much as 50 per cent of their export incomes from the export of raw materials. According to UNCTAD, the real prices of a great number of important raw materials reached only half of their 1950 price level in 1982.[96]

In the long run a decline in the proportion of raw material and food imported can be expected. (This is illustrated by the figures of Table 28.)

Under the conditions unfolded since 1970 importer countries strive to diminish their dependence on one or another major supplier and to bring about the possibility of diversification including a utilization of greater proportions of internal reserves. In that way they also try to defend themselves against the international raw material cartels.

As indicated by experience gained with international raw material agreements cartels are seldom successful in the long run. *First,* in general not all the producers are members of the cartel. The outsiders find it profitable to boost production (whereas the members of the cartel tend to restrict it). Thus, the strength of the cartel is sapped, its market share and profits are diminished. At the same time, the outsiders are stimulated by their possibilities of not joining the cartel which is the more successful the greater the part of production that is concentrated in its hand. *Second,* it is much easier to organize and hold together the cartel if the number of producers remains small. A great part of production has to be concentrated among a few producers to bring about a successful operation of the organization. *Third,* price flexibility of production outside the cartel has to be negligible. If the non-member producers are capable of raising considerably their supply following the price rise, the cartel cannot be long-lived. (The oil producers outside the OPEC were able to increase their production for export significantly despite contrary expectations.) *Fourth*, the price flexibility of demand for products turned out by the cartel has to be relatively low. If demand drops significantly as a result of prices raised by the cartel, the cartel itself disrupts its organization since the incomes of its members dwindle away. The product in question, therefore, has to be one which cannot be readily substituted. Incidentally, even successful cartels call into life forces which lead to their eventual disintegration.

All this is borne out instructively by the activities of OPEC. At the time of its founding, i.e. in 1960, OPEC controlled 37.6 per cent of global crude oil production, and this percentage reached 55.8 per cent in 1973. However, the share of OPEC has dwindled to 45.5 per cent by 1980.[97]

The development of the relationship between oil producing and oil exporting countries has undergone quite a few phases. During the first stage some oil producing countries at different stages of development successfully exploited their economic and political chances and quadrupled oil prices between October 1973 and the end of 1974. The reaction of the oil importing countries was generally unambiguously hostile in that phase (contrary to that of the oil companies). It was expected that similarly to all cartels, OPEC, too, would disintegrate relatively soon. The second phase was characterized by the recognition of the OPEC structure, the acceptance of the oil producing and exporting countries as partners in the world economy. Both parties attempted to exploit the favourable possibilities opening up before them. For the oil producing countries new vistas were opened up on the international commodity and money markets by their oil revenues. As a result of the significant development programmes of the oil countries huge investments were put into effect and in the majority of the OPEC countries domestic consumption, too, increased. The former price ratios between oil and industrial products were practically restored in this stage. The third stage was introduced by the second oil price explosion and lasted until oil prices began to drop once again. The present (fourth) stage is characterized by lower oil prices and the internal tensions of OPEC. Owing to world economic recession and to the successful conservation programs in consumption, the international oil market actually became saturated. In addition, the relatively monopolistic position of the oil cartel, too, has been shattered by non-OPEC oil-producing states. Nevertheless, an overt and rapid disintegration of OPEC does not seem likely in the present conditions of the world economy. Despite conflicts and tensions the member states share the view that the maintainance of cooperation is in their common interest. However, within OPEC "covert" price reducing or production boosting by the individual member states resulting in a weakening of their common front may become more frequent and marked.

It is an open and highly debated question how far the raw material producers will be able to strengthen the raw material market and improve their bargaining position in a world of declining material consumption intensities, slower economic growth and increasing competition. Attempts at concluding international agreements to bring about "compensatory financing" or "long-term production quotas" or maybe gradually replaced by the efforts of raw material producing states to export minerals and metals and other primary products to be found on their territories in more processed forms in the decades to follow. This may encourage the modification of the production structure of present-day users and the development of industries rendering possible a higher grade of processing.

The share of the developing countries in global raw material consumption tends to further increase in the next decades and, taking into account tendencies of industrial development and the intensities of consumption, it could reach 30–33 per cent of energy and 20–25 per cent of different important metals by the turn of the century. The proportion they might take would increase by 50–60 per cent over that of the 1980s. The share of the developing countries will continue to grow also within the raw material importing countries. Their share of global metals and minerals imports will increase from 17 per cent in 1984–86 to 21 per cent by 2000.

The significance of material sciences increases all over the world (particularly in the developed industrial countries) contributing in a complex way to the expansion of material stocks available to mankind. The progress of material sciences is going in the following directions:

— a better understanding of mineralogy, improvement in the technology of exploration;
— development of new advanced materials and new production processes (e.g. amorphous materials, synthetic polymers, ceramics, magnetic materials, special gasses, semiconductors);
— improvement in the physical efficiency of mining;
— turning out cheaper and more efficient substitute materials and the perfection of the quality indices of different alloys;
— utilization of the achievements of biotechnology in the growing and processing of materials of agricultural origin;
— developing the technologies of recycling (also for new materials).

Electronics and the defence industries are of outstanding importance for the stimulation of the development of material sciences. The development of a great number of new materials has been made possible by the special demands of microelectronics, military technologies and research work aimed at meeting such demands.

The Changing Structure in Manufacturing and the Conditions, Factors and Directions of the Development of Internationalization

The transformation of manufacturing industry takes place as part of the process of structural and organizational changes all over the world in the last part of this century. The frontiers of well-defined manufacturing activities are getting more and more uncertain, partly as a consequence of the development of the interbranch links; partly because scientific research and industry are increasingly interlinked multiply, and partly because of some services, too, are closely interwoven with industrial activities (as pointed out earlier in this book).

As a result of technological progress, the traditional branches of industry and the emerging new branches are interconnected. Around the new industries and under the effect of the new technological and economic conditions and requirements, industrial production and service blocks or complexes emerge. The most typical organizing forces are the complexes of information (electronics), energy, biology and military industry.

From the end of World War II until 1980 world trade in industrial products has expanded twice as fast as the output of manufacturing industries—an important indicator of the internationalization of industrial activities.

The share of imported products in the consumption of industrial goods rose particularly quickly in the developed industrial countries. According to UNCTAD statistics for manufacturing, imports as a percentage of apparent consumption in the EEC, North America and Japan rose between 1976 and 1985 from 8.0 to 14 per cent Within the machinery group the share of imports in consumption increased from 18 to 26 per cent. Scientific and technological cooperation have strengthened considerably. Joint ventures and other forms of industrial inter-industrial relations expanded. The internationalization of industrial relations among the major centres of the world (USA, Canada, Western Europe and Japan) also influenced the industrializing developing and socialist countries through the conditions of technology imports and export possibilities. Significant changes characterize the regional location and global structure of industrial production. It is particularly the industrial-servicing complexes in the new-tech groups which are of outstanding importance from the aspect of the establishment of the new international industrial relations. Technological changes, internationalization, specialization and the various forms of industrial cooperation transform the organizational patterns of enterprises: flexibility, faster adaptation and more rapid changes in production are becoming important principles in this respect too. The role of size is changing in many areas. Smaller firms and units are emerging, which are able to compete more effectively since the cost of modifying their products to changes in market forces and national differences is lower than those of the larger firms. While they cannot compete with the large companies in terms of marketing resources, new production technologies and cooperation may facilitate their competitiveness in certain segments of the market.

The other major factor in the process of global changes in manufacturing is the shift in branch composition under the impact of new technology, new demand conditions and sharpening international competition.

World economic changes have been especially strongly influenced by the transformation of the structure of industrial production. The main trends point basically in a similar direction in the developed Western countries, the developing countries and the European socialist states. The following changes relate to the period from 1963 to 1979–1980.

a) The share of light industry has diminished, and that of the heavy industry has increased in all three regions: the share of light industry has dropped in the developing countries (taking 47 Third World countries) from 69 to 57 per cent, in the developed Western countries (the average of 23 countries) from 47 to 40 per cent while in the European CMEA countries (the average of 7 countries) from 49 to 36 per cent. By the early 1980s 64 per cent of manufacturing output came from the heavy industry in the socialist countries, 60 per cent in the developed capitalist countries and 43 per cent in the developing countries.

b) Taking into consideration final consumption, the share of industrial consumer goods has dropped from 45 to 37 per cent in the developed industrial Western countries, from 46 to 34 per cent in the socialist countries, and from 66 to 54 per cent in the developing countries. Intermediary production in these three country groups has developed as follows:

It has increased:

from 19 to 34 per cent in the developed Western countries;

from 17 to 20 per cent in the socialist countries;

from 21 to 27 per cent in the developing countries.

In 1980 the share of capital goods (durable industrial consumer goods included) in manufacturing came to 40 per cent in the developed Western countries, to 46 per cent in the socialist countries and to 19 per cent in the Third World countries.[98] Among the branches of industry triggering off structural changes three branches of chemical industry (industrial chemicals (ISIC 351), other chemicals (ISIC 352), plastics (ISIC 356), as well as three branches of capital goods, non-electric engineering (ISIC 382), electrical engineering (ISIC 383), production of scientific instruments (ISIC 385), were of outstanding importance. The increased weight of these six branches of industry represented the most dynamic element of the structural changes.

c) The ratio of branches with a declining share in industrial production in the period under survey (from the beginning of the 1960s to the end of the 1970s) developed as follows:

It shifted:

from 46.7 to 60.6 per cent in the developed Western countries, reflecting important
            structural changes;

from 51.4 to 43.6 per cent in the socialist countries;

from 52.0 to 50.0 per cent in the developing countries.

Thus, the following branches of industries belonged to the category of declining industries in the 1960s: food, textile, leather, paper and printing industries. These were joined, among others, by the iron and steel, rubber and wood industries in the 1970s. There is no comparable data for the 1980s available. The statistics for the first half of the 1980s indicate, however, changing trends: the share of food and printing industries increased and the proportion of petroleum refineries declined. In connection with the global distribution of declining industries it is necessary to specify, that in the socialist and developing countries certain industrial branches are still in the growing category that are declining in the developed Western countries, reflecting the differences in development level. In spite of this fact, with a few exceptions the direction of changes was similar in all the three country groups, though the differences in general and within the branches should not be underestimated. For instance, one-third of manufacturing output originated from the machinery industry in the developed Western countries in 1980. This percentage was 35 per cent in the socialist countries, and in the developing countries the share of machinery in industrial production was a mere 15 per cent. Within that branch, however, the share of high-tech machinery varied according to the technological level of the three country groups.

The share of food industry in the production of the manufacturing industry was 15 per cent in the developed Western countries, 14 per cent in the European socialist countries, but 29 per cent in the developing countries. The highly capital and research intensive branches occupied a major role in the Western industrialized countries.

Among the declining branches of manufacturing industry there are some which had developed in the earlier periods of economic development. As a consequence of changing domestic and world market demand their production is shrinking sometimes in terms of absolute volume, too, often going hand in hand with significant internal economic transformations in the developed industrial countries and the increasing competitiveness of many developing countries in those branches in the world market. The share of the declining industries and the difficulties in phasing them out in the developed industrial world is a major cause of structural problems in the late twentieth century and it is a constant source of protectionist pressures.

Both in the developed Western countries and in the socialist states the intensity of the structural changes in the period under review was more significant within the single industries than among the branches of industries and was carried out on a greater scale between 1960 and 1970 than in the subsequent decade. In compliance with the characteristics of the individual industries the "structure" of production technologies has often changed to a greater extent than that of the final product, i.e. a final product of identical or similar composition has been turned out with a considerably more efficient technology. The two tendencies were frequently combined. Thus, in the steel industries of the developed Western countries with the overall decline of the branch, the ratio of the production of special steel products has increased concurrently, with the transformation of the production technologies as the size and nature of operations in steel mills have changed.

In connection with the structural changes of production and utilization the structure of the world trade in manufactured goods, too, has altered. The ratio of capital goods and durable consumer articles of heavy industrial origins has increased in the foreign trade of all the country groups of the world (it reached 46 per cent of the total global exports of manufactured goods in 1980).[99]

Changes in connection with the differing intensity of production factors represent a further dimension of structural transformation. Classification according to the intensity of labour, capital intensity, material intensity and degrees of quality or the combination of these categories—these were the basis on which UNCTAD economists made their computations of structural changes. In the period between 1970 and 1980 the production of industries demanding a high degree of capital intensity and a highly qualified labour force registered the fastest expansion in Western Europe and the United States. In Japan industries with high qualifications and low capital intensity developed most rapidly. A typical example of the first was the chemical industry, of the second, electrical engineering. In the coming decades, the changing importance of the relative factor shares will create even more important structural shifts. They will change the patterns of output towards knowledge intensive branches and many transform labour or capital intensive industries into highly "knowledge intensive" ones, with very high R & D content.

The patterns of further changes could be characterized in a simplified way by two coexisting types of manufacturing industries: the material intensive ones and the R & D intensive ones. These latter, however, are increasingly influencing the former branches as well. Still, for a longer time they will differ in many ways, not only in their technological characteristics or competitive position. The products of R & D intensive industries are traded in the world market in the form of products and services, the

Table 29.
**Share of the Multinational Corporations in the
Industrial Production and Exports of Some Countries,
1980s (per cent)**

	Share in manufacturing	Share in the exports of manufactured goods
Hong Kong	13.9	16.5
India	7.0	below 10
Pakistan	no data	below 10
South Korea	19.3	28.0
Singapore	62.9	89.7
Argentina	31.0	30.0
Brazil	32.0	32.3
Columbia	28.0	30.0
Mexico	28.0	42.4

Source: UNCTAD: *Trade and Development Report,* 1982. New York, 1982. p 77.
U.N. *Transnational Centre,* 1988. p. 159.

others are entering into market as products. While the share of the developed Western industrial countries is declining in global production and exports of material intensive industries, it is growing rapidly in the R & D intensive branches or product groups. Their competitiveness is being eroded, however, not only in many "traditional" branches but even in some of the R & D intensive ones.

The main reason for the rapid advance of some developing countries in world trade and the deterioration of the competitiveness of certain industries of the developed industrial countries can be explained by the fact that some developing countries (South Korea, Taiwan, Singapore, etc.) were able to combine their relatively qualified and cheap labour with highly developed technologies and organizational methods purchased mainly from Western industrial states, and Western marketing systems. This process was sometimes significantly furthered by transnational corporations which try to achieve the most favourable combinations of professional training, prices of materials, capital effectiveness and wage level in their global systems, and naturally exploit the advantages of customs, tax and other benefits as well, offered by different competing governments to attract foreign investment.

As reflected by Table 29, the measure of the control of the production and exports of the manufacturing industries of some developing countries by transnational corporations is rather significant. The changing role of different countries and regions in the global output of manufacturing industries and the structural shifts in production are taking place in the environment of increasing internationalization:

a) The introduction of new industries in the great majority of the countries depends on the import of technology and services—as has been already indicated in Part Three of this book. This is often connected with different forms of long-term international industrial cooperation.

Giant companies play a major role in these industrial transactions through exports of foods and services and inter-group investments.

b) The most important single factor of internationalization in manufacturing industries is the role of the transnational corporations in the distribution of global economic activities and in the performance and competitiveness of many countries. The acceleration of technological change, the increasing development costs and the partial globalization of tastes and standards are leading to the globalization or continentalization of industrial strategies and competition. These changes promoted global concentration and especially in research-intensive industries there are now only about ten to fifteen major competitors, globally. The global strategies of transnational corporations control a large part of technology transfer and establish new patterns of industrial specialization beyond the scope of industrial policies formulated by national governments. The proportion of overseas production is on the increase in all the major industrial countries (not only that of the United States). By 1985 international production contributed approximately 45 per cent of the turnover of West German multinationals and about one third of that of the UK firms.

The various actual or anticipated new protectionist measures are stimulating the establishment of new industrial firms abroad even in such countries as the US. The aim of these forms is to produce in the protected markets, instead of exporting there. (Japanese enterprises in the USA are especially motivated by this factor.)

c) Export orientation, as a basic aim of industrial development is playing an increasingly important role in the policies of many countries. The new industries are working for different international markets, sometimes as parts of global marketing and production systems.

The internationalization of industrial development has contributed to the expansion of the international division of labour. The share of exports of manufactured goods has increased in the gross national product in the majority of the countries of the world. (Table 30.)

Efforts to develop export-oriented industries in the developing countries have especially strengthened ever since the second half of the 1970s. These countries tried to attract foreign capital by means of different incentives. An instrument of increasing importance has become the establishment of special zones producing for export goods. Since they represent a small but more and more important form of internationalization we shall deal with it at a somewhat greater length in the next section.

Export Processing Zones—Special Zones—and the Internationalization in Industry

"Export processing zones for free production"—special zones—are gaining ground in international production and trade—mostly in the developing world. The establishment of these zones was encouraged by some international development agencies in order to further the industrialization of the Third World countries. The spread of export zones is closely linked to the expansion of the operations of transnational corporations in developing countries as well as to the expansion of off-shore processing and assembly. These zones offer minimal immediate economic advantages to the governments of the countries where they have been established but for foreign firms low local wages are highly attractive cost reducing factors. For this reason such zones offer great possibilities for transnational corporations.

The structure of industrial production of this nature is characterized by breaking up the production process into various operations, products or product groups which are manufactured or assembled at different places. A number of developing countries, which otherwise would have not been able to lure foreign investment, can together offer all the preconditions of efficient and competitive production to transnational corporations. Such conditions are

— well-equipped infrastructure (especially transport) and various services,
— abundant and cheap labour,
— efficient administration.

The conception of free zones for goods transfer, storage and re-exporting dates back more than two hundred years. Free trade zones established by the colonial powers in the past century at converging points of international trade, e.g. in Gibraltar and Hong Kong. At the same time, there have been centres of storage and re-exports right up to this date, which were established by cities and ports to entice some international trade.

The new form of export processing zone has appeared in the past decade or so. The first was established in Shannon, Ireland, in 1959. The original aim of the Shannon zone was to support employment at the airport by means of attracting processing activities which could stimulate air transport. As a result, Shannon has become a centre of gravitation of export oriented industries.

Enterprises operating within the confines of "duty-free zones" take advantage of a great number of different benefits guaranteed by the host country. As a rule, the region is well-protected, disposes of advantageous transport possibilities and, in some cases, has a police force of its own to guard the territory. The different incentives may include some of the following possibilities:

— full exemption from duty and taxes for imported and exported raw materials, capital goods and spare parts;
— full exemption from taxes for companies and/or dividends;
— omission of controlling foreign trade, free or only slightly restricted repatriation of profits, the deferment of amortization costs for the time of exemption from taxes;
— preferential financial possibilities, e.g. short-term, medium-term and long-term credits at favourable interest rates for those locating industry in the zone;
— favourable low cost transport facilities between the free zone and the sea ports or the airports, as well as price reductions for services, building sites, buildings and general services;
— low wages costs as one of the most obvious financial incentives;
— simplified procedures: simplified administrative rules inclusive of rules on customs, investments and labour relations;
— standard buildings suitable for production or offices. (In addition, other services are offered e.g. repair shops, medical care, bank, post, telecommunications, gas stations, storehouses, transport vehicles, insurance.)

While duty-free zones proliferate rapidly, the favourable impact on the host country is rather limited. The overall volume of output and trade generated in these zones is relatively small. The relations between the zones and the rest of the economy of the host countries are sometimes even of an adverse nature (black market operations, smuggling etc.). The diffusion of new technology, managerial talent, or entrepreneur-

Table 30.

Ratio of the Exports of Manufactured Goods in the Gross National Product

	Exports as a percentage of the GNP							
	below 10	10–20	20–30	30–40	40–50	50–60	60–70	above 70
World								
1960	27.1	34.5	19.8	9.9	2.5	2.5	—	3.7
1970	18.8	35.9	21.7	3.8	6.6	3.8	1.9	7.5
1980	16.1	25.3	24.0	12.0	8.0	4.0	5.3	5.3
Industrial countries								
1960	20.0	45.0	25.0	10.0	—	—	—	—
1970	15.0	35.0	40.0	5.0	—	—	—	—
1980	10.0	20.0	45.0	10.0	10.0	5.0	—	—
Oil-exporting countries								
1960	16.6	50.0	16.7	16.7	—	—	—	—
1970	—	10.0	40.0	—	—	10.0	10.0	30.0
1980	—	—	—	20.0	—	—	40.0	40.0
Other developing countries								
1960	30.9	29.1	18.2	9.1	3.6	3.6	—	5.5
1970	22.3	39.4	14.5	4.0	7.9	4.0	1.3	6.6
1980	20.0	30.0	18.0	12.0	8.0	4.0	4.0	4.0

Source: IMF, International Financial Statistics Supplement of Trade Statistics, 1982.

ship beyond the zone is also difficult to achieve. Still, this is an increasingly popular form of creating new jobs and establishing potential export industries, which can increasingly utilize local materials and even machinery and equipment. In certain cases special supporting industries can be established outside the zone for these purposes. Some of the products can be used also in the domestic market of the host country.

According to the estimates of the author based on various national statistics, about 2.5–3 million workers are engaged in the different free trade zones all over the world. The great majority of them are working in Asia. The most developed free trade zones are in China, Malaysia, South Korea and the Philippines. Enterprises active in such zones are nearly all operating in the electronic, textile and clothing sectors.

Global Shifts: Electronics and the Automobile Industry as Case Studies

Technological changes, the shifts in demand, growing internationalization, the increasing competition and industrial policies influence the branches of industry in many different ways. Here we select two industries; electronics and motor vehicles to illustrate some aspects of the changes. One is a new high-tech industry, the other is an important large branch with long traditions.

Certain high-technology industries may become of outstanding importance in manufacturing. Owing to their dynamism and wide-spread interbranch relations, they have a broad influence on the development of the sector as a whole, and beyond that they may develop into central branches, determining the other branches and sectors technologically over a given period of time.

a) Electronics: a major factor in global industrial transformation

In the last part of the twentieth century, among the new technologies micro-electronics has been the most significant restructuring factor in manufacturing industry. Electrical equipment and electronic industries have been important branches from the point of view of innovations and technological changes since the late nineteenth century. The utilization of electric power was the fundamental factor which led to the development of the electrical equipment industry. Electronics, and in our era microelectronics, operate on the information content. Its role originates partly in its fundamental technological characteristics, i.e. in the manipulation, transmission and storage of information, which has facilitated its application in almost all areas. In the past 10–15 years extremely fast technological progress has been achieved in electronics and by the application of the innovations (both as regards products and production processes), in different areas. Electronic industry is broad and diversified. The different branches of electronics develop under specific technological-economic and political conditions. There are no universally accepted statistical groups. The branch is spread into inherited and new categories in the industrial and trade statistics. Its main groups fall under the headings "electrical machinery and computer equipment", tele-communication equipment, electronic components and equipments, industrial and scientific instruments, electromedical equipments. These are fast-growing industries, the share of which is increasing in manufacturing output. Their total share in the developed industrial countries was around 14–15 per cent in the mid-1980s. The

Table 31.
Structure of the Electronic Complex in the United States
(business turnover in billion dollars)

	1981		1982		1983		1986*	
Semi-conductors	6.7	5.3	7.5	5.2	9.2	5.6	15.8	6.4
Component parts	12.0	9.5	12.8	8.9	14.3	8.7	19.9	8.1
Entertainment electronics	20.0	12.4	21.3	14,8	22.7	13.8	29.9	12.0
Data processing	44.3	35.0	52.1	36.2	61.8	37.5	105.0	42.7
Experimental and guaging instruments	3.2	2.5	3.6	2.5	4.2	2.5	6.6	2.6
Telecommunication equipments	6.4	5.1	7.0	4.9	8.3	5.0	12.3	5.0
Medical and control instruments	4.0	3.2	4.6	3.2	5.3	3.2	7.6	3.0
Industrial electronics	3.4	2.7	4.0	2.8	4.6	2.8	8.1	3.2
Military electronics	26.5	24.3	31.0	21.5	34.6	20.9	40.3	17.0
	126.5	100.0	143.9	100.0	165.0	100.0	245.0	100.0

* Estimates
Source: Electronics, January 1983.

organization of electronics is most complex in the United States. The structure of the electronics industry in the United States and its development in the early 1980s is set out in Table 31.

According to calculations and estimates based on the industrial statistics about the electronics complex in the USA, the group represented 16–18 per cent of industrial production in the mid-1980s, thus approaching the ratio of the automobile industry. The share of the same branches in Japan surpassed 30 per cent of manufacturing output in 1983, i.e. it outstripped that of the automobile-industry.

Microelectronics result in decisive changes in the production processes of all industries: with automation, with the application of industrial robots, flexible manufacturing systems are emerging: the production of goods with the shortest possible delivery time for constantly changing demand and heterogeneous consumer preferences. Computer-aided design represents major qualitative changes in many areas, not only in engineering work. Control by means of electronic sensors gives greater security to the product users. The size of labour force needed and its professional composition, too, are influenced by these changes in many ways. In countries where the cost of labour is high (USA, Japan, FRG) considerable efforts are made to substitute human labour in labour-intensive processes by industrial robots.

A great number of new branches of services were called into life by the use of computers linked with industrial production, labour organization, education, public administration, etc. Yet, the most important change has been the emergence of the so-called "information industry", the services of which are required on an increasing scale. In many countries national data banks have been established for various purposes. Some of them hold taxation, legal, social security, education, employment, information on all citizens. Incidentally, the volume of this information and the fact that it is centrally stored is highly important both for political and for business purposes and therefore the criteria of "availability" or "accessibility" of information should be separately regulated with regard to the right information.

There are other national and international data banks which collect and disseminate scientific and technological information. The application of electronic computers in scientific research has become increasingly widespread.

Computers are widely put to use not only to store economic information collected to help commercial and financial transactions, and also to control the stock flow within enterprises and companies. With the help of computers information on the demand for goods, prices, sales conditions, etc. can be quickly and exactly analysed by enterprises. Microelectronics has brought about revolutionary changes in telecommunications (let us only mention artificial satellites or fibre optics). About one-third of the value of a modern aircraft is the "electronic content" of it.

The development of microelectronics in world economy has evolved from three main centres: the United States, Japan and Western Europe. In 1986, 98 per cent of the global output of semiconductors came from those centres (44 per cent from the U.S., 45 per cent from Japan and 9 per cent from Western Europe). As the global spread of microelectronics is extremely fast, the above ratios might have changed considerably even within a few years. The progress of the international division of labour within this branch of industry is extraordinarily intensive. The individual phases of production or the production of component parts are deployed in different countries by the great international corporations. Smaller users, too, often tend to integrate with one or another main centre, as regards fundamental technologies.

The share of the most important Western European countries in the output of electronics was as follows in 1983 (percentage of sales value):

FRG	31%
Great Britain	23%
France	20%
Italy	6%
Benelux states	6%
Scandinavian states	8%
Spain	4%
Switzerland	2%

Source: see Table 31.

As clearly demonstrated by the above data, a considerable potential is concentrated in the Western European region though it is rather fragmented and lags far behind that of the USA and Japan.

The structure of the electronic industries in the three regions cannot be compared directly, however due to differences in the statistical bases. (Military electronics are dealt with separately in the USA, whereas in the other two regions it is not separated in the statistics.) The share of easily separable consumer's electronics was about 28 per cent in Western Europe and 29 per cent in Japan in 1983 (considerably higher than in the USA). The ratio of medical electronics was 2.8 per cent in Western Europe and 3.3 per cent in Japan (similar to its proportion in the USA).

The products of electronic industries have very rapidly penetrated into civilian consumption in the developed industrial countries. In addition to more traditional products (such as radios, television sets, tape recorders, audio-equipment), a wide range of video equipment, electronic toys and automatic devices have become widespread in households. The turnover in electronic musical instruments already surpasses that of the traditional ones. The increase in the sale of microwave ovens and grills, different household signal, alarm and other equipment as well as of calculators has been considerable. Personal computers have created new markets and demand. The turnover in auto-electronics has registered an increase, too. This part of electronics reached or approached saturation level by the early 1980s, and global competition has become even stronger as a result of the increasing role of new producers from among the developing countries. The lower prices which give them the competitive edge, are not due only to lower labour costs, but also to new products and product design. As a result of these changes the share of the developing countries in electronic consumer goods increased dramatically. In certain products, like in radio-sets, it surpassed one third of world exports by 1985.

Together with the saturation of the market in consumer electronics, a new phase of development unfolded in the field of innovation. One of the characteristics of this market is the "compression" of the cycle of innovation-production-consumption, i.e. models and series follow quickly in each others footsteps. Changes always go hand in hand with the reduction of prices despite the fact that research and development as well as investment costs per unit of output are increasing. The large companies react to the changes with the diversification of the final products based on identical components. The three main production phases of consumer electronics are the elaboration of new ideas, the development of new products and the renewal of production processes (inclusive of domestically necessary applied research). The relatively highly capital-intensive production of component elements (electronic components) represents the building blocks of electronic equipment. The electronic elements of computers, industrial control systems, digital displays, switches and audiovisual devices are basically identical. A highly complex and ramified, manifold "final product" demanding great labour intensity is turned out by production. The production of such goods becomes more and more automatized. The number of basic components by 1985 has been reduced from 5,000 to 40 within a few years. Average production time has been diminished to one tenth within a single decade. The simplification of production has also resulted in the location of production spreading into various countries.

The 1970s were characterized by the fact that the production of components and assembly bases were established for labour-intensive processes by the transnational corporations in South-East Asia, Latin America and the other industrializing Third World regions, while research and capital intensive processes remained in the developed industrial countries. In the 1980s, however, the labour intensive processes were shifted to even less developed regions: in addition to turning out component elements, the formation of complete production cycles of consumer electronics has been started by South Korea, Taiwan, Singapore and some other countries (i.e. they attempt to "rise" to a higher level in the production process). Production of electronics in the developing countries, of course, is still controlled to an overwhelming extent by transnational corporations.

At the same time, protectionism against the new producers—particularly against Japan—has increased in the industrially developed Western countries. As a consequence, the large Japanese companies—and recently the corporations of other

Asian countries, too—make great efforts to achieve more a favourable position by establishing directly producing or assembling enterprises in areas protected by customs duties. Consumer electronics progress faster since the first half of the 1980s in the European CMEA countries. This is based partly on their own R & D activities, partly on imports of technology. Their greater role in the world market is hampered by the bottlenecks in component manufacture and the slow product innovation.

Consumer electronics is closely linked with electronics serving complex industrial investment and services. The core of production-oriented electronics is the computer. In the mid-1980s there were about 1 million computers installed globally. The global production of computers has developed and diversified very rapidly, particularly in the industrialized countries. The spread of the computer industry was taking place in an atmosphere of extremely fast technological progress. Development has been especially fast and large-scale in the United States: while a mere 50 computers had been in operation in 1953, their number reached 155.000 by 1975, 400.000 by 1983 surpassed half a million in 1985. The number of personal computers in the USA surpassed 22.5 million by 1985, in Western Europe the number was about 3 million. In 1953 the capacity of computers was hardly greater than that of a high-quality present-day manual calculator, their price was $ 3 million their weight amounted to one ton, they had to be installed in a large room and their electricity consumption equalled that of an engine. In 1952 the cost of 100.000 computer operations was $ 1.25 whereas in 1980 the costs were reduced to 0.0025 cents. Memory capacity per dollar multiplied 44 times between 1950 and 1970, to more than 80 times by 1980, and to 800 times by 1985.[100]

The American computer industry continues to be the most significant and competitive of those of the developed Western countries, with 47.5 per cent of the global sales in 1984. The four biggest corporations in electronics control 44 per cent of production. More than half of the 932 enterprises operating in the field of computer production are small companies emloying less than 20 people. The major companies are integrated: they are engaged in basic and applied research, production of semiconductors, component elements and computers of various purposes, computerized services and software development alike. In 1985 42 per cent of the total research was accounted by one US company.

As mentioned before, Japanese companies have not only caught up with the United States but in some cases even surpassed them, e.g. in the fields of high-capacity processors, magnetic memories and printers. Their share in global sales was 12.2 per cent in 1984. As a result of the cooperation of industry, government and large corporations a ten-years' programme is scheduled in Japan to develop the "fifth generation" of computers.

The spread of the so-called supercomputers is one of the most important new phenomena in the market. Supercomputers are designed primarily for scientific and engineering applications. They are extremely fast (2 gigaflops in 1988), far exceeding the performance of commercial mainframe. US companies hold 90 per cent of the world market in the mid-1980s.

Technologically the unit costs, the increasing reliability, the spread of application and the availability of software are the most important factors in competition. Plug compatibility has become also an essential element.

Table 32.
The World Computer Market*—1987

	Domestic sales as per-cent of global sales
United States	46.5
Japan	10.8
FRG	6.3
United Kingdom	5.7
France	5.0
China	3.4
Italy	2.8
Canada	2.7
Brazil	2.3
Sweden	2.1
Australia	2.2
Finland	1.2
Netherlands	1.2
South Africa	1.0
Denmark	0.6
Spain	0.6
Belgium	0.6
Israel	0.6
India	0.5
Norway	0.4
Total of 20 countries	96.5

Source: US. Industrial Outlook 1986, 28–7 Without European Socialist Countries.

Owing to considerable inequalities of technological development potentials, the computer industry of the West has become extremely internationalized despite the fact that most of these countries have tried to boost their national companies by public subsidies. The countries of the European Common Market, where 26 per cent of the computers of the world were concentrated in 1984, was responsible for a mere 23.4 per cent of global sales. (Only about 45 per cent of their requirements of semiconductors were covered by their own production.)[101]

The United States is the only developed Western country which exports considerably more of its total computer production than it imports of the same item. (See Table 32.)

In Western Europe there were very few globally competitive local computer firms. By the mid—1980s several national programmes were introduced and implemented in order to strengthen their competitive position. In 1982 a joint effort, the European Strategic Programme of Research in Information Technology (ESPRIT) got under way, to lessen their international dependence in the field of electronics. On the level of the larger firms joint ventures were initiated—mainly Japanese and American enterprises. The companies and governments of the different countries try to further joint research and development activities among their national corporations, too. Joint research laboratories have been organized, the achievements of which can be made use of by all participant enterprises. The acceleration of computerization is one of the priority programmes in the USSR and other CMEA countries. The long delays and the bottlenecks in the output of different component parts, the shortcomings in standardization and other problems were the reasons for slower progress in these areas. In the second half of the 1980s the plans and the international cooperation programmes envisaged qualitative improvements in supplies and performance. Some countries of the region, like Hungary, developed software on a globally competitive basis.

Since the 1970s there has been a striking rise in the electronics industries in a number of developing countries. Their programmes were to a great extent government guided, with very active private sector role. Ten or twelve developing countries are especially characterized by relatively rapid development in the field of microelectronics which in certain cases also includes computers. The production of the microelectronics industry of South Korea increased for example at an annual average of 30 per cent in the 1970s. Highly efficient productive plants came into being in other developing countries of the Pacific region, too (Taiwan, Singapore, Hong Kong). Built on the basis of consumer electronics and having established the necessary technological conditions the electronics industry of India has entered the road of fast development. Twenty new computer producing companies were founded here in the 1970s, and five of them succeeded in acquiring rather a significant share of the software market. India has a unique opportunity since she is in the position of offering a great number of highly qualified experts to develop special software for foreign companies. Indian companies have become significant factors on the computer market. Thus the Tata Corporation began to turn out giant computers in 1983 the performance of which equalled that of the biggest Western ones though only one-fifth in size. The country invited many Indian experts employed in the computer industries of the Western countries to return, offering them high salaries and brilliant opportunities in development activities and the organization of production. She also established relations with smaller Western companies which are short of capital but have great experience in research and organization work, and are keen to expand. India was offering them joint ventures on the subcontinent. A somewhat similar strategy is employed in the development of the electronics industry in the People's Republic of China in striving to expand production capacities in order to establish a comprehensive foundation of microelectronics. This is based on the production of microprocessors. Thirty plants turning out microprocessors were in operation in the People's Republic of China at the beginning of 1984, and about 24 million integrated circuits were produced annually. Hundreds of Chinese experts studied at enterprises and institutions abroad. The target was set to double production by 1990 (as compared to the production level of 1983) mainly by importing foreign production equipment. As regards technology exports to China, the Japanese firms are ranking first since they sell entire production lines; a number of major American companies, too, participate in the development programme of the Chinese electronics industry. The forms of cooperation are rather diversified ranging from simple "standard agreements" to joint ventures. Electronics are playing an increasing role in the production processes.

The introduction and diffusion of electronics in the capital goods sector takes different forms. Various automated machine-building technologies, numerically controlled machine tools, flexible manufacturing systems, computer aided design and industrial robots are increasingly influencing the different branches of manufacturing, mainly in engineering industries. Within "process electronics" industrial robots are outstandingly important with respect to future developments. The International Organization for Standardization defined industrial robots as automatic position-controlled reprogrammable multi-functional manipulators. In the mid-1980s the third generation of robots, the "intelligent robots" with sensory ability and capacity to react to changes, required the broadening of the above definition. The American Robot Institute also defined robots from the point of view of users. According to this definition a robot is a tool programmable for a number of tasks, used for moving materials, component parts, tools or special equipment and instruments by means of different variable, programmized movements.[102] In 1987, 141.000 robots were in operation in Japan, 29.000 in the United States, 40.000 in Western Europe and about 23.000 in the rest of the world, including CMEA countries.[103]

From among the three groups of application (handling, process, assembly) their role was different in the main using countries. In the USA more than 70 per cent of the robots were applied in handling, in Japan about half of the robots were applied also in this field. In the UK and FRG most of the robots were used in processing operations.

The spread of robots was restricted in the developed Western countries until the early 1980s by the highly limited practicability (flexibility) and the relatively high investment costs. Such restrictions were reduced by the considerable progress achieved since the first half of the 1980s. However, the effect of the application of robots on employment is still a serious problem. The spread of robots is not furthered by the high rate of unemployment. Further gains in robot technics cannot be expected without measures aimed at the easing of structural unemployment (e.g. reduction of working hours, planned regrouping and vocational retraining). Robot technology, however, is not restricted to production. Its spread will most likely be more rapid in the years to come in services (banking, insurance, etc.).

Progress in robot technology occupies a major part in the joint technological development programme of the CMEA countries. The target adopted at the XXXVI session of the CMEA council, was to introduce 20.000 units by 1990. The implementation of such robot technology programmes, however, requires faster progress not only in the national research and development but also in the mechanism of international cooperation.

Microelectronics represents an important area in the global arms race. The two global powers, the USSR and the USA produced electronic systems in these areas which were performing by and large with similar efficiency in the mid-1980s, especially in such areas as remote control, automatic targeting, satellite communication and remote sensing.

The growing demand for increased research, development and professional training plays an important part in microelectronics, too, and therefore in countries where the ratio of military applications is high the position and international competitiveness of the electronics industry as a whole is strongly influenced by this single factor.

From this aspect it seems instructive to compare the United States and Japan. The decisive part of electronic research and development in Japan is initiated and financed by private companies, but these activities are comprehensively supported by the government furthering cooperation among the corporations, international expansion and even granting significant direct research aid in some cases. (In the 1970s, 50 per cent of research work on microprocessors was financed by the government.) Microelectronics in Japan is rather market-oriented and the enhancing of the market competitiveness of such firms is supported by the state. Since most of the achievements in microelectronics have a double (civilian and military) capacity of application, many Japanese achievements are important also from the strategic point of view. The position of the USA is determined by the fact that about 33 per cent of military procurement in the United States is channelled to military electronics.[104] About 50 per cent of it serves experimental and maintainance objectives and has a strong direct influence on the American electronics industry. In addition, the Pentagon participates in the development of complex integrated circuits, industrial robots and high-capacity computers. Military procurements have brought special advantages to the largest corporations and influenced their direct competitiveness accordingly. Owing to strategic restrictions, the large American corporations are subject to considerable export restrictions which in certain areas affect their international competitiveness adversely.

An essential branch of electronic research with military objectives is the so-called VHSIC Programme (Very High Speed Integrated Circuits). The aim of this programme is the development of high-speed integrated circuits sensitive to heat, light and radio waves, rendering possible the processing of systems capable of automatically reacting to changes in the environment (e.g. in the field of guided missile control). The greatest success of research would be a breakthrough on the so-called "half-micron barrier", i.e. if it were possible to transfer configurations smaller than half a micron on to silicon semiconductors, thus highly accelerating their performance.

The SDI programme of the USA also has important consequences in electronics research. The structure of industry and international relations will also be influenced, and to a certain extent further distorted by military interest in the leading electronic power of the world. The SDI programs, as other previous military programs, will of course have civilian implications as well. While they may subordinate even more extensively the electronics industries (including R & D) to military purposes, some of the achievements, like further miniaturization or remote control and sensing, may lead to improvements in civilian areas as well and increase US competitiveness.

This overview of the electronics industry has proved the complex interrelations of political and economic factors in its development. It has indicated the nature of international competition, leading to fast technological changes, surpluses and new growth potentials. In the process the role of the "electronic block" has been expanding all over the world.

b) *Motor vehicles: decline or dramatic transformation?*

The motor vehicle industry, which includes the manufacturing of passenger cars, trucks and buses and their parts represents another special case indicating the problems connected with structural change.

This industry has long traditions and it occupies a very important position in manufacturing.

It is not a new industry in the real sense of the world but it is a branch of manufacturing which has been transformed several times over the past 100 years of its existence. Since World War II it has become an important factor in accelerating industrial development as a result of rapidly increasing demand for its products and its structural interrelations with other branches of manufacturing. The motor vehicle industry is a highly concentrated one in every country. It has very high and mounting capital costs and it is increasingly difficult for new enterprises to enter into the business. Together with the intense competition, international cooperation is also intensified. Due to the relative saturation of the market, the motor vehicle industry belongs to a sector with slow growth potential. Its research intensity is higher than the industrial average.

In the years following the energy crisis during the 1970s the motor vehicle industry faced two major recessions, a shift in slow-growing consumer demand and growing international competition. The effects on the industry of the traditional car manufacturing countries were devastating. In the first half of the 1980s the motor vehicle industry, however, changed. Dramatic restructuring took place. The industry responded to the shift in demand for more efficient cars. Factories were modernized and the production processes streamlined. These changes resulted in reduced costs and major increases in productivity.

In the world economy the USA has the largest motor vehicle production and its role in the US economy is also very important. The prosperity of the motor vehicle industry is felt in the national economy of the USA as a whole. Cars comprise 95 per cent of traffic between American cities. The motor vehicle industry purchases 21 per cent of the steel production of the United States, 30 per cent of its pig-iron output, 60 per cent of the synthetic rubber production, 11 per cent of the aluminium production and 20 per cent of the machine tool production. About 4 million people are employed by the branch industry and in the related services. Of these 0.8 million work in direct production, 1.4 million in cooperating enterprises, 2.6 million in sales departments and the servicing industry.[105] According to other sources nearly 13 million people are employed directly or by some connected industries by the American motor vehicle industry. More than 10 per cent of the total American labour force is employed by the motor industry and its related branches.[106]

The role of the motor vehicle industry is also substantial in the UK, in the FRG, Italy, Sweden and France from among the Western European countries. Worldwide 28 to 35 million workers and employees work in the motor industry, and approximately 100 million work in connected industries. Two-thirds of all these people are concentrated in the developed Western industrial countries.[107]

In 1980 the share of motor vehicle production in value added by the manufacturing industry was 8 per cent in the developed industrial countries, 6 per cent in the European socialist countries and 3.8 per cent in the Third World countries.

The share of the three country groups in the world production of public vehicles was as follows: developed Western countries 68 per cent, European socialist countries 24 per cent, developing countries 8 per cent.[108]

The greatest effect of this branch of industry on the economy is exerted by the production of passenger cars.

The motor vehicle industry first became important in the United States in the pre-war years. After World War II the significance of the production of motor vehicles kept on growing under different circumstances, i.e. in connection with the considerable transformation of the way of life. Soon it went through an acceleration in Western Europe, too. In the European socialist countries and the developing regions these marked changes came later, beginning with the 1960s.

Car ownership is widely spread in the industrial world. There were 2 persons per passenger car in the USA, 4 in the developed Western countries of Europe, whereas in 1983 the average of the European CMEA countries was 14 with a range of 6 (GDR) to 24 (Soviet Union). The transformation of the way of life has been influenced by the use of cars most significantly in the United States. Cars played a great part in the transformation of the settlement pattern and the emergence of suburbia. As a result of increasing mobility the massive exodus from the cities became possible for a considerable portion of the population. The consumer's network, too, has been transformed. In the United States "motorized" housewives with mechanized households at their disposal drive to do their shopping once a week in the self-service food markets of shopping centres located about 20–30 kilometres from their homes. Food is stored in refrigerators and deep-freezers (often stocks even of perishable foodware sufficient for several weeks are stored). Retail trade is thus released from part of the costs of stockpiling and shifts such costs on the consumers. Cars have thus contributed to the fact that refrigerators have become standard accesories of American homes ever since the middle of the century. This, however, is but one side of the coin.

It was the way of life based on cars resulting in enhanced mobility which made it possible for the outskirts and suburbs of towns and cities to expand to regions far from the centre and to incorporate greenbelt areas as well. Due to this change, both individuals and society had to face a number of serious problems. For the individual cars have ceased to be luxury commodities and have become indispensable means of commuting to one's workplace, shops, schools for the children, etc. Many families contemplated, particularly if they lived in satellite towns, buying a second car. Buying and keeping a second car, however, brought about increased financial burdens. The dependence of families on cars has increased and thus the motor vehicle industry has become—from the aspect of consumption, too—a vitally important branch of industry.

The spread of cars created new conditions for society, too. The problems of traffic have been multiplied: urban traffic slowed down, public transport was made more difficult because of the great mass of cars. A great burden was laid on society by automobilism: the development of the road network, the regulation and control of traffic demanded exorbitant investment. The style of life based on cars has had additional adverse effects, too: further pollution of the air of the cities, constantly high noise level, parking difficulties, growing number of traffic accidents, etc.

Naturally the changes in civilian consumption mentioned above have not followed the American example to the same extent in other countries of the world. Individual countries have coped with the unfavourable consequences of changes, too, to varying degree. As regards, however, the production and consumption models of the production of passenger cars, the tendencies have been essentially identical and the "pulling" role of the industry has asserted itself in a similar way, too. As a result, when the unfavourable factors influencing the development of the motor vehicle industry began to show in the 1970s and 1980s, the economic effects of the difficulties made themselves felt far beyond the range of the industry itself.

The industry of the developed Western countries had to face the saturation problem in the market for passenger cars as early as the end of the 1960s though saturation has occurred in the different countries at different times. The degree of saturation is obviously the function of changes in incomes to a certain extent. However, additional demands crop up in the process of meeting requirements, and thus the market can be extended in new directions. For instance, at a time when one car per household is regarded as saturation, the sales departments can set the objective of meeting the demand of all persons with a driving licence and can begin to elaborate the conditions of a new saturation level (advertisements, financing, price level, etc.). Diversification (e.g. the appearance of smaller cars besides the big ones in the United States) can also become a factor reducing the saturation degree of the market. The major demand factor of the car market had been replacement or change in the majority of the developed Western countries in the early 1970s. Thereby, however, demand became to some extent cyclical, making it more difficult to expand the market. Thus saturation— prior to the effect of other factors—restrained the dynamism introduced by the motor industry in post-war economic development.

A further problem from the point of view of market relations was the appearance of new producers and the sharpening of international competition. It was first of all the extraordinarily fast and successful thrust of Japan which caused serious worries. Japanese car production had not reached one million in the early 1960s, i.e. it had lagged behind that of West European countries with a developed motor vehicle industry (France, Great Britain, FRG, Italy) and, naturally, far behind that of the United States. At that time the share of Japan in global passenger car production had been 6.3 per cent and 2.9 per cent in world exports, whereas the share of West European countries in global passenger car exports had reached 70 per cent. The situation took a marked turn by the early 1980s.

As illustrated by the data of Table 33, the new producers have surged ahead and the competition between the traditional great producers (USA) and exporters (Western Europe) has sharpened. The decline of the USA and the ratio of imports in covering its domestic demand has become particularly significant. The developing countries are not listed in the table, though keen competition is going on for their markets. In the second half of the 1980s the increasing role of South Korea represents one of the important changes. True, the domestic production of these countries increases but the overwhelming majority of their plants in the motor industry are assembly plants founded by big Japanese, Western European or American companies. Thus 40 car factories were operated by Japanese companies in the Asian developing countries alone in 1980. In other regions of the Third World, too, Japan was in the forefront in setting up local motor industries. West Germany has also been an important agent in the internationalization of car production. In 1960 only 2 per cent of the overall output of passenger cars came from subsidiaries abroad: in the first half of the 1980, this figure stood at 25 per cent.

Some Western corporations had a part in the establishment or development of the car industries of the European CMEA countries, too. (Thus Fiat had a part in the

Table 33.
**Share of the Major Producers
in the Production and Exports of
Passenger-cars (1985)**

	Production	Exports	Imports
Japan	30.2	24.5	5
USA	33.4	13.2	35.6
FRG	10.9	18.1	5.0
France	7.4	6.0	4.2
Italy	3.9	2.7	n.a.
Spain	3.5	2.0	n.a.
United Kingdom	3.2	3.2	5.3
Soviet Union	5.0	n.a.	n.a.
Developing countries	1.2	3.0	14.0

Source: Economic Commission for Europe, *Techno-economic Aspects of the International Division of Labour in the Automative Industry,* ECE/Eng, Aut. 11, New York, 1983; *Le Commerce International en 85–86,* AGTDC, Geneva, 1986.

establishment of car industries in the Soviet Union and Romania, Renault in the Soviet Union and Bulgaria, Volkswagen in the GDR, Citroen in Romania).

The major dilemma of the motor vehicle industries of the developing countries is that their import costs are increased by the operation of assembly plants while less than 10 per cent of their export earnings originate from the products of that industry. The growth of domestic demand and production exerts only a minimal dynamizing effect on other industries.

The "dynamizing" effect of the production of the motor industry has been considerably reduced by the sharpening international competition in the majority of the mature producer countries. The nature of competition is characterized by the fact that due to the rapid transformation of technology 4,000 workers were needed in 1985 whereas a mere 2,000 were needed at the end of the decade to turn out 1,200 cars a day in Japan. To produce the same amount of cars, 6,000 workers were used by the Italian Fiat and 8,000 by the French car producers in 1984. Owing to the above facts, among others, competition resulted in increasing protectionism and other measures affecting production and competition strategies in Western Europe and the United States.

A further important factor affecting the motor vehicle industry was the rise of oil prices in the 1970s. As demonstrated by data on different developed Western countries 25 per cent of energy was consumed by road transport there. The rise of oil prices in 1973–74 and then in 1979 resulted first and foremost in the postponement of expected car changes by the owners of older cars and in the fact that new buyers sought for smaller low fuel-consumption cars. This has become the source of significant technological transformation in the car industry.

Motor vehicle corporations are generally powerful international enterprises, and tend to have a significant part in the world economy in the future, too. Even these corporations were not capable of implementing major changes of a significant character under the world economic conditions of the late twentieth century, without using special supporting measures. Some of the largest companies have been supported by subsidies or favourable loans by the governments of a number of leading Western countries in this difficult economic situation. Protectionist measures have been taken by almost all governments in order to help their producers. The appearance of competitors on national markets has been restricted by a number of measures (rules on environmental protection, voluntary quotas and so forth). All over the world motor vehicle companies have put into force comprehensive rationalization and marketing programmes, reducing costs also by international regrouping of the production of component parts. The large companies, through their international marketing and servicing networks, offered various additional favours and advantages to the buyers. As a result of adopting materials of lighter weight, considerable technological transformation has been going on as regards the quality of products. Fuel consumption has been reduced by new solutions and more exact setting. Almost all the important parts of the cars are affected by the new technological solutions. Frontwheel drive is gaining ground. Revolutionary changes have begun in the range of fuels (as indicated by the rapid improvement of the quality properties of Diesel engines). Considerable research has been done to develop alternative fuels or fuel combinations. The application of microelectronics to perfect motors and the functions of speed-gear systems has gained ever greater momentum (regulation of the air-fuel ratio, timing, speed-control, recycling of exhaust gas, etc.). The solution of the technological problems of the efficient operation by electric cars may open up new vistas for the motor vehicle industry. A worldwide race is going on in this respect.

Technological change would imbue the motor industry with greater dynamism if the industry were on a rapid upgrade. The motor industry, however, being a "mature" industry, technological change does not mean already such a major dynamizing power in the economy such that it could be instrumental in the acceleration of general growth. And this holds true not only for the production of passenger cars but also for that of buses and trucks in the developed industrial countries. In the developing and the European socialist countries, on the other hand, where growth potential is still substantial, the dynamizing power of the motor vehicle industry is uncertain due to the general situation of the economy and the problems of income growth.

The Structural Implications of the Defence Sector

The military industrial complex plays a peculiar and significant part in the expected transformation of the industrial structure in the late phase of the twentieth century. It is not a homogeneous branch of industry but comprises various product groups and, owing to the complex requirements of armies, it is linked up with almost all the branches of industry.

Military spending influences, structural changes first of all through direct purchases mostly from manufacturing industries. It also affects long-term industrial strategies in certain branches by stimulating research and development. Through the international arms trade military expenditures promote specialization.

The investment activities created by the military expenditure ripple through the different branches of the economy. This multiplier effect makes defence outlays an important instrument of government policy in stimulating economic growth. The patterns of growth which emerge as a result of military expenditure favour and stimulate high technology industries, the innovative sectors where special performance is the basic requirement. Table 34 indicates the increasing share of military procurement in certain branches of the US economy during the implementation of the accelerated spending programme of the Reagan administration.

The military driven patterns of structural changes both weaken the competitive potential of civilian sectors and subordinate industrial development (up to a point) to political cycles.

The benefits of such developments are also highly concentrated in the oligopolistic sectors of the economy. This sector works, however, by subcontracting, and the number of subcontractors in countries like the USA or the UK is very high.

A considerable part of the defence industry is publicly owned in Western Europe, but such enterprises have to compete in certain cases with private firms. The Japanese defence industry has developed in a peculiar way. The production of traditional weapons was founded mainly on American licences whereas a highly significant independent structure has developed the means of electronic warfare, and such weapons are in many respects more sophisticated than the American ones (e.g. a three-dimensional radar system, special materials).

The important defence programmes are concentrated in the big corporations. Thus in the United States the most important 15 programmes representing 90–100 per cent of total production were "in the hands" of 6–8 big companies in the early 1980s. Research and development, too, are concentrated: 45 per cent of all research and development expenditure of a defence character was channelled to eight big companies. The very same eight companies received 25 per cent of all defence contracts. However, tens of thousands of subcontractors, too, are interested in carrying into effect these programmes. It often happens that as a result of the re-alization of such programmes some subcontractors are bought up by the prime contractor and thus the subcontracting activity becomes a mere formality. In the economies of the developed Western countries vertical integration is furthered by the long-range programmes of the defence industry. Vertical integration takes place in two ways: by "swallowing up" the subcontractors and by concentrating a programme—from research to mass-production—in a single enterprise. In Japan, for instance, the decisive part of the defence industry is in the hands of four or five big concerns.

Why is the defence industry concentrated in the largest corporations? Such corporations have great traditions and prestige in the economic life of the country in question, have immense funds at their disposal, can take the initial risks relatively easily, and are in a position to influence the government effectively when defence contracts are dealt out. They also have adequate research facilities, technical design networks, marketing organizations, are well provided with capital and are thus able readily and quickly to react to defence orders or even to suggest the production of new weapons independently, i.e. to become in all respects "reliable partners" of the military. The majority of them had proved their "loyalty" to the military establishment in the course of past wars.

Incidentally, big corporations are more reliable from the point of view of state security, too. They maintain huge security forces of their own to protect their own

Table 34.
The Share of Defence Orders in Different Industrial Branches of the USA

SIC code	Title	Defence share of output			Defence output growth
		1979	1982	1987	1982/87
		(%)	(%)	(%)	(%)
15—17	Construction of new military facilities	100.0	100.0	100.0	21.6
3795	Tanks and tank components	78.1	93.8	95.0	47.2
3483	Ammunition, esc. small	95.1	90.9	93.2	55.6
3489	Ordnance, nec	85.1	79.7	81.2	35.3
3761	Complete missiles	71.0	67.5	79.4	64.4
3731	Shipbuilding and repair	47.9	61.7	62.1	24.1
3662	Radio and TV communication	44.8	58.0	62.5	54.2
3724	Aircraft and missile engines	42.3	53.5	56.1	32.9
3728	Aircraft and missile equipment	43.4	41.2	44.2	34.9
3721	Aircraft	35.0	40.4	46.1	58.7
2892	Explosives	19.5	34.3	41.2	58.7
383	Optical instruments	21.6	28.0	30.7	38.0
3811	Engineering instruments	23.5	27.7	33.6	59.9
3163	Non-ferrous forgings	18.0	27.0	29.8	43.3
3482	Small arms ammunition	25.4	25.0	39.9	129.5
3676—9	Electric components	12.0	17.0	19.8	49.3
3369	Non-ferrous foundries, nec	20.3	15.8	17.8	44.5
3484	Small arms	19.3	13.8	6.5	−43,3
3715	Truck trailers	6.4	13.3	15.4	52.4
3471	Plating and polishing	9.6	12.8	15.4	55.4
3674	Semiconductors	9.5	12.5	12.5	51.4
3399	Primary metal products, nec	6.4	11.9	13.8	48.3
3599	Machinery, esc. elec.	5.7	9.7	11.8	52.6
3361	Aluminium foundries (castings)	7.9	9.1	11.2	58.5
3364	Water transportation	6.5	8.7	10.4	47.3
3356	Non-ferrous rolling and drawing	11.6	8.6	10.1	48.6
3825	Instruments to measure elec.	5.6	8.4	9.8	49.7
3398	Metal heat treating	7.5	8.3	9.7	47.8
2441	Wooden containers	12.0	8.0	10.0	51.2
3624	Carbon and graphite products	6.1	7.7	9.3	51.4
3362	Brass, bronze and copper castings	5.0	7.5	9.3	51.4
45	Air transportation	7.1	7.5	10.2	64.2
3334	Aluminium production	5.8	7.5	9.0	51.4
3299	Non-metallic mineral products	6.6	7.5	8.6	45.0
3469	Metal stampings	5.8	7.3	9.1	60.3
3671—3	Electron tubes	8.3	7.3	11.3	105.3
3573	Computers	3.6	7.1	12.7	141.0
3443	Fabricated platework	7.3	6.9	8.6	62.4
345	Screw machine products	5.6	6.9	8.6	57.5
3462	Iron and steel forgings	7.9	6.9	7.6	31.4
3333	Zinc smelting	9.0	6.8	8.2	41.9
47	Transportation services	6.9	6.7	7.7	37.5
3541	Machine tools—cutting	6.1	6.2	7.5	54.4

(Table 34. cont)

SIC code	Title	Defence share of output			Defence output growth
		1979	1982	1987	1982/87
		(%)	(%)	(%)	(%)
3544—5	Special dies and tools	4.9	6.0	7.5	45.4
3562	Ball bearings	4.6	5.8	6.8	45.4
3499	Fabricated metal products	5.0	5.6	7.1	53.3
3312	Blast furnace steel mills	4.5	5.6	6.7	45.6
3339	Refining on non-ferrous nec	6.6	5.6	6.5	39.3
3351	Copper rolling and drawing	5.5	5.5	7.1	66.3
3313	Electrometallurgical products	4.9	5.4	6.3	26.7
101	Iron mining	5.7	5.0	6.0	43.8
32	Lead smelting	6.2	5.0	6.8	70.0
3542	Machine tools forming	5.0	4.8	6.3	70.0
332	Iron and steel foundries	3.9	4.5	5.2	45.1

Sources: U. S. Industrial Outlook 1983. XXXIX—XLVII D. Henry Defense spending: a growth market for industry. *International Journal of Urban and Regional Research,* 1986. Vol. IV. No. 1. p. 110.

business secrets, and this apparatus has long-standing experience in industrial counter-intelligence work (naturally in certain cases in industrial espionage as well). This latter factor has greatly contributed in the USA to the fact that following the end of the Vietnam war the so-called innovative small enterprises—which have contributed considerably to the development of military technologies—were increasingly ousted from the circle of defence contractors.

Another important factor is that such big corporations dispose of a significant civilian production basis, too, and can therefore continue their business as military expenditure is reduced and make use of part of their capacities for civilian production.

Defence industries (or the military industries) as a special sector of different branches produce not only for the internal demand of the armed forces but for exports as well and, in addition, in most of the firms in this sector dual-purpose (military and civilian) products are turned out. In high-tech industries it is often impossible to separate the two, since the same technologies serve both purposes. The basic difference in the production for military needs is that the ultimate purpose is not necessarily commercial success. Marketing and production costs are not the primary concern. While defence industries are in many ways similar to other areas of big business, they play a unique role in the given countries and their position differs in many ways from companies producing for the civilian market:

— they do not run any market risks while producing for military purposes (there is but a single buyer, sales are guaranteed by long-term orders);

— the decisive part of research and development is financed by the government, but the producer simultaneously has the possibility to use such research achievements with certain restrictions in civilian production as well (new technology is therefore achieved practically cost-free or at an extremely low price);

— as a rule, the volume of transactions is substantial, and it is a truism that a certain sale worth many billions is attractive even at a lower profit rate (often, however, the rate of profit tends to be high);

— the managers of the producing enterprises gain considerable experience in the organization of mass production, the costs of which are also covered by the government (it is not by chance that many top managers of international concerns have started on their career in the defence industry);

— orders are of a long-term nature and the big companies are therefore in the position to be able to plan production for 5 to 10 years in advance (3 to 5 years running-in period and 5 years uninterrupted production);

— prices are agreed on the basis of production costs, subsequent correction being possible;

— the capital for new programmes is made available by the state to the firms participating in production.

The rate of growth and the structural changes of the defence industry have a multiple spillover effect on other industries as well. Surveys on the effects of major shifts in defence expenditure, on the closeness of inter-branch relations in some industrially developed capitalist countries (e.g. USA, Great Britain) have indicated that some industries and branches of industries are interrelated in rather a complex way. Thus in the metalworking industry the majority of all orders placed are of a military character whereas in other industries (e.g. textiles, chemical engineering, etc.) the share of military orders is much lower (though not at all negligible).

The structure of the defence industry and the conditions under which it operates have developed in a peculiar way in many respects. The chief client is the government (either that of the country in question or—in the case of exports—that of some other country), and defence orders are closely connected with the public purchasing practices of the country in question. It is characteristic of the defence industry that it is only slightly sensitive to price fluctuations and is connected with very large programmes.

The development programmes of the defence industry have two important sources. One is the army demanding ever more sophisticated weapons thus making concrete claims on science, the other is the new technology offered by the large firms, research institutes, etc., constituting more efficient weapons. In both of these the military efficiency of the new weapon systems is of fundamental importance whereas prices are of secondary significance. The development of the defence industry is also influenced by the way military expenditure is appropriated in the countries in question. In most of the countries the "authorization" for defence expenditure is given annually by the parliament. However, such annual appropriations of budgets bring about con-siderable uncertainty for the defence industry for long-term planning and, therefore, lobbying has become a must for the military and the industrial companies interested in such production, i.e. it has become necessary to maintain a public relations machine influencing both public opinion and the legislators.

The structural implications of defence industries are also causing major shifts in the composition of the labour force. Manpower employed in the defence industries of the developed Western countries has two characteristics. First, fluctuation goes hand in hand with the frequent changes in defence programmes (a long "learning" process is necessary for the new programme, and many enterprises react to changes in programmes by lay-offs or hiring new employees instead of expensive retraining of the existing manpower). Second, such programmes need a highly qualified labour force, therefore the wages of those employed in the defence industry are usually higher than those employed in many civilian high-tech industries.

The special situation of the defence industry is also influenced by the mobilization programme of the economy. The economic mobilization plans of the developed countries naturally call for the reorganization and readjustment of part of the branches of industry producing for civil consumption. This in itself is an extremely complex task in the fulfiment of which enterprises producing for national defence in peacetime have an eminent role. Such companies are regarded as specific central units around which all other branches of industry could be grouped in case of war and the top managers of them are often drawn into the management of defence production.

The enterprises of the defence industries of the developed capitalist countries also have significant international business interests. (It is a well-known fact that in the major NATO countries there are some subcontractors who are involved in the defence industries of other countries as well, producing specialized component parts or supplying certain services.)

The defence sector influences structural changes also on an international scale. One of the sources of such influences is the production specialization within NATO. Special integration of military and civilian industrial activities has been carried into effect internationally within the framework of cooperation and specialization among the subcontractors, particularly in the domain of electronics in American-Japanese relations. American-Japanese cooperation in military electronics is of particular importance for the USA. Japan was encouraged by the United States in 1983 to sign an agreement on the mutual utilization of research achievements in military engineering. By means of this agreement American corporations get hold of a great number of research result which can be used for civilian purposes as well. Incidentally, this agreement is advantageous to Japan, too. Some Western European corporations have also joined in both the civil and military production of electronic equipment in the United States.

Naturally every government strives to reserve the contracts originating from national armaments for its own enterprises. Many Western countries tried to put legal obstacles in the way of public purchases from abroad even in recent years. International standardization, specialization and cooperation within NATO has developed rather slowly. The efforts of the European member states of NATO to bring about reciprocity in the arms trade within the alliance system have incurred the embittered resistance of the American defence industry. The American industry is rather unwilling to share the arms market with its European partners. In 1963 the European NATO partners had bought 27 times more war material from the USA than vice versa. This ratio became more favourable to the European partners by 1984 (6.5:1) but the US surplus originating from the arms trade was still 1.8 billion dollars.[109]

The influence of the arms industry on structural changes in the less developed countries has become an important issue in debates on development policies. Do these industries represent an isolated segment in the economy (thus their impact is limited) or are they important factors contributing to the major structural development of arms industries in the economy? The material has been stepped up in the developing countries since the 1970s. The establishment of an arms industry in some developing countries had begun at the time of or even before World War II. Several attempts had been made, for instance by Brazil, even prior to 1940 to establish a national aircraft industry; several prototypes had been designed but owing to a lack of technological experience and financial difficulties, all their attempts had met with failure. In Argentina the production of military aircraft started as early as 1927. In India the British initiated the building up of an arms industry in order to meet the demands of their own army in India many years before the outbreak of World War II. The accelerated development of the arms industries of the other developing countries started only in the 1960s.

At the beginning of the 1980s arms production was carried on in 16 developing countries mainly on the basis of licences from abroad. There are ten developing countries (Argentina, Brazil, Egypt, India and Indonesia among them) who have arms industries which turn out independent designs.

Both from the economic and defence aspects, the aircraft industry is of outstanding importance in the developing countries: nine Third World countries have aircraft industries but it is only India that has been able to construct jet motors and to turn out jet fighters independently. However, India, too, is dependent on foreign design and a supply of components from abroad.

Helicopters and light aircraft (mainly for reconnaissance) are produced in a number of developing countries, but this is done exclusively on the basis of foreign licences and mostly by using imported component parts. Of all Third World countries it is only Argentina which produces locally designed tanks and armoured vehicles.

Warships above 500 tons are built—exclusively on the basis of foreign licences—by Argentina, Brazil, Peru, India and South Korea. The latter two countries dispose of the most significant shipbuilding capacity but none of the warships built there register more than 2,000 gross tons.

Anti-tank weapons and anti-aircraft guns were produced—mostly on the basis of foreign licences and with imported production plant—at the beginning of the 1980s in seven developing countries (Brazil, Argentina, Kuwait, South Korea, India, Pakistan, the Philippines). Light arms, infantry weapons, submachine guns—as well as ammunition, handgrenades and mines—are turned out by a great number of developing countries, but once again almost entirely on the basis of foreign licences.

The rapid spread in the Third World of technology suited for the production of atomic weapons is a new phenomenon giving rise to considerable anxiety. At the end of the 1970s India, Argentina, Brazil and Pakistan were technologically capable of producing atom bombs and these states had adequate amounts of fissile material at their disposal. By the end of the first half of the 1980s five or six further developing countries have become capable of producing the A-bomb. The scientific and technological conditions necessary for the production of atom bombs developed relatively fast.

The establishment of independent defence industries in the developing countries is stimulated by a number of factors. The efforts made to call into being an independent defence industry must be emphasized. The slogan to become "independent" of the

developed industrial countries is highly popular in the armed forces and admini-
strations of all Third World countries. Independence is regarded by many as an
important measure of national sovereignty. The establishment of a national defence
industry has often been started by the manufacture of primitive weapons by forces
fighting against imperialism or local oppression. National defence industries carry out
often the strategy of import substitution and in certain cases they become export
industries.

The development of a defence industry has been encouraged also by local economic
interests since local entrepreneurs would like to make greater profits as a result of
defence expenditure. Though the defence industry is publicly owned in the majority of
the countries some local private enterprises can also join in with production as
subcontractors or suppliers. Efforts are made by some countries with relatively
significant defence industries to draw local private enterprises increasingly into the
orbit of arms production. The greater part of arms production in Brazil is concentrated
in two state-owned companies: the *Industria de Material Belico* controlled by the
Ministry of Defense, and the *Empresa Brasilaria de Aeronautica* controlled by the
Army. However, the privately owned *Engenheiros Especializados,* too, participates in
the production of aircraft and vehicles meeting both civil and military demands.

Profits originating from military contracts are particularly high in the developing countries since the control on low-efficiency production tends to be rather slack.
The reasons for production costs surpassing those of the developed industrial
countries by 50–100 per cent are the following:
— backwardness of local research and development,
— rather slow organization of the necessary production and technological
   knowledge,
— exorbitant investment input in small-volume production,
— high prices of imported service parts and other component parts,
— insufficient quality control,
— the need to employ foreign experts,
— excessive profits made by local entrepreneurs and subcontractors.

The transnational corporations make great efforts to gain control of the defence
industries developed in the Third World countries. The majority of the developing
countries which have just begun to establish their independent defence industries
cooperate with one or another Western transnational corporation. These
corporations—fearing nationalization—have chosen forms of cooperation which
minimize risks, and partly perpetuate control. The most common form of cooperation
is the licence agreement which they try to combine with the exact definition of the
quantitative and qualitative parameters of the products turned out, with the import of
foreign equipment (machinery), component parts and experts as well as the technical
servicing of the armed forces. (Italian Aermacchi MN 326 type aircraft and British
Rolls-Royce turbojet engines are produced on the basis of licence agreements in Brazil;
Jaguar aircraft are produced—among others—on the basis of British Aerospace
licences in India; British Sheffield-type destroyers are built in Argentina; and West
German Cobra-type rockets are turned out in Pakistan.)

Another frequent form of cooperation has been the foundation of joint companies.
Thus, of the Arab states Saudi Arabia, Egypt, Qatar and the United Arab Emirates

established in 1974 a joint international arms industrial enterprise under the name of *Arab Organization for Industrialization* with an initial capital of approximately $ 4 million. Within the framework of this company and with the participation of the American Motors Co. they established—among others—a joint enterprise for the production of light military vehicles, an Arab-British joint company for the production of rockets, another one for building helicopters, and finally an Arab-French joint company for the production of light fighters. Some other Arab enterprises have set up the military electronic industry together with certain Western firms.

In conformity with the specific features reflected by other branches of technological transfer the following stages can be pointed out in the development of the defence industries of developing countries:

— establishment of local repair-shops to service imported military equipment,
— establishment of local plants in accordance with licence agreements to assemble weapons from imported component parts,
— establishment of factories turning out component parts on the basis of licences,
— domestic production on the basis of licences but built on locally produced service parts and component parts,
— full production processes on the basis of local adaption of licences purchased,
— production of domestically designed weapons partly from imported component parts,
— development of full-scale production of locally designed weapons and armaments.

The above mentioned stages could naturally differ according to the specific features of the production of certain war material, weapons and so forth.

Despite the rapid growth of national defence industries the volume of arms production in the developing countries is negligible. According to estimates based on defence budget expenditures and the 1980 production figures of global arms production only about 0.2 per cent of world production fall to the share of the developing countries. Trends in the production of war materials and the envisaged armament programmes, however, indicate a faster future increase of the share of Third World countries than ever before. We have to reckon with the doubling of the present ratio in the 10–15 years to follow, nevertheless the share of the developing countries of this sector will remain rather negligible and will cover only a fraction of their own demand.

As far as the structural implications are concerned, from among the developing countries India has the widest domestic base for an arms industry. This sector represents about 10 per cent of the total industrial output. In 1985 there were 33 production facilities run by the armed forces. In addition 34 large research and development institutions are administered by the ministry of defence. They employ more than 6,000 scientists. Nine major state-owned industrial enterprises produce sophisticated weapon systems and military equipment. Approximately 300,000 persons were employed in the arms production sectors in 1985. The defence industries in India are by and large self-sufficient, with relatively well developed supporting firms. Brazil has the second largest arms industry in the "developing market economies" and is more dependent on external sources of licences and know-how than the Indian defence sector. It also has broad structural interrelations with other (civilian) branches. The development of defence industries even in those two countries has not strengthened their position in modern civilian technologies in world trade. Rather the opposite seems to have happened. A large part of modern technology imports was absorbed by the defence sector. The absorption of an important part of skilled manpower by arms industries is another cost which the economies of the developing countries have to carry.

The arms trade tends to be an important factor in international relations of the defence industries. Due to their very nature, data on the volume of the international arms trade are unreliable; generally contradictory figures are published by different sources. Estimates by experts, too, are suitable only for the demonstration of trends and orders of magnitude. According to some of these estimates about two thirds of global arms exports originated from NATO countries, and 43–44 per cent of world exports are delivered by the United States (SIPRI Yearbook 1981). Arms and defence material exports are held to be almost double of the above figure by other American sources. According to 1980 data of the US Armaments Control and Disarmament Agency the cumulative value (current prices) of global arms and defence material exports had been $112 billion between 1969 and 1978, representing 1.8 per cent of total world exports..Almost 60 per cent of this—amounting to 1.6 per cent of their total exports—originated from the developed Western countries. The ratio of arms exports within the total exports of the USA was considerably higher: on an average of the past ten years it came to 6.3 per cent. At the same time, arms made up only 0.1 per cent of the total exports of Japan.[110]

Of all arms exported 74 per cent were purchased by the developing countries (coming to 6 per cent of their total imports on average in the past ten years).[111]

The export of arms to the developing countries (more precisely: the export of goods and services for military objectives) also shows a markedly expanding tendency. Three times as much arms had been imported by the developing countries as by the developed industrial countries in the 1970s. More than two thirds of total arms exports had been purchased (or received) by the Third World countries at that time. (Part of the arms exports had been given to the recipient countries in the form of aid programmes, but the ratio of such grants was decreasing recently.)

The items in the statistical tables do not reflect total imports of a military character. More often than not military equipment is defined in foreign trade statistics as "transport vehicles" or "other equipment".[112]

Imported weapons and defence material listed as such in the official statistics made up 6–7 per cent of the total imports of the developing countries in the annual average of the 1970s. Within that the import ratio of the Middle East countries was particularly high reaching 30 per cent of total imports in some years. Military imports increased fivefold within the total imports of Africa in the 1970s. Nearly one-third of all arms importers of the world were Middle East countries in the 1970s (their arms imports amounted to almost twice as much as that of the NATO countries). Africa bought about one-sixth of arms sold on the world market. A considerable part—about 40 per cent—of arms exports to the developing countries originated from the United States, one-fifth from Great Britain and France.

As·a result of the rising prices of weapons and other defence material, as well as the more complex weapon systems, the purchasing costs of the developing countries have increased rapidly. Expenditure on spare parts is particularly high, often reaching 50 per cent of total imports.

Arms are exported to some developing countries by the Soviet Union and other socialist countries, too. It is mostly progressive countries which appeal to the socialist countries for weapons. These countries would be unable to defend themselves without weapons and ammunition received from the socialist countries since the leading Western arms-exporting countries reject their pleas for arms. National liberation movements, too, frequently call upon the socialist countries for arms. It also happens that important non-aligned countries purchase arms and ammunition from socialist countries in order to diminish their dependence on one supplier.

The role of the socialist countries in the supply of modern weapons has brought about major changes in international relations and has contributed to the consolidation of the position of many developing countries. Arms deliveries from socialist countries rendered considerable help to the organization of national defence in India, Egypt, Iraq, Syria, Angola and Mozambique.

Some of the developing countries have appeared in recent years as exporters, too, in the international market for arms and ammunition. The most significant exporters are those developing countries which have built up a relatively large defence industry (as compared to their domestic demands) and have purchased great quantitites of foreign licences and know-how related to arms production. In such countries (e.g. in Brazil) the maintainance and development of the defence industry is of vital importance from the point of view of exports.

Of the developing countries Brazil, India and Argentina were the outstanding arms and ammunition exporting countries in the 1970s. In 1984 Brazil exported rockets and rocket launching pads, tanks, armoured vehicles, aircraft and patrol-boats to an annual amount of $ 1 billion to South America and the Middle East as well as Africa, altogether to 35 countries. Thus it ranks first on the list of arms exporters of the Third World. In addition, Brazil gives technical help, too, to a number of countries (e.g. to Saudi Arabia) on the establishment of certain branches of their defence industries. The main buyers from Argentina are the Latin American countries (Bolivia, Paraguay) whereas India has sold weapons first and foremost to Bangladesh and Nepal. Arms exports from South Korea have rapidly increased since the second half of the 1970s. The South Korean export of light infantry arms, tactical rockets and patrolboats is directed mainly to Indonesia.

However, the bulk (about 80 per cent in the 1970s) of arms exports from the developing countries does not originate from local production but is merely re-exporting activity.

The developed Western countries, particularly the United States, made serious efforts to restrict the export and re-export of arms produced on the basis of licences purchased from them. Their basic aim is to exclude potential competitors from the market. Some Third World countries evade such regulations by the modification of arms produced on the basis of licences. However, the export potential of the arms and war material from the developing countries is still minimal and therefore they are not serious rivals of the developed capitalist countries.

The People's Republic of China, too, has a certain part in arms exports to the developing countries. Two per cent of the arms and ammunition imports of the Third

World countries originated from China in the 1970s. In some years of the past decade arms and ammunition exports made up 10–15 per cent of total Chinese exports.

Lacking substantial disarmament agreements, the arms industry sector will continue to play an important part in shaping the industrial structure of the world in the years to come. The arms production and the new scientific and technological revolution have been closely linked by the new wave of the arms race in the 1980s. The structural policies of the governments, too, are influenced in many ways by the changes in the pattern and composition of defence technologies.

4. Economic Policies and Structural Changes in International Perspectives

As indicated by the analysis of the structural relations of world production the solution or mitigation of conflicts of different intensity and character which arise in the course of industrial growth and in the process of the differentation of production and consumption cannot be left to market forces alone. The world economy of the late twentieth century is far too complex and highly heterogeneous as to structure and development both of which require policy coordination and concerted action. These are, however, extremely difficult. Not only because the scale and material composition of consumption and accumulation are dissimilar, but also because the size of the countries, varies and their natural endowments are different. There are considerable differences in priorities due to social patterns, balance of power among the social classes and the effect of all these on the political institutions. The two groups of countries (states which have a determinant part in the structural changes of the world economy, and those which primarily adapt themselves to structural changes) of course occupy different positions in their approach to international policy coordination.

In the absence of an internationally coordinated approach to structural change, most of the tasks of adaption or structural adjustment emerge on a national level, in national economic policies.

The importance of structural policies has increased and gained an increasingly central role in economic policy even in states where planning on the state level has not developed. (True, the concept of that policy is different from country to country.) In many countries it is identified with the national industrial policy. In the United States it has been debated for many years whether an industrial policy existed at all or to what extend such a policy is needed. According to the views of experts in other countries there is no such notion as a structural policy but the structure and pattern of production and consumption are automatically influenced by the economic policy. It may be true that the economic policy influences structural changes in general but the objectives and means of the economic policy especially aimed at affecting structural changes represent a well-defined framework. Structural policy as such has a number of special characteristics, the most important of which are as follows.

a) Structural policy is not an autonomous domain but a necessary part of economic policy since neither its general aims nor the means needed to carry them into effect can be separated from the general framework and conditions of the economy.

b) In the structural policy the general socio-political, socio-economic objectives are interlinked closely with technological-economic aims and conditions. Structural policy therefore has a key role among the general objectives of economic (social) policy and in the shaping of the conditions for their realization.

c) The two basic levels of decisions, the macro and the micro spheres, are connected by the structural policy. Naturally, depending on the specific characteristics of the social and economic system different instruments are used. The relative importance of the two spheres in decision-making and implementation could be different whereas the connections between the two levels in structural policy is always an issue of vital importance from the point of view of adaptation and adjustment.

d) Since structural policy also shapes the position of a given country within the international division of labour, it exerts an influence on the whole system of international economic relations as well. These aspects of the structural policy are of outstanding importance especially in countries which cannot influence world economic changes but have to adapt themselves to such changes.

As regards the national objectives of structural policy related to production, there are two basic groups of problems: one is connected with the growth of output in some product groups or industries, the other is related to the tasks of phasing out product groups or industries.

An economic policy connected with consumption as well as the proportion and composition of consumption and investment may set the aim of modifying the system of distribution and may also imply various partial preferences.

Ends and means of a structural policy are closely linked, particularly in the life of highly developed industrial countries.

Three main groups of means can be defined in the implementation of structural policies:

— means related to production inputs,
— means regulating demand (incomes, market, distribution),
— means shaping international conditions.

The definition of the objectives mentioned and the utilization of means is particularly difficult if a change in international conditions is the direct reason for the necessary structural adjustment.

Adjustment, like many other economic terms has various meanings. It is used in many different ways. Basically it means the process of restoring correct relationships. In the vocabulary of international economics in past decades, the concept of adjustment was closely related to external imbalances and to indebtedness and the conditionalities established by the IMF and the policies of the World Bank. The meaning of adjustment, however, is not confined to this notion.

Adjustment as a set of policy measures is also used in cases when the difficulties are of internal origin. Rapid growth of government expenditure may result in a budget deficit, leading to domestic cost and price increases, inflation, declining competitiveness and finally balance of payment difficulties.

The restoration of the national, let alone international balance of supply and demand often requires drastic stabilization measures. Technological change requires far-reaching adjustment measures. In order to survive, countries have to adjust.

In the framework of the OECD the concept of "positive adjustment" was developed as the one which facilitates shifts from declining sectors to the growing ones and from the less efficient branches to the more efficient ones. According to their definition, adjustment policies can be regarded as positive if they facilitate such shifts or if they are directed to achieving other governmental objectives, such as improving the social and physical environment, the distribution of income or the fair sharing of the burdens. Adjustment is an integral and necessary phase of the economic growth process.

In a flexible economic system adjustment is not an alien concept, it is a more or less permanent requirement in economic policies. Since the domestic and external environment is changing constantly, economic policies have to accommodate to the changes sooner or later. Depending on the intensity and the nature of the changes, adjustment requirements may differ greatly.

Structural adjustment is a strategic task. It is a comprehensive set of policy measures which take place in a macroeconomic framework and includes not only external measures but also internal changes in development policies and priorities, structural shifts in output, consumption, etc. Short-term adjustment policies and measures reacting mostly to external shocks may be parts or beginnings of strategic adjustment. The interrelation between short-term adjustment measures and strategic changes may be especially strong in those cases where the factors requiring adjustment are of major importance and of a lasting nature. In those cases the short-term steps must be followed by longer-term policies. These requirements seem to be especially strong in the contemporary world economy. The new technological revolution, the long-term imbalances in international finance, the structural changes in world output and trade indicate that short-term imbalances reflect long-term development problems. Therefore adjustment policies must be implemented with a longer-term view and with a new development horizon. The changes which have taken place in the past decade have altered the operating mechanism of the world economy. Competition has increased in an interdependent world, with the spread of the rapid international transmission of economic disturbances and structural changes in the industrial countries. In an increasingly hierarchical structure of world economy, global distributive mechanisms and pressures are reproducing and strengthening inequalities without any clear sign of an increase in international economic solidarity. Technological progress makes the achievements of earlier industrialization increasingly obsolete in the global division of labour.

The failures and the partial successes of shorter-term adjustment policies proved the necessity of planning for longer-term changes.

From among the recent national and international debates and practices concerning the problems of structural adjustment especially, the following issues were raised on an economic policy level:

— which are the best ways to minimize the costs of adjustment, especially human costs,

— how to improve the adjustment capacity of individual countries,

— how to increase the efficiency of public administration, especially that branch which is responsible for the elaboration and implementation of adjustment programmes,

— what are the best ways of providing international institutional support for the national adjustment policies.

The overcoming of internal opposition to structural adjustment is not an easy task either. Opposition is generally connected with fear of changes in the system of distribution, modification of incomes, unemployment or other shocks.

As mentioned in another part of this book, policies aimed at the transformation of structure have an effect on the level of profits, wages and employment even within national frameworks. If the economic policies of the states or the business strategies of enterprises attempt to influence the direction of structural changes in the interest of solving some other conflict, they generally tend to create additional conflicts. Similar problems of international efforts aimed at the coordination of structural changes (both initiated by inter-governmental organizations or by transnational corporations).

It is often the changes in the relative capacity for economic performance, industrial structure and competitiveness of the states which result in structural problems, tensions and troubles.

In an open economy domestic products always compete potentially with imported goods meeting similar demands. Naturally the national producers try to create more favourable conditions for their products against competitive imports. If, however, an attempt is made to protect the declining industries in the national economic structure by import restrictions, then production or even the expansion of production is rewarding for low-productivity units, too. Since economic growth tends to be an uneven process, the competitiveness of some industries (or enterprises) decreases permanently whereas that of others increases. Persistence in the maintenance of declining industries, backward management methods, obsolete technologies and unfavourable product patterns inevitably result in import restrictions and encourage the policy of "national isolation".

Business Strategies and the Process of Structural Changes in the World Economy

One of the outstanding experts of management science, Peter Drucker set seven conceptual foundations for the modern firm: 1) the scientific management of work as the key to productivity; 2) decentralization as a basic principle of organization; 3) personnel management, embracing job descriptions, appraisals, wage and salary administration and human relations; 4) management development; 5) managerial accounting which may be described as "the use of analysis and information, as the foundation for managerial decision-making"; 6) marketing; 7) long-range planning.[113]

While it is, of course, true that structural factors operating on an international scale are basically the same as in a national framework, long-range planning on a global scale must take into account the main trends in the world economy and in its different sectors and regions. From the point of view of structural changes it is necessary to take into account the industrial (structural) policies of different governments, the factors influencing the position and policies of international competitors (including the pool of potential new-comers).

Long-run planning or long-term business strategies are important not only because of the competition. In most modern industries at least two years are needed to bring significant investment decisions to fruition and in the case of developing new products an even longer time is needed. (Small and medium-size enterprises naturally react faster and more flexibly to direct market impulses and therefore are able to plan the expansion or transformation of their production within a shorter time-span.)

But for large firms, especially the international corporations holding key positions in different global industrial sectors, development plans spanning 3–15 years have become common. They have to take into account the activity of the whole corporation in question (comprising the technological aspects of production, too). It is the rate and volume of profits, of course, which determines what, how, and where should be produced in the final analysis.

At the beginning of the "golden age" of the 1960s a leading economist of the Du Pont concern, one of the biggest American chemical corporations, stressed the point that for a big modern enterprise it is the long-terms decisions not the short-term ones which are of vital importance. Decisions on research or investments imply long-term consequences. The managers of the enterprises can influence developments but to a very small measure in the short run and have to react mainly to circumstances beyond their control. Only long-term decisions can determine the fate of business companies.[114]

Long-term planning of enterprises was greatly hindered by the world economic conditions arising from inflation during the 1970s and 1980s, rising oil prices, the recessions of 1974 and the early 1980s, the uncertainty of exchange rates and some other factors, which made earlier long-term investment decisions irrelevant to the new situation. In this environment long-range planning as a feasible exercise was widely questioned by many business leaders. Some of them went so far as to abolish the relevant departments of their firms. It is, however, precisely the new environment which makes long-range planning more important than before, especially for the large, international firms, where technology and marketing skills are combined with a coordinated, world-wide production system.

The nature and the tasks of long-range planning is of course changing. In the framework of long-range planning in international firms, such important issues are increasingly dealt with as:

— How to promote innovations and apply the new technologies more widely, and efficiently within the given international system.

— How to develop management structures globally so as to attract and retain creative people from different countries.

— How to select the best choice (strategic groups) from among the different alternatives without wasting resources in the process of the structural transformation of the firm. How to combine divesting and investing in international operations.

— How to reduce risks while accepting the necessity of permanent changes and shifts in input and output structures in different parts of the world.

— What strategic alternatives should be used or combined: what broad produce line should be maintained; should the firm concentrate on a given product for a particular region how to differentiate between national and global operations.
— How to live with different national economic polices while maintaining world-wide operations and integrating human resources, finance, production and marketing on a global scale.
— How to channel the requirements of business into the political process.
— How to establish global alliances (joint ventures, industrial cooperation, etc.) in what areas and for what purpose. With which firms should strategic partnership be established.
— How should the identity of the company develop globally and in various parts of the world.

Scientific research and development is another very important part of long-range strategic planning, also on an international scale. Such issues must be dealt with as: on what areas should the research work of a given company concentrate in order to increase future competitiveness; where to locate research activities in the international system, in order to secure the greatest possible lead time.

The problems of integration are also vital strategic issues for the large firms. The advantages of integration (both in national and in international scale) are well known. In the case of vertical integration important gains can be achieved by putting technologically distinct operations together. The costs of scheduling and coordinating operations may be lower in an integrated firm. The firms may also avoid or reduce the costs of market transactions and information. Supply and demand are also assured. There are of course important disadvantages of integration, which can be quite substantial in a period of rapid technological change. The mobility and the flexibility of the firms in changing partners is reduced. Capital costs are usually high and the exit from the given business may be more difficult. Vertical integration implies a more or less captive relationship. Typical examples of the problems of vertically integrated firms would be the large US steel companies which controlled steel making from the coal and iron mines to finished sheet steel, blooms and ingots. With the declining demand, these firms suffered great losses in the 1980s. Their non-integrated competitors, the minimills using the latest technologies, made their products mostly from cheap steel scrap, grabbed about 20 per cent of the market and expanded rapidly.

As a reaction to the accelerated changes in technology, demand patterns and competition in certain countries, especially in the US a new entrepreneurial form has developed, under the name of network corporations. These use the latest information technology and with a small central organization rely on small independent or semi-independent units or firms which perform manufacturing, distribution, marketing and other crucial business functions on a contract basis. This organizational form is more flexible, requires less capital, carries lower overhead costs, and can easily use the least expensive global sources and tap the best technologies. Companies working like this are, however, more vulnerable to competition from suppliers, have less control over production and can lose design and manufacturing expertise.[115]

While the spread of the network companies was rather fast in the 1980s, their role is still limited. It is highly probable that the traditional form of diversification, i.e.

"vertical integration" will be combined with the *horizontal diversification* used in the network form.

The latter is often characterized also by the fact that efforts are made by the large companies to organize production to serve some well-defined consumer or technology "system" in a complex way (e.g. full-scale business machine development or enterprises turning out hospital equipment). Through these forms the expansion of industrial companies in the service sector has also assumed increasing dimensions.

As regards the international aspect of the problem, joint enterprises—as opposed to parallel fully-owned subsidiary company forms—have achieved a greater role in carrying into effect the strategic objectives mentioned; such firms comprise all the spheres from research to production of goods or services.

The patterns of integration among the subsidiaries of the international corporations operating in different countries influence the structure of the division of labour and the adjustment process in the world economy. Accordingly, the debate in the developed Western countries that centres around the problem of whether the large or the small and medium-sized enterprises are playing a greater role in structural adjustment is basically of an "academic" nature. In theory it is naturally true that it is easier and faster to establish smaller firms and that closing down such enterprises implies smaller economic shocks. However, under the conditions of the modern Western economy it is the large corporations and the mechanisms developed between them and the state which determine the main trend of technological progress and economic processes. (The small and medium-sized enterprises are largely dependent on these relationships. The capital needed for their operations, too, is generally supplied by the large banks or by the "entrepreneurial funds" created by them.) On the other hand it is undeniable that when furthering the flexible functioning of the economy, the speed of innovation and the product pattern of small and medium-sized enterprises have played a significant part.

In the 1980s the strategic decisions of the large enterprises are linked more than ever with scientific activities. Not only product development but also sales strategies have strong scientific foundations. New requirements were formulated in connection with market research, too, and in marketing activities the utilization of a great number of social sciences (economics, mathematics, psychology and even neurology) is taking place in the spheres of advertising, packaging, predicted and planned durability and so forth. These impacts are of particular importance in the market for consumer goods but are by no means restricted solely to this sphere. On the market for capital goods it is naturally the product and process development aspects which are much more important.

In connection with structural changes, economic research has become more widespread in the large corporations, beyond the traditional areas of market research. The management expects economists and research on economics to support efficient business strategies linked with the changes and technological-economic transformations. "The organization of changes", the control of the switch-over, requires an analysis of all the factors influencing such processes from the national economic policy to the different trends in technological development. In addition to experts on marketing and operations research, the big corporations are compelled to employ in increasing numbers specialists who are able to make sense of general macro-economics for micro-environments to increase the profitably of the enterprises by understanding and anticipating factors in long-term changes, within the national economies and on a global scale.

Structural Adjustment Policies and External Changes

Structural adjustment is of course a necessary step in every country. The different external and domestic changes, however, may require completely different measures in each country and their need for international supportive policies may also greatly vary. There are great differences in the capacities of the countries to adjust to the changes. The potential and actual costs and benefits of the adjustment process may depend on factors which can be controlled by one country more than by another, depending on the economic and political power, the structure of the economy, the achieved level of economic and social development, etc. There are important systemic factors influencing the concrete policies of adjustment. In the socialist countries the problems of output, consumption and trade are receiving greater attention from the beginning. In spite of the great differences, there are also important similarities in the tasks, in the causes of success or failure, in the factors determining the costs and also in social conditions and consequences.

Structural adjustment is especially urgent where there are difficulties. These difficulties may be limited to one country, to a group of countries or they may be of a general, global nature. When only a couple of countries are facing serious structural problems requiring major adjustment measures, the external environment can be more supportive than it would be for widespread and long-term difficulties. For many countries the "world economy" may represent in such cases a hostile environment. External forces may undermine or destabilize national economic structures, may force countries to give up social priorities and change the dominating system of values. The weaker the countries are, the more limited are the international efforts to help those countries, the greater the shocks will be.

During the great depression the "beggar-my-neighbour" concept characterized policies by which the different countries wanted to shift the burden of adjustment to their partners. The main burden was thrown on the debtor countries. Adjustments, according to Keynes' analysis forced the countries "in the direction most disruptive of social order, and threw the burden on the countries least able to support it, making the poor poorer".[116]

Prior to the 1970s some industrially developed Western countries—under the conditions of favourable economic growth interrupted only by short recession periods—had reacted to structural disturbances generally by implementing short-term measures. These had mainly been policies of wait-and-see thus gaining time until the next period of recovery. Thus, structural problems were permitted to increase to a dangerous extent. These countries were not willing to accept the costs of long-term adjustment measures. Their situation had become rather difficult at the time of the 1974 recession. The dangers of such policies became even more marked at the time of the recession of the early 1980s. It was clearly demonstrated that by delaying structural changes no country can evade shocks shifting great and lasting burdens on to sectors which have to stand their ground on the world market.

In most of the developed Western countries measures taken by the state in connection with structural policies have corrected or shaped the pattern of the economy without, however, destroying market relations. In the 1970s and 1980s the need for structural adjustment has induced new and often very serious challenges to economic policies. The question of the necessity of phasing out or incidental international redeployment of industries lagging behind was raised as early as the end of the 1960s. The reasoning was that if such changes were not carried out the adverse influence on the national economy and the costs of measures following such a delay would be far higher (e.g. subsidies, permanent structural unemployment). It was also understood that relocation to other countries could become an important incentive in the development of economic relations both with developing and developed countries.

A massive redeployment of declining branches, however, was not taking place since in the leading Western countries, also, development had slowed down.

As proved by the recessions of 1974 and 1981, the different factors do not affect the states in a uniform way. Not only their intensity is different, but also the structural "immunity" of the states to external problems which emerge at the time of a recession is dissimilar. The exact surveying and evaluation of external effects are indispensable for the definition of the character of the measures and the intensity of the reaction necessary for the solution of the problems which have emerged. Even in the case of the so-called normal functioning of the world economy problems may crop up in some countries which have an adverse influence on the partners of these states.

The unfavourable effects of sudden changes in economic policies, economic strategies and, as a consequence, in the economic situation of countries having a major part in world economic relations can spread to other countries as well. In the first half of the 1980s, for instance, the serious disturbances in the national economic policy of the United States, the huge budget deficit and the high interest rates caused serious troubles in a great number of industrially developed Western countries, too.

In the 1970s and 1980s external disturbances in the relations of the Western industrial countries were connected not only with international monetary relations (overvalued dollars, problems of the balance of payments, etc.). Problems which were particularly troublesome originated from internal structural imbalances in the production and consumption structures of large countries which affected other states as well. "Traditional" producers and exporters had to face difficulties also because of the sudden "change" of technology or production branch in other countries. Similar problems were encountered as a result of the backlog in some important sectors of industry and the "rigidity" of some national economic structures. Structural problems assumed particularly serious dimensions in states dependent on the production and export of only a few products. Structural dependence is also the chief means of the transfer on international difficulties to other countries in the world economic system. Economic difficulties stemming from this fact are often concealed or manifest themselves on the surface as "technical" problems.

Major structural problems emerged in the economies of the socialist countries, too. Some of them were of external origin, others were rooted in internal imbalances.

The individual countries reacted to the effects of the external shocks in different ways and took different courses.

a) Restrictive measures were introduced (import and foreign exchange restrictions, import substitution, reduction of domestic production and consumption).

b) Attempts were made to limit the impact of external shocks by short-term measures, and at the same time medium and long-term plants were moderated to modernize production structures.

c) Imports were reduced temporarily (by means of economizing, by the slowdown of production growth, the cutting back of consumption) and simultaneously attempts were made to increase exports by all means.

d) As a result of common interests attempts were made to reach international agreements by establishing transitory or lasting groupings, and joint measures were taken to settle problems.

e) Efforts were made within the framework of regional cooperation organizations to mitigate unfavourable external effects.

f) Measures were taken to produce a global international settlement for countries with different interests (i.e. both those profiting and those losing as a result of changes) and attempts were made to reconcile contradictory interests by reaching compromises.

Thus the adjustment experiences of the 1970s and 1980s were not completely dissimilar to the process characterized by Keynes. The economic and social costs of adjustment were high in most countries, particularly in developing ones. The poorer and more dependent the countries were, the higher were the costs, the more domestic problems they had. In the developed Western countries it has been emphasized in policies and often implemented in practical terms, that adjustment presupposes the alleviation of the burden of those directly affected by compensation payments, unemployment benefits, training programmes, assistance for moving, etc. Such facilities were hardly available in the developing countries, where the costs of adjustment were relatively higher. The acceleration of inflation reduced real wages. The decline in real wages was sometimes 30–40 per cent. Import restrictions and the declining demand resulted in major losses in output and employment. Underemployment also increased and the informal sector grew rapidly. There was a general deterioration of social conditions. Public expenditure for the extension and maintenance of social infrastructure declined sharply. Health and education expenditures were cut in real terms in many countries.

According to the estimates of the author, calculating the differences between the actual and potential output during 1975–85, taking also into account the losses on the terms of trade and the higher interest rates, the combined total loss of the developing countries equalled their GNP for one year in 1980. This was, of course, not the cost of the adjustment programmes but the result of cumulative losses suffered by the countries. But part of it was connected with the adjustment policies.

Experience shows that it is, of course, very difficult to develop a cost-minimizing adjustment strategy, especially for a single country. Costs are often not even calculated by the countries. Some lessons, however, could be learned from the experiences of the past decades.

a) Adjustment policies became especially costly for countries in an international environment, when the economic policies of the larger Western industrial countries were dominated by neo-conservative ideologies, accepting the idea of "global belt-tightening", emphasizing the need for economic policy autonomy in an interdependent world. The developing countries were not able to build efficient defence lines against the burden switching effects of those policies.

b) While it is correct to state that in countries where prices and exchange rates were greatly distorted and low-efficiency import-substituting policies were adopted, where too much was borrowed and not enough was exported in relation to their external obligations, adjustment proved to be more difficult. Adjustment policies in basically outward-oriented economies were in many cases faster. As for the costs and benefits, the division is not on the line of the world market orientation but according to the abilities to develop and implement proper and comprehensive policy packages. Changes in development strategies (shifts from import substitution to export orientation) as adjustment policies are very difficult to implement even on a medium-term horizon, due to the different structural, skill, managerial and marketing requirements.

c) Smaller countries are in general more exposed to external shocks as a result of high trade intensity and relatively weak structural position in the world economy. In those countries the growth process must be organized in a more flexible way. When the shocks have already occurred, it is much more difficult to act. Economic adjustment is much more difficult amidst major socio-economic problems, stagnation and tensions. The speed of the measures is also an important issue. Some economists suggest that when external shocks or inappropriate domestic measures created disequilibrium, the necessary corrective actions should be taken as quickly as possible. External financial sources should be used to speed up adjustment and not for postponing it.

Certain economies, however, do not respond to sudden changes in policies or regulations rapidly. Usually more developed and flexible economies can implement rapid shifts in policies more easily. The political implications are more favourable where the economic feasibility of change is greater. The sacrifices are brief, there is less time for the opposition buildup against the programmes and with some early results they can even generate considerable support. The impact of the adjustment programme on the different social classes of the population creates less social tension and it is more manageable. Gradualism in principle facilitates more flexibility in the implementation of the programme and the distribution of the burdens. But it may create long periods of austerity with very little concrete changes, diminishing popular support and increasing discontent.

e) Since the ability of any given country to develop and implement such adjustment programs which minimize the costs and mitigate the burdens of adjustment and do not lead to political tension depends to a great extent upon the efficiency of public administration, strengthening its capacity is a major task of a longer-term nature. Of course there must be strong executive leadership and the staff of the economic or development administration must also be motivated. The economic and social goals of the adjustment process must also be well and clearly defined. Priorities in the adjustment process should be properly selected. In the government agencies there must be clear responsibilities for each of the adjustment policies. The tasks must be well coordinated and separated with minimum overlapping. The issues of "centralization" or "decentralization" during the adjustment process must be treated flexibly in a pragmatic way.

Adjustment tasks and their implementation usually cause tensions within the administration. Such issues as necessary cuts in budget, the reallocation of resources, etc. increase existing differences. The weaknesses of the administrative structure, the inconsistencies, etc., may become more conspicuous. An administrative reform may become essential. While it is not easy to implement administrative reforms during the adjustment process, in certain cases this may become a fundamental condition for success.

In difficult adjustment periods it is even more important than under normal circumstances of the growth process that the participation of the population should be encouraged by the changes.

The stability of the societies depends not only on the economic successes or adverse consequences of the adjustment process. If the priorities are correctly selected and the political structure facilitates broad popular participation, even the difficulties are better tolerated.

f) The proper choice of economic partners can be a vitally important asset, especially in the adjustment process. The complementarity of economic structures, the character and norms of relations, mutual advantages, their reliability and readiness to provide assistance, if necessary, prove to be especially relevant issues in this respect. Due to the fact that the principal partners of any country are determined by historical, geo-economic, political and structural factors, the freedom of a small country to make sudden shifts is very limited in the short term. Sudden shifts are possible only among marginal partners. Of course, there can be exceptions when a larger country is ready to help smaller partners through deliberate action, such as providing special market facilities. This practice, which is not completely unknown in the world economy, usually has strong political motivations.

g) Small countries are especially interested in those forms of multilateral cooperation which could strengthen their economic position by collective measures, taking into acount the interests of all partners involved, in which the partners share responsibilities. The present international institutions, like the IMF, the IBRD or regional bodies, were not able properly to fulfil the functions of a growth-oriented collective economic adjustment supporting system.

Sectoral Adjustment:
The Case of the Developing Countries

Sectoral adjustment problems represent an especially difficult task and indicate the limitations of many developing countries in this respect.

In the first half of the 1980s, in the majority of the countries the task of adjustment emerged as a structural problem: to change the role and place of the given sectors in the economy or to introduce adjustment measures within the given sectors to increase exports in order to achieve the required increase in import capacity, and to change the domestic environment scarcities to improve supplies to the domestic market and increase employment. Within the general international framework, the developing countries had to face greater difficulties:

a) In agriculture, the main task was to increase domestic food production and non-traditional export products. Since the capacity for food imports in many countries declined, due to the great socio-political importance of food supplies, various incentives were supposed to be introduced in many countries. While the measures in principle should have had a moderately favourable impact on the agricultural sector, in practice this was sometimes more than neutralized by the declining prices of traditional agricultural export products. Agricultural incomes in general were not increasing, and even in the case of larger farms, purchases of tractors and other agricultural machinery were deferred as a result of the relative high costs.

Medium-term adjustment assistance, like institutionalized credits, helped the larger farms and estates more then smaller ones. The small farmers and the landless agricultural workers had great difficulties. Agricultural poverty was on the increase and the shrinking purchasing power of the agricultural population was adversely influencing other sectors also.

In the agricultural sector of many developing countries there are of course major, long-term structural problems, like the forms of ownership, the low level of the agrotechnological base, the lack of institutional infrastructure for marketing, financing, etc. All those and other problems limit the possibilities of efficient adjustment. The solution to the problems, however, goes beyond adjustment tasks and requires major agricultural reforms.

b) In the mining sector (other than fuel) the long-term impact of the world economic changes required major steps in adjustment to reduced demand and declining prices. Even where price increases were expected later, it was necessary to consolidate and rationalize the existing operations, to increase the efficiency of investments, to rely on small-scale activities more heavily, and to increase the value added by expanding vertical integration. It was also important to find areas where the mining sector could efficiently increase its relations with the domestic economy, through different inputs. Since the mining sector is often the most important source of external earnings and non-agricultural employment, the success of adjustment measures influences the general economic situation in many countries and regions. If deterioration continues, the adverse effects on incomes and public expenditures will be increasingly felt.

c) Due to the "not so bright" outlook in the agriculture and mining sector, the problems and tasks of adjustment in manufacturing were especially important for the majority of the developing countries. The manufacturing sector was affected by the world economic problems and their domestic consequences in many ways. The obsolescence of production capacities installed earlier increased as a result of postponed investment. Upgrading of machinery and equipment was deferred and technology imports were reduced. Industrial infrastructural projects were postponed or completely abandoned. Expenditure on domestic research and development and on technical education was reduced during the adjustment period. Since it is highly improbable under the conditions of the expected technological development and investment constraints that the autonomous job-generating capacity of industrial development will be sufficient for recovery, it will be necessary to develop special job-generating strategies especially in certain highly urbanized regions of the Third World.

Employment problems will increase due to the continuing rapid urbanization in the developing world. According to UN estimates, in addition to the 840 million urban population, by the turn of the century another 1.0–1.2 billion people will have to be absorbed by the cities of the Third World. Most of them will be poor and unskilled. About 50 per cent of them come as a consequence of population growth, the rest will migrate from the agricultural regions.

Adjustment measures must therefore include job-creating programs at low capital investment cost. Projects which are labour intensive and at the same time justified on economic grounds must be developed in the industrial sector. Most of the possibilities which are open in manufacturing and satisfy the above needs are concentrated in the small-scale industrial sector. (In urban services there are of course such facilities too.)

d) The role and especially the potential role of the transnational corporations (TNCs) in the strategic adjustment process is often discussed by experts. Their possible positive role is mentioned in such important areas as:
— bringing in, reallocating and investing capital, thus helping to alleviate the debt problem;
— innovating, adopting, perfecting and transferring technology, which may help to upgrade technological capabilities;
— bringing in new and useful knowledge about organization and management, which are important in the domestic structural changes;
— facilitating international marketing and promotion;
— providing new job facilities for the local labour force;
— educating and upgrading workers, professionals and managerial staff;
— through the international vertical organizations they can promote the more effective progression of goods from one stage to another, outside the free market, which may imply greater stability of export earnings;
— to some extent they may stimulate local services and output.

There are of course great differences between the actual and potential role of TNCs, since their activities are not guided by altruistic motivation or public interest but profit motives.

The points listed above may help adjustment efforts, especially export increases. The subordination of a large segment of the national economy to international strategies or interests may, of course, hamper such aims in the adjustment process as:
— the increase in export surplus and import-saving;
— maximizing external earning potentials;
— creating new jobs for the masses by labour-intensive operations;
— increasing international competitiveness in those areas which are not in the interest of the given TNCs.

The outflow of resources through the price mechanism, in the form of profit remittances, royalties, etc., was in many cases excessively high. Transnationals also promoted the outflow of highly skilled professionals (brain drain). Experiences with transnationals proved also that in the adjustment period they often reduced operations or completely withdrew activities. There were, of course, counter-examples as well when the reduced real wages, devalued currencies and different direct incentives offered especially favourable conditions.

Structural Imbalances: The Trade Policy Response

The problems of the 1970s and 1980s proved that a model of economic policy which deals only with national economic conditions and does not reckon with international interrelationships inevitably leads to sharp domestic and even international conflicts in a world of strengthening interactions and interdependence. It is also a fact, however, that there has been very little international institutional reaction to the changes in the world economy (these problems are discussed in the last part of this book) and there are no international norms on government reaction to abrupt—and from their point of view disadvantageous—changes in the economic policies of other countries. To this very day international trade policy is the most significant means for the settlement of problems.

Trade policy in itself is not a direct and effective instrument to increase industrial competitiveness or to correct structural imbalances within national economies. Protectionism naturally influences the volume and the structure of trade and through its consequences, output and consumption patterns in the various national economies. (There may be greater production, higher wages and profits as the result of protection.) It usually helps less competitive industries (or firms) and it is not a long-term response to structural imbalances. Liberalization may be a helpful policy to crowd out inefficient, less competitive activities but it helps the stronger and move competitive actors and countries, and it puts the burden of structural adjustment on the weaker and poorer participants in international economic relations.

For almost 40 years after World War II an international trade policy was practised by the developed industrial countries which could be characterized as restricted or moderate liberalism. Practical decisions and trade-policy systems have developed as a result of the mixture of liberal and interventionist-protectionist measures. The proportions of that "mixture" have changed from time to time according to the problems encountered by these countries. The character and timing of changes was virtually in harmony with the practice of the various Western governments. This is partly to be explained by the fact that they were motivated by similar events, influences and ideals. Their attitudes were influenced also by the fact that they attempted to pursue policies which could—through bilateral and multilateral channels—operate the prevailing system, as well as taking part in further consultations, talks and agreements. Thus, to understand Western trade policies it is necessary to grasp the essence of liberal and protectionist arguments since both of these are permanently present in and exert their influence on the international trade policy. Significant lobbies back up such tendencies in all of these countries and ever since the end of World War II none has proved able to oust the other.

Practical trade policies have developed as compromises in the conflicts between the different groupings, and the continuity of the two tendencies is strong though often covered up by extremely intense propaganda for certain periods. It is often stated, for instance, that from the 1944 Bretton Woods agreement until the early 1970s liberalization had dominated international economic relations and trade policy was under the influence of that trend. This statement, however, disregards all the contradictory tendencies which were also present in that period. Besides, liberalization was more characteristic of the developed world and it scarcely asserted itself in the developing world.

The system of GATT in the 1950s and 1960s was characterized by the "golden age": six tariff-reducing "rounds" were held in that time. As a result, the quantitative restrictions on imported industrial goods were virtually abolished by the Western countries, their customs duties, too, were considerably reduced according to the agreements characterized by multilateral negotiations and bargaining in the course of the "rounds". The last of these agreements was reached at the so-called Tokyo round concluded in 1977, the realization of which is in progress. The relations among the European states have been considerably liberalized by the calling into life and extension of the European Economic Community and later on by the conclusion of various agreements between the Community and other European countries furthering the flow not only of goods but also of capital. Institutionalized international rules, agreements and statutes were elaborated within the frameworks of OECD, GATT (General Agreement on Tariffs and Trade) and IMF (International Monetary Fund) the aim of which was to influence national trade policies in the interest of the implementation of liberal principles.

Trade policy has not become a vital issue of national party politics. One element supporting liberal tendencies was the general recognition that international trade offers possibilities founded on mutual advantages, another one was the fear that the prosperity of all the countries could be jeopardized by unilateral trade and currency restrictions. This latter conclusion was regarded as one of the most definite lessons of the 1930s. All this explains the effort made by the individual countries to take a consistent and predictable line in international relations. It is also obvious that the new international division of labour, too, demands an approach of that kind.

The "triumph" of liberalism, however, was not absolute and neither was development unambiguous. Significant parts of the trade policies of the countries involved were kept safe from liberalization. Thus, agriculture was everywhere taken out of the scope of liberalization, and until recently government purchases and trade in services, too, was beyond the sphere of liberalization. Thus, direct liberalization has been centred mainly on industrial goods but even within that sector new restrictions have appeared and been valid ever since the end of the 1950s.

First the export of textiles, later that of clothing were affected by trade restrictions referring to the stipulations of the 1961 and 1962 cotton-textile agreements and the 1974 so-called multi-fibre arrangement (MFA).

A number of industrial countries have enacted discriminatory import quotas on certain Japanese goods. Such restrictions have been defined as "voluntary export restricting agreements" since the middle of the 1970s. Though it was Japan at the beginning which had to bear the lion's share of export restrictions, later the developing countries and even the socialist countries were compelled to adapt themselves to more and more of these restrictions. Such "exceptions" set a limit to the spread of liberalization and weakened the system of GATT. The multi-fibre arrangements were elaborated within the framework of GATT, nevertheless they did not harmonize with the rules of GATT. All other restrictions were worked out outside GATT,

The GATT structure has been weakened further by two developments since the end of the 1950s. First, the system established within the framework of the European Economic Community, particularly the mobile customs duties levied on agricultural exports and the preferential agreements. Second, in 1964 a dual category membership had been introduced in the GATT according to which rules lifting trade restrictions do not pertain to Third World countries, and Western countries renounced the principle of reciprocity in their trade with developing countries.

The above tendencies appeared prior to 1973, and illustrate the fact that the process of liberalization in the Western world had been rather weak and contradictory even at a time when trade policies had been founded generally on liberal principles. Owing to the particular mixture of liberalism and protectionism, no "general" trend had taken shape which could have made possible a global regulation of world trade relations. High-sounding statements on an open world trade order remained just popular slogans, whereas in practice just the opposite was carried into effect by the economic policies. A specific kind of dualism has endured in the relationships of the industrial countries.

Other tendencies prevailed in the developing countries in their trade with the developed industrial states. Beginning with the 1960s (the establishment of the developing countries) a new world has emerged representing another kind of trade order. While restrictions were partly lifted by the developed countries, almost all the developing countries introduced administrative control on international economic transactions. The objectives, endeavours and effects of this control were of a protectionist nature since the developing countries tried to overcome in this way their difficulties derived from an unfavourable balance of payments. The policy was influenced by the concept of the protection of domestic industry by customs duties, quotas and prohibitions at a time of competition and pressure through trade by the more developed countries because a free trade policy was definitely favourable only to the rich and strong countries. The socialist countries, too, developed their foreign trade system setting off from such considerations.

Thus, the contrast between the industrial and the developing countries exists still. In the developing countries, however, highly variegated and often differing trade systems have been established. At one end of the spectrum there are countries which have strictly controlled all international transactions. The other extreme is represented by Hong Kong which approached the liberal ideal closer than many a Western country. The 1970s brought little change to the situation of the developing world. No new protectionist wave emerged in this region.

Despite the significant differences the developing countries more often than not took a common stand on issues of trade policy and international economic diplomacy. In order to achieve more favourable bargaining positions, they organized the so-called Group of 77 which has grown to a membership of 125. This group exerted pressure on the developed industrial countries and attempted to have them accept a package deal on economic reforms the principles of which were included in the declaration "New International Economic Order" passed in 1974. Most of the ideas regarding such a new world economic order have taken shape since 1946 at different international meetings. The main suggestions on international trade contained two elements of vital importance: the integrated programme relating to commodities (including financial structures to be developed to stabilize prices) and the offering of free or preferential possibilities to exported goods of the developing countries on the markets of the Western countries. This latter proposal was based on the principle (and was in harmony with the dual-type membership in the GATT) according to which a liberal trade policy by the developed countries as regards the poor countries was an obligation assumed unilaterally. Trade negotiation on the problems mentioned above have achieved, however, only negligible results.

A new protectionist wave emerged in the 1970s as a result of the radical changes which had taken place in the world economy first of all in consequence of stagflation (i.e. simultaneous stagnation and inflation). Interventionist and protectionist tendencies pursued by non tariff means had strengthened everywhere in the world economy between 1974 and 1978.

The percentage of world trade affected by various administrative restrictions increased from 40 per cent in 1974 to 48 per cent in 1980. In 1985 more than 3 million restrictive measures were in effect in 170 countries. This increase was due everywhere to the global turnover of industrial goods. The volume of trade in industrial goods affected by protectionism has grown considerably. Whereas protectionist measures introduced by the industrial countries afflicted only 3 per cent of the global industrial goods trade in 1974, this percentage grew to 24 per cent in 1980. Such measures were taken overwhelmingly against the exports of the developing and— to a certain extent—the socialist countries.

Besides the phenomena mentioned above (related mainly to import restrictions), considerable changes have taken place on the export side, too. The most substantial of these has been the increase in export subsidies. Of outstanding importance was the fact that the support of agricultural exports was increased by the European Economic Community. It should be stressed that the EEC has become one of the leading exporters of a number of agricultural products by the early 1980s.

Public support of export credits was increased, too, mainly as a result of the fact that the interest rates on export credits were kept low while nominal interest rates increased. So-called "mixed credits" were granted from the middle of the 1970s on, chiefly to Third World countries. Low interest "aid funds" were combined with standard interest export credits to make the exports of capital goods attractive.

Thus export competition has become sharper and has shifted in the direction of administrative advantages. An agreement was reached at the OECD in 1978 on the principles of government supported export credits but this agreement had several loopholes. Though Western economic literature still contains the catchword "liberalism" a number of marked changes of contrary tendency and serious practical consequences have taken place at various international meetings.

The general features of the protectionist measures taken since the 1970s are the following:
— they are of an extremely discriminative nature;
— they are arbitrary and are changed frequently;
— they comprise a great number of differences according to products and sectors of industry;
— they distort price fluctuations (thus deepening the gap between national and international prices);
— they restrict competition (not only through protectionism and subsidies but by means of stimulating cartellization).

Protectionist measures assert themselves as a rule through central administrative mechanisms and, therefore, the significance of political bargaining has increased in world trade. At the same time, strategic restrictions (pointed out above) have strengthened in world trade.

The changes mentioned have made themselves felt not only within the individual countries but have expanded to the international system as a whole increasing inter-governmental tensions. This is emphasized, for instance, by the fact that the European Economic Community has come up against the other parts of the world and concurrently tensions have grown within the Community itself. It is mainly on the exports of steel and agricultural products that tensions have grown between the Community and the other parts of the world. With a few important exceptions, trade among the developed Western countries has been restricted only to a minor extent by the new protectionism, the unfavourable consequences of which are felt mainly by the developing and the socialist countries.

Protectionist policy has undermined the structure of the system which brought about the new conditions for the development of world trade in the post-war years. As a rule, governments do not want to change this system but often attempt to circumvent it. The disintegrating effects of protectionism are manifested not only in interstate relations but also in the functioning of the world markets. The internal development of the states has become increasingly isolated from the world economy mainly in the spheres of agriculture, the textile and garment industry, the steel industry, shipbuilding, the motor industry and consumer's electronics. International shipping has received increasing public support. Such sectoral measures result in isolated trade systems for some products rendering world trade extremely unstable. The new round of the GATT negotiations, the "Uruguay Round", was initiated and started against this background. It has to deal with several new issues, beyond the traditional problems. Agriculture and the service sector are the most difficult problems of the negotiations. The outcome of these negotiations will be extremely important in the global adjustment process.

In the first half of the 1980s the market conditions and economic policies which took shape following the recession did not greatly encourage the elimination of structural and equilibrium disturbances in the leading countries of the world economy. Incidentally, these countries have played a decisive part in determining development. The lack of necessary and coordinated economic policies or the insufficiency of these policies could also magnify the structural problems of the world economy. Even those few countries which from their own point of view succeeded in overcoming the structural problems within their national economies were able to step up growth only partially. In other countries—first of all in the Third World—it is the increasing structural problems and the continuation of imbalances which seem the most likely scenarios for the 1980s. The easing of the structural problems of econo-mies of the CMEA countries, too, could only be achieved be an accelerated interna-tional cooperation supporting and guaranteeing more efficient development.

The structural troubles and disturbances of the individual countries and the world economy as a whole reflect the likely development of the situation of the major sectors as well.

The simultaneous presence of overproduction and starvation on our planet is the reflection of the structural crisis of the whole world economy and agriculture in particular. Structural disturbances are reflected and occasionally aggravated by agrarian protectionism in the developed Western countries, which has a great effect on the world market of agrarian products and particularly encourages the agrarian exporter countries to bring about a structural switch-over.

The analysis of the factors influencing the consumption, production and international market of raw materials and energy sources has emphasized the lasting character of uncertainty, and considerable fluctuations in demand, supply and prices. In this respect major changes which could stabilize conditions in the 1980s according to the interests of the producing or exporting countries or bring about an improvement in conditions on the basis of compromises between producers and consumers seems highly improbable.

This, too, impedes the efforts to bring about more harmonious world economic conditions.

Overproduction—as compared to the increase of demand—will remain permanent in a number of important industries, too. International cooperation in manufacturing is not efficient enough to eliminate this, and neither does the intensity and structure of the expansion of the expected effective demand make it possible to ease the problems significantly.

The foreseeable consequences of technological-scientific progress, too, will agggravate the effects of the above on employment. Thus, structural unemployment in the developed industrial countries will be reduced only very slowly. In the developing countries new social and economic tensions will develop owing to the fact that nearly one billion additional people will attain employment age and the difficulties or even hoplessness of employing them have to be faced.

Serious troubles and tensions in the structure of the individual countries and in the world economy will therefore remain which could even take the form of a full-fledged crisis; moreover the cumultive effect of certain conditions could result in the breaking up of the world economic system. Such a situation could evolve if the strengthening of protectionism in the industrial countries, particularly in the leading countries of the world economy, should coincide with the aggravation of the problems of international finance, the further deterioration of the position of the debtor countries and the further growth of deficiencies in the international monetary system.

Part Five

New Conditions and Tasks in Global Economic Cooperation

Any given system of international economic cooperation is a result of various, sometimes highly complex, factors. The needs and the possibilities of the countries, the power structure of the period, political conflicts and coinciding interests, the experiences and actions of international institutions established for functional activities on a global or regional level are some of the main components forming the system. The constant changes in those components lead to minor or major transformations in international cooperation. The system however is usually a rather rigid one. In the late twentieth century, the problems of the world indicate that major changes are needed in the scope and effectiveness of international cooperation, to facilitate the solution or management of the present problems and to promote progress towards an institutionalized global collective economic security system.

How could a well-functioning international system be characterized in the late twentieth century? In political terms, in the maintenance of world peace, the contractual and peaceful guarantees for the security of each individual country based on the obligations undertaken according to the U.N. Charter, the peaceful solution of international debates, the absence of massive violation of human rights are the most important general requirements. From the economic point of view the international system is functioning effectively and well if it promotes a relatively widespread development for the national economies which comprise the system, through the maximum international flow of goods, services and capital, management, and to the necessary degree, labour. It should help to avoid international crises and such uncertainties and problems which may disrupt international economic transactions and cause trade wars.

The international economic system is dysfunctional if it causes widespread instability, restrains in international transactions, or results in serious structural and other imbalances.

It is generally agreed, that a well-functioning international system in the present and future world must be of a multilateral nature.

There is a narrower and a broader concept for multilaterism. Multilaterialism in a narrower understanding is a system which emerged after the Second World War in international trade and monetary matters, as the result of multilateral agreements which replaced the chaotic, disintegrated pre-Second World War regime, based on bilateralism. These multilateral agreements on one hand created such obligations for the member countries as to reduce barriers to promote freer and fairer trade and capital movements and to improve conditions for international economic relations. On the other hand, they established international organizations to oversee and to provide certain safeguards (IMF, GATT) in fulfilment of the obligations. The principle of equal treatment was the basis of this multilateral approach, and the major actors in world trade and monetary affairs which took part in it, went through a series of bargaining rounds.

Multilateralism in the broader understanding is an instrument for joint global (or regional) management of different regimes, first of all trade and monetary systems, but also the collective utilization of the seas and the oceans, the peaceful use of outer space, a special regime for commodities, etc.

In the global system of the late 20th century multilateralism has often been considered as a necessity, dictated by the process of internationalization and by the new global problems of humankind. This source of multilaterialism is increasingly important.

1. Incentives of and Barriers to International Cooperation and the Problems of Global Economic Security

The system of international cooperation which evolved in the years following World War II is today only capable to a very limited extent of promoting the joint solution of the problems and troubles which have been facing mankind in the 1970s and 1980s. It is true that the world economy has not collapsed and no such serious events have taken place as occurred during the Great Depression of the 1930s. It is also a fact, however, that world economic conditions and requirements, too, have changed since the 1920s and 1930s or even the 1950s and 1960s. One of the most significant changes—as pointed out—has been the strengthening of interdependence under specific conditions. Internationalization and the perpetuation of traditional conflicts within national limits have not only survived but have taken new forms in the late twentieth century. An important and often mentioned characteristic of the present-day global order is the existence of more than 170 countries. Never in the course of the modern history of mankind have there existed so many countries simultaneously on our globe. With their specific national, economic and social structures, their interests, strength and weaknesses, the states have remained fundamental factors in the world of the late twentieth century.

The role of the state frameworks is so great that even expected changes and possible economic and political shifts in the next 30 to 40 years will not influence the survival of states as fundamental political, organizational units in our world. Thus, the significance of states has not ceased, their role has not diminished. However, at the end of the twentieth century it is impossible, even in principle, to maintain and support the nineteenth century conception which regarded states as isolated economic units. Under normal conditions no modern state could exist—whatever its social system—if it did not participate in international economic relations. Any accepted system of international cooperation sets limits for the states. However, particularly for smaller countries, economic realities and necessities have created conditions from the very outset to which they have to adapt.

The development of the process of internationalization, the precondition of which is the raising of the standards of production, science, technology, transport and telecommunication, as well as the international division of labour cannot do without those mechanisms which transmit the various effects and impacts experienced in inter-state relations. Such effects can be advantageous or disadvantageous, premediated or spontaneous, desired or undesired. Some mechanisms function only in the economy while others go far beyond the bounds of the economic sphere. Some effects maintain the survival of states, whereas others are the sources of conflict in the contemporary world system. Not only are the forms of conflict different, but the possibilities of the individual states overcoming conflicts are highly dissimilar as well. The differences originate from the form in which such conflicts manifest themselves, from the nature of the systems in question and from the size and development level of the countries. The process of internationalization evolves not in some kind of an abstract world but under given political and economic conditions. Its development—as pointed out—is influenced to a great extent by international power relations.

The economic, political and military realities of our time have brought about specific and often difficult conditions for small countries and have stressed even more than before the significance and responsibility of major—particularly global—powers.

As a consequence of the structure of current world political and economic relations, the process of internationalization is not irreversible. Nevertheless, the danger of the disintegration of the world economy, the collapse of the international structure has not ceased. This, however, could ensue only in the wake of extremely serious political shocks, if the states were neither capable of nor willing to create the necessary level, depth, forms and organizations of international cooperation while the units which have greatest influence on the development process of the world economy pursued a policy contrary to the interests of the others and also to the general needs of world development. The disintegration of international relations could also take place if mankind, i.e. the states of our world, were not to develop a policy of necessary cooperation in order to solve crises, tensions and conflicts.

The possibility of the collapse of world economic relations and structures as a real danger first came up come up (since World War II) in the 1970s and 1980s. Particularly in the first half of the 1980s the weaknesses of the international organizational system came to the fore. Also the world economic recession of the early 1980s showed that the states tend to adopt a policy of isolationism in difficult situations thus ignoring all other parts of the world, and seeking solutions for their own problems on the basis of their domestic preferences. The lessons of the 1930s faded away thinking of governments guided by neo-conservative ideas. Even integrated organizations which attempted to shape qualitatively new relations of international cooperation in the 1960s were shaken or became temporarily paralysed by the events of the 1970s and 1980s.

The processes of internationalization and the shocks experienced may lead, however, to other conclusions than those above. Contrary to the traditional system of objectives and means, i.e. a system defined from the point of view of the individual countries, a global policy approach (according to many experts) may offer better and lasting solutions.

The approach based on the needs of the national economy considers international cooperation as the continuation of national economic decisions and economic policy. Actually every country has (and always had) some kind of international economic policy and foreign policy, the aim of which is to influence under specific conditions the relations of the country in question to other countries. Characteristic objectives and the means of this policy were rooted in national interests, values and ideas. Some decades ago a new branch of international policy took shape—multilateral economic policy. While this, also, reflected what was basically a national approach it was an important step forward in the harmonization of interest, policies and actions on an international level. This change brought about a multilateral framework for international cooperation on the basis of some of the collective interests, which could be utilized for joint efforts.

GATT (General Agreement on Tariffs and Trade), OECD, the specialized agencies of the UNO and the CMEA are characterized by policies defined on multilateral terms and realized within national frameworks. The first international organization to take some steps towards a supranational policy was the European Economic Community (Common Market).

The past and recent experiences of international cooperation, and especially of international organizations, revealed some of the basic problems and constraints of taking a global policy approach contrary to national policies as the foundation of international cooperation within international organizations and beyond.

The great philosophers, the great humanists in the past, analysed the world on a universal scale. The outstanding politicians of our century have done the same. The great powers of modern times, too, adopted policies which had global consequences. The global approach in philosophy and political thought has a long history. The question was often put by philosophers in the following way: what does the word humankind mean? Is it a concept for decision-makers on the basis of which policies could be formed?

Such general interests can be defined less ambiguously in our time as a result of the development of internationalization. Because of the various developments threatening the very existence and survival of mankind, an obviously common interest of our globe is the maintenance of the survival and further development (i.e. not only of the vital biological conditions) of mankind making possible further progress. On the basis of these comprehensive objectives and interests it is, of course, extremely hard to draw up practical programmes of action acceptable to everybody. It is almost impossible to define generally accepted prospects and solutions. One of the main reasons for this is the present division of the world, the different interests and values, the contradictory definition of the roots of the problems. It is also essential to clarify in the interest of international cooperation whether the states are sufficiently motivated to seek for the definition of global policies deliberately, make efforts in this direction and help the implementation of such policies. A further practical question is how such global policies could be formed? In connection with the above mentioned points, we must clarify what kind of conflicts hamper or impede such decisions.

To be realistic we must take into account that the inhabitants of our globe live within the frameworks of states and that they are loyal to national state institutions and not to global organizations. Naturally, within the states they belong to different social groups, political and church organizations, tribes, etc. States are not equally capable of influencing international conditions, and the capacity and possibility of the different groups to shape and mould state policies are also unequal. All their efforts are motivated by specific interests and objectives. On an international scale they hold some of these objectives and interests in common. No country would encourage a nuclear disaster or a devastating natural catastrophe. None of them is interested in an international system which would put the seas, the oceans or space at the mercy of some new pirates. None of the countries wishes global economic chaos.

However, as regards the actual realization of these common interests, the position taken by the individual countries is not at all the same. In the view of some Western countries, economic chaos can be avoided by the assertion of market relations. Others regard the "organized world" as more acceptable, meaning economic cooperation based on a network of international organizatuons and comprehensive agreements. The differences between these two points of view have became stronger in recent years. The individual countries, the interests of which manifest themselves in different ways, are affected in highly specific ways by the concrete questions. Thus, Zaire or India, though they are both developing countries dependent on raw material production, have different demands for the regulation of the character and conditions of the international commodity markets. The situation gets even more entangled when producers and consumers, debtors and creditors come up against each other. Nevertheless, a certain community of interests can evolve even under such circumstances. The UN Conference on the Law of the Sea, for instance, has proved that conflicting interest resulting from different positions taken can be highly differentiated, and has also thrown a light on the fact that it is very difficult to reach a compromise in merits between the leading states and smaller countries or between non-maritime powers and naval powers.

According to some, the global system could be established most easily "from above", i.e. by the initiative of one of the great powers. Such views were dominant in the leading circles of the United States in the postwar years, and—as pointed out—the international organizational system has been shaped accordingly after World War II.

The founder of the Club of Rome, an indefatigable adherent of global cooperation, the statesman Aurelio Peccei, was motivated by quite different ideals. In one of his last studies, he suggested a common Soviet–American initiative in the interest of the future of mankind. In this connection he pointed out that it is necessary to answer criticism according to which this would lead to the rule of the superpowers over the other parts of the world, which would be intolerable. Peccei stressed the point that such dominance was an established fact anyway. But scientists and researchers of other countries, too, could join in the efforts and the common East-West initiative. In this way certain guarantees could be obtained, and the threat of a confrontation between the superpowers could be diminished, at least temporarily. According to Peccei, it would be worthwhile taking the risk, though there would be a possibility that the superpowers themselves could get some special advantages from such a process.[117]

It stands to reason that under the present power relations the establishment of a system of comprehensive international cooperation seems to be hopeless without the cooperation and agreement of the most powerful and influential countries of the world. This, however, is not identical with imposing their will on the other parts of the world.

Setting out from the present-day situation and adding up the most likely alternatives to be expected it can be pointed out that if the establishment of any real global cooperation between the different global systems succeeded the problems of mankind, this new order could be realized not as a dictate enforced by a few great powers but only by means of a series of partial agreements. Compromises between state-centred and globally oriented solutions will not take identical forms as regards all questions either. In periods of economic and social troubles and difficulties decision makers will be less inclined to support globally oriented solutions. (This was clearly borne out by the crises of the 1970s and 1980s.) In the long run, however, it is still the global approaches which are of greater importance, at least if the disintegration of the world economy can be prevented. The reasons for this are the following:

a) As a result of world economic—particularly industrial and financial—development, interdependence and the influence of the actions of some countries on other states is increasing, and therefore rules and mechanisms are needed which would diminish the possibility of confrontations and conflicts, and would bring about the basis of the solution of problems rooted in conflicting interests—and all this in a mutually acceptable and advantageous way.

b) Since most of the international phenomena are of a highly complex nature (e.g. world trade or international finance) it seems impossible to establish lasting and functioning methods founded on the interests of a single country or group of countries. It is necessary to coordinate the interests, to initiate measures based on the functional conditions of the global system which would further the more efficient development of the world economy.

c) It has become increasingly expedient to impose global control over the universally accessible goods (seas, space, etc.) in order to prevent—in the interest of mankind—certain dangers and crises. As a consequence of the increased diversification and dividedness of the states, these tasks have become highly urgent.

d) As a result of the growing influence of functioning international institutions, inter-state organizations, international associations and international social organizations it has become necessary to control and supervise these on a regional and global scale, and this, too, needs to be based on joint, global solutions.

For the time being there is no global government or supranational global authority, and it seems unlikely that any such organization would emerge in the foreseeable future. Yet, it seems probable that as a result of minor compromises regarding a common policy, measures coordinated within national frameworks or the activities of international organizations, global cooperation will gradually be established, the strengthening of which is going to bring about progress in the late twentieth century. Such prospects suit the realities and structure of the present world order. The interests, political mentality, strategies and opportunities of the major powers—particularly of the two greatest powers—are more of a global character than those of the smaller countries, and therefore their responsibility is also much greater as regards furthering global economic security.

The problems of security on a global level are connected with the existence of common global interests of mankind in survival and progress. Small countries often blame their larger partners in the international system for sometimes disregarding the interests of the rest of the world when they formulate military or economic security policies or when their global approach projects national priorities and interests into the international system. Sometimes smaller countries are blamed for their irresponsible attitude to global security issues. The famous sentence of a French politician in the post World War I period, that "small countries are as bad as the larger ones but they cannot afford it", is mentioned sometimes in this context. In any case, the experiences of smaller countries has clearly proved that there was not one single area of national security policies which could have been dealt with in an isolated framework. In the present, and even more in the future, world system the links are certainly getting stronger. The idea that security is primarily an issue of national military power or economic strength is challenged by the environment and conditions in which the individual states have to exist. The countries are and will have to live in a world in which:

— in their efforts to increase their national security they are facing problems beyond their direct control, such as the threat caused by the nuclear arms race, by the deterioration of the natural environment, by the increase of the population of the globe, by the problems of resources, etc.;

— the unrestrained pursuit of policies by certain states justified by their perceived national security interests are increasingly undermining the security interests of mankind as a whole;

— due to the increased interactions of different states in the present and future world system, which is full of existing and potential tensions and is divided by ideologies, economic interests and military alliances and tied together through many channels, actions of small countries can have great regional or even global consequences, jeopardizing global peace.

The growing interrelations between national and global security issues require a new approach to security policies both on the national and on the global level.

It is necessary, first of all, to deal with the concept of security in a comprehensive way, to understand all the implications of interrelations between its different aspects. This includes the better understanding and appreciation of the security problems and interests of other countries, the acceptance of important notions, which derive from the words and the spirit of the UN Charter, that all nations have a legitimate right to security, that military force is not a legitimate instrument for resolving international disputes, that restraint is necessary in pursuing national policies in an interdependent world, that neither military superiority nor military means in general offer the right answer to security issues emerging in the present or future world on different levels, etc.

As the second requirement of the new approach, while understanding the comprehensive, multidimensional nature of security issues, special priorities must be given to the resolution of such problems, which are endangering the very survival of mankind. The qualitative and quantitative development of the nuclear arms race, especially between the two leading nuclear powers, presents the most serious danger to world peace and human survival at this stage. Policies which lead to the further intensification of this process must be stopped and reversed. It is the reduction or elimination of the most serious dangers to human security which could pave the road towards the resolution of all the other serious military, political and economic issues of global security, through the relaxation of tensions, increasing confidence, promoting international cooperation in other areas and releasing resources for the satisfaction of other human needs.

As a third important requirement of a comprehensive approach on a global level, one must understand the great diversity of security interests among the individual countries or groups. Without understanding these diversities, no global compromises will be possible. The legitimate security interests of the two global powers present an extremely important set of issues within the overall context. The understanding and reconciliation of the political, military and economic security interests of the individual countries and their global interrelations in a comprehensive framework will also be an important condition in the creation of a global security system. In this context, it is also very important to understand, that any effort by countries or by their groups to maximize their security in general or that of any of the components of national security at the expense of the others or at the expense of another component of national security is condemned to failure in the long run. On a short-term basis such efforts may also create serious problems for all the countries.

The fourth requirement is the understanding of the fact that while global economic security issues in a comprehensive framework are connected with all the other aspects mentioned so far, they have their own logic. In the present structure of global economic relations, the main actors of the world market are interested in pursuing policies which are based on the special, often dominating, position of the stronger countries. In this context, it is not global stability and progress but the security of the main actors, their interests in expansion, profits, in control of international flows and technology which is at the centre of their efforts. These efforts often have a disastrous effect on the other parties, especially on the small or developing countries. Economic stagnation or decline is taking place. External economic forces trigger tensions, create dissatisfaction, protest, often violence against governments not capable of providing economic relief, being themselves subordinate to the situation in the world market: the progress towards a new international economic order, which would take the interests of the weaker countries also into account, and be organized more on the basis of mutual interest, would also be an important step towards a greater global economic security.

The necessity of maintaining and strengthening global institutional arrangements for the increase of global security represents the fifth requirement. The United Nations Organization was established in 1945 as a collective global security system. According to the Charter, its main purpose is "to maintain international peace and security" and to that end "to take effective collective measures for the prevention and removal of threats to peace" (UN Charter, Chapter I. Article 1.).

Security was understood by the founders of the UN in a comprehensive way which included also the security of individuals. The concept of security was also developed in a multidimensional framework, since it has included the importance of political and military, as well as of economic security. The sovereign equality of states within the system implied also that all states, regardless of size, geographic location, social system or level of development, have a legitimate right to security.

While the world organization during years of its existence has not been able to play the role of a collective security system to the extent which was envisaged in its

Charter, so as to effectively deter or counter aggression, it has still made substantial contributions to the maintenance of peace and international security. There has been no world war since 1945 and thus the fundamental promise of the founders has been fulfilled so far. It is correct to state, or course, that the danger of a new world war has not disappeared from international life. But none of the more than 130 international armed conflicts which broke out between 1945 and 1989 widened into global or broader regional wars. This was a substantial achievement in a tense and divided world.

The organization could report achievements in many areas. Important agreements on international military, political and legal issues were concluded within its framework. Economic and social cooperation was promoted. In the process of decolonization the UN also proved to be an important actor. It has played a part in the struggle against the massive violation of human rights, the promotion of the anti-apartheid struggle, etc. Unfortunately, many common actions aimed at the settlement of urgent global security problems were blocked by the increasing international tension. It has been demonstrated that any genuine advance in those fields depends on the cooperation of the major powers.

Although the United Nations, particularly in the field of major global military security issues, could only take measures which were not vetoed by any of the leading powers, namely it could not take any step contrary to the interest of any of the five powers (with some exceptions), for example in peace-keeping operations, the organization had a fairly wide range of possibilities in those fields which were more neutral in the context of confronting global interests or even developing some common ground or interest in their solution.

As a consequence of strengthening interdependence, which requires a higher level of economic cooperation in a world of 170 states and of growing inequalities, the future importance of the United Nations in the struggle for global economic security is also beyond doubt. It remains to be seen whether the world organization will be able to cope with the difficult political conditions, and with the consequences of asymmetrical international interdependence, namely with the enormous differences in the extent and consequences of dependence for the different states. This asymmetrical interde-pendence causes vast inequalities and exacerbates the tensions of attempts at international cooperation. The UN is the only universal international organization at the end of the twentieth century which would be capable of dealing with the problems of the world economy in a collective framework. The structural changes which took place in the early 1980s within the framework of the UN could promote the exploration of major world economic problems and the more efficient treatment of these problems.

The UN has a comprehensive institutional structure to deal with the most important issues of global economic security and cooperation, as is indicated by the following examples:

— *Nutrition, development of agriculture*. UN General Assembly, UN Economic and Social Council (ECOSOC), World Food Council, Food and Agriculture Organization of the UN (FAO) as well as regional economic commissions.
— *Economic growth, economic security, economic planning*.
  UN General Assembly, ECOSOC, UNCTAD and almost all other specialized UN agencies and regional economic commissions.

— *Energy, utilization of natural resources, industrialization.*
   UN General Assembly, ECOSOC, International Atomic Energy Agency,
   UNCTAD, UNIDO and other specialized agencies.
— *World trade.*
   UN General Assembly, ECOSOC, GATT, UNCTAD and regional economic
   commissions.
— *Employment.*
   International Labour Organization (ILO), UNESCO, regional economic
   commissions.
— *International finances, capital flow.*
   UN General Assembly, ECOSOC, UNCTAD.
— *Communications and transport.*
   UN General Assembly, ECOSOC, ICAO, IMCO, UNCTAD, regional
   economic commissions, etc.
— *Environmental protection.*
   UN General Assembly, ECOSOC, UNEP, FAO, IAEA, IMCO, WHO, regional
   economic commissions.
— *Science and technology transfer.*
   UN General Assembly, ECOSOC, UNCTAD, UNIDO, UNESCO, WIPO.

So far, the different forms and agencies of the UN have dealt mainly with world
economic questions related to progress and the chances of improving the position of
the developing countries. Representatives of many countries are inclined to think that
UN forums are not suitable for discussing the merits of and reaching agreements on
world economic problems because of the great number of the member states, their
antagonistic interests and the political nature of the problems involved. Unquestionably in the overwhelming majority of issues dealt with by UN agencies up till now,
sharp conflicts were unavoidable. Such issues were, for instance, the democratic restructuring of the world economy on the basis of the declaration on "the new international economic order", the problems of the stabilization of the raw material markets,
the regulation of the activities of transnational corporations and of international
technology transfer, etc. As regards East-West relations, the essential differences of the
two systems have rendered it rather difficult to strengthen the part of the UN in the
problems involved.

The differences of interests have a characteristic influence in general on the
multilateral framework and talks. As a rule, compromises are based on the smallest
common denominator. However, if the states are capable of and willing to surrender
their interests in certain questions and reach compromises as a result of which they
presumably lose something today only to gain something perhaps in the future (or
losses and gains are balanced in a way which cannot be realized immediately)—then
the smallest common denominator is not an absolute necessity.

There was a widespread view in the mid-1970s that it would be necessary and useful
to call a new global conference in order to settle the comprehensive problems of the
world economy. As a result, a new-type world economic organization could be
established which would meet the requirements of the last decades of this century as
well as of the twenty-first century. This new organization would facilitate the smoother
working of international commodity markets (those of industrial finished goods and

raw materials included), to further the structural changes within the states with international financial support, to redefine and assert in new way the general rules of international monetary cooperation, to control the activities of transnational corporations and to regulate the conditions of the international flow of new technologies. Experts have been discussing also how these goals could be achieved. The unification of GATT and UNCTAD and also the merging of a number of other organizations in the new structure was suggested.

The possibility of shaping world economic relations in a more planned way has been considered by experts in international organizations for decades. As early as at the beginning of the 1960s the ideas of an international "development decade" and "development strategy" were formulated in the UN and resolutions were passed accordingly. Originally such concepts served as a basis for these ideas which set the aim of elaborating and approving of a "world plan" primarily to alleviate the problems of the developing countries and to promote their progress. Important experts, for instance Jan Tinbergen from the Netherlands, and politicians, among them U Thant, former General Secretary of the UN, have come to the conclusion that within the framework of a world plan the redistribution of investment resources would be possible together with the coordination of production and consumption in each country by satisfactorily harmonizing interests. Though the ideas relating to a world plan were based on real problems they formulated unrealistic objectives. The interests of the individual states, the unavoidable conflicts between real and alleged interests, the clashes of short-term and long-term interests as well as world political relations were not taken into consideration. The designation of the UN as the chief executive organ of the world plan was proposed but the capabilities of the UN were not understood correctly, although it is a well-known fact that within the UN no system of means has been developed which could create the preconditions for the accomplishment of even an indicative world plan.

In spite of all this it is an undeniable fact that the first and second development decade or the development strategy for the 1980s had a positive part in the international dialogues and programmes within and outside the scope of the UN. These schemes directed attention to many important correlations and contradictions of the contemporary world economy, such as the connection between the struggle for disarmament and the trend in conditions of development, the definition of the actual interests and needs of the developing countries regarding the stabilization of the prices of raw materials and earnings from their exports, the restricted nature of the development and aid policy of the developed Western countries, the activities of the transnational corporations in the developing countries.

It is only natural that when listing the global objectives and the recommendations for the individual countries all those problems must be pointed out which would seem necessary for changing the world economic conditions and for improving the situation. Outstanding among these are the following:
— national and coordinated international economic policies aiming at the establishment of more flexible and more efficient world economic relations;
— reaching long-term agreements to improve the system of world trade;
— decisions on capital flows and technology transfer in order to bring about more favourable conditions for the developing countries;

— further development of the international financial system which would serve the interests of the developing nations in a more efficient way;

— measures to improve the domestic economic, organizational conditions of the states and the efficiency of the national economies.

Obviously there is a close structural relationship among the five tasks mentioned above. Particularly the problems connected with world trade and international finance (which are closely interwined) have to be dealt with and solved by concerted action.

The conflict between the needs and possibilities of international cooperation is reflected in a particularly obvious way in the case of the future of the international monetary system. These problems are dealt with in more detail because the functioning of the system may serve as an instructive example of conflicts between the state centered and global approaches and the chances of surmounting such difficulties. At the same time, the prospects throw a light on other problems too, which have to be faced by the countries of the world.

2. The Past, Present and Future of the International Monetary System

In its broader definition the international monetary system is a global network of inter-governmental organizations and agreements, money markets, different state and private banks and other financial institutions as well as international financial centres. (Such international financial centres are, for instance, New York, London, Zurich or Singapore.) Institutionalized and informal relations established within the monetary system comprise a network of great importance as regards the economic life and international economic relations of the states. Transactions carried out in the framework of the monetary system—governmental as well as private transactions— exert an influence on all economic units, and in case of convertible currencies the international consequences of such transactions are also unambiguous. (E.g. almost the whole world economy felt the impact of the budgetary deficit of the United States in the 1980s.)

Though the international monetary system is closely interrelated with other areas of the world economy, the issues emerging in this sector are in many cases very specific ones, because international money markets are internationalized to a much higher degree than the markets for other commodities. It is the international monetary system which links individual national economic policies. Governments—whether they like it or not—are compelled to seek for cooperation resolutely in this field. The frontiers between domestic and international finance have been progressively disappearing in the developed Western industrial countries. International institutions such as the International Monetary Fund or the Bank for International Settlements, which have long traditions in organizing cooperation and practical transactions, and are much more powerful than other international organizations, are parts of this system. Economics and sciences too devote greater attention to the globalization of the international monetary system in order to harmonize its requirements and possibilities with the present and expected realities of the world. International monetary relations are also influenced by conflicting interests and differing economic power relations. However, as a result of the disintegration of the Bretton Woods system, international finance is still rather chaotic in the middle of the 1980s.

The Bretton Woods system represented the state-centred approach to international monetary affairs. It was based on the assumption that through the state budget and the control of the banking institutions national governments were able fully to control national finances and thus virtually the fundamental processes of their national economies. Accordingly, the basis for establishing international monetary harmony were interstate agreements. However, even the original system functioning at the end of the 1950s was not able to control the increasingly great volume of speculative capital flows in the wake of liberalization, and governments could react only by restoring previous restrictions if they thought that the "destructive" economic consequences had assumed too dangerous proportions.

Even more serious problems arose following the collapse of the pillars of the system. Changes in Western monetary relations resulted in the abandonment of the basic principles of the Bretton Woods Agreement at the end of the 1960s and the early 1970s. According to official explanations the system changed because the United States was no longer in the position to meet the demands of foreign countries to satisfy their dollar claims in gold. Under the changing economic power relations, fixed exchange rates were not regarded as suitable either to reflect or assert the realities. So-called "floating" was thought to be more viable for this purpose. The Bretton Woods system has been the source of serious concern in Western Europe, too, since the beginning of the 1950s. Actually the dollar, functioning as the key currency of the Western international monetary system, linked up international monetary affairs and, thus, virtually the entire economic situation of the Western European countries with the fluctuations of the domestic economic policy of the United States. Under the conditions of the "organized" economic hegemony of the United States, the functioning of the dollar as a key currency compelled the USA to respect certain rules though these were never fully adhered to. After the problems caused by the dollar shortages, the international monetary system went through three major crises. The first one, at the end of the 1960s, was a dollar glut crisis and influenced more the developed countries. The second crisis was connected with the increase of oil prices influencing all countries. The third crisis is the ongoing international debt crisis. Following the collapse of the supporting pillar of the international monetary system in 1971, the American government was actually not obliged to take into consideration the international consequences of its national economic policy decisions. Subsequent agreements have not changed this situation either.

Yet, the international monetary system has contributed in the postwar years to the avoidance of large-scale world economic troubles and has had a major part in bridging over temporary imbalances. However, tensions which cropped up in the past fifteen years in the sphere of finance extended to other branches of economic activity as well. Thus, indebtedness has reached such dimensions in the 1970s that according to my calculations, world debt (piled up in convertible currencies both national and international) surpassed in the middle of 1987 the value of the full annual material production of our globe. Servicing these debts imposed immense burdens on the individuals, enterprises and governments concerned. Particularly, a great number of countries were put into a difficult financial situation by the second explosion of oil prices at the end of the 1970s (the second oil shock), so much so that they were forced to restrain their economic growth and imports considerably.

The increasing vulnerability of the international monetary system is the result of several factors. One of the main factors is the considerable expansion of international commercial credits and the increase in the number of banks involved. To bring about the so-called "recycling" of incomes originating from oil sales (i.e. their re-pumping into the international monetary system) the commercial banks of the Western world have joined in the international credit and loan transactions to a far greater extent than before—and not only the major banks of the traditional financial centres, which had a great part in such transactions from the very start. The credit-granting capacity of these latter was enhanced by deposits pouring in from the oil states. Smaller American, Japanese and European commercial banks were increasingly drawn into the orbit of international credit transactions by the mammoth banks.

International credits grew annually by 25 per cent on average between 1973 and 1981. Prior to the first oil shock only some hundred banks had participated to a greater extent in international credit and loan transactions whereas from 1973 on the number of such banks grew by an annual average of about hundred (e.g. in 1981 already 1,640 banks participated in talks about the rescheduling of the Mexican debt). Practically any country could obtain loans and credits with acceptable interest rates (sometimes with negative real interest rates) and annuities. Under such conditions little attention was paid to the International Monetary Fund since there was scarcely any need for it. The increase in the number of banks participating in international credit granting and the growth of the amount of credits granted was accompained by the extension of the Euromarket (it grew from an annual $ 20 billion in 1960 to $ 2000 billion in 1983).[118] And this happened in such a way that no significant organizational improvements were introduced on the international money market. By the extension of credit-granting activities and by the participation in credit transactions of banks without adequate experience of such transactions the liability and vulnerability of the monetary system increased.

The overwhelming part of international debt falls on the developing countries. Their indebtedness increased from $ 100 billion in 1973 to more than $ 800 billion by 1985. Two-thirds of these were raised from commercial banks under normal market conditions. The share of developing countries which were not members of the OPEC in loans to the Euro foreign exchange market in 1981 exceeded 60 per cent (in 1974 it had been 35 per cent) while the average interest rate on loans increased from 4 per cent in 1973 to 20 per cent by the end of 1980. (Eighty per cent of the total debts belonged to twenty developing countries and half of the loans were drawn by five countries: Brazil, Mexico, Argentina, South Korea and the Philippines.)[119]

The international hard-currency debts of the socialist countries, too, have increased considerably: by 1982 they were ten times what they were in 1971. Of this, two-thirds belonged to three countries: Poland, Hungary and the GDR. Under such circumstances the changes considerably disturbed the normal functioning of international finance and have thrown a light on the deficiencies of the monetary system.

a) Since World War II the actual threat of the collapse of the international monetary structure arose for the first time in the early 1980s. The interlocking of banks, insurance companies and investment companies is extremely great in a world of interdependence. Under conditions of uncertainty and anxiety a great number of financial institutions, banks and foreign currency exchanges would be compelled to close down if a major banking house collapsed. Such a collapse is highly improbable within a national framework since it can be prevented by the government with the help of the central bank. This was clearly illustrated when the Continental Illinois Bank was rescued by an emergency loan of $ 7.5 billion by the Federal Reserve Bank in 1984. However, there are no such guarantees for the international private bank network. As was shown by the bankruptcy of the Luxembourg-affiliated firm of Banco Ambrosiano, an Italian banking house, in the autumn of 1982, there are serious deficiencies in agreements between central banks on international transactions. One of the major unsolved problems in which institutions should render help in the case of bankrupticies as a consequence of international transactions. There are no international agreements or national obligations regarding this problem. It would seem an obvious solution to link up the IMF with the international private bank network in some way to provide guarantees. Moreover, a system of international "liquidity insurance" could be established under the auspices of IMF or BIS.

b) For the first time in the postwar years several major debtor countries defaulted at the same time. At the end of the 1970s and at the beginning of the 1980s for political and economic reasons, several major debtor countries were unable to meet not only total debt servicing, but even their interest payment obligations. Interest payment and amortization payment difficulties were experienced—due to economic recessions or political troubles—by Iran, Nigeria, Chile, Argentina, Mexico and Brazil and even by some socialist countries which drew attention to increasing risks in this new dimension. By the end of June 1984 of the international debts amounting to $ 1.2 billion about $ 250 were under negotiation for rescheduling. While it must be recognized that the debt situation in fact is a longer-term development crisis, the short and medium-term financial management of the problems is vitally important. The question arose as to what extent the international banking system would be willing to accept the rescheduling of debts without any institutional changes or to what an extent it would be able to do so (without initiating restrictions resulting in the collapse of world economic relations). Such problems as where to find the new money for the system in order to support the countries which, in spite of the rescheduling, were in a difficult position, and how to raise the resources to support international financial organizations were encountered: measures taken to internationalize the yen held out promises of a possibility of extending international sources in the spring of 1984.

The existing structure demonstrated that commercial banks were ready to strengthen the informal cooperation with BIS and the International Monetary Fund in those cases when the parties agreed that it seemed feasible to help governments of countries in a temporarily difficult situation. No doubt, creditors are not interested in enforcing the bankruptcy of the debtors and are inclined to make some sacrifices. However, they were neither capable of rendering nor willing to render lasting support because they would not have enough international guarantees in case of major crises.

   c) The problems of the international monetary system are related also to the character and scale of exchange rate fluctuations. There are several reasons for increasing fluctuations in the present system. In the case of floating rates, unforeseen economic troubles influencing the demand and supply of the currency of some countries have a considerable effect on the exchange rates. The increase or decrease in exchange rates take place generally as a consequence of tight money, raising of interest rates or expansive economic policy decisions. The position of countries which are in a difficult situation is further aggravated by the so-called "overshot" phenomenon (i.e. the overestimating of the changes in the exchange rate). A similar situation arises in case of domestic economic difficulties influencing the trade balance of the country in question (a considerable surplus or deficit). Another reason for liability is brought about by the economic—and also non-economic—uncertainty influencing the changes in exchange rates. It is quite obvious that views exaggerating the problems of the European countries and overrating the relative stability of the USA had a considerable part in the overvaluation of the dollar. Speculation in the hope of drawing profits from the movements of the exchange rates has also become a significant factor; it has strained the situation on the foreign exchange markets often to the verge of irrationality in the mid-1980s. As a factor influencing the relative movements of the exchange rates the hypothetical risk can bring about extremely difficult situations since it can trigger off very strong speculative waves against a specific currency (as has happened in the case of the French franc). Under the influence of the factors mentioned the extent of the fluctuations in the exchange rates of some currencies sometimes has exceeded 30 per cent and has caused serious confusion in world trade. Such fluctuations cannot be counterbalanced by direct intervention because this would need such enormous reserves that only a few countries could hold them. Moreover, short-term capital movements—resulting from real or anticipated changes in interest rates—also contribute to a great extent to fluctuations in the exchange rates. The overvaluation of the dollar was mainly related to this phenomenon. Any form of fixing the rates of the leading currencies would require coordinated measures and substantial intervention funds. Such an intervention fund could in practice be created only by a common action since the expected result could be achieved only by the continual utilization of a great amount of money. The daily turnover of the international foreign exchange markets was actually $125–130 billion, i.e. twenty-times as much as the volume of world trade in the mid-1980s.

Under such circumstances there would be no sense in returning to the original Bretton Woods agreement. The agreement of the five leading Western countries about the changes in exchange rates between the US dollar and other currencies proved that the international coordination of monetary policies was necessary, since the central banks were unable to bring about regulation within the frameworks of the present mechanisms by themselves. The turnover of the money markets is too great and interrelated as compared with the amounts that the central banks functioning in isolation can provide. An administrative and isolated international control of the money markets (that is one which does not reckon with national monetary conditions) would result in the paralysis of the money markets and would become the source of serious disturbances.

The various forms of cooperation within the framework of the international monetary system and their deficiencies exert a considerable influence on international trade. Currencies revalued or devalued as a result of speculation or manipulated floating distort the conditions of international competitition. Since there are no comprehensive agreements, the readiness of governments to cooperate is not very strong, especially in difficult economic situations. Even the European monetary system based on relatively closer cooperation is facing considerable difficulties. The world trade system is weakened by the liability of the leading currencies. Under the conditions of high interest rates and difficult financing terms, the indebted countries try to seek for new markets and restrict their imports.

The international monetary system is not a neutral institution but is, among others, the means of the global redistribution of incomes; almost all of its functions are related directly to this role. The multiple character of the functions of the international monetary system demand the establishment of conditions which would allow of a better national management of public finances, more efficient international coor-dination and global agreements. But the conditions prevailing in the second half of the 1980s in the world economy do not seem very favourable for such a turn of events. Nevertheless, there are some chances for new initiatives.

A number of factors can be expected in the following years to reshape the international monetary system.

a) In defining the tendencies of the international monetary system and the operational mechanism of this system the developed Western countries will continue to play a vital part. Disturbances and problems in the world economy will facilitate and even require the formation of long-term or temporary coalitions to an even greater extent than before, and in such coalitions other countries too, can have a considerable role, especially in such issues as how to increase monetary discipline, how to improve the international equilibria, how to stabilize exchange rates and maintain sufficient flexibility, how to coordinate their economic policies better, especially in the struggle against inflation and in promoting economic growth. The relative role of the leading currencies of the monetary system will also change.

b) Most of the leading countries of the international monetary system will assume a defensive position in the future to reduce the vulnerability of their national economies to dangerous external effects (inflation, influx of speculative capital, crises, etc.), which they have to take into account as a consequence of the open character of their economies. For a time they will try to fend off adverse effects by forming blocks (like the Group of Seven), establishing special target zones, or by building various guarantees and backdoor clauses into the system.

c) Governments participating in the system are still motivated by their short-term national interests rather than longer-term national, international or global considerations. If in addition, their national policies aim to realize the main priorities of their economies at the expense of the "rest of the world", they may hamper the solution of their domestic problems, and will create the sources of serious economic conflicts.

d) Non-economic problems (e.g. political or military problems, relations with the socialist countries, the political stability of the developing countries) will also play a major part in shaping the system. The interrelations between international monetary arrangements and measures in the field of trade, services and other areas of international cooperation will also be strengthened.

e) The probability that the leading powers of the world economy would increasingly be inclined to create a new comprehensive international monetary system within the next five or ten years is not too big. The conflicting interests of the different countries in the world would prevent such a development. The concrete domestic needs of the individual countries and country groups are also rather different in many respects. The further reforming of the present system by means of more or less significant agreements seems to be the most feasible alternative. These reforms would affect chiefly the mechanism and conditions of exchange rate changes, the strengthening of international liquidity and the terms of credits. The mechanisms of the present institutions could also be modified.

f) In the view of many experts, order in international monetary relations could best be restored by returning to the gold standard. Under the world political and economic conditions of the last stage of the twentieth century, however, an international monetary system could not be based on the gold standard. Gold production is concentrated in a few countries of the world, and the meagre gold resources as well as their unequal distribution make it impossible to rely on such a measure. Yet, there is naturally a close relation between movements in gold prices and changes in the international situation. One of the major factors of this is inflation (not only the given but anticipated inflationary pressure). The other factor lies in political tensions. The price of gold increases in the wake of major international political tensions, regional armed conflicts (short-term price fluctuations too, are explained to a certain extent by such events). Oviously, as a result of gold purchases by certain oil exporting countries, a specific correlation could be noticed between the changes in oil prices and in gold prices. (Gold prices are also influenced by international currency speculations and by supply and demand conditions.) All those factors above indicate that while it is impossible to demonetize gold, it is equally unrealistic to think about the restoration of any system based upon it.

g) The evolution of the international monetary institutions (the International Monetary Fund, the World Bank, the Bank for International Settlements (BIS)) and the interrelations between them are also highly relevant for the future of the monetary system. Under the present—practically unchanged—institutional conditions the means available to the International Monetary Fund need to be increased. In order to strengthen the security of the international monetary system and, first of all, to be able to avoid short-term difficulties, the countries themselves have dared to make bolder measures. The problem of further development of the institutions is more complex. The International Monetary Fund was authorized to render aid to bridge temporary problems of the balance of payments by the Bretton Woods Agreement in 1944. When elaborating this construction only the position and short-term problems of the developed industrial countries were reckoned with. International financing needs related to economic development, as well as dealing with the international monetary consequences of structural changes or adjustment, were not considered fully in the institutional scope. The World Bank (International Bank for Reconstruction and Development) was given the task of participating in the long-term financing of the reconstruction of the economies of Europe and Japan. At that time this had meant general import financing and not project financing. Following the emergence of the Third World countries, certain changes took place and a new organizational network was established within the framework of the World Bank. In the 1970s the World Bank had a considerable part in the financing of the infrastructural projects of middle-level countries and certain groups of the developing countries, with the assumption that the middle-level countries would be able to cover their long-term financing requirements from the international capital markets. By the end of the 1980s world economic conditions had demonstrated that this was possible only in a favourable international economic environment.

The activities of the World Bank in overall development financing have been expanding also in other areas. It is playing an important role in bringing new capital and technology to the developing countries beyond its own resources though the Multilateral Investment Guarantee Agency and the special joint financing programme with private financial institutions. The Structural Adjustment loans which are aimed at the assistance of changes in output patterns are increasingly serving general economic purposes. Thus the loans of the World Bank are in a way overlapping but in fact supplementing IMF assistance. This practice proves the necessity of reformulating relations between the two intsitutions in the future with the aim of coordinating their role in the new global environment, characterized by the high level of indebtedness and the difficulties of debt servicing. The role of the World Bank in solving the long-term problems of the international monetary system ought to be increased.

The role and the functioning of the International Monetary Fund is of outstanding importance from the point of view of the future of the monetary system since of all global international economic organizations it is the IMF which has the greatest responsibilities. Yet, there is a considerable divergence of opinion as regards its future. Some experts have suggested that the International Monetary Fund should be transformed into a global central bank with the following functions:
— the release and handling of the common reserve currency of the world;
— control of the international banking institutions;
— furthering the coordination of international economic policies;
— functioning as a lender of last resort.

Though the necessity of these functions is accepted by many countries, views diverge considerably on certain principles. Due to their interests, the states (i.e. the entities shaping the system) will presumably not choose the course of restrictions.

However, the criteria of a smoothly functioning international monetary system are judged differently by the developed Western nations and the developing countries, and even by the leading countries and country groups within these categories. Developed Western countries regard an international monetary system as well functioning which furthers the free flow of commodities and international capital and makes it possible for the individual countries to settle the surplus or the deficit of their balance of payments in a way that neither they nor their partners should incur losses. Among such countries the distribution of international reserves and the credits available ought to assume a form which would render them capable of adequately financing the deficits on their balances of payments. The chief requirement is that deficit countries should not be compelled to take emergency measures, to stop debt servicing, to declare import restrictions or to increase their external incomes in a way causing potential damage to their own national economies or to other countries.

The criteria mentioned above seem insufficient for the majority of the developing nations. These countries deem it necessary to bring about an international monetary system which gives more direct attention to interrelations of international finance, trade and development. This means first of all that the international monetary system has to provide long-range financing even to countries plagued by a chronic budget deficit (such financing ought to be effected from loans from various special funds, international aid as well as from loans by the International Monetary Fund and private banks). At the same time, the international monetary system ought to be authorized to raise additional liquid funds (e.g. by connecting the issue of special drawing rights with development aid). Stable exchange rates are especially important for developing countries since this renders it possible to maintain the stability of their reserves and facilitates planning.

The decision-making mechanisms and the right to intervention are also important for the interests of the developing countries. Great importance is attributed by these nations to the universal character of the system and to the modification of the present voting structure. It is also considered significant that conditions of adjustment (e.g. reduction of domestic consumption) should be imposed not only on debtors and countries in difficult positions but more serious attention should be paid to the international effects of the domestic economic policies of the developed Western countries. Frequent criticism is voiced about the International Monetary Fund and the World Bank concerning the way in which they destabilize the political system of the developing country in question by their recommendations relating to their economic policies.

While there is an organized system of settlements among the socialist countries and there are international financial institutions within the CMEA, many important conditions of a well-functioning regional monetary system are still to be developed. The participation of those countries in the international monetary system is expanding.

Of the European socialist countries, four (Hungary, Romania, Poland, and Yugoslavia) were members of the International Monetary Fund in 1988. The interests and the international financial requirements of the European socialist countries are similar to those of the developing nations. To what an extent the system is capable and willing to take into consideration the different endowments and development levels of countries with different social and economic systems is regarded as an important criterion. It is stressed by the socialist countries that conditions should be created which guarantee equal rights, i.e. that no country should be able to dominate international monetary relations or should exploit them for its own sake. Efforts should be made so that the development of all the member countries of the international monetary system should be promoted and no country should be able to act unilaterally outside or against the system. Thus, the socialist countries are interested in a well-organized system functioning in a disciplined way, capable of preventing inflation and international monetary disturbances. As regards the structure of the new international monetary system, certain views were expressed according to which it would be easier to coordinate the interests of all the country groups if regional groupings were brought about (e.g. similar organizations as the present European Monetary System), and these would cluster around a regional key currency; the system as a whole would consist of the organizational network of these groupings. Regional commodity and capital movements would probably benefit from such solutions; global cooperation, however, would become more difficult.

It is obvious from the above that owing to their complex nature, international monetary affairs are fundamentally important for all the branches of economic cooperation and, therefore, the formation of new institutions of global approach and character is an extremely difficult task. The debate about creating a new international monetary system has been going on for about 10–15 years at a number of international economic conferences. The recession of the 1980s has increased the necessity of such a system, however, the chances for its establishment have not improved. Though the solutions reached up till now from the point of view of global cooperation cannot be regarded as optimal ones, in the current international situation they have managed to adjust the system to the new circumstances by slowly modifying the previous structure.

3. Global and Regional Conditions for Change

Since World War II certain groups of countries have established not only global but also regional organizations to facilitate the realization of their objectives. Integrated regional organizations also serve as the instrument of the international economic policies of their member countries if common solutions seem more feasible or the means of national economic policies are not sufficient for solving the problems. Integration, however, presumes that states within its framework have essential common interests and therefore are ready to give up a certain degree of their sovereignty. The interdependence of such countries tends to be so strong that they are in a position to call into life "supranational" institutions. One of the most characteristic examples of such integration is the European Common Market which has a significant part in the international economic policies of its member countries.

The readiness to set up supranational institutions and to give up the decision-making right of the national state is not identical even in the member countries of the Common Market. The community of interest is different too, since it evolved under the influence of different economic and political factors as a result of problems the solution of which was sought for by each of the member countries. The more problems were thought solvable the easier it was for the domestic economic and social interest groups to reach compromises regarding international economic policy pointing in the direction of supranationalism but, at the same time, the lower has been the "integration threshold" for the countries in question in the macro-economic sphere, i.e. in the range of the national economy.

Economic development, however, is not a steady process and thus, interests are not constant either, and the conditions of carrying into effect such interests are also modified in the course of realization. Changes in the interests of a given country bring about the restructuring of the elements of common interests as well. Such changes in common interests resulted in serious crises in the functioning of the Common Market in the 1970s. It turned out that if the links forged by the community of interests are not strong enough and there is a lack of deliberate and constant efforts to settle problems cropping up in the course of development, the integration programmes are not only slowed down by unavoidable conflicts but can be paralysed by them, thus constantly reproducing the forces of disintegration. In principle it cannot be ruled out that as a consequence of sharpening conflicts some countries would quit the European Economic Community and—if this seemed to be their real interests—re-establish their national customs frontiers and other defensive economic means. It was not by chance that in the 1980s the problem came up as to whether the European Economic Community as an integrated unit could reach the point of no return as regards the reestablishment of national markets and the 1992 programme was formed.

The events of the crisis of the 1980s answered the questions about whether this organizational form developed according to the ideas of the participating nations, solved the contradiction between the national frameworks and needs of the internationalization of economic and scientific-technological development or would it be stranded on the rocks of disaccord. It became evident beyond argument that the process of merging national economies was a slow and painful course. Serious difficulties are caused by the unevenness of development, political problems are related to these inequalities as well as "neo-nationalism" which strengthens parallel with economic difficulties. The discussion connected with the establishment of a unified international market by 1992 ended with an important compromise. However, the member countries did not give up the possibility of making use of the benefits of integration in the fields of finance, industry and agriculture.

The situation of the CMEA, too, was rendered difficult as a result of economic difficulties. Relations have assumed an increasingly bilateral character. The common aims agreed on in order to further the process of integration and embodied in the Complex Programme of 1971 and the new long-term agreements based on that programme were realized only to a small degree. It was later realized, however, that without a radical reform of the CMEA, no meaningful progress could be achieved in integration or even in cooperation.

The integrated institutions of the developing countries have also come to a standstill or have even regressed. Thus, under the impact of recession, trade among a group of Latin American countries (the Andean Group) diminished by 50 per cent in 1983, and protectionism gained ground. Similar phenomena could be observed in the cooperation of the member states of the Central American Common Market. The integrated development of the ASEAN countries, which are in a rather more advantagous position, has slowed down. Thus, the problems of the world economy have also affected those regional organizations the members of which assumed that there would open up brighter vistas as a consequence of the failures of global cooperation. The satisfying of new requirements is rendered more difficult by the insufficiencies of global and regional cooperation.

As a result of changing international relations in the late twentieth century the countries of the world have had to face qualitatively new requirements. These new factors have not emerged all of a sudden, overnight; all countries were affected in many ways by the problems piling up relatively slowly, sometimes almost imperceptibly, and by the fact that relations based on interdependence among the individual countries have strengthened. The interrelations between economic and political processes have become more intensive, by the increasing and novel priority of natural conditions and by the unfolding of a new scientific and technological revolution. The leading states of the world economy have not become isolationist but sought for the solution of their problems by giving priority to their national objectives and means. Not only in these but in all countries national economic policy has been upgraded and also more thought has been given to the efficiency of the institutions and concurrently to all the factors influencing efficiency. Such factors can be defined as follows:

— *scientific research* which can react rapidly to change and produce adequate suggestions and recommendations for solutions, and the achievements of which back up technological development and social action;
— *a national political environment* capable of stimulating research on adapting new development work, of adapting new developments (even in cases when this contradicts dominating views and concepts) and acting accordingly (acceptance of political risks included);
— *macro and micro-economic institutions* capable of flexible action to implement the necessary changes, to revitalize themselves and to act energetically, quickly and efficiently both in the national and in the world market;
— *social and economic mechanisms* transmitting the effects and requirements of changes, and suitable for stimulating necessary action;
— *the human factor* (education, qualifications, production experiences, production culture of people and the aptitude to shape all these flexibly);
— the emergence of *cooperative organizations* aiding the international economic security of smaller countries and capable of a more efficient support of national priorities;
— *international economic partners* cooperating so that economic tasks can be solved more efficiently;
— *international political conditions* facilitating the functioning of all the factors mentioned.

The way of thinking and acting as required by the new situation is naturally not at all synchronous with needs either within the bounds of any single country or in the network of international cooperation. This is due mainly to the differing interests of the states—and particularly of the leading powers in the world economy—in international cooperation, and also to the policy by means of which these countries try to solve their domestic problems. However, the changes which have taken place up till now—and particularly in the 1970s and the 1980s—and experiences gained in this process are highly significant both in the present and for the future.

National economic policies are much more aware of the world economic environment in which they have to operate than in earlier periods. States have acquired considerable practical knowledge regarding the handling of the structural disturbances of international cooperation. The international organizational network functions in all the significant branches of economic cooperation. But it is true that the efficiency of these organizations has not improved and has even deteriorated in some cases. The world would have to pay dearly if the boat of mankind were standed on the rocks of conflicting interests, international strife and power ambitions as a result of which the international cooperation could not be realized at the necessary level. The inadequacy of international cooperation has already caused serious harm to those countries which for structural reasons are highly dependent on world economic changes but could not adapt themselves to these transformations. The changes which have taken place under the conditions of world economic recessions and political tensions since the beginning of the 1970s have not improved the chances of cooperation. Some important experiences of the past fifteen years indicate the direction of action on an international scale:

— The world has been unable—and probably will be unable—to call into being better institutions than the present international global and regional organizations.

— Therefore, in the interest of the common future of mankind the operative efficiency of the international organizations has to be improved. Countries hope to receive support from the organized network of international cooperation mainly in such important fields as better utilization of human and material resources, the maintenance of a growth-oriented development of national economies, the elaboration of methods for the prevention of disadvantageous changes or economic disturbances spreading from one country to another, causing serious harms thereby. International organizations should also be enabled to predict world economic "storms" in advance and should seek for possible solutions in order to avoid them or at least to mitigate their effects. Under the conditions of the coexistence and interactions of 170 countries it has to be realized that this is an increasingly difficult task in a rigid and stagnant world economy.

— The furthering of economic development and not the joint "managing" of stagnation is the common and mutual interest of the states. We are warned by the economic shocks of the past decades that structural changes in the world economy, the emergence of new producers and their activities on the world markets result in serious conflicts and emergency situations which can be avoided only if it becomes possible to set into action an appropriate mechanism of international adaptation and change. These also have essential preconditions. Such are, first of all, better international coordination of national economic policies and establishment of "buffer" funds which could render some temporary assistance to countries in difficult positions to accomplish the required adjustment.

— Owing to the deficiencies of the present international organizations, it seems inevitable that new "rules of the game" in world trade and international monetary matters must be developed which would reflect the close and organic connections between these two important forms of cooperation, and would hold out promises of security and stability while, at the same time, would be flexible enough to take into consideration the rapidly changing conditions.

— International cooperation has to reckon with the regional organizations too, in order that these should be able to integrate adequately with the global system. Thus, such forms and forums of consultation should be developed which would make it possible—often in an antagonistic system of requirements—to reach temporary or lasting compromises.

Such requirements and new norms of cooperation could be brought to pass only in a world where the necessary standards of inter-state confidence and reliance evolved by taking into account mutual interests and where actions are not distorted by the escalation of the arms race or tensions and confrontations which are frequently provoked artificially in its background. Since policies resulting in international tension and mistrust disregard the justified interests of other countries, they undermine the structure of the global system to a higher degree than in the past when the level of interdependent relations was lower. A more secure and efficient global cooperation could emerge only as the result of joint political actions, through different sub-systems. In principle there could be different alternatives for such progress. In the realities of the last part of our century the United Nations and its specialized agencies have the mandate and offer the only global framework for mankind to build up the structure of cooperation required by the complex and difficult tasks of our common future.

Notes

1. *Economic Survey of Europe, 1982, 1983,* United Nations, New York
2. *Economic Survey of Europe, 1983.*
3. Chemical Bank, Economic Research Department, March 25, 1983, *Weekly Economic Package.*
4. *International Management,* January 1983, June 1984. Different issues of the OECD *Observer.*
5. United Nations, *World Economic Survey,* 1983, Vol. 1, pp. 1–2, New York, 1983 (L/1983/43 St. ESA 131).
6. Institute for International Economics, *Promoting World Recovery. Statement of Global Economic Strategy,* Washington, 1982, pp. 1–4.
7. The Brandt Commission, *Common Crisis: North-South Cooperation for World Recovery.* Pan Books, London, 1983.
8. 7th World Congress of Economists, Madrid, September 1983, Mimeo.
9. UNCTAD, *Trade and Development Review,* 1982, No. 4, pp. 1–3.
10. O. Bogomolov, "Interdependence, Structural Change". 7th World Congress of the IEA, Madrid, 1983, Colegio de Economistas de Madrid, p. 1.
11. T. Szentes, "Global Nature, Origins and Strategic Implications of the World Economic Crisis", UNCTAD, *Trade and Development Review,* 1982. No 4. pp. 25–42.
12. N. D. Kondratiev, "Die langen Wellen der Konjuktur", *Archiv für Sozialwissenschaft und Sozialpolitik,* Tübingen, Vol. 56, 1926.
13. A. H. Parvus, *Die Handelskrise und die Gewerkschaften,* München, 1901, pp. 26–27.
14. I. A. Schumpeter, *Business Cycles: A Theoretical Historical Analysis of the Capitalist Process,* McGraw Hill, New York, 1939.
15. G. Mensch, *Das technologische Patt,* Frankfurt, 1975.
16. W. W. Rostow, "Japan, United States and the Pacific Basin", Tokyo, 1983, Mimeo.
17. M. Simai, *A harmadik évezred felé* (Towards the Third Millennium), Kossuth Könyvkiadó, Budapest, 1971, 1976.
18. On this problem see in detail: I. Lesourne: "The Specific Problems of the European Community", 7th World Congress of the IEA, Madrid, 1983, Mimeo, *Industrial Change and Public Policy,* Federal Reserve Bank of Kansas City, 1983.
19. Computations of the author on the basis of the Statistical Yearbooks of the U.N.
20. A. Wagner, *Finanzwissenschaft,* Teil 1, 3. Auflage, Leipzig, 1983.
21. *National Westminster Bank Quarterly Review,* London 1984, p. 28.

22. *Economic Survey of Europe*, 1982, 1983.

23. *US News and World Report*, May 21, 1984, "Inflation and National Survival", 1979, No. 4.

24. *Inflation and National Survival*, 1979, p. 99.

25. *Inaccuracy of Department of Defense Weapons. Acquisition Cost Estimates*, U.S.G.P.O., Washington, D. C., 1979.

26. *Industrial Change and Public Policy*, The F.R.B. of Kansas City.

27. Quoted by *National Westminster Bank Quarterly Review*, February 1984, pp. 16–17.

28. SIPRI, *World Armaments and Disarmament Yearbook*, and computed on the basis of data of U.N. statistics.

29. Sources of data: U.N. Disarmament Centre, *UNCTAD Trade and Development Report*, 1982, pp. 118–24, UNCTAD TDR/2, Rev. 1. *Defense Spending and the Economy*, Congress of the U.S., U.S.G.P.O., Washington D.C., 1961.

30. President D. Eisenhower, *Farewell Address*, 1961, U.S.G.P.O, Washington, D.C., 1961.

31. S. Ostry, "The World Economy: Marking Time", Foreign Affairs, Council on Foreign Relations, New York 1981., p. 544.

32. O. Emminger, "Investment and Government Policy", In: *Investing in Europe's Future*, pp. 72–3, Basil Blackwell, London, 1983.

33. *Frankfurter Rundschau*, April 27, 1984.

34. UNCTAD: *Trade and Development Report 1982., pp. 1–5.*

35. UNCTAD: *Trade and Development Report, 1982.*

36. *The State of the World's Children*, 1984. U.N. Oxford University Press, 1984.

37. Data computed on the basis of estimates by U.N. Economic Commission for Latin America, and UNCTAD. Profits and interests paid to abroad in the early 1980s came to 5 per cent of the gross national product. A further 2 per cent resulted from deteriorating terms of trade. Computations by UNCTAD on the Third World reflected by and large similar proportions. *CEPAL Review*, 1983, No. 19, *UNCTAD: Trade and Development Report*, 1983, p. 18.

38. CEPAL *Review*, 1983, No. 19, p. 57, Santiago, Chile.

39. *World Development Report*, The World Bank, Washington, 1979.

40. K. Marx and F. Engels, *Kommunista Kiáltvány* (Manifest of the Communist Party), Szikra, Budapest, 1948. p. 16.

41. R. Aron: *Peace and War*, Doubleday, New York, 1966.

42. See: I. Wallenstein, *The Capitalist World Economy*, Cambridge University Press, New York, 1979.

An interesting debate has unfolded in the Soviet Union in the past decade on the notion of world order but on the unity of the world economy (the two are similar in many respects). Soviet economist J. Shishkow reported the following on the debate in the Soviet periodical *Mirovaja Ekonomika i Mezhdunarodnije Otnoshenija*, Moscow No. 4. 1984.

"Under the conditions of the cold war unleashed by the imperialists, the sharp political and ideological confrontation between the two world systems, the breaking off of their mutual trade and economic relations has caused some confusion with some theoreticians of that period. The idea that the unified, all-comprising world market had disintegrated into two opposed—socialist and capitalist—markets began to spread from the early 1950s on. It was but a single step from there to the total negation of the world economy as such; the category world economy disappeared from the pages of scientific publications, encyclopedia and economic dictionaries.

Thanks to Marxist theoretical thought, this misconception could be overcome in due course. The world economy, which has developed as a result of a long historical development of the productive forces and production relations of human society could, of course, not disintegrate, it could not "evaporate" even in the heat of the struggle between the two socio-economic systems. It simply passed over to a new qualitative state. "The breaking away of all the new countries from capitalism does not terminate the (global) world economy, it only changes its economic substance,"— wrote Academician A. M. Rumiantzev in 1969. The economy of our era comprises both capitalism, which has been transformed from economy on a global scale into a world economy... and socialism which has developed from a national economy to a socialist world economy and socialist economy on a global scale. (A. M. Rumiantzev, *The Problems of Modern Social Sciences,* Moscow, 1969, p. 196, in Russian.) Quite a few Soviet researchers put forward similar views on the global economy of our period. (I. A. Sokolow, *world Economy and Revolutionary Process,* Moscow, 1971, M. Maksimova, "The World Economy and International Cooperation, *Mirovaja Ekonomimika i Mezhdunarodnije Otnoshenija,* No. 4, 1974, "world Economy, Scientific-Technological Revolution and International Relations", Mirovaja Ekonomika i Mezhdunarodnije Otnoshenija, No. 4, 1979; "Some Problems of the Marxist-Leninist Conception of the World Economy". *Mirovaja Ekonomika i Mezhdunarodnija Othoshenija,* No. 7, 1983, E. Plentniev, "The Leninist Theory of World Economy and its Immense Vitality". *Mirovaja Ekonomika i Mezhdunarodnije Othoshenija,* NO. 10, 1979; "Marxism on the Unity of the World Economy: Retrospection and Present", *SShA—ekonomika, politika, ideologia,* No. 12, 1983; O. Bogomolov, "Economic Relations between the Socialist and the Capitalist Countries", *Mirovaja Ekonomika i Mezzdunarodnije Otnoshenija,* No. 3, 1980: All in Russian.)

The aim of the above cited definitions (and many others not quoted) is naturally not the declaration of some kind of absolute truth. Nevertheless all of these definitions reflect to a certain extent the following truth: despite its complex character and contradictory nature, the modern economic world represents a certain uniform system held together by the historically reached level of the international socialization of production. Thus, every regular world-scale economy, too, has some general laws of development characteristics of all of its subsystems (disregarding here the qualitative characteristics of the subsystems constituting the system as a whole) defining the basic direction of its further developement. This author is inclined to think that it is only on the basic of this conception that the tendencies of the contemporary processes of the world economy can be understood and an explanation offered for the new situation which has evolved under the effect of the increasing internationalization of economic life, greatly enhanced by the scientific-technological revolution, and as a result of the pressure of global problems, as well as the fact that the economic utilization of the nearest parts of the cosmos and the deep oceans has begun."

43. These problems will be touched upon in detail in Part Five.

44. R. Väyrinen, "Economic Cycles, Power Transition and Political Management", *International Studies Quarterly*, Stoneham, Mass. 1983, No. 27, pp. 389–418.

45. The global deposits of some of the most important mineral substances are concentrated in a relatively great percentage in the United States. According to data relating to the end of the 1970s 30.7 per cent of global coal reserves, 7.5 per cent of natural gas reserves, 4.1 per cent of oil reserves, 19 per cent of uranium, 18.5 per cent of copper and 35.6 per cent lead reserves are to be found in the United States.

46. *The Nation*, New York, August 2, 1980, 9, p. 114,

47. *Transnational Relations and World Politics*, Harvard University Press, Cambridge, Mass., 1972, p. 4.

48. D. Holzman, "International Trade under Communism", *Politics and Economics*, Macmillan, London, 1976, p. 54.

49. F. Perroux, *L'economie du XX*^{eme} *siecle*, paris, Presses Universitaires de France, 1961, pp. 27–56.

50. *The Economic Report of the President*, 1981, Washington D.C., U.S.G.P.O, 1982.

51. *Newsweek*, December 14, 1981.

52. Figures are computed by the author on the basis of statistics of the U.N., UNCTAD and the World Bank. Conversion from net material product to gross domestic product has been made taking into account statistics of countries which use both of these categories.

53. UNIDO: *Industrial Development Survey*, and on the basis of UN statistics.

54. Data from the UN Economic Commission for Europe and *Iron and Steel Engineer*, August 1981, p. 60.

55. H. P. Bowen, U.S. Office of Foreign Economic Research, U.S. Department of Labour, 1980, *Changes in the International Pattern of Factor Abundance*, p. 14.

56. U.S. National Science Board, *Science Indicators*, Washington, D.C, 1979.

57. *The Japan Economic Journal*, November 8, 1983.

58. See note 16.

59. *Bulletin of Statistics on World trade in Engineering Products*, U.N. New York, 1982.

60. See e.g. J. Willoughby, "The Changing Role of Protection in the World Economy", *Cambridge Journal of Economics*, 1982, No. 6.

61. S.D. Cohen, *The Making of U.S. International Economic Policy*, Praeger, New York, 1977, pp. 10–1.

62. Embassy of the United States, Budapest. "Wireless File", Mimeo, September 16, 1981 (Eur. 4.)

63. Ch. Royen, "Wirtschaftssanktionen als Instrument der Ost-West Auseinandersetzung", *Europa Archiv*, Bonn, 1983, No. 4, pp. 112–14.

64. Institute for International Economics: *Economic Sanctions in Support of Foreign Policy Goals*, Washington, 1983.

65. S.K. Padover, *Wilson's Ideals*, Washington (American Council on Public Affairs), 1942, p. 108.

66. Congressional Research Service, *An Assessment of the Afghanistan Sanctions: Implications for Trade and Diplomacy in the 1980s*, U.S.G.P.O, Washington, 1981, pp. 44–5.

67. *Népszabadság* (Budapest), June 16, 1984.

68. M. Boretsky, *Concerns about Present American Position: Technology and International Trade.* American Academy of Sciences, Washington, 1971; R. K. Kelly, *Technology Intensity of U.S. Output and Trade in Manufactures,* George Washington University, 1974; L. A. Davis, *Technology Intensity of U.S. Output and Trade, U.S. Department of Commerce, 1982.*

69. *Quantification of Western Export of High Technology Products to Communist Countries,* U.S. Department of Commerce, 1981.

70. "National Science Foundation, U.S, 1977," *The Conference Board: World Business Perspectives, New York No. 53, February 1980, pp. 3–4.*

71. *Business Week,* New York August 3, 1981.

72. Report of the President on the U.S. Competitiveness, U.S.G.P.O, 1981; also computations by the author.

73. *Bulletin économique mensuel de la Banque Paribas,* Paris October 1982.

74. U.N. ECE, *The Transfer of Disembodied Technology with Special Regards to Licencing,* Sc(TEch) R. III. 27 May, 1981.

75. U.N. General Assembly, A(Res. 3362/S—VII), September 19, 1975, Chapter III, paras, 1,3,5,6.

76. "Technology Imports into the United States", *The Conference Board,* New York, 1983.

77. *Human Resources Implications of Robotics,* Ann Arbor, Michigan, Upjohn Institute for Employment, 1983.

78. E. Zaleski and H. Wienert, *Technology Transfer between East and West,* Paris, OECD 1980; *Technology and East-West Trade* U.S. Congress, Office of Technology Assessment, Washington, 1983.

79. UNESCO 1979, and computations based on national statistics.

80. Secretariat of the U.N. Economic Commission for Europe, *Economic Survey of Europe 1982,* New York, U.N, p. 220.

81. *U.S. News World Report,* January 17, 1983.

82. *U.N. Yearbook of National Account Statistics,* various volumes.

83. *Finance and Development,* Washington, D.C. March 1984.

84. UNCTAD, *Trade and Development Report,* 1982, 1983.

85. FAO, *World Food Report, 1983,* Rome 1984.

86. FAO, *The State of Food and Agriculture* 1982, Rome, 1983.

87. Computations by the author on the basis of FAO, *The State of Food and Agriculture, 1982.*

88. *Lloyds Bank Review,* London January 1970.

89. L. R. Brown, *By Bread Alone,* New York, 1974, p. 24.

90. UNIDO, *Industry in a Changing World,* U.N., New York, 1973, II. B. 6. p. 21.

91. UNCTAD: *Trade and Development Report, 1982,* p. 101. U.N. New York, 1982, 1988

92. S. Kuznets, "Level and Structure of Foreign Trade: Long Term Trends", *Economic Development and Cultural Change,* Vol. 15, No. 2, Part 11, January 1967, Chicago.

93. These are as follows: iron, ore, bauxite, copper, phosphorus, potassium and sulphur.

94. Computations by the author based on U.N. statistics.

95. *World Energy Supplies; World Metal Statistics.*

96. UNCTAD: VI.T.D. 273.

97. OPEC *Annual Statistical Bulletin,* Vienna, 1985.

98. UNIDO, *Industry in a Changing World,* U.N. New York 1983.

99. See note 98.

100. *The Economic Impact,* Vol. 2. U.S.I.A, Washington, D. C, 1983.

101. *The Economist,* London, December 19, 1981.

102. *The Economist Impact,* Washington, D. C. 1982. 1., p. 20.

103. UNCTAD(TT)65, 6.E. 85, 57218. Geneva 1985, p. 17, U.S. Industrial Outlook, 1986, 21.5. Annual Review of Engineering Industries. U.N.E.C.E. 1987.

104. *Electronics,* February 24, 1982.

105. *The U.S. Automobile Industry 1980,* January 1981, "Golschmidt Report", p.1.

106. Motor Vehicle Manufacturers Association of the U.S.A, Inc. *Motor Vehicle Facts and Figures,* 1982.

107. K. Bhaskar, *The Future of the World Motor Industry,* London, Kogan & Paul, Nichols Publishing Co., 1980.

108. UNIDO: *A Statistical Review of the World Industrial Situation,* Vienna 1982, UNIDO, I. S, p. 292.

109. *Business Week,* New York, March 26, 1984.

110. U.S. Arms Control and Disarmament Agency, *World Military Expenditures 1969*–1978, Washington, D.C, 1981.

111. The sources of the statistics and information given are various publications of the U.S. Arms Control end Disarmament Agency. *The Military Balance* (various numbers), various volumes of the International Institute of Strategic Studies, *World Armaments and* Disarmament Yearbook, SIPRI, Stockholm; various publications of the Center for Strategic and International Studies, Georgetown University, Washington. The frequently contradictory information by these sources were compared with U.N. data and local sources and corrected by the author.

112. See e.g. A. G. Frank, "Arms Economy and Warfare in the Third World", *Third World Quarterly,* London, April 1980.

113. *International Management,* London, August 1986. p. 23.

114. *Commercial and Financial Chronicle,* New York, November 23, 1967.

115. *The Business Week,* March 3, 1986.

116. D. Moggridge, ed., *The Collected Writings of John Maynard Keynes,* Macmillan, London 1980, Vol. 25, p. 29.

117. A. Peccei, *One Hundred Pages for the Future,* Futura, London, 1982, pp. 158—9.

118. Sources of the data: Chemical Bank, New York, Economic Research Department.

119. I.M.F. *World Economic Outlook,* Washington, D.C. 1982, 1983.